Confessing the International Rights of Children

Confessing the International Rights of Children: The Basic Documents with Analysis

Farhad Malekian and Kerstin Nordlöf

CAMBRIDGE
SCHOLARS
PUBLISHING

Confessing the International Rights of Children:
The Basic Documents with Analysis,
by Farhad Malekian and Kerstin Nordlöf

This book first published 2012

Cambridge Scholars Publishing

12 Back Chapman Street, Newcastle upon Tyne, NE6 2XX, UK

British Library Cataloguing in Publication Data
A catalogue record for this book is available from the British Library

Cover illustration: Massacre of the Innocents by Masreliez, Louis, 1748-1810
Permission obtained from the Carolina Rediviva Library, Uppsala University, Sweden

ISBN (10): 1-4438-3981-7, ISBN (13): 978-1-4438-3981-5

To the sources of our inspiration

Afrang
Cariz
Paliz
Alvan

TABLE OF CONTENTS

PREFACE

It has always been our plan to collect the most important documents which are relevant to the protection of the rights of children within national, regional and international legislation. One of the essential reasons for the presentation of those basic documents relating to the rule of law applicable to the rights of children, minors or juveniles is to make their contents as accessible as possible to all readers. Thus, one of the core reasons for the presentation of these documents in a single volume is to protect the voice of all those victims whose rights have been violated, purely on the basis that they were minors. Justice cannot be done within the social structure of any society as long as the basic elements of that society do not appropriately protect the rights of children. This is because social justice cannot properly survive if the members of a society and the machinery of justice prejudice the protection of the rights of children or juveniles. Our aim with this collection is thus twofold. The purpose is firstly to protect the rights of our children, and secondly to emphasize that the development of the principles of international democracy is also based on the appropriate implementation of the rights of children. This means that inequality and violence cannot be reduced during peace or war as long as we have not modified our understanding of the meaning of rights for all persons of all ages. As the 1968 Proclamation of Tehran states, "The aspirations of the younger generation for a better world, in which human rights and fundamental freedoms are fully implemented, must be given the highest encouragement. It is imperative that youth participate in shaping the future of mankind"; and is further emphasized in the 2000 United Nations Millennium Declaration: "As leaders we have a duty therefore to all the world's people, especially the most vulnerable and, in particular, the children of the world, to whom the future belongs".

Farhad Malekian
Kerstin Nordlöf
Carolina Rediviva Library
Uppsala, May 2012

INTRODUCTION

In order to describe, understand and analyse the rule of law[1] for the protection of children, one has to understand the intention of the philosophy of law; this philosophy is itself the subject of much debate. In short, legal philosophy deals with the theoretical analysis of the nature of law, norms of law and the relationship between law and morality, and what the values underpinning of the various regulations. Thus, when we talk about different values, we are simultaneously talking about different combinations of norms which are supposed to protect society. This criterion distinguishes law norms from non-juridical norms, such as ethical one. An appropriate rule of law is hence a legal framework under which decisions about various matters of interest have to be impartially applied. The system of law must create and preserve equality, justice, fairness, reciprocity, mutual understanding and not least should be based on human values integrated with documents on human rights law. "International justice can refer to adherence to the rule of law generally, i.e., accepting that 'there is an international society within which every state accepts that the same basic principles of international norms are applicable to every other state and that they are all equal before the law and the international legal system. They can neither modify the rules by their own will nor ignore them.'[2] Adherence to the rule of law includes application of norms of equity *infra legem*".[3] Therefore, when we deny or ignore the rule of law, which is based on the fundamental principles of human rights law, we are not only violating the rules of the national or regional spheres, but of the international legal community as a whole. This means that states are under an obligation to implement the principles of human rights law, including those protecting the integrity of children. Furthermore, there is

---

[1] The Preamble to the Universal Declaration of Human Rights states that human rights should be protected by the rule of law.

[2] F. Malekian, "Emasculating the Philosophy of International Criminal Justice in the Iraqi Special Tribunal," 38 *Cornell Int'l L. J.* 638, 678 (2005)

[3] Dinah Shelton, Of Means and Ends: Poverty Alleviation and Environmental Protection (Manatt/Ahn Professor of International Law, The George Washington University Law School Mexico City, November 11, 2008). Shelton has quoted F. Malekian *ibid.* www.iucnael.org/component/option,com_docman/task,doc_download /gid,228/Itemid,/lang,english/.

actually a growing tendency towards the recognition of the rules of law governing the protection of children as an integral part of obligatory *erga omnes*.

Laws to protect the rights of children have been existed since antiquity. These protections have been integrated into other laws such as criminal law or theological rules. Criminal law also meant civil law, family law and human rights law. This was because the body of criminal law dealt with most areas of domestic jurisdiction. Protection of children was thus not in itself a separate area of law, but an integral part of domestic legislation, the identification of which was rather problematic. The fact was that every matter came under the same concept of law. More significantly, provisions of natural law spoke about the rights of genders in which rights of children were combined. But the serious problem with these forms of protection was that children's rights were not recognised separately, and violations of their rights were therefore frequent. Yet, certain negative decisions could also be taken with regard to the natural rights of children by those who had law-making power or were regarded as the most authoritative body to carry out extraordinary measures. Those decisions could, as in the contemporary position of children, be taken in war or peacetime. In connection with a study on the confessing the international rights of children only a few examples out of millions concerning the violation of children's rights will be mentioned below, where the contradictions of such practice are more than obvious.

One historical example is the Thirty Years War in Europe (1618-1648) during which thousands of children were killed, and some even eaten.[4] This was mostly the consequence of theological atrocities beginning in Germany and going through most of central and northern Europe. But massacres against children were not just carried out in seventeenth century Europe. The 1917 Russian Revolution stands as one of the most terrible examples of genocide, including children. In 1921, the Committee of The Save the Children Fund from Canada insisted on the importance of relief for six million Russian children who were suffering from famine and malnutrition.[5] For instance, the famine in the Ukraine (1932-1933), which was the result of forced collectivization by the Russian communists, caused the starvation of seven million, a large number of which were

[4] Farhad Malekian, International Criminal Law, Vol.2 (1991).
[5] www.savethechildren.ca/page.aspx?pid=384. Visited 28 February 2012.

undoubtedly children.[6] These inhuman decisions were a direct consequence of Stalinist policies, rather than of Marx and Engel's theories.

The same is true in the case of famine and starvation during the Second World War in Bengal, India. Millions knowingly perished because of Winston Churchill's diplomacy, causing the huge murder of Indian children.[7] The basic reason for this murder was to use the resources of India in order to wage war against Germany and Japan which were fighting against most European States. Churchill himself mentions that the British victory was carried out on the "shoulders of our small Island" namely Bengal.[8] Or perhaps it is best to say on the small shoulders of babies, juveniles, and young children. These killings were surely against children's rights in peace or war, and in disregard of the duties of the colonial powers of the time.

Atrocities and criminal actions were also committed against Jewish children during the Second World War (1939–1945). The crimes were mostly carried out by Nazi criminals. The result was that the natural and legal rights of Jewish children were seriously violated during the war and they were brutally killed. This brutality against Jewish children even occurred in other countries, including Russia, and occurred when Germany occupied Poland in 1939. Almost 1000 children were forced from Russia to escape to Iran and obtain temporary asylum in Tehran. They were called Tehran Children.[9]

The Vietnam War (1955–1975) is another instance of violation of children's rights and their humiliation.[10] It was generally a war between two super powers—the United States and the USSR. The former supported South Vietnam, and the latter North Vietnam. Over one million Vietnamese were slaughtered, a large number of whom were children. One of the most horrible ongoing legacies of this war is the children who were born as a result of the rape of Vietnamese women, or of close relations with American Soldiers. They were called *children of the dust.* The rights of these children were long denied, not only by the American authorities,

---

[6] James E. Mace, Communism and the Dilemmas of National Liberation: National Communism in Soviet Ukraine, 1918-1933 (1983); Borys Martchenko, La Famine-genocide en Ukraine: 1932-1933 (1983).

[7] Madhusree Mukerjee, Churchill's Secret War: The British Empire and the Ravaging of India during World War II (2010).

[8] Winston Churchill, The Second World War, 6 volumes (2002).

[9] Henryk Grynberg, Children of Zion (Jewish Lives - Nonfiction), (1998).

[10] Richard Falk, The Vietnam War and International Law, Vol.1 (1968), Vol.2 (1970), Vol.3 (1972). Richard Falk, The Vietnam War and International Law: The Concluding Phase, Vol.4 (1976).

but also by the Vietnamese. Even those children who emigrated to the United States faced problematic questions on their arrival. These problems even occurred in 1991, for the children, who were now grown up, had themselves had children, and those children now had an American background.[11] One of the most famous photos of the war, demonstrating the horrors suffered by children (and which also won the Pulitzer Prize), is the photo recording the running of five children between 5–12 years, three of whom are two brothers and a sister, and two others their cousins. It shows the 9-year-old sister running naked in order to flee a South Vietnamese napalm attack on Trảng Bàng village.[12]

The use of children by Iranian armed forces in the war between Iran and Iraq (1980–1988) and offering them the key to paradise is another illustrative example of ignoring of children's rights by two of the Middle East's oil powers. The violations of Kurdish children's rights in Halabja in Iraq by Saddam Hussein (1988), and their killing with chemical weapons, imply the systematic machinery of ignoring children's rights. The tragedy of the killing of Kurdish children was internationally condemned, but without any particular steps taken in the cause of victims. Saddam Hussein was hanged in 2006, but not for the destruction of Kurdish children's rights.

In fact, Iraqi children went into more horrible and unfinished wars after the war with Iran. This is known as the First and Second Gulf Wars. The first started by a coalition of states led by the United States. It ended in 1991. The intention was to drive out the Iraqi army from Kuwait.[13] The Second war started in 2003 and ended in 2011.[14] This was led by the United States and the Great Britain aggressive armed activities. In 1995 the Food and Agriculture Organization of the United Nations report Crop and Nutrition Status Assessment Mission pointed out that the mortality among Iraqi children had increased almost fivefold since 1990. According

[11] Carol Lawson, Sheltering Children Of the Vietnam War, The New York Times, April 18, 1991. www.nytimes.com/1991/04/18/garden/she. Visited 28 February 2012.

[12] en.wikipedia.org/wiki/Vietnam_War. Visited 28 February 2012.

[13] Iraq had conquered its neighbour country – Kuwait. This was based on the fact that the discussion for oil settlement was failed between the two countries.

[14] In short, Saddam Hussein had been working for the CIA. It is today generally agreed by a majority of writers that the resolutions of the Security Council did not permit the use of armed force, although the invasion of Kuwait was a strong reason for armed attacks. For an examination of the Gulf War See Farhad Malekian, Condemning the Use of Force in the Gulf Crisis (2ed, 1994); See also Farhad Malekian, 'Emasculating the Philosophy of International Criminal Justice in the Iraqi Special Tribunal,' 38:3 *Cornell International Law Journal* (2005) 673-723.

to the 1996 United Nations Children Found (UNICEF), every month 4,500 children under five years old died from hunger in Iraq. As a result, millions of children were starving and still are suffering as a consequence of the Gulf Wars.[15]

These violations of children's rights are intensified in other parts of the globe. For instance, according to the Human Rights Watch Report, the use of child soldiers as young as 11 in Burma constituted 20 per cent of the total military. However, this figure did not however include the recruitment of children by opposition political parties.[16]

Until recent decades, children in Latin America were not recognized as an independent social group. However, the 1989 Convention on the Rights of the Child has developed the idea of the recognition and protection of the rights of children. Nevertheless "it is a constant struggle for families to protect the rights of their children".[17] One of the serious reasons is the economic poverty which creates practical problems for the protection of children, in particular those who do not have any guardian or custodian. The problem is greater in Brazil, where street children are reportedly killed by police officers. In addition, children are still the victims of social or political violence because of their vulnerability. The consequences of this poverty are clear even today.

In 2010, the estimated global number of childhood deaths was 7.6 million, half of which was, at least, due to poor nutrition. It is also estimated that 4 per cent of malnourished children live in Latin America and the Caribbean, 26 per cent in Africa and 70 per cent in Asia.[18] The

---

[15] Farhad Malekian, 'Emasculating the Philosophy of International Criminal Justice in the Iraqi Special Tribunal,' 38:3 *.Cornell International Law Journal* (2005) 673-723.; See also Report of the Secretary-General on children and armed conflict in Iraq, S/2011/366, 15 June 2011. The report emphasises the patterns of grave violations committed against children. It lists the killing and injury of a large number of children in various situations and conflicts such as recruitment and use of children by armed forces and armed groups, detention of children for alleged association with armed groups, killing or maiming of children, rape or other grave sexual violence against children, abduction of children, attacks on schools or hospitals, denial of humanitarian access and sexual violence perpetrated against children.

[16] My Gun Was as Tall As Me: Child Soldiers in Burma (2002).

[17] Maria Cristina Salazar and Felicia Marie Knaul, Children Without Rights in Latin America, pangaea.org/street_children/world/rights.htm, visited on 1 March 2012.

[18] www.worldhunger.org/.../world%20hunger%20facts%202002.htm. Visited on 1 March 2012.

under-nourishment of children is not necessarily due to food shortages,[19] but incorrect economic division; insufficient income among families thus endangers the physical health of children, and violates their rights to a healthy childhood which is repeatedly stated in United Nations documents.[20]

The majority of the Afghan population are children. Afghan children not only suffer from poverty (and therefore nutrition problems), but also from 30 years of war and the extreme risk of violence, abuse, exploitation, gender discrimination, attacks and air strikes by insurgent groups, international military and armed forces and the Afghan National Army.[21] Boys face recruitment and sexual abuse by the armed forces. To take a few examples, 93 children died in United States air strikes in 2009; almost 1.6 million children have been orphaned and are condemned also to hunger, sickness, and deprivation because of the NATO war. In addition, the children of refugees, and refugee children are homeless and experience many social problems. Registration of births is very limited (90 per cent are not registered at all), and a large number of children die before their fifth birthday. Lack of proper education is damaging children, in particular girls who face multiple discrimination. Almost 70 per cent of girls in Afghanistan do not attend school.[22]

The denial of children's rights can also be seen in the policy of the Chinese government against its own children, or its forceful occupation of Tibet, for example in discrimination of social services or prevention of distribution of medicine to hundreds of thousands of children who are at risk of permanent mental and physical disabilities because of factory

---

[19] Black RE, Morris SS, Bryce J. "Where and why are 10 million children dying every year?" Department of International Health, Johns Hopkins Bloomberg School of Public Health, Baltimore (2003).

[20] www.worldhunger.org/articles/Learn/child_hunger_facts.htm. Visited on 1 March 2012.

[21] Report of the Secretary-General on children and armed conflict in Afghanistan, S/2011/55, 3 February 2011.

[22] David Swanson & David Swanson, Afghanistan: worst place for children to be born and raised: Not only do children die, they can also be recruited and used to fight in armed forces and groups (October 2011), stopwar.org.uk/.../afghanistan.../839-afghanistan-the-worst-place-on-earth-for-children. Visited on 1 March 2012. Visited on 1 March 2012; David Swanson & David Swanson The Children of Afghanistan: An analysis of children's rights in Afghanistan Report (2011), stopwar.org.uk/.../afghanistan.../839-afghanistan-the-worst-place-on-earth-for-children. Visited on 1 March 2012. Visited on 1 March 2012.

pollution.[23] Discrimination between boys and girls is also a serious problem in Chinese society. Similarly, gender discrimination against girls in India constitutes another aspect of the violation of children's rights.[24]

Although Australia has stated that it supports human rights law, the United Nations's Human Rights Committee has handled 50 cases relating to Australia since 1990. The Committee has found that in 17 decisions Australia violated its obligations of human rights law, including mistreatment of children or family unity by immigration authorities or the like.[25] Despite this, the Australian government wholly denied the decision of Human Rights Committee arguing that the Committee was not a Court, and that its decision was therefore not judicially binding. The Australian authorities have, however ignored the fact that Australia does not have a Bill of Rights, and that Australian courts are not therefore empowered to hear complaints about violations of international human rights law.[26]

Australia, Canada and the United States do not accept the Human Rights Committee's interpretation of Article 19 of the Convention on the Rights of the Child disallowing the corporal punishment of children.[27] Nevertheless, the most recent event is that the third Protocol to the Convention on the Rights of the Child empowers the United Nations Child Rights Committee to examine violations of children's rights. The Protocol allows children and young people to report violations of their rights directly to the Committee. It opened for signature and ratification on 29 February 2012. The hope is that the Protocol will be signed by all states. This is exclusively for the protection of children and gross violations of their rights under different domestic legal machinery. However, we are aware that the Convention on the Rights of the Child has not yet been ratified by the United State or Somalia. The former claims that its national

---

[23] My Children Have been Poisoned, Human Rights Watch Report (2011), www.hrw.org/news/.../china-children-poisoned-lead-and-denied-treatment. Visited on 1 March 2012.

[24] Navdeep Kour Sasan, The Indian Perspective of Gender Discrimination on Girl Children and Foeticide in Farhad Malekian and Kerstin Nordlöf, The Sovereignty of Children in Law (2012), pp. 178-ff.

[25] Winata v Australia (2002): UN Doc CCPR/C/72/D/930/2000 (16 August 2001); Bakhtiyari v Australia (2003)UN Doc CCPR/C/79/D/1069/2002 (29 October 2003); Madafferi v Australia (2004): UN Doc CCPR/C/81/D/1011/2001 (26 August 2004). *Visited on 2 March 2009.*

[26] www.nswccl.org.au/issues/hr_violations.php. Visited on 2 March 2012.

[27] Simalis, Linda (21 March 2010): "Aussie parents to defy UN smacking ban". *The Sunday Telegraph* (Sydney). http://www.heraldsun.com.au/news/national/aussie-parents-to-defy-un-smacking-ban/story-e6frf7l6-1225843384853?from=public_rss. Visited on 2 March 2012.

legislation protects the rights of children, although there is evidence proving that there are a considerable number of problems regarding child abuse, juvenile law and health services. For instance, there are 3 million reported cases of child abuse, including physical and sexual ones. And some individual states in the United States have not yet abolished the application of the death penalty to those who were minors at the time of the commission of the crime. In 2009, the Human Rights Watch even found that 2500 children received life imprisonment although they were under 18 at the time of the crime. In addition, although the United States has ratified the Optional Protocol to the Convention on the Rights of the Child on the Involvement of Children in Armed Conflicts, it has not completely fulfilled its provisions and has even armed countries such as Chad, The Democratic Republic of Congo, Sudan and Yemen which notoriously use children in armed conflicts.[28]

Serious violations and horrible chemical killing of children in the Gaza Strip (2008) by Israeli armed forces implies the illegality of unlawful violations of the rights of children.[29] The violations of the Gaza Strip children's rights can be read in the statement by Richard Goldstone on behalf of the Members of the United Nations Fact Finding Mission on the Gaza Conflict before the Human Rights Council. It concludes *inter alia* that: "The truth and accountability are also essential to prevent ascribing collective guilt to a people. Many people in Gaza deplore the firing of thousands of rockets at civilians in Southern Israel and the terror that it has caused to innocent children, women and men." [30] It further states that "And many in Israel, Jews and Palestinians, deplore the actions by the Israel Defense Force that caused unjustifiable civilian deaths and injuries on a very large scale. They do not approve of the damage to the food and commercial infrastructure of Gaza that will take many years to repair".[31] The report of the mission specified that in the Gaza Strip 20 per cent of children suffer from post-traumatic stress disorders, and that:

> From the facts gathered, the Mission finds that numerous violations of international humanitarian law and human rights law were committed in the context of ... detentions. Civilians, including women and children, were

[28] childrensrightsportal.org/united-states-of-america/. Visited on 2 March 2012.

[29] For example see HUMAN RIGHTS SITUATION IN PALESTINE AND OTHER OCCUPIED ARAB TERRITORIES, A/HRC/10/22, 20 March 2009.

[30] Statement by Richard Goldstone on behalf of the Members of the United Nations Fact Finding Mission on the Gaza Conflict before the Human Rights Council, Human Rights Council 12th Session – 29 September 2009.

[31] Ibid.

> detained in degrading conditions, deprived of food, water and access to sanitary facilities, and exposed to the elements in January without any shelter. ... In the al-Atatra area in north-western Gaza, Israeli troops had dug out sandpits in which Palestinian men, women and children were detained. Israeli tanks and artillery positions were located inside the sandpits and around them and fired from next to the detainees...The razing of farmland and the destruction of greenhouses are expected to further worsen food insecurity despite the increased quantities of food items allowed into Gaza since the beginning of the military operations. Dependence on food assistance increases. Levels of stunting and thinness in children and of anaemia prevalence in children and pregnant women were worrying even before the military operations. The hardship caused by the extensive destruction of shelter (the United Nations Development Programme reported 3,354 houses completely destroyed and 11,112 partially damaged) and the resulting displacement particularly affects children and women. Children's psychological learning difficulties are compounded by the impact of the blockade and the military operations on the education infrastructure. Some 280 schools and kindergartens were destroyed in a situation in which restrictions on the importation of construction materials meant that many school buildings were already in serious need of repair.[32]

The violation of children's rights can also be examined in other parts of the world. A clear example of these violations is the various illegal uses of children in conflicts in Sierra Leone, Somalia, Uganda and Chad.[33] In all regions, children have been physically and physiologically employed to carry out adult orders and works. They have also been forced in recruitment and use of children in armed forces and groups, into sex slavery, to commit crimes, and to kill civilians. In the Uganda conflicts as in many other conflicts in Africa or other parts of the world, children were stigmatized in order not to be able to return to their own society, for example by being forced to kill members of their own family. It is reported that many child soldiers in Uganda, Nepal and Sri Lanka are girls. They are raped, sexually violated and forced to marry military commanders. Although the Special Sierra Leone Court (SCSL) and the hybrid court are working with all relevant issues governing violations of children's rights, the legacy of conflicts has been seriously harmful, and rehabilitation and returning children to normal social life has not been easy. The SCSL has even worked with the aim of proving that children should always be regarded as victims and not as perpetrators. It has therefore strongly

---

[32] *Ibid., paras.*57, 58, 67, 70.

[33] For example see Report of the Secretary-General on children and armed conflict in Chad, S/2011/64, 9 February 2011.

avoided applying any punishment at all. However, the application of capital punishment to children has been employed in other parts of the world. A clear example and very extensive form of this illegal punishment has been carried out under the Islamic Republic of Iran. In addition, trafficking, as well as the sexual exploitation of children in many countries, and the unlawful use of children for work purposes in a large number of countries, are still some of the most unpleasant violations of children's rights.

All the above examples show the injustice against children and their vulnerable position as victims.[34] The Basic Principles and Guidelines on the Rights to a Remedy and Reparation for Victims of Gross Violations of International Human Rights Law and Serious Violations of International Humanitarian Law has to some extent described the word "victim" by emphasising that:

> Victims are persons who individually or collectively suffered harm, including physical or mental injury, emotional suffering, economic loss or substantial impairment of their fundamental rights, through acts or omissions that constitute gross violations of international human rights law, or serious violations of international humanitarian law. Where appropriate, and in accordance with domestic law, the term "victim" also includes the immediate family or dependants of the direct victim and persons who have suffered harm in intervening to assist victims in distress or to prevent victimization.[35]

Protection of children's rights under the rule of law undoubtedly constitutes one of the most important questions of justice and morality, which cannot be ignored by any national or international lawyer. The juridical protection of these rights has been especially emphasized in a number of international documents formulated under the supervision of the United Nations Organization. There are therefore many international documents dealing directly or indirectly with the rights of juveniles, youths, minors or children. A very significant convention relating to the rights of children is the Convention on the Rights of the Child, and its very valuable additional protocols. The convention is a milestone in the protection of various rights of children. Similarly, there are other

---

[34] Report of the Special Representative of the Secretary-General for Children and Armed Conflict, A/66/256, 3 August 2011.

[35] Basic Principles and Guidelines on the Rights to a Remedy and Reparation for Victims of Gross Violations of International Human Rights Law and Serious Violations of International Humanitarian Law. G.A. Res. 60/147, U.N. Doc.A/RES/60/147 (Mar. 21, 2006).

international conventions which protect the rights of children before various types of jurisdiction, when the question of juvenile criminality arises, and in other situations such as discrimination.

Within different continents, a number of documents directly and indirectly protecting the rights of children have been developed; the relevant sections of these documents are presented here. The presentation is divided into different sections depending on the direct or indirect intention of the relevant document. They may also be divided according to the particular child protection. Each document presented in this issue has an introductory description. Some documents are presented in their entirety, and others, because of their wider application than child protection, only partly. The introduction to each document illustrates and furnishes important explanations to aid understanding of the legal position of the document and the reasons underlying its formulation or ratification in the international or regional arena. Our hope is that the rule of law protecting the rights of children, will be positively worked out in their interests.

CHAPTER I

INTERNATIONAL LEGISLATIONS INDIRECTLY SUPPORTING VARIOUS RIGHTS OF CHILDREN

1. Universal Declaration of Human Rights, 1948

The Universal Declaration of Human Rights, which was adopted by the United Nations General Assembly in 1948, is one of the most significant instruments in the field of human rights.[1] Although the Declaration does not have the legal effect of an international convention, its norms are an integral part of customary international law. The norms of the Declaration are also regarded as an important part of the international law of *jus cogens*, which means that they have to be respected by all states and should not be violated by their national legislations. The Declaration contains many provisions regarding the fundamental rights of individuals that should not be ignored by state organs or authorities. Some of the rights listed in the Declaration are of a general, and some of a particular, character. Two of the most important Articles of the Declaration on the rights of children are numbers 25 and 26: these bring together some of the essential principles that are of decisive social value in the protection of children. They state:

Article 25

1. Everyone has the right to a standard of living adequate for the health and well-being of himself and of his family, including food, clothing, housing, and medical care and necessary social services, and the right to security in the event of unemployment, sickness, disability, widowhood, old age or other lack of livelihood in circumstances beyond his control.

2. Motherhood and childhood are entitled to special care and assistance. All children, whether born in or out of wedlock, shall enjoy the same social protection.

---

[1] Resolution 217 A (III) of 10 December 1948. It was a unanimously adopted by the 48 member states of the U.N.

Article 26

1. Everyone has the right to education. Education shall be free, at least in the elementary and fundamental stages. Elementary education shall be compulsory. Technical and professional education shall be made generally available and higher education shall be equally accessible to all on the basis of merit.

2. Education shall be directed to the full development of the human personality and to the strengthening of respect for human rights and fundamental freedoms. It shall promote understanding, tolerance and friendship among all nations, racial or religious groups, and shall further the activities of the United Nations for the maintenance of peace.

3. Parents have a prior right to choose the kind of education that shall be given to their children.

2. Proclamation of Tehran, 1968

The words of the Universal Declaration of Human Rights regarding the protection of children are also contained within the Proclamation of Tehran, constituting one of the significant instruments of the recognition of the protection of the rights of the child. The Proclamation was adopted at an international conference on human rights in Tehran, 1968, and the intention was to strengthen human rights values within national and international systems. The Proclamation particularly stated that "Since human rights and fundamental freedoms are indivisible, the full realization of civil and political rights without the enjoyment of economic, social and cultural rights is impossible. The achievement of lasting progress in the implementation of human rights is dependent upon sound and effective national and international policies of economic and social development".[2] The Proclamation paved the way for the adoption of a number of new international instruments.

One of the Proclamation's 19 sections states the importance of the protection children's rights by the international political and legal community as a whole. In other words, the Proclamation internationalizes the rights of children, and emphasises the obligations of the international community to seriously deal with the rights of children at a universal level.[3] It read that:

---

[2] Section 13.

[3] Proclamation of Tehran, Final Act of the International Conference on Human Rights, Teheran, 22 April to 13 May 1968, U.N. Doc. A/CONF. 32/41 at 3 (1968), United Nations, May 1968.

14. The existence of over seven hundred million illiterates throughout the world is an enormous obstacle to all efforts at realizing the aims and purposes of the Charter of the United Nations and the provisions of the Universal Declaration of Human Rights. International action aimed at eradicating illiteracy from the face of the earth and promoting education at all levels requires urgent attention;

15. The discrimination of which women are still victims in various regions of the world must be eliminated. An inferior status for women is contrary to the Charter of the United Nations as well as the provisions of the Universal Declaration of Human Rights. The full implementation of the Declaration on the Elimination of Discrimination against Women is a necessity for the progress of mankind;

16. The protection of the family and of the child remains the concern of the international community. Parents have a basic human right to determine freely and responsibly the number and the spacing of their children;

17. The aspirations of the younger generation for a better world, in which human rights and fundamental freedoms are fully implemented, must be given the highest encouragement. It is imperative that youth participate in shaping the future of mankind.

:::::::::

Therefore,

The International Conference on Human Rights,

1. Affirming its faith in the principles of the Universal Declaration of Human Rights and other international instruments in this field,

2. Urges all peoples and governments to dedicate themselves to the principles enshrined in the Universal Declaration of Human Rights and to redouble their efforts to provide for all human beings a life consonant with freedom and dignity and conducive to physical, mental, social and spiritual welfare.

3. Declaration on Social Progress and Development, 1969

Another relevant instrument concerning safeguarding of the rights of children is the Declaration on Social Progress and Development, recalling the principles of the Declaration of the Rights of the Child. The Declaration was adopted and proclaimed by General Assembly Resolution 2542 (XXIV) of 11 December 1969. The Declaration has several goals for the protection of social rights of human beings under the legal machinery of states. Its aims are to create some sort of norms regarding the duties of governments in the protection of children's rights. It therefore included several principles relating to the rights of children, with the hope that they will be respected by the legal authorities of states. Some of the applicable provisions of the Declaration are contained in Articles 4, 11, 19, 21 and 22. They state:

Part I
PRINCIPLES
Article 4

The family as a basic unit of society and the natural environment for the growth and well-being of all its members, particularly children and youth, should be assisted and protected so that it may fully assume its responsibilities within the community. Parents have the exclusive right to determine freely and responsibly the number and spacing of their children.

Part II
OBJECTIVES
Article 11

(a) The provision of comprehensive social security schemes and social welfare services; the establishment and improvement of social security and insurance schemes for all persons who, because of illness, disability or old age, are temporarily or permanently unable to earn a living, with a view to ensuring a proper standard of living for such persons and for their families and dependants;

(b) The protection of the rights of the mother and child; concern for the upbringing and health of children; the provision of measures to safeguard the health and welfare of women and particularly of working mothers during pregnancy and the infancy of their children, as well as of mothers whose earnings are the sole source of livelihood for the family; the granting to women of pregnancy and maternity leave and allowances without loss of employment or wages;

(c) The protection of the rights and the assuring of the welfare of children, the aged and the disabled; the provision of protection for the physically or mentally disadvantaged;

(d) The education of youth in, and promotion among them of, the ideals of justice and peace, mutual respect and understanding among peoples; the promotion of full participation of youth in the process of national development;

(e) The provision of social defence measures and the elimination of conditions leading to crime and delinquency, especially juvenile delinquency;

(f) The guarantee that all individuals, without discrimination of any kind, are made aware of their rights and obligations and receive the necessary aid in the exercise and safeguarding of their rights.

Social progress and development shall further aim at achieving the following main objectives:

Part II
MEANS AND METHODS
Article 19

(a) The provision of free health services to the whole population and of adequate preventive and curative facilities and welfare medical services accessible to all;

(b) The enactment and establishment of legislative measures and administrative regulations with a view to the implementation of comprehensive programmes of social security schemes and social welfare services and to the improvement and co-ordination of existing services;

(c) The adoption of measures and the provision of social welfare services to migrant workers and their families, in conformity with the provisions of Convention No. 97 of the International Labour Organisation and other international instruments relating to migrant workers;

(d) The institution of appropriate measures for the rehabilitation of mentally or physically disabled persons, especially children and youth, so as to enable them to the fullest possible extent to be useful members of society-these measures shall include the provision of treatment and technical appliances, education, vocational and social guidance, training and selective placement, and other assistance required-and the creation of social conditions in which the handicapped are not discriminated against because of their disabilities.

Article 21

(a) The training of national personnel and cadres, including administrative, executive, professional and technical personnel needed for social development and for over-all development plans and policies;

(b) The adoption of measures to accelerate the extension and improvement of general, vocational and technical education and of training and retraining, which should be provided free at all levels;

(c) Raising the general level of education; development and expansion of national information media, and their rational and full use towards continuing education of the whole population and towards encouraging its participation in social development activities; the constructive use of leisure, particularly that of children and adolescents;

(d) The formulation of national and international policies and measures to avoid the "brain drain" and obviate its adverse effects.

Article 22

(a) The development and co-ordination of policies and measures designed to strengthen the essential functions of the family as a basic unit of society;

(b) The formulation and establishment, as needed, of programmes in the field of population, within the framework of national demographic policies and as part of the welfare medical services, including education, training of personnel and the provision to families of the knowledge and means necessary to enable them to exercise their right to determine freely and responsibly the number and spacing of their children;

(c) The establishment of appropriate child-care facilities in the interest of children and working parents.

4. Universal Declaration on the Eradication of Hunger and Malnutrition, 1974

The Universal Declaration on the Eradication of Hunger and Malnutrition is a key instrument protecting the rights of children to food, and condemning starvations. The Declaration was adopted by the World Food Conference in 1974, having been strongly supported by General Assembly Resolution 3180 (XXVIII) in 1973. One of the most important parts of the Declaration concerns the inalienable and indisputable rights of children to food for their daily life. Other provisions of the Declaration emphasise the responsibility of governments for achieving the aims of eradicating hunger, malnourishment and starvation among children. According to Jean Ziegler, the United Nations Special Rapporteur on the Right to Food from 2000 to March 2008, starvation of children is one of the main reasons for the high mortality in this group: “In the world, approximately 62 million people, all causes of death combined, die each year. One in twelve people worldwide is malnourished. In 2006, more than 36 millions died of hunger or diseases due to deficiencies in micronutrients". Although the provisions of the Declaration encourage protecting children from starvation or hunger, the international community is still challenged by the problems. Some of the relevant provisions of the Declaration on the Eradication of Hunger and Malnutrition state:

The Conference consequently solemnly proclaims:

1. Every man, woman and child has the inalienable right to be free from hunger and malnutrition in order to develop fully and maintain their physical and mental faculties. Society today already possesses sufficient resources, organizational ability and technology and hence the competence to achieve this objective. Accordingly, the eradication of hunger is a common objective of all the countries of the international community, especially of the developed countries and others in a position to help.

2. It is a fundamental responsibility of Governments to work together for higher food production and a more equitable and efficient distribution of food between countries and within countries. Governments should initiate immediately a greater concerted attack on chronic malnutrition and deficiency diseases among the vulnerable and lower income groups. In order to ensure adequate nutrition for all, Governments should formulate appropriate food and nutrition policies integrated in overall socio-economic and agricultural development plans based on adequate knowledge of available as well as potential food resources. The importance of human milk in this connection should be stressed on nutritional grounds.

3. Food problems must be tackled during the preparation and implementation of national plans and programmes for economic and social development, with emphasis on their humanitarian aspects.

4. It is a responsibility of each State concerned, in accordance with its sovereign judgement and internal legislation, to remove the obstacles to food production and to provide proper incentives to agricultural producers. Of prime importance for the attainment of these objectives are effective measures of socio-economic transformation by agrarian, tax, credit and investment policy reform and the reorganization of rural structures, such as the reform of the conditions of ownership, the encouragement of producer and consumer co-operatives, the mobilization of the full potential of human resources, both male and female, in the developing countries for an integrated rural development and the involvement of small farmers, fishermen and landless workers in attaining the required food production and employment targets. Moreover, it is necessary to recognize the key role of women in agricultural production and rural economy in many countries, and to ensure that appropriate education, extension programmes and financial facilities are made available to women on equal terms with men.

5. Declaration on the Elimination of All Forms of Intolerance and of Discrimination Based on Religion or Belief, 1981

Another remarkable international document, which indirectly relates to the protection of the rights of children, whether minors, young or juveniles, is the Declaration on the Elimination of All Forms of Intolerance and of Discrimination Based on Religion or Belief, adopted by the General Assembly in 1981. One of the chief purposes of the Declaration is to restrict provisions of the constitutions of states which interfere with basic rights of individuals, and discriminate between different beliefs. The Declaration has in fact strengthened the norms of the Universal Declaration of Human Rights. The 1981 Declaration was formulated during a time when there were movements in some of the states against the inalienable rights of individuals in the matter of freedom of religion, such as the Iranian constitution of 1979. It must not be forgotten that one of the major criticisms of the Declaration is its legal structure, which is formulated as a resolution and not as a law-making treaty. Some of the most important parts of the Declaration relating to the rights of children state:

Article 5

1. The parents or, as the case may be, the legal guardians of the child have the right to organize the life within the family in accordance with their religion or belief and bearing in mind the moral education in which they believe the child should be brought up.

2. Every child shall enjoy the right to have access to education in the matter of religion or belief in accordance with the wishes of his parents or, as the case may be, legal guardians, and shall not be compelled to receive teaching on religion or belief against the wishes of his parents or legal guardians, the best interests of the child being the guiding principle.

3. The child shall be protected from any form of discrimination on the ground of religion or belief. He shall be brought up in a spirit of understanding, tolerance, friendship among peoples, peace and universal brotherhood, respect for freedom of religion or belief of others, and in full consciousness that his energy and talents should be devoted to the service of his fellow men.

4. In the case of a child who is not under the care either of his parents or of legal guardians, due account shall be taken of their expressed wishes or of any other proof of their wishes in the matter of religion or belief, the best interests of the child being the guiding principle.

5. Practices of a religion or belief in which a child is brought up must not be injurious to his physical or mental health or to his full development, taking into account article 1, paragraph 3, of the present Declaration.

6. Declaration on the Human Rights of Individuals Who are not Nationals of the Country in which They Live, 1985

The Declaration on the Human Rights of Individuals Who are Not Nationals Of The Country in Which They Live was adopted by the General Assembly in Resolution 40/144, in December 1985. The aim of the Declaration is to maintain high human rights standards for those who for one reason or another are classified as aliens. Among others, it seeks to protect the rights of children of aliens within the legislation of different states. These rights, such as the right to life, equality, security and protection before the court, are listed in various Articles of the Declaration. This Declaration, like many other similar instruments, refers to the important character of the Universal Declaration of Human Rights and the functions of its norms. Several direct references to minors or children's rights can be seen in the content of the 1985 Declaration. Articles 1 and 5 of the Declaration state:

Article 1

For the purposes of this Declaration, the term "alien" shall apply, with due regard to qualifications made in subsequent articles, to any individual who is not a national of the State in which he or she is present.

Article 5

1. Aliens shall enjoy, in accordance with domestic law and subject to the relevant international obligation of the State in which they are present, in particular the following rights:

....

4. Subject to national legislation and due authorization, the spouse and minor or dependent children of an alien lawfully residing in the territory of a State shall be admitted to accompany, join and stay with the alien.

7. Declaration on the Protection of all Persons from Enforced Disappearance, 1992

The question of the disappearance of persons under the unlawful machinery of governments or states has been discussed from different angles within the system of international law, and the question has also been closely examined under the authority of the United Nations General Assembly. The Declaration on the Protection of all Persons from Enforced Disappearance was therefore adopted by the Assembly in order to protect the rights of those persons who have, for one reason or another, been the victims of these criminal actions. The disappearance of persons originally occurred under the legal authority of certain Latin American governments, such as Guatemala, and military regimes in Argentina, Chile, El Salvador, Honduras, Colombia and Nicaragua.The machinery of justice within these countries unfortunately thus had a very significant role in the application of unlawful decisions regarding torture, rape, murder or the killing of innocent individuals. Although the Declaration was mostly adopted for the prevention of the enforced disappearance in Latin American regimes, it has equal force and validity with respect to the disappearance of persons under the political authority of other regions such as Saudi Arabia and Libya, in the Middle East. Thus, enforced disappearance is not just a Latin American phenomenon, but a particular practice within many different, for example the disappearance of human activists in China. Some of the most important provisions of the Declaration regarding children state:

Article 20

1. States shall prevent and suppress the abduction of children of parents subjected to enforced disappearance and of children born during their mother's enforced disappearance, and shall devote their efforts to the search for and identification of such children and to the restitution of the children to their families of origin.

2. Considering the need to protect the best interests of children referred to in the preceding paragraph, there shall be an opportunity, in States which recognize a system of adoption, for a review of the adoption of such children and, in particular, for annulment of any adoption which originated in enforced disappearance. Such adoption should, however, continue to be in force if consent is given, at the time of the review, by the child's closest relatives.

3. The abduction of children of parents subjected to enforced disappearance or of children born during their mother's enforced disappearance, and the act of altering or suppressing documents attesting

to their true identity, shall constitute an extremely serious offence, which shall be punished as such.

4. For these purposes, States shall, where appropriate, conclude bilateral and multilateral agreements.

8. Guiding Principles on Internal Displacement, 1997

The Guiding Principles on Internal Displacement was first submitted to the United Nations Commission on Human Rights. It is not an officially enforceable law-making treaty, and does not have even the legal status of a resolution by the General Assembly.[4] It is simply a guiding instrument for the protection of certain civilians. The Guiding Principles have focused on the protection of the rights of those who are intentionally displaced by national authorities. In general, the instrument is against any arbitrary action. The philosophy behind the adoption of the Guiding Principles was not, however, welcomed by many governments, because it criticised their internal policies. Some of the more relevant provisions of the instrument concerning children are:

Principle 4

1. These Principles shall be applied without discrimination of any kind, such as race, colour, sex, language, religion or belief, political or other opinion, national, ethnic or social origin, legal or social status, age, disability, property, birth, or on any other similar criteria.

2. Certain internally displaced persons, such as children, especially unaccompanied minors, expectant mothers, mothers with young children, female heads of household, persons with disabilities and elderly persons, shall be entitled to protection and assistance required by their condition and to treatment which takes into account their special needs.

[4] Guiding Principles on Internal Displacement, U.N. Doc. E/CN.4/1998/53/Add.2 (1998), noted in Comm. Hum. Rts. res. 1998/50. Consult the Report of the Representative of the Secretary-General, Mr. Francis M. Deng, submitted pursuant to Commission Resolution 1997/39.

Principle 11

1. Every human being has the right to dignity and physical, mental and moral integrity.

2. Internally displaced persons, whether or not their liberty has been restricted, shall be protected in particular against:

(a) Rape, mutilation, torture, cruel, inhuman or degrading treatment or punishment, and other outrages upon personal dignity, such as acts of gender-specific violence, forced prostitution and any form of indecent assault;

(b) Slavery or any contemporary form of slavery, such as sale into marriage, sexual exploitation, or forced labour of children; and

(c) Acts of violence intended to spread terror among internally displaced persons.

Threats and incitement to commit any of the foregoing acts shall be prohibited.

Principle 13

1. In no circumstances shall displaced children be recruited nor be required or permitted to take part in hostilities.

2. Internally displaced persons shall be protected against discriminatory practices of recruitment into any armed forces or groups as a result of their displacement. In particular any cruel, inhuman or degrading practices that compel compliance or punish non-compliance with recruitment are prohibited in all circumstances.

Principle 17

1. Every human being has the right to respect of his or her family life.

2. To give effect to this right for internally displaced persons, family members who wish to remain together shall be allowed to do so.

3. Families which are separated by displacement should be reunited as quickly as possible. All appropriate steps shall be taken to expedite the reunion of such families, particularly when children are involved. The responsible authorities shall facilitate inquiries made by family members and encourage and cooperate with the work of humanitarian organizations engaged in the task of family reunification.

4. Members of internally displaced families whose personal liberty has been restricted by internment or confinement in camps shall have the right to remain together.

Principle 23

1. Every human being has the right to education.

2. To give effect to this right for internally displaced persons, the authorities concerned shall ensure that such persons, in particular displaced children, receive education which shall be free and compulsory at the primary level. Education should respect their cultural identity, language and religion.

3. Special efforts should be made to ensure the full and equal participation of women and girls in educational programmes.

4. Education and training facilities shall be made available to internally displaced persons, in particular adolescents and women, whether or not living in camps, as soon as conditions permit.

9. United Nations Millennium Declaration, 2000

At the start of the millennium in 2000, the General Assembly of the United Nations adopted a Resolution on 8 September,[5] emphasizing the commitments of the Organization, and in particular to the children to whom future society belongs. The areas which are specially mentioned in connection with children are poverty, education, HIV/AIDS, armed conflicts, sale, prostitution and pornography. These have all been fundamentally important to the effective consideration of the situation of children across the world. In particular, the physical health of children in relation to HIV/AIDS, widely broadcasted seen as essential to their future. The Millennium provides:

2. We recognize that, in addition to our separate responsibilities to our individual societies, we have a collective responsibility to uphold the principles of human dignity, equality and equity at the global level. As leaders we have a duty therefore to all the world's people, especially the most vulnerable and, in particular, the children of the world, to whom the future belongs.

...

Freedom. Men and women have the right to live their lives and raise their children in dignity, free from hunger and from the fear of violence, oppression or injustice. Democratic and participatory governance based on the will of the people best assures these rights.

...

19. We resolve further:

---

[5] Resolution 55/2.

· To halve, by the year 2015, the proportion of the world's people whose income is less than one dollar a day and the proportion of people who suffer from hunger and, by the same date, to halve the proportion of people who are unable to reach or to afford safe drinking water.

· To ensure that, by the same date, children everywhere, boys and girls alike, will be able to complete a full course of primary schooling and that girls and boys will have equal access to all levels of education.

· By the same date, to have reduced maternal mortality by three quarters, and under-five child mortality by two thirds, of their current rates.

· To have, by then, halted, and begun to reverse, the spread of HIV/AIDS, the scourge of malaria and other major diseases that afflict humanity.

· To provide special assistance to children orphaned by HIV/AIDS.

· By 2020, to have achieved a significant improvement in the lives of at least 100 million slum dwellers as proposed in the "Cities Without Slums" initiative.

VI. Protecting the vulnerable

26. We will spare no effort to ensure that children and all civilian populations that suffer disproportionately the consequences of natural disasters, genocide, armed conflicts and other humanitarian emergencies are given every assistance and protection so that they can resume normal life as soon as possible.

We resolve therefore:

· To expand and strengthen the protection of civilians in complex emergencies, in conformity with international humanitarian law.

· To strengthen international cooperation, including burden sharing in, and the coordination of humanitarian assistance to, countries hosting refugees and to help all refugees and displaced persons to return voluntarily to their s, in safety and dignity and to be smoothly reintegrated into their societies.

· To encourage the ratification and full implementation of the Convention on the Rights of the Child and its optional protocols on the involvement of children in armed conflict and on the sale of children, child prostitution and child pornography.

10. Norms on the Responsibilities of Transnational Corporations and Other Business Enterprises with Regard to Human Rights, 2003

The Norms of Business Enterprises with Regard to Human Rights were formulated and adopted under the authority of the Sub-Commission on the Promotion and Protection of Human Rights.[6] The norms deal with the areas of private, national or transnational cases. They aim to prevent transnational corporations and any other business enterprises from violating the basic principles of human rights law in the pursuit of making profits for their shareholders or other owners, among which national interests are often to be found. The Norms stipulate the importance of acting in accordance with recognized responsibilities and norms contained in United Nations treaties and other international instruments relating to human rights law. The Norms have also taken into serious account the provisions of the Convention on the Rights of the Child. The intention is to prevent various forms of exploitation of children under the power of corporations or other multilateral companies. The relevant parts of the Norms state:

> *Realizing* that transnational corporations and other business enterprises, their officers and persons working for them are also obligated to respect generally recognized responsibilities and norms contained in United Nations treaties and other international instruments such as the Convention on the Prevention and Punishment of the Crime of Genocide; the Convention against Torture and Other Cruel, Inhuman or Degrading Treatment or Punishment; the Slavery Convention and the Supplementary Convention on the Abolition of Slavery, the Slave Trade, and Institutions and Practices Similar to Slavery; the International Convention on the Elimination of All Forms of Racial Discrimination; the Convention on the Elimination of All Forms of Discrimination against Women; the International Covenant on Economic, Social and Cultural Rights; the International Covenant on Civil and Political Rights; the Convention on the Rights of the Child; the International Convention on the Protection of the Rights of All Migrant Workers and Members of Their Families; the four Geneva Conventions of 12 August 1949 and two Additional Protocols thereto for the protection of victims of war; the Declaration on the Right and Responsibility of Individuals, Groups and Organs of Society to Promote and Protect Universally Recognized Human Rights and Fundamental Freedoms; the Rome Statute of the International Criminal Court; the United Nations Convention against Transnational Organized

[6] U.N.Doc.E/CN.4/Sub.2/2003/12Rev.2.

> Crime; the Convention on Biological Diversity; the International Convention on Civil Liability for Oil Pollution Damage; the Convention on Civil Liability for Damage Resulting from Activities Dangerous to the Environment; the Declaration on the Right to Development; the Rio Declaration on the Environment and Development; the Plan of Implementation of the World Summit on Sustainable Development; the United Nations Millennium Declaration; the Universal Declaration on the Human Genome and Human Rights; the International Code of Marketing of Breast milk Substitutes adopted by the World Health Assembly; the Ethical Criteria for Medical Drug Promotion and the "Health for All in the Twenty-First Century" policy of the World Health Organization; the Convention against Discrimination in Education of the United Nations Education, Scientific, and Cultural Organization; conventions and recommendations of the International Labour Organization; the Convention and Protocol relating to the Status of Refugees; the African Charter on Human and Peoples' Rights; the American Convention on Human Rights; the European Convention for the Protection of Human Rights and Fundamental Freedoms; the Charter of Fundamental Rights of the European Union; the Convention on Combating Bribery of Foreign Public Officials in International Business Transactions of the Organization for Economic Cooperation and Development; and other instruments,

B. Right to equal opportunity and non-discriminatory treatment

2. Transnational corporations and other business enterprises shall ensure equality of opportunity and treatment, as provided in the relevant international instruments and national legislation as well as international human rights law, for the purpose of eliminating discrimination based on race, colour, sex, language, religion, political opinion, national or social origin, social status, indigenous status, disability, age - except for children, who may be given greater protection - or other status of the individual unrelated to the inherent requirements to perform the job, or of complying with special measures designed to overcome past discrimination against certain groups.

…

D. Rights of workers

…

6. Transnational corporations and other business enterprises shall respect the rights of children to be protected from economic exploitation as forbidden by the relevant international instruments and national legislation as well as international human rights and humanitarian law.

11. The Declaration on the Rights of Indigenous Peoples, 2007

The Rights of indigenous peoples have at various times unfortunately often been disregarded by political and even legal authorities, and these rights have been considered of less importance than other social matters. In fact, in a large number of cases, it has been proved that indigenous people and their cultural heritage are of secondary value, and of inferior quality. The humiliation of the social status of indigenous peoples has also caused serious harm to the children of these groups. Consequently, indigenous peoples have long struggled for their rights and solidarity, with the hope of receiving an effective contribution by the international community for the reestablishment of those rights. The Draft United Nations Declaration on the Rights of Indigenous Peoples is one of the UN's finer achievements, governing the rights of minorities. The draft is recognized as the first positive stage in the creation of an instrument which focuses solely on the protection of indigenous peoples and the promotion of their rights. The Declaration was adopted in 1994 by the Sub-Commission on Prevention of Discrimination and Protection of Minorities and became a guideline for the protection of indigenous peoples who have been discriminated against by national authorities.[7] It also opened the way for the adoption of a final declaration by the General Assembly.

The work on the rights of indigenous people in protecting their lands and their unique cultures and traditions was, after decades of negotiations, finally adopted in a Declaration by the General Assembly on 13 September, 2007.[8] It involves the individual as well as collective rights of 370 million native peoples. Even if the Declaration is considered as a landmark in protecting the rights of indigenous people, they still face marginalisation, extreme poverty and violations of their rights.[9] The intention of the Declaration has thus not been fulfilled, and many indigenous groups are suffering from illegal acts by governments and activities of multilateral companies. These cause the victimization of

---

[7] Adopted without a vote. See chap. XVI. E/CN.4/Sub.2/1994/56

[8] Resolution 61/295 by a vote of 143 in favour to 4 against (Australia, Canada, New Zealand and the United States), and with 11 abstentions. Those who voted against stated that it was out of concern over provisions on self-determination, land and resources rights and language, giving indigenous peoples a right of veto over national legislation and State management of resources. The convention had previously been adopted by the Human Rights Council in June 2006.

[9] See also 8. Draft United Nations Declaration on the Rights of Indigenous Peoples, 1994.

indigenous people by the unlawful and corrupt exploitation of their natural environmental resources. One of the most identifiable ways is when government authorities appropriate the resources or the land of indigenous peoples for their own individual interests. The corruption has also occurred when governments have ignored the rights of indigenous people and permitted private individuals to appropriate their resources. All this particularly affects their children, not only by threatening their way of life, but also their access to health care and education. The Articles of the Declaration which deal with children of indigenous people have positive and humanitarian aims, but they are insufficient to prevent direct or indirect harm to these peoples. The provisions of the Declaration have been objected by Australia, Canada, New Zealand, and the United States based on the fact that they are against their national legislations. However, Australia modified its political position and signed the UN Declaration on 3rd April 2009. The relevant parts of the declaration state:

The General Assembly,

…

Recognizing in particular the right of indigenous families and communities to retain shared responsibility for the upbringing, training, education and well-being of their children, consistent with the rights of the child,

…

Solemnly proclaims the following United Nations Declaration on the Rights of Indigenous Peoples as a standard of achievement to be pursued in a spirit of partnership and mutual respect:

Article 7

1. Indigenous individuals have the rights to life, physical and mental integrity, liberty and security of person.

2. Indigenous peoples have the collective right to live in freedom, peace and security as distinct peoples and shall not be subjected to any act of genocide or any other act of violence, including forcibly removing children of the group to another group.

Article 14

1. Indigenous peoples have the right to establish and control their educational systems and institutions providing education in their own languages, in a manner appropriate to their cultural methods of teaching and learning.

2. Indigenous individuals, particularly children, have the right to all levels and forms of education of the State without discrimination.

3. States shall, in conjunction with indigenous peoples, take effective measures, in order for indigenous individuals, particularly children, including those living outside their communities, to have access, when possible, to an education in their own culture and provided in their own language.

Article 17

1. Indigenous individuals and peoples have the right to enjoy fully all rights established under applicable international and domestic labour law.
2. States shall in consultation and cooperation with indigenous peoples take specific measures to protect indigenous children from economic exploitation and from performing any work that is likely to be hazardous or to interfere with the child's education, or to be harmful to the child's health or physical, mental, spiritual, moral or social development, taking into account their special vulnerability and the importance of education for their empowerment.

3. Indigenous individuals have the right not to be subjected to any discriminatory conditions of labour and, inter alia, employment or salary.

Article 21

1. Indigenous peoples have the right, without discrimination, to the improvement of their economic and social conditions, including, inter alia, in the areas of education, employment, vocational training and retraining, housing, sanitation, health and social security.

2. States shall take effective measures and, where appropriate, special measures to ensure continuing improvement of their economic and social conditions. Particular attention shall be paid to the rights and special needs of indigenous elders, women, youth, children and persons with disabilities.

Article 22

1. Particular attention shall be paid to the rights and special needs of indigenous elders, women, youth, children and persons with disabilities in the implementation of this Declaration.

2. States shall take measures, in conjunction with indigenous peoples, to ensure that indigenous women and children enjoy the full protection and guarantees against all forms of violence and discrimination.

CHAPTER II

REGIONAL LEGISLATIONS INDIRECTLY SUPPORTING VARIOUS RIGHTS OF CHILDREN

African States

1. African Charter on Human and Peoples' Rights, 1981

The African Charter on Human and Peoples' Rights was formulated in 1981, and came into force in 1986. The Charter constitutes one of the significant instruments in the legislations of African states. It speaks about many rights for all individuals in the territories of African States. It refers, *inter alia*, to social rights, economic rights, and, not least, cultural rights of different groups. It states that "Every individual shall be entitled to the enjoyment of the rights and freedoms recognized and guaranteed in the present Charter without distinction of any kind such as race, ethnic group, colour, sex, language, religion, political or any other opinion, national and social origin, fortune, birth or other status".[1] Although the Charter does not have any particular section concerning the protection of juveniles, children, youths or minors, the general interpretation of the Charter implies this key protection. In particular, it states:

Article 18

1. The family shall be the natural unit and basis of society. It shall be protected by the State which shall take care of its physical health and moral.

2. The State shall have the duty to assist the family which is the custodian of morals and traditional values recognized by the community.

---

[1] The provisions of the Convention are strengthened by the provisions of the Protocol to the African Charter on Human and Peoples' Rights on the Establishment of an African Court on Human and Peoples' Rights of 1988.

3. The State shall ensure the elimination of every discrimination against women and also ensure the protection of the rights of the woman and the child as stipulated in international declarations and conventions.

4. The aged and the disabled shall also have the right to special measures of protection in keeping with their physical or moral needs.

2. Protocol to the African Charter on Human and Peoples' Rights on the Rights of Women in Africa, 2003

The Protocol to the African Charter on Human and Peoples' Rights on the Rights of Women in Africa was adopted by the Second Ordinary Session of the Assembly of the African Union, Maputo, Mozambique in 2003. The aims of the Protocol are to give legislative protection to women and to increase the value of integrity of women within African states. With these, the Protocol intends to bring to an end various forms of violations against women and to safeguard their civil, social, cultural, political, economic, and any other rights within African states. For the same reasons, the Protocol prohibits and condemns all forms of discrimination against women and female children. As a result, the exploitation of women and female children is strongly prohibited. This includes, *inter alia*, various sexual exploitation of women and female children. As a whole, the key purpose of the Protocol is to protect women in times of war and peace. But this key purpose of the Protocol has been violated by many African states in various ways. The result is that the Protocol has not been effective as it was supposed to be, and that the protection of women and children remains one of the most serious questions of implementation within the jurisdiction of the various states of the African continent. The relevant parts of the Protocol state:

Recalling that women's rights have been recognised and guaranteed in all international human rights instruments, notably the Universal Declaration of Human Rights, the International Covenant on Civil and Political Rights, the International Covenant on Economic, Social and Cultural Rights, the Convention on the Elimination of All Forms of Discrimination Against Women and its Optional Protocol, the African Charter on the Rights and Welfare of the Child, and all other international and regional conventions and covenants relating to the rights of women as being inalienable, interdependent and indivisible human rights;

Article 6 Marriage

States Parties shall ensure that women and men enjoy equal rights and are regarded as equal partners in marriage. They shall enact appropriate national legislative measures to guarantee that:

a) no marriage shall take place without the free and full consent of both parties;

b) the minimum age of marriage for women shall be 18 years;

c) monogamy is encouraged as the preferred form of marriage and that the rights of women in marriage and family, including in polygamous marital relationships are promoted and protected;

d) every marriage shall be recorded in writing and registered in accordance with national laws, in order to be legally recognised;

e) the husband and wife shall, by mutual agreement, choose their matrimonial regime and place of residence;

f) a married woman shall have the right to retain her maiden name, to use it as she pleases, jointly or separately with her husband's surname;

g) a woman shall have the right to retain her nationality or to acquire the nationality of her husband;

h) a woman and a man shall have equal rights, with respect to the nationality of their children except where this is contrary to a provision in national legislation or is contrary to national security interests;

i) a woman and a man shall jointly contribute to safeguarding the interests of the family, protecting and educating their children;

j) during her marriage, a woman shall have the right to acquire her own property and to administer and manage it freely.

Article 7: Separation, Divorce and Annulment of Marriage

States Parties shall enact appropriate legislation to ensure that women and men enjoy the same rights in case of separation, divorce or annulment of marriage. In this regard, they shall ensure that:

a) separation, divorce or annulment of a marriage shall be effected by judicial order;

b) women and men shall have the same rights to seek separation, divorce or annulment of a marriage;

c) in case of separation, divorce or annulment of marriage, women and men shall have reciprocal rights and responsibilities towards their children. In any case, the interests of the children shall be given paramount importance;

d) in case of separation, divorce or annulment of marriage, women and men shall have the right to an equitable sharing of the joint property deriving from the marriage.

Article 11: Protection of Women in Armed Conflicts

1. States Parties undertake to respect and ensure respect for the rules of international humanitarian law applicable in armed conflict situations which affect the population, particularly women.

2. States Parties shall, in accordance with the obligations incumbent upon them under the international humanitarian law, protect civilians including women, irrespective of the population to which they belong, in the event of armed conflict.

3. States Parties undertake to protect asylum seeking women, refugees, returnees and internally displaced persons, against all forms of violence, rape and other forms of sexual exploitation, and to ensure that such acts are considered war crimes, genocide and/or crimes against humanity and that their perpetrators are brought to justice before a competent criminal jurisdiction.

4. States Parties shall take all necessary measures to ensure that no child, especially girls under 18 years of age, take a direct part in hostilities and that no child is recruited as a soldier.

Article 13: Economic and Social Welfare Rights

States Parties shall adopt and enforce legislative and other measures to guarantee women equal opportunities in work and career advancement and other economic opportunities. In this respect, they shall:

a) promote equality of access to employment;

b) promote the right to equal remuneration for jobs of equal value for women and men;

c) ensure transparency in recruitment, promotion and dismissal of women and combat and punish sexual harassment in the workplace;

d) guarantee women the freedom to choose their occupation, and protect them from exploitation by their employers violating and exploiting their fundamental rights as recognised and guaranteed by conventions, laws and regulations in force;

e) create conditions to promote and support the occupations and economic activities of women, in particular, within the informal sector;

f) establish a system of protection and social insurance for women working in the informal sector and sensitise them to adhere to it;

g) introduce a minimum age for work and prohibit the employment of children below that age, and prohibit, combat and punish all forms of exploitation of children, especially the girl-child;

h) take the necessary measures to recognise the economic value of the work of women in the home;

i) guarantee adequate and paid pre and post-natal maternity leave in both the private and public sectors;

j) ensure the equal application of taxation laws to women and men;

k) recognise and enforce the right of salaried women to the same allowances and entitlements as those granted to salaried men for their spouses and children;

l) recognise that both parents bear the primary responsibility for the upbringing and development of children and that this is a social function for which the State and the private sector have secondary responsibility;

m) take effective legislative and administrative measures to prevent the exploitation and abuse of women in advertising and pornography.

Article 14: Health and Reproductive Rights

1. States Parties shall ensure that the right to health of women, including sexual and reproductive health is respected and promoted. This includes:

a) the right to control their fertility;

b) the right to decide whether to have children, the number of children and the spacing of children;

c) the right to choose any method of contraception;

d) the right to self protection and to be protected against sexually transmitted infections, including HIV/AIDS;

e) the right to be informed on one's health status and on the health status of one's partner, particularly if affected with sexually transmitted infections, including HIV/AIDS, in accordance with internationally recognised standards and best practices;

f) the right to have family planning education.

2. States Parties shall take all appropriate measures to:

a) provide adequate, affordable and accessible health services, including information, education and communication programmes to women especially those in rural areas;

b) establish and strengthen existing pre-natal, delivery and post-natal health and nutritional services for women during pregnancy and while they are breast-feeding;

c) protect the reproductive rights of women by authorising medical abortion in cases of sexual assault, rape, incest, and where the continued pregnancy endangers the mental and physical health of the mother or the life of the mother or the foetus.

Article 20: Widows' Rights

States Parties shall take appropriate legal measures to ensure that widows enjoy all human rights through the implementation of the following provisions:

a) that widows are not subjected to inhuman, humiliating or degrading treatment;

b) a widow shall automatically become the guardian and custodian of her children, after the death of her husband, unless this is contrary to the interests and the welfare of the children;

c) a widow shall have the right to remarry, and in that event, to marry the person of her choice.

American states

1. American Declaration of the Rights and Duties of Man, 1948

The American Declaration was adopted by the Ninth International Conference of American States in Bogota, Colombia in April 1948. The Conference also adopted the Charter of the Organization of American States. The Declaration is a model of the Universal Declaration of Human Rights, and presents the modest human rights provisions accepted by a nation at the time. Chapter 1 of the Declaration lists a record of civil and political rights, economic, social and cultural rights to be demanded by the citizens of the participating states. In its second chapter, the Declaration also sets forth a catalogue of duties which have to be carried out by citizens. The preamble of the Declaration states that "All men are born free and equal, in dignity and in rights, and, being endowed by nature with reason and conscience, they should conduct themselves as brothers one to another." Further, "The fulfilment of duty by each individual is a prerequisite to the rights of all. Rights and duties are interrelated in every social and political activity of man. While rights exalt individual liberty, duties express the dignity of that liberty". In two separate Articles, the Declaration dealt with the rights of children. The intention of the provisions of the articles is to protect the rights of children and their various social developments. However, it must be stressed that both articles are interconnected, and their intentions cannot be read in isolation. In addition, the chief aims of the American Declaration of the Rights of Man should be the starting point for the interpretation of both articles. The articles contain:

Right to protection for mothers and children

Article VII. All women, during pregnancy and the nursing period, and all children have the right to special protection, care and aid.

Duties toward children and parents

Article XXX. It is the duty of every person to aid, support, educate and protect his minor children, and it is the duty of children to honour their parents always and to aid, support and protect them when they need it.

2. American Convention on Human Rights, 1969

Since the American Declaration of the Rights and Duties of Man, 1948 was not effective and its legal validity was based solely on a declaration and could not therefore create the merit of treaty law, the need for another binding instrument was as seen necessary. Consequently, the American Convention on Human Rights was adopted at the Inter-American Specialized Conference on Human Rights in 1969. The Convention aims to recognise the different rights of individuals and groups which live under the jurisdiction of American states .The Convention came into force in 1978. One of the significant functions of the Convention was the creation of the Inter-American Court of Human Rights, which was finally created in San José, Costa Rica 1979. Since its creation, the Court has attempted to defend the rights of individuals within different American states. The Convention has dealt with the rights of children, and aims to protect them from various social and political problems. According to it, the rights stated in its statute should not be derogated by the parties. This means that any deviation from its norms for reasons lik war or state of emergency is invalid, and violates the conventional obligations of the party *i.e. pacta sunt servanda*. Some of the more relevant parts of the Convention on the protection of children relate to the following Articles. They state:

Article 12. Freedom of Conscience and Religion

1. Everyone has the right to freedom of conscience and of religion. This right includes freedom to maintain or to change one's religion or beliefs, and freedom to profess or disseminate one's religion or beliefs, either individually or together with others, in public or in private.
2. No one shall be subject to restrictions that might impair his freedom to maintain or to change his religion or beliefs.
3. Freedom to manifest one's religion and beliefs may be subject only to the limitations prescribed by law that are necessary to protect public safety, order, health, or morals, or the rights or freedoms of others.

4. Parents or guardians, as the case may be, have the right to provide for the religious and moral education of their children or wards that is in accord with their own convictions.

Article 17. Rights of the Family

1. The family is the natural and fundamental group unit of society and is entitled to protection by society and the state.

2. The right of men and women of marriageable age to marry and to raise a family shall be recognized, if they meet the conditions required by domestic laws, insofar as such conditions do not affect the principle of non-discrimination established in this Convention.

3. No marriage shall be entered into without the free and full consent of the intending spouses.

4. The States Parties shall take appropriate steps to ensure the equality of rights and the adequate balancing of responsibilities of the spouses as to marriage, during marriage, and in the event of its dissolution. In case of dissolution, provision shall be made for the necessary protection of any children solely on the basis of their own best interests.

5. The law shall recognize equal rights for children born out of wedlock and those born in wedlock.

Article 19. Rights of the Child

Every minor child has the right to the measures of protection required by his condition as a minor on the part of his family, society, and the state.

Article 27. Suspension of Guarantees

1. In time of war, public danger, or other emergency that threatens the independence or security of a State Party, it may take measures derogating from its obligations under the present Convention to the extent and for the period of time strictly required by the exigencies of the situation, provided that such measures are not inconsistent with its other obligations under international law and do not involve discrimination on the ground of race, color, sex, language, religion, or social origin.

2. The foregoing provision does not authorize any suspension of the following articles: Article 3 (Right to Juridical Personality), Article 4 (Right to Life), Article 5 (Right to Humane Treatment), Article 6 (Freedom from Slavery), Article 9 (Freedom from Ex Post Facto Laws), Article 12 (Freedom of Conscience and Religion), Article 17 (Rights of the Family), Article 18 (Right to a Name), Article 19 (Rights of the Child), Article 20 (Right to Nationality), and Article 23 (Right to Participate in

Government), or of the judicial guarantees essential for the protection of such rights.

3. Any State Party availing itself of the right of suspension shall immediately inform the other States Parties, through the Secretary General of the Organization of American States, of the provisions the application of which it has suspended, the reasons that gave rise to the suspension, and the date set for the termination of such suspension.

3. Additional Protocol to the American Convention on Human Rights in the Area of Economic, Social and Cultural Rights "Protocol of San Salvador", 1988

This Protocol, which came into force in 1999, has an important role within the provisions of human rights in the American states. It develops many principles—economic, social and cultural—relating to the protection of individuals,. The purpose of this is to create as much individual protection as possible; this relates to both gender, and the rights of children within the territories of the American States. But, it must be stated that neither this Protocol, nor other documents concerning human rights law, have been sufficiently effective in creating just and fair treatment for the population of the American States. They have suffered not only from economic problems, but also from the deprivation of many other social rights under the authority of different governments. The Convention lists a number of inalienable children's rights. These include, *inter alia*, the right to grow under the direct protection of parents, that a young age child should not be separated from his/her mother, the right to the educational system within the country, and to have legal rights in various juridical procedures. The Protocol states:

Article 13 Right to Education

1. Everyone has the right to education.

2. The States Parties to this Protocol agree that education should be directed towards the full development of the human personality and human dignity and should strengthen respect for human rights, ideological pluralism, fundamental freedoms, justice and peace. They further agree that education ought to enable everyone to participate effectively in a democratic and pluralistic society and achieve a decent existence and should foster understanding, tolerance and friendship among all nations and all racial, ethnic or religious groups and promote activities for the maintenance of peace.

3. The States Parties to this Protocol recognize that in order to achieve the full exercise of the right to education:

a. Primary education should be compulsory and accessible to all without cost;

b. Secondary education in its different forms, including technical and vocational secondary education, should be made generally available and accessible to all by every appropriate means, and in particular, by the progressive introduction of free education;

c. Higher education should be made equally accessible to all, on the basis of individual capacity, by every appropriate means, and in particular, by the progressive introduction of free education;

d. Basic education should be encouraged or intensified as far as possible for those persons who have not received or completed the whole cycle of primary instruction;

e. Programs of special education should be established for the handicapped, so as to provide special instruction and training to persons with physical disabilities or mental deficiencies.

4. In conformity with the domestic legislation of the States Parties, parents should have the right to select the type of education to be given to their children, provided that it conforms to the principles set forth above.

5. Nothing in this Protocol shall be interpreted as a restriction of the freedom of individuals and entities to establish and direct educational institutions in accordance with the domestic legislation of the States Parties.

Article 15 Right to the Formation and the Protection of Families

1. The family is the natural and fundamental element of society and ought to be protected by the State, which should see to the improvement of its spiritual and material conditions.

2. Everyone has the right to form a family, which shall be exercised in accordance with the provisions of the pertinent domestic legislation.

3. The States Parties hereby undertake to accord adequate protection to the family unit and in particular:

a. To provide special care and assistance to mothers during a reasonable period before and after childbirth;

b. To guarantee adequate nutrition for children at the nursing stage and during school attendance years;

c. To adopt special measures for the protection of adolescents in order to ensure the full development of their physical, intellectual and moral capacities;

d. To undertake special programs of family training so as to help create a stable and positive environment in which children will receive and develop the values of understanding, solidarity, respect and responsibility.

Article 16 Rights of Children

Every child, whatever his parentage, has the right to the protection that his status as a minor requires from his family, society and the State. Every child has the right to grow under the protection and responsibility of his parents; save in exceptional, judicially-recognized circumstances, a child of young age ought not to be separated from his mother. Every child has the right to free and compulsory education, at least in the elementary phase, and to continue his training at higher levels of the educational system.

Arab States

1. The Cairo Declaration of Human Rights in Islam, 1990

Historically, Islamic law has contributed to the development of the principles of human rights law between the Islamic nations since its revelation approximately fourteen centuries ago. It aimed to create equality between all men, regardless of race, ethnic origin, language, nationality, religion or cultural attitudes. However, this was interpreted differently with the development of Islamic law, or *Sharia*, based on the provisions of the *Qur'an*. The various interpretations and practices of Islamic law in different periods of time have been very controversial because of the political and economic interests of the authorities in force. Clear examples of the serious political violations of the Islamic jurisprudence can be seen in Yemen, Saudi Arabia, Iran, Libya, Iraq, and Afghanistan.

The Cairo Declaration of Human Rights in Islam was originally based on Islamic law *sharia*, and interprets the Islamic values of human rights law. The Declaration was adopted by the Organization of the Islamic Conference at Cairo, in August 1990. The purpose of the Declaration is implicitly and explicitly to guide Islamic states towards implementation of Islamic human rights law and prevent misinterpretation and misapplication of Islamic law. Therefore, the Declaration encourages the entire fulfilment of the principles of human rights in the Islamic states. Some of the relevant provisions of the Declaration regarding the protection of the rights of children can be examined in its Articles 3 and 7. With respect to this matter, the Declaration states:

Article 3

(a) In the event of the use of force and in case of armed conflict, it is not permissible to kill non-belligerents such as old men, women and children. The wounded and the sick shall have the right to medical treatment; and prisoners of war shall have the right to be fed, sheltered and clothed. It is prohibited to mutilate dead bodies. It is a duty to exchange prisoners of war and to arrange visits or reunions of the families separated by the circumstances of war.

(b) It is prohibited to fell trees, to damage crops or livestock, and to destroy the enemy's civilian buildings and installations by shelling, blasting or any other means.

Article 7

(a) As of the moment of birth, every child has rights due from the parents, society and the state to be accorded proper nursing, education and material, hygienic and moral care. Both the fetus and the mother must be protected and accorded special care.

(b) Parents and those in such like capacity have the right to choose the type of education they desire for their children, provided they take into consideration the interest and future of the children in accordance with ethical values and the principles of the Shari'ah.

(c) Both parents are entitled to certain rights from their children, and relatives are entitled to rights from their kin, in accordance with the tenets of the Shari'ah.

2. Arab Charter on Human Rights, 2004

The first Arab Charter on Human Rights is one of the most important ever accepted within the Islamic states. The aim of the Charter is to regulate human rights rules and to emphasise that those rights should not be violated by the Arab states. The Charter refers to many individual rights which are originally based not only on Islamic rules, principles and regulations, but also on the most significant principles of international human rights law accepted under the United Nations Charter. In any event, the Charter underlines certain important principles regarding the interpretation and application of human rights law. It refers to social values and the full respect of different opinions. Agreement between the Arab states on the provisions of the first Charter was not initially easy, and there were consequently different interpretations by the members of the Council of the League of Arab States. This means, in practice, that the first Charter was merely adopted in 1994, but not signed. It was revised in 2002, and accepted without any amendment by the Summit of Heads of Member States of the Arab League Council at Tunis, on 22 May 2004, and entered into force on 15 March 2008. The Charter reaffirms several human rights documents which have been adopted under United Nations' supervision, such as the principles of the Charter of the United Nations, the Universal Declaration of Human Rights and the provisions of the International Covenant on Civil and Political Rights and the International Covenant on Economic, Social and Cultural Rights, and the Cairo Declaration on Human Rights. The new edition, like the former, has many rules concerning the protection of children's rights within the legislation of Arab states. It particularly emphasises the protection of children in court procedures. According to it, "a special legal system for minors in all stages of investigation, trial and enforcement of sentence" should be created by the member states. Some of the more relevant parts of the Arab Charter relating to the protection of children are:

Article 10

1. All forms of slavery and trafficking in human beings are prohibited and are punishable by law. No one shall be held in slavery and servitude under any circumstances.

2. Forced labour, trafficking in human beings for the purposes of prostitution or sexual exploitation, the exploitation of the prostitution of others or any other form of exploitation or the exploitation of children in armed conflict are prohibited.

Article 17

Each State party shall ensure in particular to any child at risk or any delinquent charged with an offence the right to a special legal system for minors in all stages of investigation, trial and enforcement of sentence, as well as to special treatment that takes account of his age, protects his dignity, facilitates his rehabilitation and reintegration and enables him to play a constructive role in society.

Article 29

1. Everyone has the right to nationality. No one shall be arbitrarily or unlawfully deprived of his nationality.

2. States parties shall take such measures as they deem appropriate, in accordance with their domestic laws on nationality, to allow a child to

acquire the mother's nationality, having due regard, in all cases, to the best interests of the child.

3. Non one shall be denied the right to acquire another nationality, having due regard for the domestic legal procedures in his country.

Article 33

1. The family is the natural and fundamental group unit of society; it is based on marriage between a man and a woman. Men and women of marrying age have the right to marry and to found a family according to the rules and conditions of marriage. No marriage can take place without the full and free consent of both parties. The laws in force regulate the rights and duties of the man and woman as to marriage, during marriage and at its dissolution.

2. The State and society shall ensure the protection of the family, the strengthening of family ties, the protection of its members and the prohibition of all forms of violence or abuse in the relations among its members, and particularly against women and children. They shall also ensure the necessary protection and care for mothers, children, older persons and persons with special needs and shall provide adolescents and young persons with the best opportunities for physical and mental development.

3. The States parties shall take all necessary legislative, administrative and judicial measures to guarantee the protection, survival, development and well-being of the child in an atmosphere of freedom and dignity and shall ensure, in all cases, that the child's best interests are the basic criterion for all measures taken in his regard, whether the child is at risk of delinquency or is a juvenile offender.

4. The States parties shall take all the necessary measures to guarantee, particularly to young persons, the right to pursue a sporting activity.

Article 34

1. The right to work is a natural right of every citizen. The State shall endeavour to provide, to the extent possible, a job for the largest number of those willing to work, while ensuring production, the freedom to choose one's work and equality of opportunity without discrimination of any kind on grounds of race, colour, sex, religion, language, political opinion, membership in a union, national origin, social origin, disability or any other situation.

2. Every worker has the right to the enjoyment of just and favourable conditions of work which ensure appropriate remuneration to meet his essential needs and those of his family and regulate working hours, rest

and holidays with pay, as well as the rules for the preservation of occupational health and safety and the protection of women, children and disabled persons in the place of work.

3. The States parties recognize the right of the child to be protected from economic exploitation and from being forced to perform any work that is likely to be hazardous or to interfere with the child's education or to be harmful to the child's health or physical, mental, spiritual, moral or social development. To this end, and having regard to the relevant provisions of other international instruments, States parties shall in particular:

(a) Define a minimum age for admission to employment;

(b) Establish appropriate regulation of working hours and conditions;

(c) Establish appropriate penalties or other sanctions to ensure the effective endorsement of these provisions.

4. There shall be no discrimination between men and women in their enjoyment of the right to effectively benefit from training, employment and job protection and the right to receive equal remuneration for equal work.

5. Each State party shall ensure to workers who migrate to its territory the requisite protection in accordance with the laws in force.

Article 43

Nothing in this Charter may be construed or interpreted as impairing the rights and freedoms protected by the domestic laws of the States parties or those set force in the international and regional human rights instruments which the states parties have adopted or ratified, including the rights of women, the rights of the child and the rights of persons belonging to minorities.

European States

1. European Convention for the Protection of Human Rights and Fundamental Freedoms of 1950 as amended by Protocol No. 11 of 1998 and Protocol No. 14 of 2010

One of the key works of the Council of Europe is the 1949European Convention for the Protection of Human Rights and Fundamental Freedoms . The Convention was signed in Rome in 1950, and entered into force in 1953. The member states of the Council are parties to this Convention, and are under obligation to carry out their conventional duties regarding certain matters. However, the provisions of the Convention were not completely implemented by some European states, so these provisions have subsequently been strengthened by many other documents. The 1950 European Convention has also been amended by Protocol No.11 of 1998 in order to update its provisions. One of the valuable outcomes of the Convention was the establishment of the European Court of Human Rights, which has the power to examine different cases submitted by individuals relating to breaches of human rights law under the jurisdiction of the parties. The decisions of the Court are binding on the parties, and the Court may also call for damages. The relevant provisions of the above Convention on the protection of the rights of juveniles state:

Article 5
Right to liberty and security

1. Everyone has the right to liberty and security of person. No one shall be deprived of his liberty save in the following cases and in accordance with a procedure prescribed by law:

a. the lawful detention of a person after conviction by a competent court;

b. the lawful arrest or detention of a person for non-compliance with the lawful order of a court or in order to secure the fulfilment of any obligation prescribed by law;

c. the lawful arrest or detention of a person effected for the purpose of bringing him before the competent legal authority on reasonable suspicion of having committed an offence or when it is reasonably considered necessary to prevent his committing an offence or fleeing after having done so;

d. the detention of a minor by lawful order for the purpose of educational supervision or his lawful detention for the purpose of bringing him before the competent legal authority;

e. the lawful detention of persons for the prevention of the spreading of infectious diseases, of persons of unsound mind, alcoholics or drug addicts or vagrants;

f. the lawful arrest or detention of a person to prevent his effecting an unauthorised entry into the country or of a person against whom action is being taken with a view to deportation or extradition.

2. Everyone who is arrested shall be informed promptly, in a language which he understands, of the reasons for his arrest and of any charge against him.

3. Everyone arrested or detained in accordance with the provisions of paragraph 1.c of this article shall be brought promptly before a judge or

other officer authorised by law to exercise judicial power and shall be entitled to trial within a reasonable time or to release pending trial. Release may be conditioned by guarantees to appear for trial.

4. Everyone who is deprived of his liberty by arrest or detention shall be entitled to take proceedings by which the lawfulness of his detention shall be decided speedily by a court and his release ordered if the detention is not lawful.

5. Everyone who has been the victim of arrest or detention in contravention of the provisions of this article shall have an enforceable right to compensation.

Article 6
Right to a fair trial

1. In the determination of his civil rights and obligations or of any criminal charge against him, everyone is entitled to a fair and public hearing within a reasonable time by an independent and impartial tribunal established by law. Judgment shall be pronounced publicly but the press and public may be excluded from all or part of the trial in the interests of morals, public order or national security in a democratic society, where the interests of juveniles or the protection of the private life of the parties so require, or to the extent strictly necessary in the opinion of the court in special circumstances where publicity would prejudice the interests of justice.

2. Everyone charged with a criminal offence shall be presumed innocent until proved guilty according to law.

3. Everyone charged with a criminal offence has the following minimum rights:

a. to be informed promptly, in a language which he understands and in detail, of the nature and cause of the accusation against him;

b. to have adequate time and facilities for the preparation of his defence;

c. to defend himself in person or through legal assistance of his own choosing or, if he has not sufficient means to pay for legal assistance, to be given it free when the interests of justice so require;

d. to examine or have examined witnesses against him and to obtain the attendance and examination of witnesses on his behalf under the same conditions as witnesses against him;

e. to have the free assistance of an interpreter if he cannot understand or speak the language used in court.

2. European Social Charter, 1961, revised 1996

The European Social Charter, Strasbourg, adopted in 1961 and revised in 1996, is another instrument protecting the rights of children , and it came into force in 1999. This instrument, like other European regional instruments, aims to protect social rights of individuals. It guarantees rights concerning education, health, employment, housing, legal and social protection, the movement of persons and non-discrimination between genders. It was intended to fill a gap left by the Convention for the Protection of Human Rights and Fundamental Freedoms, which essentially covers only civil and political rights.

The instrument is also strongly focused on children's rights. Accordingly, the integrity of children has to be protected by the provisions of human rights law, and states parties to the treaty are responsible for the maintenance of children's rights. One of the instrument's significant values is that it has updated and developed the principles set out in the 1960 Charter, such as education, and social and legal protection, and strengthened the fundamental rights of children at a regional level. Although the Charter has certain aims regarding the social protection of individuals from various forms of inequalities, its aims have not been completely fulfilled, and so the implementation of social rights of children have been varied and depended on the individual decisions of different national bodies. Some of the instrument's most significant provisions are:

Preamble
Part I
::::::::::::::::::::::::

1. Children and young persons have the right to a special protection against the physical and moral hazards to which they are exposed.

::::::::::::::::

11. Children and young persons have the right to appropriate social, legal and economic protection.

Article 7 – The right of children and young persons to protection
With a view to ensuring the effective exercise of the right of children and young persons to protection, the Parties undertake:

1. to provide that the minimum age of admission to employment shall be 15 years, subject to exceptions for children employed in prescribed light work without harm to their health, morals or education;

2. to provide that the minimum age of admission to employment shall be 18 years with respect to prescribed occupations regarded as dangerous or unhealthy;

3. to provide that persons who are still subject to compulsory education shall not be employed in such work as would deprive them of the full benefit of their education;

4. to provide that the working hours of persons under 18 years of age shall be limited in accordance with the needs of their development, and particularly with their need for vocational training;

5. to recognise the right of young workers and apprentices to a fair wage or other appropriate allowances;

6. to provide that the time spent by young persons in vocational training during the normal working hours with the consent of the employer shall be treated as forming part of the working day;

7. to provide that employed persons of under 18 years of age shall be entitled to a minimum of four weeks' annual holiday with pay;

8. to provide that persons under 18 years of age shall not be employed in night work with the exception of certain occupations provided for by national laws or regulations;

9. to provide that persons under 18 years of age employed in occupations prescribed by national laws or regulations shall be subject to regular medical control;

10. to ensure special protection against physical and moral dangers to which children and young persons are exposed, and particularly against those resulting directly or indirectly from their work.

Article 17 – The right of children and young persons to social, legal and economic protection

With a view to ensuring the effective exercise of the right of children and young persons to grow up in an environment which encourages the full development of their personality and of their physical and mental capacities, the Parties undertake, either directly or in co-operation with public and private organisations, to take all appropriate and necessary measures designed:

1.

a) to ensure that children and young persons, taking account of the rights and duties of their parents, have the care, the assistance, the education and the training they need, in particular by providing for the establishment or maintenance of institutions and services sufficient and adequate for this purpose;

b) to protect children and young persons against negligence, violence or exploitation;

c) to provide protection and special aid from the state for children and young persons temporarily or definitively deprived of their family's support;

2. to provide to children and young persons a free primary and secondary education as well as to encourage regular attendance at schools.

3. Charter of Fundamental Rights of the European Union, 2000

The Charter of Fundamental Rights of the European Union was proclaimed by the European Council, the European Parliament and the European Commission in 2000. The text of the Charter was signed and solemnly proclaimed by the presidents of the European Parliament, and the Council and Commission on the behalf of their respective institutions at a meeting in Nice at the end of the same year. On 12 December 2007 an adopted version was proclaimed in Strasbourg, and became legally binding on 1 December 2009 under the Lisbon Treaty. The Charter speaks of many rights including the economic, civil, political, and social rights of European citizens. It has six important principles governing humanity, human rights and its subjects. These are dignity, freedom, equality, solidarity, the rights of citizens and justice. Some of the relevant provisions of the Charter regarding the protection of children, youth, minors or juveniles are:

Article 14 Right to education

1. Everyone has the right to education and to have access to vocational and continuing training.

2. This right includes the possibility to receive free compulsory education.

3. The freedom to found educational establishments with due respect for democratic principles and the right of parents to ensure the education and teaching of their children in conformity with their religious, philosophical and pedagogical convictions shall be respected, in accordance with the national laws governing the exercise of such freedom and right.

Article 21 Non-discrimination

1. Any discrimination based on any ground such as sex, race, colour, ethnic or social origin, genetic features, language, religion or belief, political or any other opinion, membership of a national minority, property, birth, disability, age or sexual orientation shall be prohibited.

2. Within the scope of application of the Treaty establishing the European Community and of the Treaty on European Union, and without prejudice to the special provisions of those Treaties, any discrimination on grounds of nationality shall be prohibited.

Article 24 The rights of the child

1. Children shall have the right to such protection and care as is necessary for their well-being. They may express their views freely. Such views shall be taken into consideration on matters which concern them in accordance with their age and maturity.

2. In all actions relating to children, whether taken by public authorities or private institutions, the child's best interests must be a primary consideration. Every child shall have the right to maintain on a regular basis a personal relationship and direct contact with both his or her parents, unless that is contrary to his or her interests.

Article 32 Prohibition of child labour and protection of young people at work

The employment of children is prohibited. The minimum age of admission to employment may not be lower than the minimum school-leaving age, without prejudice to such rules as may be more favourable to young people and except for limited derogations. Young people admitted to work must have working conditions appropriate to their age and be protected against economic exploitation and any work likely to harm their safety, health or physical, mental, moral or social development or to interfere with their education.

Article 33 Family and professional life

1. The family shall enjoy legal, economic and social protection.

2. To reconcile family and professional life, everyone shall have the right to protection from dismissal for a reason connected with maternity and the right to paid maternity leave and to parental leave following the birth or adoption of a child.

CHAPTER III

INTERNATIONAL LEGISLATIONS INDIRECTLY DEFENDING PARTICULAR SITUATIONS OF CHILDREN

1. The International Labour Organization Declaration Concerning Aims and Purposes, 1944

The ILO was established on 28 June 1919. It is a specialized agency working for the regulation of many rules for the protection of men and women; it also has a connection to the United Nations. The work of the organization should, according to the preamble of its Constitution, aim at creating universal social justice. It has successfully formulated several international treaties protecting the fundamental principles of human rights including the rights of children. The ILO adopted the Declaration Concerning Aims and Purposes on 10 May 1944. The Declaration does not necessarily deal with the rights of children, but does include them within the rights of parents. This can be seen in the following section of the Declaration:

III

The Conference recognizes the solemn obligation of the International Labour Organisation to further among the nations of the world programmes which will achieve:

(a) full employment and the raising of standards of living;

(b) the employment of workers in the occupations in which they can have the satisfaction of giving the fullest measure of their skill and attainments and make their greatest contribution to the common well-being;

(c) the provision, as a means to the attainment of this end and under adequate guarantees for all concerned, of facilities for training and the transfer of labour, including migration for employment and settlement;

(d) policies in regard to wages and earnings, hours and other conditions of work calculated to ensure a just share of the fruits of progress to all, and a minimum living wage to all employed and in need of such protection;

(e) the effective recognition of the right of collective bargaining, the co-operation of management and labour in the continuous improvement of productive efficiency, and the collaboration of workers and employers in the preparation and application of social and economic measures;

(f) the extension of social security measures to provide a basic income to all in need of such protection and comprehensive medical care;

(g) adequate protection for the life and health of workers in all occupations;

(h) provision for child welfare and maternity protection;

(i) the provision of adequate nutrition, housing and facilities for recreation and culture;

(j) the assurance of equality of educational and vocational opportunity.

2. The Convention on the Prevention and Punishment of the Crime of Genocide, 1948

The Convention on the Prevention and Punishment of the Crime of Genocide was adopted by the General Assembly Resolution 260 (III) A on 9 December 1948, and came into force on 12 January 1951. The reason for the convention was the massacre of millions of people because of their race, faith, language, nationality or membership of specific groups during the Second World War. The convention is a part of the statutes of the *ad hoc* or permanent international criminal tribunals and the Court (ICC). Its provisions also regarded as an integral part of customary, as well as conventional international human rights law, including international criminal law. Furthermore, the provisions of the Convention are a fundamental part of *jus cogens*. It should be emphasized that the provisions of the Convention have often been violated during different national or international conflicts. In particular, these violations have also been directed against children, including unborn children. In Article 2 of the Convention lists a number of acts classified as genocide are listed, such as forcibly transferring children of one group to another group. The Article states:

Article 2

In the present Convention, genocide means any of the following acts committed with intent to destroy, in whole or in part, a national, ethnical, racial or religious group, as such:

- (a) Killing members of the group;
- (b) Causing serious bodily or mental harm to members of the group;
- (c) Deliberately inflicting on the group conditions of life calculated to bring about its physical destruction in whole or in part;
- (d) Imposing measures intended to prevent births within the group;
- (e) Forcibly transferring children of the group to another group.

3. The Convention Relating to the Status of Refugees, 1951

The Convention Relating to the Status of Refugees entered into force on 22 April 1954. It was adopted by the United Nations Conference of Plenipotentiaries on the Status of Refugees and Stateless Persons on 28 July 1951, documented in Resolution 429 (V) of the General Assembly. The provisions of the convention were enlarged by the Protocol Relating to the Status of the Refugee, which was adopted by the General Assembly on 16 December 1966. The status of refugee may be based on persecution due to his/her race, religion, nationality or membership of a particular social or political group. He/she may be outside her or his country or unable to benefit from the protection of his or her own country of nationality or habitual residence, or be unable to return to his or her own country due to the internal situation. The Convention is not as strong as it should be regarding protection of children. It nevertheless foresaw the difficult situation of refugees in which their children may be suffering from different social problems. The Convention especially encourages some of the primary rights of children, and states:

Article 4 Religion

The Contracting States shall accord to refugees within their territories treatment at least as favourable as that accorded to their nationals with respect to freedom to practise their religion and freedom as regards the religious education of their children.

Article 17 Wage-earning employment

1. The Contracting States shall accord to refugees lawfully staying in their territory the most favourable treatment accorded to nationals of a foreign country in the same circumstances, as regards the right to engage in wage-earning employment.

2. In any case, restrictive measures imposed on aliens or the employment of aliens for the protection of the national labour market shall not be applied to a refugee who was already exempt from them at the date of entry into force of this Convention for the Contracting State concerned, or who fulfils one of the following conditions:

(a) He has completed three years' residence in the country;

(b) He has a spouse possessing the nationality of the country of residence. A refugee may not invoke the benefit of this provision if he has abandoned his spouse;

(c) He has one or more children possessing the nationality of the country of residence.

3. The Contracting States shall give sympathetic consideration to assimilating the rights of all refugees with regard to wage-earning employment to those of nationals, and in particular of those refugees who have entered their territory pursuant to programmes of labour recruitment or under immigration schemes.

4. Convention Relating to the Status of Stateless Persons, 1954

The Convention relating to the Status of Stateless Persons was adopted on 28 September 1954 by a Conference of Plenipotentiaries convened by the Economic and Social Council, Resolution 526 A(XVII) of 26 April 1954 and entered into force on 6 June 1960. The provisions of the Convention relating to the protection of children are similar to the provisions the Status of Refugees. With regard to the rights of children, Article 4 is relevant:

Article 4 Religion

The Contracting States shall accord to stateless persons within their territories treatment at least as favourable as that accorded to their nationals with respect to freedom to practise their religion and freedom as regards the religious education of their children.

5. Supplementary Convention on the Abolition of Slavery, the Slave Trade, and Institutions and Practices Similar to Slavery, 1956

The Supplementary Convention on the Abolition of Slavery, the Slave Trade, and Institutions and Practices Similar to Slavery is an internationally known instrument for the abolition of the exploitation of adults, as well as children. The Convention was adopted by a Conference of Plenipotentiaries arranged by Economic and Social Council Resolution 608(XXI) in 1956 and came into force in 1957. The relevant provision of the Convention relating to the protection of children from various forms of exploitation is:

Article 1

Each of the States Parties to this Convention shall take all practicable and necessary legislative and other measures to bring about progressively and as soon as possible the complete abolition or abandonment of the following institutions and practices, where they still exist and whether or not they are covered by the definition of slavery contained in article 1 of the Slavery Convention signed at Geneva on 25 September 1926:

(a) Debt bondage, that is to say, the status or condition arising from a pledge by a debtor of his personal services or of those of a person under his control as security for a debt, if the value of those services as reasonably assessed is not applied towards the liquidation of the debt or the length and nature of those services are not respectively limited and defined;

(b) Serfdom, that is to say, the condition or status of a tenant who is by law, custom or agreement bound to live and labour on land belonging to another person and to render some determinate service to such other person, whether for reward or not, and is not free to change his status;

(c) Any institution or practice whereby:

(i) A woman, without the right to refuse, is promised or given in marriage on payment of a consideration in money or in kind to her parents, guardian, family or any other person or group; or

(ii) The husband of a woman, his family, or his clan, has the right to transfer her to another person for value received or otherwise; or

(iii) A woman on the death of her husband is liable to be inherited by another person;

(d) Any institution or practice whereby a child or young person under the age of 18 years, is delivered by either or both of his natural parents or by his guardian to another person, whether for reward or not, with a view to the exploitation of the child or young person or of his labour.

6. The Convention on the Reduction of Statelessness, 1961

The Convention on the Reduction of Statelessness was adopted on 30 August 1961 by a conference of Plenipotentiaries which met in 1959 and reconvened in 1961 in pursuance of General Assembly Resolution 896 (IX) of 4 December 1954. It entered into force in 1975. Some of the more relevant provisions of the Convention relating to the rights of children are:

Article 1

1. A Contracting State shall grant its nationality to a person born in its territory who would otherwise be stateless. Such nationality shall be granted:

(a) At birth, by operation of law, or

(b) Upon an application being lodged with the appropriate authority, by or on behalf of the person concerned, in the manner prescribed by the national law. Subject to the provisions of paragraph 2 of this article, no such application may be rejected. A Contracting State which provides for the grant of its nationality in accordance with subparagraph (b) of this paragraph may also provide for the grant of its nationality by operation of law at such age and subject to such conditions as may be prescribed by the national law.

2. A Contracting State may make the grant of its nationality in accordance with subparagraph (b) -of paragraph I of this article subject to one or more of the following conditions:

(a) That the application is lodged during a period, fixed by the Contracting State, beginning not later than at the age of eighteen years and ending not earlier than at the age of twenty-one years, so, however, that the person concerned shall be allowed at least one year during which he may himself make the application without having to obtain legal authorization to do so;

(b) That the person concerned has habitually resided in the territory of the Contracting State for such period as may be fixed by that State, not exceeding five years immediately preceding the lodging of the application nor ten years in all;

(c) That the person concerned has neither been convicted of an offence against national security nor has been sentenced to imprisonment for a term of five years or more on a criminal charge;

(d) That the person concerned has always been stateless.

3. Notwithstanding the provisions of paragraphs I (b) and 2 of this article, a child born in wedlock in the territory of a Contracting State, whose mother has the nationality of that State, shall acquire at birth that nationality if it otherwise would be stateless.

Article 5

1. If the law of a Contracting State entails loss of nationality as a consequence of any change in the personal status of a person such as marriage, termination of marriage, legitimation, recognition or adoption, such loss shall be conditional upon possession or acquisition of another nationality.

2. If, under the law of a Contracting State, a child born out of wedlock loses the nationality of that State in consequence of a recognition of affiliation, he shall be given an opportunity to recover that nationality by written application to the appropriate authority, and the conditions governing such application shall not be more rigorous than those laid down in paragraph 2 of article I of this Convention.

Article 6

If the law of a Contracting State provides for loss of its nationality by a person's spouse or children as a consequence of that person losing or being deprived of that nationality, such loss shall be conditional upon their possession or acquisition of another nationality.

7. International Covenant on Economic, Social and Cultural Rights, 1966

This Convention is one of the most important instruments of international human rights law, and promotes equality between individuals. Its intention is to apply equal social, economic and cultural rights. The Covenant of the Convention was originally the work of the General Assembly. It was adopted and opened for signature, ratification and accession by Resolution 2200A (XXI) in 1966. It came into force in January 1976. The International Covenant on Economic, Social and Cultural Rights, the International Covenant on Civil and Political Rights and the Universal Declaration of Human Right are collectively known as the International Bill of Rights. All three instruments indeed complement one another, although their intentions, aims, provisions and their highly philosophical merit have been repeatedly violated by most members of the United Nations: this includes not only the most notorious dictatorial regimes, but also the most well-known democracies. The relevant provisions of the

Covenant aim to protect children's rights from various points of view, in particular discrimination. With regard to the protection of children rights, the following articles are of importance:

Article 10

The States Parties to the present Covenant recognize that:

1. The widest possible protection and assistance should be accorded to the family, which is the natural and fundamental group unit of society, particularly for its establishment and while it is responsible for the care and education of dependent children. Marriage must be entered into with the free consent of the intending spouses.

2. Special protection should be accorded to mothers during a reasonable period before and after childbirth. During such period working mothers should be accorded paid leave or leave with adequate social security benefits.

3. Special measures of protection and assistance should be taken on behalf of all children and young persons without any discrimination for reasons of parentage or other conditions. Children and young persons should be protected from economic and social exploitation. Their employment in work harmful to their morals or health or dangerous to life or likely to hamper their normal development should be punishable by law. States should also set age limits below which the paid employment of child labour should be prohibited and punishable by law.

Article 12

1. The States Parties to the present Covenant recognize the right of everyone to the enjoyment of the highest attainable standard of physical and mental health.

2. The steps to be taken by the States Parties to the present Covenant to achieve the full realization of this right shall include those necessary for:

(a) The provision for the reduction of the stillbirth-rate and of infant mortality and for the healthy development of the child;

(b) The improvement of all aspects of environmental and industrial hygiene;

(c) The prevention, treatment and control of epidemic, endemic, occupational and other diseases;

(d) The creation of conditions which would assure to all medical service and medical attention in the event of sickness.

Article 13

1. The States Parties to the present Covenant recognize the right of everyone to education. They agree that education shall be directed to the full development of the human personality and the sense of its dignity, and shall strengthen the respect for human rights and fundamental freedoms. They further agree that education shall enable all persons to participate effectively in a free society, promote understanding, tolerance and friendship among all nations and all racial, ethnic or religious groups, and further the activities of the United Nations for the maintenance of peace.

2. The States Parties to the present Covenant recognize that, with a view to achieving the full realization of this right:

(a) Primary education shall be compulsory and available free to all;

(b) Secondary education in its different forms, including technical and vocational secondary education, shall be made generally available and accessible to all by every appropriate means, and in particular by the progressive introduction of free education;

(c) Higher education shall be made equally accessible to all, on the basis of capacity, by every appropriate means, and in particular by the progressive introduction of free education;

(d) Fundamental education shall be encouraged or intensified as far as possible for those persons who have not received or completed the whole period of their primary education;

(e) The development of a system of schools at all levels shall be actively pursued, an adequate fellowship system shall be established, and the material conditions of teaching staff shall be continuously improved.

3. The States Parties to the present Covenant undertake to have respect for the liberty of parents and, when applicable, legal guardians to choose for their children schools, other than those established by the public authorities, which conform to such minimum educational standards as may be laid down or approved by the State and to ensure the religious and moral education of their children in conformity with their own convictions.

4. No part of this article shall be construed so as to interfere with the liberty of individuals and bodies to establish and direct educational institutions, subject always to the observance of the principles set forth in paragraph I of this article and to the requirement that the education given in such institutions shall conform to such minimum standards as may be laid down by the State.

8. International Covenant on Civil and Political Rights, 1966

The International Covenant on Civil and Political Rights completes the provisions of the earlier conventions relating to the protection of individuals. The Covenant was adopted by General Assembly Resolution 2200A (XXI) in 1966. It came into force on 23 March 1976. The Covenant has many aims in protecting the rights of individuals. It speaks about the civil and political rights of all persons within a society, regardless of their ethnic origins. The Covenant has especially focused on the different aspects of children's rights. It condemns the discrimination and humiliation of children, and supports their rights without regard to race, colour, sex, religion, social origin or birth. The relevant articles of the Covenant state:

Article 14

1. All persons shall be equal before the courts and tribunals. In the determination of any criminal charge against him, or of his rights and obligations in a suit at law, everyone shall be entitled to a fair and public hearing by a competent, independent and impartial tribunal established by law. The press and the public may be excluded from all or part of a trial for reasons of morals, public order (ordre public) or national security in a democratic society, or when the interest of the private lives of the parties so requires, or to the extent strictly necessary in the opinion of the court in special circumstances where publicity would prejudice the interests of justice; but any judgement rendered in a criminal case or in a suit at law shall be made public except where the interest of juvenile persons otherwise requires or the proceedings concern matrimonial disputes or the guardianship of children.

2. Everyone charged with a criminal offence shall have the right to be presumed innocent until proved guilty according to law.

3. In the determination of any criminal charge against him, everyone shall be entitled to the following minimum guarantees, in full equality:

(a) To be informed promptly and in detail in a language which he understands of the nature and cause of the charge against him;

(b) To have adequate time and facilities for the preparation of his defence and to communicate with counsel of his own choosing;

(c) To be tried without undue delay;

(d) To be tried in his presence, and to defend himself in person or through legal assistance of his own choosing; to be informed, if he does not have legal assistance, of this right; and to have legal assistance assigned to him, in any case where the interests of justice so require, and without payment by him in any such case if he does not have sufficient means to pay for it;

(e) To examine, or have examined, the witnesses against him and to obtain the attendance and examination of witnesses on his behalf under the same conditions as witnesses against him;

(f) To have the free assistance of an interpreter if he cannot understand or speak the language used in court;

(g) Not to be compelled to testify against himself or to confess guilt.

4. In the case of juvenile persons, the procedure shall be such as will take account of their age and the desirability of promoting their rehabilitation.

5. Everyone convicted of a crime shall have the right to his conviction and sentence being reviewed by a higher tribunal according to law.

6. When a person has by a final decision been convicted of a criminal offence and when subsequently his conviction has been reversed or he has been pardoned on the ground that a new or newly discovered fact shows conclusively that there has been a miscarriage of justice, the person who has suffered punishment as a result of such conviction shall be compensated according to law, unless it is proved that the non-disclosure of the unknown fact in time is wholly or partly attributable to him.

7. No one shall be liable to be tried or punished again for an offence for which he has already been finally convicted or acquitted in accordance with the law and penal procedure of each country.

Article 18

1. Everyone shall have the right to freedom of thought, conscience and religion. This right shall include freedom to have or to adopt a religion or belief of his choice, and freedom, either individually or in community with others and in public or private, to manifest his religion or belief in worship, observance, practice and teaching.

2. No one shall be subject to coercion which would impair his freedom to have or to adopt a religion or belief of his choice.

3. Freedom to manifest one's religion or beliefs may be subject only to such limitations as are prescribed by law and are necessary to protect public safety, order, health, or morals or the fundamental rights and freedoms of others. 4. The States Parties to the present Covenant undertake to have respect for the liberty of parents and, when applicable, legal guardians to ensure the religious and moral education of their children in conformity with their own convictions.

Article 23

1. The family is the natural and fundamental group unit of society and is entitled to protection by society and the State.

2. The right of men and women of marriageable age to marry and to found a family shall be recognized.

3. No marriage shall be entered into without the free and full consent of the intending spouses.

4. States Parties to the present Covenant shall take appropriate steps to ensure equality of rights and responsibilities of spouses as to marriage, during marriage and at its dissolution. In the case of dissolution, provision shall be made for the necessary protection of any children.

Article 24

1. Every child shall have, without any discrimination as to race, colour, sex, language, religion, national or social origin, property or birth, the right to such measures of protection as are required by his status as a minor, on the part of his family, society and the State.

2. Every child shall be registered immediately after birth and shall have a name.

3. Every child has the right to acquire a nationality.

9. Declaration on the Protection of Women and Children in Emergency and Armed Conflict, 1974

The Declaration on the Protection of Women and Children in Emergency and Armed Conflict is one of the instruments of international law concerning the protection of children which directly and indirectly deals with the rights of children in armed conflicts. Although the Declaration does not have the legal character of a law-making treaty, it constitutes one of the important instruments for the protection of children's rights in war zones. This work of the General Assembly has also been one of the constructive reasons for the further development of children rights in armed conflicts and their various protection in the international legal community as a whole. The function of the Declaration is also visible within the provisions of the Convention on the Rights of the Child and their humanitarian protection during armed conflicts. The Declaration provides:

The General Assembly,

Having considered the recommendation of the Economic and Social Council contained in its resolution 1861 (LVI) of 16 May 1974,

Expressing its deep concern over the sufferings of women and children belonging to the civilian population who in periods of emergency and armed conflict in the struggle for peace, self-determination, national liberation and independence are too often the victims of inhuman acts and consequently suffer serious harm,

Aware of the suffering of women and children in many areas of the world, especially in those areas subject to suppression, aggression, colonialism, racism, alien domination and foreign subjugation,

Deeply concerned by the fact that, despite general and unequivocal condemnation, colonialism, racism and alien and foreign domination continue to subject many peoples under their yoke, cruelly suppressing the national liberation movements and inflicting heavy losses and incalculable sufferings on the populations under their domination, including women and children,

Deploring the fact that grave attacks are still being made on fundamental freedoms and the dignity of the human person and that colonial and racist foreign domination Powers continue to violate international humanitarian law,

Recalling the relevant provisions contained in the instruments of international humanitarian law relative to the protection of women and children in time of peace and war,

Recalling, among other important documents, its resolutions 2444 (XXIII) of 19 December 1968, 2597 (XXIV) of 16 December 1969 and 2674 (XXV) and 2675 (XXV) of 9 December 1970, on respect for human rights and on basic principles for the protection of civilian populations in armed conflicts, as well as Economic and Social Council resolution 1515 (XLVIII) of 28 May 1970 in which the Council requested the General Assembly to consider the possibility of drafting a declaration on the protection of women and children in emergency or wartime,

Conscious of its responsibility for the destiny of the rising generation and for the destiny of mothers, who play an important role in society, in the family and particularly in the upbringing of children,

Bearing in mind the need to provide special protection of women and children belonging to the civilian population,

Solemnly proclaims this Declaration on the Protection of Women and Children in Emergency and Armed Conflict and calls for the strict observance of the Declaration by all Member States:

1. Attacks and bombings on the civilian population, inflicting incalculable suffering, especially on women and children, who are the most vulnerable members of the population, shall be prohibited, and such acts shall be condemned.

2. The use of chemical and bacteriological weapons in the course of military operations constitutes one of the most flagrant violations of the Geneva Protocol of 1925, the Geneva Conventions of 1949 and the principles of international humanitarian law and inflicts heavy losses on civilian populations, including defenceless women and children, and shall be severely condemned.

3. All States shall abide fully by their obligations under the Geneva Protocol of 1925 and the Geneva Conventions of 1949, as well as other instruments of international law relative to respect for human rights in armed conflicts, which offer important guarantees for the protection of women and children.

4. All efforts shall be made by States involved in armed conflicts, military operations in foreign territories or military operations in territories still under colonial domination to spare women and children from the ravages of war. All the necessary steps shall be taken to ensure the prohibition of measures such as persecution, torture, punitive measures, degrading treatment and violence, particularly against that part of the civilian population that consists of women and children.

5. All forms of repression and cruel and inhuman treatment of women and children, including imprisonment, torture, shooting, mass arrests, collective punishment, destruction of dwellings and forcible eviction, committed by belligerents in the course of military operations or in occupied territories shall be considered criminal.

6. Women and children belonging to the civilian population and finding themselves in circumstances of emergency and armed conflict in the struggle for peace, self-determination, national liberation and independence, or who live in occupied territories, shall not be deprived of shelter, food, medical aid or other inalienable rights, in accordance with the provisions of the Universal Declaration of Human Rights, the International Covenant on Civil and Political Rights, the International Covenant on Economic, Social and Cultural Rights, the Declaration of the Rights of the Child or other instruments of international law.

10. International Convention on the Protection of the Rights of All Migrant Workers and Members of Their Families, 1990

The International Convention on the Protection of the Rights of All Migrant Workers and Members of Their Families is the work of the organs of the General Assembly. It was adopted under Resolution 45/158 in 1990 and came into force in 2003, and was meant to close the gap between the various laws of states and provisions of human rights law. Its intention was to deal with the increasing problems of migration, and to try to solve various issues relating to workers and family members. The Convention is, in other words, a useful instrument for protecting the rights of migrants in the countries of origin, transit and destination.. Therefore, the Convention aims to ensure the rights of migrants and includes some important rules concerning the protection of migrant children. The relevant parts of the Convention concerning the rights of children are:

Preamble

The States Parties to the present Convention,
Taking into account the principles embodied in the basic instruments of the United Nations concerning human rights, in particular the Universal Declaration of Human Rights, the International Covenant on Economic, Social and Cultural Rights, the International Covenant on Civil and Political Rights, the International Convention on the Elimination of All Forms of Racial Discrimination, the Convention on the Elimination of All Forms of Discrimination against Women and the Convention on the Rights of the Child.

Article 4

For the purposes of the present Convention the term "members of the family" refers to persons married to migrant workers or having with them a relationship that, according to applicable law, produces effects equivalent to marriage, as well as their dependent children and other dependent persons who are recognized as members of the family by applicable legislation or applicable bilateral or multilateral agreements between the States concerned.

Article 12

1. Migrant workers and members of their families shall have the right to freedom of thought, conscience and religion. This right shall include freedom to have or to adopt a religion or belief of their choice and freedom either individually or in community with others and in public or private to manifest their religion or belief in worship, observance, practice and teaching.

2. Migrant workers and members of their families shall not be subject to coercion that would impair their freedom to have or to adopt a religion or belief of their choice.

3. Freedom to manifest one's religion or belief may be subject only to such limitations as are prescribed by law and are necessary to protect

public safety, order, health or morals or the fundamental rights and freedoms of others.

4. States Parties to the present Convention undertake to have respect for the liberty of parents, at least one of whom is a migrant worker, and, when applicable, legal guardians to ensure the religious and moral education of their children in conformity with their own convictions.

Article 17

1. Migrant workers and members of their families who are deprived of their liberty shall be treated with humanity and with respect for the inherent dignity of the human person and for their cultural identity.

2. Accused migrant workers and members of their families shall, save in exceptional circumstances, be separated from convicted persons and shall be subject to separate treatment appropriate to their status as unconvicted persons. Accused juvenile persons shall be separated from adults and brought as speedily as possible for adjudication.

3. Any migrant worker or member of his or her family who is detained in a State of transit or in a State of employment for violation of provisions relating to migration shall be held, in so far as practicable, separately from convicted persons or persons detained pending trial.

4. During any period of imprisonment in pursuance of a sentence imposed by a court of law, the essential aim of the treatment of a migrant worker or a member of his or her family shall be his or her reformation and social rehabilitation. Juvenile offenders shall be separated from adults and be accorded treatment appropriate to their age and legal status.

5. During detention or imprisonment, migrant workers and members of their families shall enjoy the same rights as nationals to visits by members of their families.

6. Whenever a migrant worker is deprived of his or her liberty, the competent authorities of the State concerned shall pay attention to the problems that may be posed for members of his or her family, in particular for spouses and minor children.

7. Migrant workers and members of their families who are subjected to any form of detention or imprisonment in accordance with the law in force in the State of employment or in the State of transit shall enjoy the same rights as nationals of those States who are in the same situation.

8. If a migrant worker or a member of his or her family is detained for the purpose of verifying any infraction of provisions related to migration, he or she shall not bear any costs arising therefrom.

Article 29

Each child of a migrant worker shall have the right to a name, to registration of birth and to a nationality.

Article 30

Each child of a migrant worker shall have the basic right of access to education on the basis of equality of treatment with nationals of the State concerned. Access to public pre-school educational institutions or schools shall not be refused or limited by reason of the irregular situation with respect to stay or employment of either parent or by reason of the irregularity of the child's stay in the State of employment.

Article 44

1. States Parties, recognizing that the family is the natural and fundamental group unit of society and is entitled to protection by society and the State, shall take appropriate measures to ensure the protection of the unity of the families of migrant workers.

2. States Parties shall take measures that they deem appropriate and that fall within their competence to facilitate the reunification of migrant workers with their spouses or persons who have with the migrant worker a relationship that, according to applicable law, produces effects equivalent to marriage, as well as with their minor dependent unmarried children.

3. States of employment, on humanitarian grounds, shall favourably consider granting equal treatment, as set forth in paragraph 2 of the present article, to other family members of migrant workers.

Article 45

1. Members of the families of migrant workers shall, in the State of employment, enjoy equality of treatment with nationals of that State in relation to:

(a) Access to educational institutions and services, subject to the admission requirements and other regulations of the institutions and services concerned;

(b) Access to vocational guidance and training institutions and services, provided that requirements for participation are met;

(c) Access to social and health services, provided that requirements for participation in the respective schemes are met;

(d) Access to and participation in cultural life.

2. States of employment shall pursue a policy, where appropriate in collaboration with the States of origin, aimed at facilitating the integration

of children of migrant workers in the local school system, particularly in respect of teaching them the local language.

3. States of employment shall endeavour to facilitate for the children of migrant workers the teaching of their mother tongue and culture and, in this regard, States of origin shall collaborate whenever appropriate.

4. States of employment may provide special schemes of education in the mother tongue of children of migrant workers, if necessary in collaboration with the States of origin.

11. Basic Principles and Guidelines on the Right to a Remedy and Reparation for Victims of Gross Violations of International Human Rights Law and Serious Violations of International Humanitarian Law, 2005

The basic principles were adopted and proclaimed by the General Assembly Resolution 60/147 of 16 December 2005. It refers to the Convention on the Rights of the Child and reparation in the form of satisfaction for the identities of the children abducted. It provides that:

Preamble

The General Assembly,

Recalling the provisions providing a right to a remedy for victims of violations of international human rights law found in numerous international instruments, in particular article 8 of the Universal Declaration of Human Rights, 1 article 2 of the International Covenant on Civil and Political Rights, 2 article 6 of the International Convention on the Elimination of All Forms of Racial Discrimination, article 14 of the Convention against Torture and Other Cruel, Inhuman or Degrading Treatment or Punishment, and article 39 of the Convention on the Rights of the Child, and of international humanitarian law as found in article 3 of the Hague Convention respecting the Laws and Customs of War on Land of 18 October 1907 (Convention IV), article 91 of the Protocol Additional to the Geneva Conventions of 12 August 1949, and relating to the Protection of Victims of International Armed Conflicts (Protocol I) of 8 June 1977, and articles 68 and 75 of the Rome Statute of the International Criminal Court,

…

IX. Reparation for harm suffered

…

22. Satisfaction should include, where applicable, any or all of the following:

…

(*c*) The search for the whereabouts of the disappeared, for the identities of the children abducted, and for the bodies of those killed, and assistance in the recovery, identification and reburial of the bodies in accordance with the expressed or presumed wish of the victims, or the cultural practices of the families and communities;

CHAPTER IV

INTERNATIONAL LEGISLATIONS DIRECTLY PROTECTING THE RIGHTS OF CHILDREN

1. Geneva Declaration of the Rights of the Child, 1924

Since the beginning of the twentieth century, the international legal community has tried in various ways to increase the protection of children, and to reduce violations against them, but this has not been easy. The idea of protecting children's rights actually began in 1913, when there was in fact a strong desire to create an International Association for the protection of children. The Declaration of the Rights of the Child was therefore formulated in order to create some moral or legal obligations for states. The Declaration was later accepted by the International Save the Children Union at Geneva in 192, adopted by the League of Nations the next year, and re-approved in 1934. The intention of the Declaration is to protect children in times of armed conflict, and its provisions were the cause for the approval of other instruments for the protection of children in times of armed conflict. The Declaration provides:

By the present Declaration of the Rights of the Child, commonly known as "Declaration of Geneva," men and women of all nations, recognizing that mankind owes to the Child the best that it has to give, declare and accept it as their duty that, beyond and above all considerations of race, nationality or creed:

1. The child must be given the means requisite for its normal development, both materially and spiritually.
2. The child that is hungry must be fed, the child that is sick must be helped, the child that is backward must be helped, the delinquent child must be reclaimed, and the orphan and the waif must be sheltered and succoured.
3. The child must be the first to receive relief in times of distress.

4. The child must be put in a position to earn a livelihood, and must be protected against every form of exploitation.

5. The child must be brought up in the consciousness that its talents must be devoted to the service of its fellow men.

2. Declaration of the Rights of the Child, 1959

One of the problems of the declarations of the United Nations General Assembly, and many other declarations from other international organizations, is that they do not have the legal effect of law-making treaties, and therefore their effect or legal enforceability depends on many conditions and on the policy of different states. The Declaration of the Rights of the Child, which was adopted by the General Assembly, has a similar problem. This means that the legal character of the Declaration is very soft, and its implementation is not definite. The policies of the 1959 Declaration were developed by the provisions of Article 24 of the 1966Covenant on Civil and Political Rights. The Declaration was, in fact, adopted by General Assembly Resolution 1386(XIV) in 1959. It develops different aspects of the rights of the child and, particularly emphasises the inalienable rights of children, for example protection against all forms of exploitation, although it does not take into effective consideration all the necessary aspects of children's social. This shortcoming of the Declaration was one of the reasons why many other international instruments were subsequently adopted. The Declaration states:

Whereas the peoples of the United Nations have, in the Charter, reaffirmed their faith in fundamental human rights and in the dignity and worth of the human person, and have determined to promote social progress and better standards of life in larger freedom,

Whereas the United Nations has, in the Universal Declaration of Human Rights, proclaimed that everyone is entitled to all the rights and freedoms set forth therein, without distinction of any kind, such as race, colour, sex, language, religion, political or other opinion, national or social origin, property, birth or other status,

Whereas the child, by reason of his physical and mental immaturity, needs special safeguards and care, including appropriate legal protection, before as well as after birth,

Whereas the need for such special safeguards has been stated in the Geneva Declaration of the Rights of the Child of 1924, and recognized in the Universal Declaration of Human Rights and in the statutes of specialized agencies and international organizations concerned with the welfare of children,

Whereas mankind owes to the child the best it has to give,

Now therefore,

The General Assembly

Proclaims this Declaration of the Rights of the Child to the end that he may have a happy childhood and enjoy for his own good and for the good of society the rights and freedoms herein set forth, and calls upon parents, upon men and women as individuals, and upon voluntary organizations, local authorities and national Governments to recognize these rights and strive for their observance by legislative and other measures progressively taken in accordance with the following principles:

Principle 1

The child shall enjoy all the rights set forth in this Declaration. Every child, without any exception whatsoever, shall be entitled to these rights, without distinction or discrimination on account of race, colour, sex, language, religion, political or other opinion, national or social origin, property, birth or other status, whether of himself or of his family.

Principle 2

The child shall enjoy special protection, and shall be given opportunities and facilities, by law and by other means, to enable him to develop physically, mentally, morally, spiritually and socially in a healthy and normal manner and in conditions of freedom and dignity. In the enactment of laws for this purpose, the best interests of the child shall be the paramount consideration.

Principle 3

The child shall be entitled from his birth to a name and a nationality.

Principle 4

The child shall enjoy the benefits of social security. He shall be entitled to grow and develop in health; to this end, special care and protection shall be provided both to him and to his mother, including adequate pre-natal and post-natal care. The child shall have the right to adequate nutrition, housing, recreation and medical services.

Principle 5

The child who is physically, mentally or socially handicapped shall be given the special treatment, education and care required by his particular condition.

Principle 6

The child, for the full and harmonious development of his personality, needs love and understanding. He shall, wherever possible, grow up in the care and under the responsibility of his parents, and, in any case, in an atmosphere of affection and of moral and material security; a child of tender years shall not, save in exceptional circumstances, be separated from his mother. Society and the public authorities shall have the duty to extend particular care to children without a family and to those without adequate means of support. Payment of State and other assistance towards the maintenance of children of large families is desirable.

Principle 7

The child is entitled to receive education, which shall be free and compulsory, at least in the elementary stages. He shall be given an education which will promote his general culture and enable him, on a basis of equal opportunity, to develop his abilities, his individual judgement, and his sense of moral and social responsibility, and to become a useful member of society.

The best interests of the child shall be the guiding principle of those responsible for his education and guidance; that responsibility lies in the first place with his parents.

The child shall have full opportunity for play and recreation, which should be directed to the same purposes as education; society and the public authorities, shall endeavour to promote the enjoyment of this right.

Principle 8

The child shall in all circumstances be among the first to receive protection and relief.

Principle 9

The child shall be protected against all forms of neglect, cruelty and exploitation. He shall not be the subject of traffic, in any form.

The child shall not be admitted to employment before an appropriate minimum age; he shall in no case be caused or permitted to engage in any occupation or employment which would prejudice his health or education, or interfere with his physical, mental or moral development.

Principle 10

The child shall be protected from practices which may foster racial, religious and any other form of discrimination. He shall be brought up in a spirit of understanding, tolerance, friendship among peoples, peace and universal brotherhood, and in full consciousness that his energy and talents should be devoted to the service of his fellow men.

3. Convention on the Rights of the Child, 1989

The League of Nations was ineffective in protecting the rights of children and juveniles. The League had many problems, and its only legacy concerning the protection of children's rights was the Declaration of 1924. Children's protection was therefore brought before the United Nations Organization in the hope that it might protect children from various social, political, economic and humanitarian problems, but this was not possible in the beginning, however. Many states did not want to regulate children's rights with an international convention. One of the chief reasons for this was that the protection of children would limit their use in times of armed conflict, and another problem was that protection would limit the juridical machinery of states to bring juveniles before a criminal court. This was not welcomed in many conservative countries that treat children as secondary subjects of the law and where, traditionally, the child is entirely dependent on his/her parent or guardian's decisions. Furthermore, serious protection could also lead to the non-sanctioning of the death penalty. These and many other reasons combined to provide a strong case against formulating a convention dealing exclusively with the rights of children. But the formulation of many other international instruments of human rights law finally created the conditions for the adoption of an international convention which exclusively dealt with the rights of children. This is what is known as the Convention on the Rights of Child, adopted in 1989.The Convention on the Rights of the Child and its protocols are the most valuable instruments dealing with the social, political, economic and natural rights of children. The Convention and its protocols together form the three sides of the triangle of the law dealing solely with children. The Convention entered into force in 1990, and has created a Committee (of 10 members) on the Rights of Child under the provisions of Article 43 (2). In order to have more experts on the Committee, the Article was amended in 2002, increasing its size from 10 to 18 members.

Preamble

The States Parties to the present Convention,

Considering that, in accordance with the principles proclaimed in the Charter of the United Nations, recognition of the inherent dignity and of the equal and inalienable rights of all members of the human family is the foundation of freedom, justice and peace in the world,

Bearing in mind that the peoples of the United Nations have, in the Charter, reaffirmed their faith in fundamental human rights and in the dignity and worth of the human person, and have determined to promote social progress and better standards of life in larger freedom,

Recognizing that the United Nations has, in the Universal Declaration of Human Rights and in the International Covenants on Human Rights, proclaimed and agreed that everyone is entitled to all the rights and freedoms set forth therein, without distinction of any kind, such as race, colour, sex, language, religion, political or other opinion, national or social origin, property, birth or other status,

Recalling that, in the Universal Declaration of Human Rights, the United Nations has proclaimed that childhood is entitled to special care and assistance,

Convinced that the family, as the fundamental group of society and the natural environment for the growth and well-being of all its members and particularly children, should be afforded the necessary protection and assistance so that it can fully assume its responsibilities within the community,

Recognizing that the child, for the full and harmonious development of his or her personality, should grow up in a family environment, in an atmosphere of happiness, love and understanding,

Considering that the child should be fully prepared to live an individual life in society, and brought up in the spirit of the ideals proclaimed in the Charter of the United Nations, and in particular in the spirit of peace, dignity, tolerance, freedom, equality and solidarity,

Bearing in mind that the need to extend particular care to the child has been stated in the Geneva Declaration of the Rights of the Child of 1924 and in the Declaration of the Rights of the Child adopted by the General Assembly on 20 November 1959 and recognized in the Universal Declaration of Human Rights, in the International Covenant on Civil and Political Rights (in particular in articles 23 and 24), in the International Covenant on Economic, Social and Cultural Rights (in particular in article 10) and in the statutes and relevant instruments of specialized agencies and international organizations concerned with the welfare of children, '

Bearing in mind that, as indicated in the Declaration of the Rights of the Child, "the child, by reason of his physical and mental immaturity, needs special safeguards and care, including appropriate legal protection, before as well as after birth",

Recalling the provisions of the Declaration on Social and Legal Principles relating to the Protection and Welfare of Children, with Special Reference to Foster Placement and Adoption Nationally and Internationally; the United Nations Standard Minimum Rules for the Administration of Juvenile Justice (The Beijing Rules) ; and the Declaration on the Protection of Women and Children in Emergency and Armed Conflict,

Recognizing that, in all countries in the world, there are children living in exceptionally difficult conditions, and that such children need special consideration,

Taking due account of the importance of the traditions and cultural values of each people for the protection and harmonious development of the child,

Recognizing the importance of international co-operation for improving the living conditions of children in every country, in particular in the developing countries,

Have agreed as follows:

PART I

Article 1

For the purposes of the present Convention, a child means every human being below the age of eighteen years unless under the law applicable to the child, majority is attained earlier.

Article 2

1. States Parties shall respect and ensure the rights set forth in the present Convention to each child within their jurisdiction without discrimination of any kind, irrespective of the child's or his or her parent's or legal guardian's race, colour, sex, language, religion, political or other opinion, national, ethnic or social origin, property, disability, birth or other status.

2. States Parties shall take all appropriate measures to ensure that the child is protected against all forms of discrimination or punishment on the basis of the status, activities, expressed opinions, or beliefs of the child's parents, legal guardians, or family members.

Article 3

1. In all actions concerning children, whether undertaken by public or private social welfare institutions, courts of law, administrative authorities or legislative bodies, the best interests of the child shall be a primary consideration.

2. States Parties undertake to ensure the child such protection and care as is necessary for his or her well-being, taking into account the rights and duties of his or her parents, legal guardians, or other individuals legally responsible for him or her, and, to this end, shall take all appropriate legislative and administrative measures.

3. States Parties shall ensure that the institutions, services and facilities responsible for the care or protection of children shall conform with the standards established by competent authorities, particularly in the areas of safety, health, in the number and suitability of their staff, as well as competent supervision.

Article 4

States Parties shall undertake all appropriate legislative, administrative, and other measures for the implementation of the rights recognized in the present Convention. With regard to economic, social and cultural rights, States Parties shall undertake such measures to the maximum extent of their available resources and, where needed, within the framework of international co-operation.

Article 5

States Parties shall respect the responsibilities, rights and duties of parents or, where applicable, the members of the extended family or community as provided for by local custom, legal guardians or other persons legally responsible for the child, to provide, in a manner consistent with the evolving capacities of the child, appropriate direction and guidance in the exercise by the child of the rights recognized in the present Convention.

Article 6

1. States Parties recognize that every child has the inherent right to life.

2. States Parties shall ensure to the maximum extent possible the survival and development of the child.

Article 7

1. The child shall be registered immediately after birth and shall have the right from birth to a name, the right to acquire a nationality and. as far as possible, the right to know and be cared for by his or her parents.

2. States Parties shall ensure the implementation of these rights in accordance with their national law and their obligations under the relevant international instruments in this field, in particular where the child would otherwise be stateless.

Article 8

1. States Parties undertake to respect the right of the child to preserve his or her identity, including nationality, name and family relations as recognized by law without unlawful interference.

2. Where a child is illegally deprived of some or all of the elements of his or her identity, States Parties shall provide appropriate assistance and protection, with a view to re-establishing speedily his or her identity.

Article 9

1. States Parties shall ensure that a child shall not be separated from his or her parents against their will, except when competent authorities subject to judicial review determine, in accordance with applicable law and procedures, that such separation is necessary for the best interests of the child. Such determination may be necessary in a particular case such as one involving abuse or neglect of the child by the parents, or one where the parents are living separately and a decision must be made as to the child's place of residence.

2. In any proceedings pursuant to paragraph 1 of the present article, all interested parties shall be given an opportunity to participate in the proceedings and make their views known.

3. States Parties shall respect the right of the child who is separated from one or both parents to maintain personal relations and direct contact with both parents on a regular basis, except if it is contrary to the child's best interests.

4. Where such separation results from any action initiated by a State Party, such as the detention, imprisonment, exile, deportation or death (including death arising from any cause while the person is in the custody of the State) of one or both parents or of the child, that State Party shall, upon request, provide the parents, the child or, if appropriate, another member of the family with the essential information concerning the whereabouts of the absent member(s) of the family unless the provision of the information would be detrimental to the well-being of the child. States Parties shall further ensure that the submission of such a request shall of itself entail no adverse consequences for the person(s) concerned.

Article 10

1. In accordance with the obligation of States Parties under article 9, paragraph 1, applications by a child or his or her parents to enter or leave a State Party for the purpose of family reunification shall be dealt with by States Parties in a positive, humane and expeditious manner. States Parties shall further ensure that the submission of such a request shall entail no adverse consequences for the applicants and for the members of their family.

2. A child whose parents reside in different States shall have the right to maintain on a regular basis, save in exceptional circumstances personal relations and direct contacts with both parents. Towards that end and in accordance with the obligation of States Parties under article 9, paragraph 1, States Parties shall respect the right of the child and his or her parents to leave any country, including their own, and to enter their own country. The right to leave any country shall be subject only to such restrictions as are prescribed by law and which are necessary to protect the national security, public order (ordre public), public health or morals or the rights and freedoms of others and are consistent with the other rights recognized in the present Convention.

Article 11

1. States Parties shall take measures to combat the illicit transfer and non-return of children abroad.

2. To this end, States Parties shall promote the conclusion of bilateral or multilateral agreements or accession to existing agreements.

Article 12

1. States Parties shall assure to the child who is capable of forming his or her own views the right to express those views freely in all matters affecting the child, the views of the child being given due weight in accordance with the age and maturity of the child.

2. For this purpose, the child shall in particular be provided the opportunity to be heard in any judicial and administrative proceedings affecting the child, either directly, or through a representative or an appropriate body, in a manner consistent with the procedural rules of national law.

Article 13

1. The child shall have the right to freedom of expression; this right shall include freedom to seek, receive and impart information and ideas of

all kinds, regardless of frontiers, either orally, in writing or in print, in the form of art, or through any other media of the child's choice.

2. The exercise of this right may be subject to certain restrictions, but these shall only be such as are provided by law and are necessary:

(a) For respect of the rights or reputations of others; or

(b) For the protection of national security or of public order (ordre public), or of public health or morals.

Article 14

1. States Parties shall respect the right of the child to freedom of thought, conscience and religion.

2. States Parties shall respect the rights and duties of the parents and, when applicable, legal guardians, to provide direction to the child in the exercise of his or her right in a manner consistent with the evolving capacities of the child.

3. Freedom to manifest one's religion or beliefs may be subject only to such limitations as are prescribed by law and are necessary to protect public safety, order, health or morals, or the fundamental rights and freedoms of others.

Article 15

1. States Parties recognize the rights of the child to freedom of association and to freedom of peaceful assembly.

2. No restrictions may be placed on the exercise of these rights other than those imposed in conformity with the law and which are necessary in a democratic society in the interests of national security or public safety, public order (ordre public), the protection of public health or morals or the protection of the rights and freedoms of others.

Article 16

1. No child shall be subjected to arbitrary or unlawful interference with his or her privacy, family, home or correspondence, nor to unlawful attacks on his or her honour and reputation.

2. The child has the right to the protection of the law against such interference or attacks.

Article 17

States Parties recognize the important function performed by the mass media and shall ensure that the child has access to information and material from a diversity of national and international sources, especially those aimed at the promotion of his or her social, spiritual and moral well-being and physical and mental health. To this end, States Parties shall:

(a) Encourage the mass media to disseminate information and material of social and cultural benefit to the child and in accordance with the spirit of article 29;

(b) Encourage international co-operation in the production, exchange and dissemination of such information and material from a diversity of cultural, national and international sources;

(c) Encourage the production and dissemination of children's books;

(d) Encourage the mass media to have particular regard to the linguistic needs of the child who belongs to a minority group or who is indigenous;

(e) Encourage the development of appropriate guidelines for the protection of the child from information and material injurious to his or her well-being, bearing in mind the provisions of articles 13 and 18.

Article 18

1. States Parties shall use their best efforts to ensure recognition of the principle that both parents have common responsibilities for the upbringing and development of the child. Parents or, as the case may be, legal guardians, have the primary responsibility for the upbringing and development of the child. The best interests of the child will be their basic concern.

2. For the purpose of guaranteeing and promoting the rights set forth in the present Convention, States Parties shall render appropriate assistance to parents and legal guardians in the performance of their child-rearing responsibilities and shall ensure the development of institutions, facilities and services for the care of children.

3. States Parties shall take all appropriate measures to ensure that children of working parents have the right to benefit from child-care services and facilities for which they are eligible.

Article 19

1. States Parties shall take all appropriate legislative, administrative, social and educational measures to protect the child from all forms of physical or mental violence, injury or abuse, neglect or negligent treatment, maltreatment or exploitation, including sexual abuse, while in the care of parent(s), legal guardian(s) or any other person who has the care of the child.

2. Such protective measures should, as appropriate, include effective procedures for the establishment of social programmes to provide necessary support for the child and for those who have the care of the

child, as well as for other forms of prevention and for identification, reporting, referral, investigation, treatment and follow-up of instances of child maltreatment described heretofore, and, as appropriate, for judicial involvement.

Article 20

1. A child temporarily or permanently deprived of his or her family environment, or in whose own best interests cannot be allowed to remain in that environment, shall be entitled to special protection and assistance provided by the State.

2. States Parties shall in accordance with their national laws ensure alternative care for such a child.

3. Such care could include, inter alia, foster placement, kafalah of Islamic law, adoption or if necessary placement in suitable institutions for the care of children. When considering solutions, due regard shall be paid to the desirability of continuity in a child's upbringing and to the child's ethnic, religious, cultural and linguistic background.

Article 21

States Parties that recognize and/or permit the system of adoption shall ensure that the best interests of the child shall be the paramount consideration and they shall:

(a) Ensure that the adoption of a child is authorized only by competent authorities who determine, in accordance with applicable law and procedures and on the basis of all pertinent and reliable information, that the adoption is permissible in view of the child's status concerning parents, relatives and legal guardians and that, if required, the persons concerned have given their informed consent to the adoption on the basis of such counselling as may be necessary;

(b) Recognize that inter-country adoption may be considered as an alternative means of child's care, if the child cannot be placed in a foster or an adoptive family or cannot in any suitable manner be cared for in the child's country of origin; (c) Ensure that the child concerned by inter-country adoption enjoys safeguards and standards equivalent to those existing in the case of national adoption;

(d) Take all appropriate measures to ensure that, in inter-country adoption, the placement does not result in improper financial gain for those involved in it;

(e) Promote, where appropriate, the objectives of the present article by concluding bilateral or multilateral arrangements or agreements, and endeavour, within this framework, to ensure that the placement of the child in another country is carried out by competent authorities or organs.

Article 22

1. States Parties shall take appropriate measures to ensure that a child who is seeking refugee status or who is considered a refugee in accordance with applicable international or domestic law and procedures shall, whether unaccompanied or accompanied by his or her parents or by any other person, receive appropriate protection and humanitarian assistance in the enjoyment of applicable rights set forth in the present Convention and in other international human rights or humanitarian instruments to which the said States are Parties.

2. For this purpose, States Parties shall provide, as they consider appropriate, co-operation in any efforts by the United Nations and other competent intergovernmental organizations or non-governmental organizations co-operating with the United Nations to protect and assist such a child and to trace the parents or other members of the family of any refugee child in order to obtain information necessary for reunification with his or her family. In cases where no parents or other members of the family can be found, the child shall be accorded the same protection as any other child permanently or temporarily deprived of his or her family environment for any reason, as set forth in the present Convention.

Article 23

1. States Parties recognize that a mentally or physically disabled child should enjoy a full and decent life, in conditions which ensure dignity, promote self-reliance and facilitate the child's active participation in the community.

2. States Parties recognize the right of the disabled child to special care and shall encourage and ensure the extension, subject to available resources, to the eligible child and those responsible for his or her care, of assistance for which application is made and which is appropriate to the child's condition and to the circumstances of the parents or others caring for the child.

3. Recognizing the special needs of a disabled child, assistance extended in accordance with paragraph 2 of the present article shall be provided free of charge, whenever possible, taking into account the financial resources of the parents or others caring for the child, and shall be designed to ensure that the disabled child has effective access to and receives education, training, health care services, rehabilitation services, preparation for employment and recreation opportunities in a manner

conducive to the child's achieving the fullest possible social integration and individual development, including his or her cultural and spiritual development

4. States Parties shall promote, in the spirit of international cooperation, the exchange of appropriate information in the field of preventive health care and of medical, psychological and functional treatment of disabled children, including dissemination of and access to information concerning methods of rehabilitation, education and vocational services, with the aim of enabling States Parties to improve their capabilities and skills and to widen their experience in these areas. In this regard, particular account shall be taken of the needs of developing countries.

Article 24

1. States Parties recognize the right of the child to the enjoyment of the highest attainable standard of health and to facilities for the treatment of illness and rehabilitation of health. States Parties shall strive to ensure that no child is deprived of his or her right of access to such health care services.

2. States Parties shall pursue full implementation of this right and, in particular, shall take appropriate measures:

(a) To diminish infant and child mortality;

(b) To ensure the provision of necessary medical assistance and health care to all children with emphasis on the development of primary health care;

(c) To combat disease and malnutrition, including within the framework of primary health care, through, inter alia, the application of readily available technology and through the provision of adequate nutritious foods and clean drinking-water, taking into consideration the dangers and risks of environmental pollution;

(d) To ensure appropriate pre-natal and post-natal health care for mothers;

(e) To ensure that all segments of society, in particular parents and children, are informed, have access to education and are supported in the use of basic knowledge of child health and nutrition, the advantages of breastfeeding, hygiene and environmental sanitation and the prevention of accidents;

(f) To develop preventive health care, guidance for parents and family planning education and services.

3. States Parties shall take all effective and appropriate measures with a view to abolishing traditional practices prejudicial to the health of children.

4. States Parties undertake to promote and encourage international co-operation with a view to achieving progressively the full realization of the right recognized in the present article. In this regard, particular account shall be taken of the needs of developing countries.

Article 25

States Parties recognize the right of a child who has been placed by the competent authorities for the purposes of care, protection or treatment of his or her physical or mental health, to a periodic review of the treatment provided to the child and all other circumstances relevant to his or her placement.

Article 26

1. States Parties shall recognize for every child the right to benefit from social security, including social insurance, and shall take the necessary measures to achieve the full realization of this right in accordance with their national law.

2. The benefits should, where appropriate, be granted, taking into account the resources and the circumstances of the child and persons having responsibility for the maintenance of the child, as well as any other consideration relevant to an application for benefits made by or on behalf of the child.

Article 27

1. States Parties recognize the right of every child to a standard of living adequate for the child's physical, mental, spiritual, moral and social development.

2. The parent(s) or others responsible for the child have the primary responsibility to secure, within their abilities and financial capacities, the conditions of living necessary for the child's development.

3. States Parties, in accordance with national conditions and within their means, shall take appropriate measures to assist parents and others responsible for the child to implement this right and shall in case of need provide material assistance and support programmes, particularly with regard to nutrition, clothing and housing.

4. States Parties shall take all appropriate measures to secure the recovery of maintenance for the child from the parents or other persons having financial responsibility for the child, both within the State Party

and from abroad. In particular, where the person having financial responsibility for the child lives in a State different from that of the child, States Parties shall promote the accession to international agreements or the conclusion of such agreements, as well as the making of other appropriate arrangements.

Article 28

1. States Parties recognize the right of the child to education, and with a view to achieving this right progressively and on the basis of equal opportunity, they shall, in particular:

(a) Make primary education compulsory and available free to all;

(b) Encourage the development of different forms of secondary education, including general and vocational education, make them available and accessible to every child, and take appropriate measures such as the introduction of free education and offering financial assistance in case of need;

(c) Make higher education accessible to all on the basis of capacity by every appropriate means;

(d) Make educational and vocational information and guidance available and accessible to all children;

(e) Take measures to encourage regular attendance at schools and the reduction of drop-out rates.

2. States Parties shall take all appropriate measures to ensure that school discipline is administered in a manner consistent with the child's human dignity and in conformity with the present Convention.

3. States Parties shall promote and encourage international cooperation in matters relating to education, in particular with a view to contributing to the elimination of ignorance and illiteracy throughout the world and facilitating access to scientific and technical knowledge and modern teaching methods. In this regard, particular account shall be taken of the needs of developing countries.

Article 29

1. States Parties agree that the education of the child shall be directed to:

(a) The development of the child's personality, talents and mental and physical abilities to their fullest potential;

(b) The development of respect for human rights and fundamental freedoms, and for the principles enshrined in the Charter of the United Nations;

(c) The development of respect for the child's parents, his or her own cultural identity, language and values, for the national values of the country in which the child is living, the country from which he or she may originate, and for civilizations different from his or her own;
(d) The preparation of the child for responsible life in a free society, in the spirit of understanding, peace, tolerance, equality of sexes, and friendship among all peoples, ethnic, national and religious groups and persons of indigenous origin;
(e) The development of respect for the natural environment.

2. No part of the present article or article 28 shall be construed so as to interfere with the liberty of individuals and bodies to establish and direct educational institutions, subject always to the observance of the principle set forth in paragraph 1 of the present article and to the requirements that the education given in such institutions shall conform to such minimum standards as may be laid down by the State.

Article 30

In those States in which ethnic, religious or linguistic minorities or persons of indigenous origin exist, a child belonging to such a minority or who is indigenous shall not be denied the right, in community with other members of his or her group, to enjoy his or her own culture, to profess and practise his or her own religion, or to use his or her own language.

Article 31

1. States Parties recognize the right of the child to rest and leisure, to engage in play and recreational activities appropriate to the age of the child and to participate freely in cultural life and the arts.

2. States Parties shall respect and promote the right of the child to participate fully in cultural and artistic life and shall encourage the provision of appropriate and equal opportunities for cultural, artistic, recreational and leisure activity.

Article 32

1. States Parties recognize the right of the child to be protected from economic exploitation and from performing any work that is likely to be hazardous or to interfere with the child's education, or to be harmful to the child's health or physical, mental, spiritual, moral or social development.

2. States Parties shall take legislative, administrative, social and educational measures to ensure the implementation of the present article. To this end, and having regard to the relevant provisions of other international instruments, States Parties shall in particular:

(a) Provide for a minimum age or minimum ages for admission to employment;
(b) Provide for appropriate regulation of the hours and conditions of employment;
(c) Provide for appropriate penalties or other sanctions to ensure the effective enforcement of the present article.

Article 33

States Parties shall take all appropriate measures, including legislative, administrative, social and educational measures, to protect children from the illicit use of narcotic drugs and psychotropic substances as defined in the relevant international treaties, and to prevent the use of children in the illicit production and trafficking of such substances.

Article 34

States Parties undertake to protect the child from all forms of sexual exploitation and sexual abuse. For these purposes, States Parties shall in particular take all appropriate national, bilateral and multilateral measures to prevent:

(a) The inducement or coercion of a child to engage in any unlawful sexual activity;

(b) The exploitative use of children in prostitution or other unlawful sexual practices;

(c) The exploitative use of children in pornographic performances and materials.

Article 35

States Parties shall take all appropriate national, bilateral and multilateral measures to prevent the abduction of, the sale of or traffic in children for any purpose or in any form.

Article 36

States Parties shall protect the child against all other forms of exploitation prejudicial to any aspects of the child's welfare.

Article 37

States Parties shall ensure that:

(a) No child shall be subjected to torture or other cruel, inhuman or degrading treatment or punishment. Neither capital punishment nor life imprisonment without possibility of release shall be imposed for offences committed by persons below eighteen years of age;

(b) No child shall be deprived of his or her liberty unlawfully or arbitrarily. The arrest, detention or imprisonment of a child shall be in conformity with the law and shall be used only as a measure of last resort and for the shortest appropriate period of time;

(c) Every child deprived of liberty shall be treated with humanity and respect for the inherent dignity of the human person, and in a manner which takes into account the needs of persons of his or her age. In particular, every child deprived of liberty shall be separated from adults unless it is considered in the child's best interest not to do so and shall have the right to maintain contact with his or her family through correspondence and visits, save in exceptional circumstances;

(d) Every child deprived of his or her liberty shall have the right to prompt access to legal and other appropriate assistance, as well as the right to challenge the legality of the deprivation of his or her liberty before a court or other competent, independent and impartial authority, and to a prompt decision on any such action.

Article 38

1. States Parties undertake to respect and to ensure respect for rules of international humanitarian law applicable to them in armed conflicts which are relevant to the child.

2. States Parties shall take all feasible measures to ensure that persons who have not attained the age of fifteen years do not take a direct part in hostilities.

3. States Parties shall refrain from recruiting any person who has not attained the age of fifteen years into their armed forces. In recruiting among those persons who have attained the age of fifteen years but who have not attained the age of eighteen years, States Parties shall endeavour to give priority to those who are oldest.

4. In accordance with their obligations under international humanitarian law to protect the civilian population in armed conflicts, States Parties shall take all feasible measures to ensure protection and care of children who are affected by an armed conflict.

Article 39

States Parties shall take all appropriate measures to promote physical and psychological recovery and social reintegration of a child victim of: any form of neglect, exploitation, or abuse; torture or any other form of cruel, inhuman or degrading treatment or punishment; or armed conflicts. Such recovery and reintegration shall take place in an environment which fosters the health, self-respect and dignity of the child.

Article 40

1. States Parties recognize the right of every child alleged as, accused of, or recognized as having infringed the penal law to be treated in a manner consistent with the promotion of the child's sense of dignity and worth, which reinforces the child's respect for the human rights and fundamental freedoms of others and which takes into account the child's age and the desirability of promoting the child's reintegration and the child's assuming a constructive role in society.

2. To this end, and having regard to the relevant provisions of international instruments, States Parties shall, in particular, ensure that:

(a) No child shall be alleged as, be accused of, or recognized as having infringed the penal law by reason of acts or omissions that were not prohibited by national or international law at the time they were committed;

(b) Every child alleged as or accused of having infringed the penal law has at least the following guarantees:

(i) To be presumed innocent until proven guilty according to law;

(ii) To be informed promptly and directly of the charges against him or her, and, if appropriate, through his or her parents or legal guardians, and to have legal or other appropriate assistance in the preparation and presentation of his or her defence;

(iii) To have the matter determined without delay by a competent, independent and impartial authority or judicial body in a fair hearing according to law, in the presence of legal or other appropriate assistance and, unless it is considered not to be in the best interest of the child, in particular, taking into account his or her age or situation, his or her parents or legal guardians;

(iv) Not to be compelled to give testimony or to confess guilt; to examine or have examined adverse witnesses and to obtain the participation and examination of witnesses on his or her behalf under conditions of equality;

(v) If considered to have infringed the penal law, to have this decision and any measures imposed in consequence thereof reviewed by a higher competent, independent and impartial authority or judicial body according to law;

(vi) To have the free assistance of an interpreter if the child cannot understand or speak the language used;

(vii) To have his or her privacy fully respected at all stages of the proceedings. 3. States Parties shall seek to promote the establishment of laws, procedures, authorities and institutions specifically applicable to children alleged as, accused of, or recognized as having infringed the penal law, and, in particular:

(a) The establishment of a minimum age below which children shall be presumed not to have the capacity to infringe the penal law;

(b) Whenever appropriate and desirable, measures for dealing with such children without resorting to judicial proceedings, providing that human rights and legal safeguards are fully respected.

4. A variety of dispositions, such as care, guidance and supervision orders; counselling; probation; foster care; education and vocational training programmes and other alternatives to institutional care shall be available to ensure that children are dealt with in a manner appropriate to their well-being and proportionate both to their circumstances and the offence.

Article 41

Nothing in the present Convention shall affect any provisions which are more conducive to the realization of the rights of the child and which may be contained in:

(a) The law of a State party; or

(b) International law in force for that State.

PART II

Article 42

States Parties undertake to make the principles and provisions of the Convention widely known, by appropriate and active means, to adults and children alike.

Article 43

1. For the purpose of examining the progress made by States Parties in achieving the realization of the obligations undertaken in the present Convention, there shall be established a Committee on the Rights of the Child, which shall carry out the functions hereinafter provided.

2. The Committee shall consist of eighteen experts of high moral standing and recognized competence in the field covered by this Convention. The members of the Committee shall be elected by States Parties from among their nationals and shall serve in their personal capacity, consideration being given to equitable geographical distribution, as well as to the principal legal systems.

3. The members of the Committee shall be elected by secret ballot from a list of persons nominated by States Parties. Each State Party may nominate one person from among its own nationals.

4. The initial election to the Committee shall be held no later than six months after the date of the entry into force of the present Convention and thereafter every second year. At least four months before the date of each election, the Secretary-General of the United Nations shall address a letter to States Parties inviting them to submit their nominations within two months. The Secretary-General shall subsequently prepare a list in alphabetical order of all persons thus nominated, indicating States Parties which have nominated them, and shall submit it to the States Parties to the present Convention.

5. The elections shall be held at meetings of States Parties convened by the Secretary-General at United Nations Headquarters. At those meetings, for which two thirds of States Parties shall constitute a quorum, the persons elected to the Committee shall be those who obtain the largest number of votes and an absolute majority of the votes of the representatives of States Parties present and voting.

6. The members of the Committee shall be elected for a term of four years. They shall be eligible for re-election if renominated. The term of five of the members elected at the first election shall expire at the end of two years; immediately after the first election, the names of these five members shall be chosen by lot by the Chairman of the meeting.

7. If a member of the Committee dies or resigns or declares that for any other cause he or she can no longer perform the duties of the Committee, the State Party which nominated the member shall appoint another expert from among its nationals to serve for the remainder of the term, subject to the approval of the Committee.

8. The Committee shall establish its own rules of procedure.

9. The Committee shall elect its officers for a period of two years.

10. The meetings of the Committee shall normally be held at United Nations Headquarters or at any other convenient place as determined by the Committee. The Committee shall normally meet annually. The duration of the meetings of the Committee shall be determined, and reviewed, if necessary, by a meeting of the States Parties to the present Convention, subject to the approval of the General Assembly.

11. The Secretary-General of the United Nations shall provide the necessary staff and facilities for the effective performance of the functions of the Committee under the present Convention.

12. With the approval of the General Assembly, the members of the Committee established under the present Convention shall receive

emoluments from United Nations resources on such terms and conditions as the Assembly may decide.

Article 44

1. States Parties undertake to submit to the Committee, through the Secretary-General of the United Nations, reports on the measures they have adopted which give effect to the rights recognized herein and on the progress made on the enjoyment of those rights:

(a) Within two years of the entry into force of the Convention for the State Party concerned;

(b) Thereafter every five years.

2. Reports made under the present article shall indicate factors and difficulties, if any, affecting the degree of fulfilment of the obligations under the present Convention. Reports shall also contain sufficient information to provide the Committee with a comprehensive understanding of the implementation of the Convention in the country concerned.

3. A State Party which has submitted a comprehensive initial report to the Committee need not, in its subsequent reports submitted in accordance with paragraph 1 (b) of the present article, repeat basic information previously provided.

4. The Committee may request from States Parties further information relevant to the implementation of the Convention.

5. The Committee shall submit to the General Assembly, through the Economic and Social Council, every two years, reports on its activities.

6. States Parties shall make their reports widely available to the public in their own countries.

Article 45

In order to foster the effective implementation of the Convention and to encourage international co-operation in the field covered by the Convention:

(a) The specialized agencies, the United Nations Children's Fund, and other United Nations organs shall be entitled to be represented at the consideration of the implementation of such provisions of the present Convention as fall within the scope of their mandate. The Committee may invite the specialized agencies, the United Nations Children's Fund and other competent bodies as it may consider appropriate to provide expert advice on the implementation of the Convention in areas falling within the scope of their respective mandates. The Committee may invite the specialized agencies, the United Nations Children's Fund, and other United

Nations organs to submit reports on the implementation of the Convention in areas falling within the scope of their activities;

(b) The Committee shall transmit, as it may consider appropriate, to the specialized agencies, the United Nations Children's Fund and other competent bodies, any reports from States Parties that contain a request, or indicate a need, for technical advice or assistance, along with the Committee's observations and suggestions, if any, on these requests or indications;

(c) The Committee may recommend to the General Assembly to request the Secretary-General to undertake on its behalf studies on specific issues relating to the rights of the child;

(d) The Committee may make suggestions and general recommendations based on information received pursuant to articles 44 and 45 of the present Convention. Such suggestions and general recommendations shall be transmitted to any State Party concerned and reported to the General Assembly, together with comments, if any, from States Parties.

PART III

Article 46

The present Convention shall be open for signature by all States.

Article 47

The present Convention is subject to ratification. Instruments of ratification shall be deposited with the Secretary-General of the United Nations.

Article 48

The present Convention shall remain open for accession by any State. The instruments of accession shall be deposited with the Secretary-General of the United Nations.

Article 49

1. The present Convention shall enter into force on the thirtieth day following the date of deposit with the Secretary-General of the United Nations of the twentieth instrument of ratification or accession.
2. For each State ratifying or acceding to the Convention after the deposit of the twentieth instrument of ratification or accession, the Convention shall enter into force on the thirtieth day after the deposit by such State of its instrument of ratification or accession.

Article 50

1. Any State Party may propose an amendment and file it with the Secretary-General of the United Nations. The Secretary-General shall thereupon communicate the proposed amendment to States Parties, with a request that they indicate whether they favour a conference of States Parties for the purpose of considering and voting upon the proposals. In the event that, within four months from the date of such communication, at least one third of the States Parties favour such a conference, the Secretary-General shall convene the conference under the auspices of the United Nations. Any amendment adopted by a majority of States Parties present and voting at the conference shall be submitted to the General Assembly for approval.

2. An amendment adopted in accordance with paragraph 1 of the present article shall enter into force when it has been approved by the General Assembly of the United Nations and accepted by a two-thirds majority of States Parties.

3. When an amendment enters into force, it shall be binding on those States Parties which have accepted it, other States Parties still being bound by the provisions of the present Convention and any earlier amendments which they have accepted.

Article 51

1. The Secretary-General of the United Nations shall receive and circulate to all States the text of reservations made by States at the time of ratification or accession.

2. A reservation incompatible with the object and purpose of the present Convention shall not be permitted.

3. Reservations may be withdrawn at any time by notification to that effect addressed to the Secretary-General of the United Nations, who shall then inform all States. Such notification shall take effect on the date on which it is received by the Secretary-General

Article 52

A State Party may denounce the present Convention by written notification to the Secretary-General of the United Nations. Denunciation becomes effective one year after the date of receipt of the notification by the Secretary-General.

Article 53

The Secretary-General of the United Nations is designated as the depositary of the present Convention.

Article 54

The original of the present Convention, of which the Arabic, Chinese, English, French, Russian and Spanish texts are equally authentic, shall be deposited with the Secretary-General of the United Nations.

IN WITNESS THEREOF the undersigned plenipotentiaries, being duly authorized thereto by their respective governments, have signed the present Convention.

4. Optional Protocol to the Convention on the Rights of the Child on a Communications Procedure, 2011 (2012)

The international legal community has long suffered from the non-existence of an instrument which could, to some extent, secure children's rights under civil or criminal justice procedures. The movement for the adoption of a new protocol which could establish a communications procedure for the violations of children's rights was started by a group of children's rights organizations in 2006. After several years of discussions, meetings and negotiations between different groups working for the rights of children in the world, and positive contributions by states as well as the United Nations on the question of the protection of children, the final draft Optional Protocol establishing a communications procedure for children's rights violations was drafted in 2011. The text of the draft, which was transmitted to the UN General Assembly by the UN Human Rights Council, was well received by the Third Committee of the Assembly. In fact, the text was adopted by *consensus* in the General Assembly on 19 December 2011. The signature and ratification of the Protocol was begun during the Human Rights Council Session in Geneva on 28th February 2012.

There are very many reasons for the adoption of the Protocol by the General Assembly. One of the strongest is a lack in the complaints mechanism. Although there have been several complaints mechanisms which can be used by children at an international level, they have been insufficient, and not recognized all children's rights. Another potential reason is that complaints are usually examined by a body that is not familiar with children's rights and has no special expertise concerning legal attitudes towards children as a whole. This is especially so within the domestic systems of countries which are not strong enough to defend children's rights. Domestic systems constitutionally based on Islamic law are particularly notable. Thus, one of the core intentions in the draft of the Optional Protocol establishing a communications procedure for children's rights violations is to enable individuals and groups to present violations of their rights within a national system directly to the Committee. Obviously, complaints should only be brought before the Committee when domestic remedies have been entirely exhausted or been unsuccessful. However, this may constitute one of the serious problems of the Optional Protocol, and limits children's petitions before the Committee, because exhaustion of all domestic remedies may hinder the complaints mechanism of the Optional Protocol. It would have been much more practical if the Protocol had also encouraged the parties to the Protocol to create certain procedural measures according to which a child's petition would be given particular priority and speediness under national legal systems.

Although it may be too soon to say that the provisions of the Optional Protocol to the Convention on the Rights of the Child on a Communications Procedure is one of the most significant instruments protecting those rights, the value of the instrument cannot be realistically denied by any international lawyer. The fact is that the Protocol not only creates complementary provisions governing the child's rights at an international level, but it also opens the window to the effective protection of the sovereignty of children in law which has long been established by the norms of international law and international human rights law.[1]The Protocol therefore constitutes an excellent international treaty with the force of *pacta sunt servanda* and treaty-making power.

The text of General Assembly Resolution provides:

Optional Protocol to the Convention on the Rights of the Child on a Communications Procedure[2]

The States parties to the present Protocol,

Considering that, in accordance with the principles proclaimed in the Charter of the United Nations, the recognition of the inherent dignity and the equal and inalienable rights of all members of the human family is the foundation of freedom, justice and peace in the world,

Noting that the States parties to the Convention on the Rights of the Child (hereinafter referred to as "the Convention") recognize the rights set forth in it to each child within their jurisdiction without discrimination of any kind, irrespective of the child's or his or her parent's or legal guardian's race, colour, sex, language, religion, political or other opinion, national, ethnic or social origin, property, disability, birth or other status,

---

[1] Farhad Malekian and Kerstin Nordlöf (eds.), *The Sovereignty of Children in Law* (2012).

[2] Adopted and opened for signature and ratification by General Assembly resolution 66/138 of 19 December 2011.

Reaffirming the universality, indivisibility, interdependence and interrelatedness of all human rights and fundamental freedoms,

Reaffirming also the status of the child as a subject of rights and as a human being with dignity and with evolving capacities,

Recognizing that children's special and dependent status may create real difficulties for them in pursuing remedies for violations of their rights,

Considering that the present Protocol will reinforce and complement national and regional mechanisms allowing children to submit complaints for violations of their rights,

Recognizing that the best interests of the child should be a primary consideration to be respected in pursuing remedies for violations of the rights of the child, and that such remedies should take into account the need for child-sensitive procedures at all levels,

Encouraging States parties to develop appropriate national mechanisms to enable a child whose rights have been violated to have access to effective remedies at the domestic level,

Recalling the important role that national human rights institutions and other relevant specialized institutions, mandated to promote and protect the rights of the child, can play in this regard,

Considering that, in order to reinforce and complement such national mechanisms and to further enhance the implementation of the Convention and, where applicable, the Optional Protocols thereto on the sale of children, child prostitution and child pornography and on the involvement of children in armed conflict, it would be appropriate to enable the Committee on the Rights of the Child (hereinafter referred to as "the Committee") to carry out the functions provided for in the present Protocol,

Have agreed as follows:

Part I
General provisions
Article 1
Competence of the Committee on the Rights of the Child

1. A State party to the present Protocol recognizes the competence of the Committee as provided for by the present Protocol.

2. The Committee shall not exercise its competence regarding a State party to the present Protocol on matters concerning violations of rights set forth in an instrument to which that State is not a party.

3. No communication shall be received by the Committee if it concerns a State that is not a party to the present Protocol.

Article 2
General principles guiding the functions of the Committee

In fulfilling the functions conferred on it by the present Protocol, the Committee shall be guided by the principle of the best interests of the child. It shall also have regard for the rights and views of the child, the views of the child being given due weight in accordance with the age and maturity of the child.

Article 3
Rules of procedure

1. The Committee shall adopt rules of procedure to be followed when exercising the functions conferred on it by the present Protocol. In doing so, it shall have regard, in particular, for article 2 of the present Protocol in order to guarantee child-sensitive procedures.

2. The Committee shall include in its rules of procedure safeguards to prevent the manipulation of the child by those acting on his or her behalf and may decline to examine any communication that it considers not to be in the child's best interests.

Article 4
Protection measures

1. A State party shall take all appropriate steps to ensure that individuals under its jurisdiction are not subjected to any human rights violation, ill-treatment or intimidation as a consequence of communications or cooperation with the Committee pursuant to the present Protocol.

2. The identity of any individual or group of individuals concerned shall not be revealed publicly without their express consent.

Part II
Communications procedure
Article 5
Individual communications

1. Communications may be submitted by or on behalf of an individual or group of individuals, within the jurisdiction of a State party, claiming to be victims of a violation by that State party of any of the rights set forth in any of the following instruments to which that State is a party:

(a) The Convention;

(b) The Optional Protocol to the Convention on the sale of children, child prostitution and child pornography;

(c) The Optional Protocol to the Convention on the involvement of children in armed conflict.

2. Where a communication is submitted on behalf of an individual or group of individuals, this shall be with their consent unless the author can justify acting on their behalf without such consent.

Article 6
Interim measures

1. At any time after the receipt of a communication and before a determination on the merits has been reached, the Committee may transmit to the State party concerned for its urgent consideration a request that the State party take such interim measures as may be necessary in exceptional circumstances to avoid possible irreparable damage to the victim or victims of the alleged violations.

2. Where the Committee exercises its discretion under paragraph 1 of the present article, this does not imply a determination on admissibility or on the merits of the communication.

Article 7
Admissibility

The Committee shall consider a communication inadmissible when:

(a) The communication is anonymous;

(b) The communication is not in writing;

(c) The communication constitutes an abuse of the right of submission of such communications or is incompatible with the provisions of the Convention and/or the Optional Protocols thereto;

(d) The same matter has already been examined by the Committee or has been or is being examined under another procedure of international investigation or settlement;

(e) All available domestic remedies have not been exhausted. This shall not be the rule where the application of the remedies is unreasonably prolonged or unlikely to bring effective relief;

(f) The communication is manifestly ill-founded or not sufficiently substantiated;

(g) The facts that are the subject of the communication occurred prior to the entry into force of the present Protocol for the State party concerned, unless those facts continued after that date;

(h) The communication is not submitted within one year after the exhaustion of domestic remedies, except in cases where the author can demonstrate that it had not been possible to submit the communication within that time limit.

Article 8
Transmission of the communication

1. Unless the Committee considers a communication inadmissible without reference to the State party concerned, the Committee shall bring any communication submitted to it under the present Protocol confidentially to the attention of the State party concerned as soon as possible.

2. The State party shall submit to the Committee written explanations or statements clarifying the matter and the remedy, if any, that it may have provided. The State party shall submit its response as soon as possible and within six months.

Article 9
Friendly settlement

1. The Committee shall make available its good offices to the parties concerned with a view to reaching a friendly settlement of the matter on the basis of respect for the obligations set forth in the Convention and/or the Optional Protocols thereto.

2. An agreement on a friendly settlement reached under the auspices of the Committee closes consideration of the communication under the present Protocol.

Article 10
Consideration of communications

1. The Committee shall consider communications received under the present Protocol as quickly as possible, in the light of all documentation submitted to it, provided that this documentation is transmitted to the parties concerned.

2. The Committee shall hold closed meetings when examining communications received under the present Protocol.

3. Where the Committee has requested interim measures, it shall expedite the consideration of the communication.

4. When examining communications alleging violations of economic, social or cultural rights, the Committee shall consider the reasonableness of the steps taken by the State party in accordance with article 4 of the Convention. In doing so, the Committee shall bear in mind that the State party may adopt a range of possible policy measures for the implementation of the economic, social and cultural rights in the Convention.

5. After examining a communication, the Committee shall, without delay, transmit its views on the communication, together with its recommendations, if any, to the parties concerned.

Article 11
Follow-up

1. The State party shall give due consideration to the views of the Committee, together with its recommendations, if any, and shall submit to the Committee a written response, including information on any action taken and envisaged in the light of the views and recommendations of the Committee. The State party shall submit its response as soon as possible and within six months.

2. The Committee may invite the State party to submit further information about any measures the State party has taken in response to its views or recommendations or implementation of a friendly settlement agreement, if any, including as deemed appropriate by the Committee, in the State party's subsequent reports under article 44 of the Convention, article 12 of the Optional Protocol on the sale of children, child prostitution and child pornography or article 8 of the Optional Protocol on the involvement of children in armed conflict, where applicable.

Article 12
Inter-State communications

1. A State party to the present Protocol may, at any time, declare that it recognizes the competence of the Committee to receive and consider communications in which a State party claims that another State party is not fulfilling its obligations under any of the following instruments to which the State is a party:

(a) The Convention;

(b) The Optional Protocol to the Convention on the sale of children, child prostitution and child pornography;

(c) The Optional Protocol to the Convention on the involvement of children in armed conflict.

2. The Committee shall not receive communications concerning a State party that has not made such a declaration or communications from a State party that has not made such a declaration.

3. The Committee shall make available its good offices to the States parties concerned with a view to a friendly solution of the matter on the basis of the respect for the obligations set forth in the Convention and the Optional Protocols thereto.

4. A declaration under paragraph 1 of the present article shall be deposited by the States parties with the Secretary-General of the United Nations, who shall transmit copies thereof to the other States parties. A declaration may be withdrawn at any time by notification to the Secretary-General. Such a withdrawal shall not prejudice the consideration of any

matter that is the subject of a communication already transmitted under the present article; no further communications by any State party shall be received under the present article after the notification of withdrawal of the declaration has been received by the Secretary-General, unless the State party concerned has made a new declaration.

Part III
Inquiry procedure
Article 13
Inquiry procedure for grave or systematic violations

1. If the Committee receives reliable information indicating grave or systematic violations by a State party of rights set forth in the Convention or in the Optional Protocols thereto on the sale of children, child prostitution and child pornography or on the involvement of children in armed conflict, the Committee shall invite the State party to cooperate in the examination of the information and, to this end, to submit observations without delay with regard to the information concerned.
2. Taking into account any observations that may have been submitted by the State party concerned, as well as any other reliable information available to it, the Committee may designate one or more of its members to conduct an inquiry and to report urgently to the Committee. Where warranted and with the consent of the State party, the inquiry may include a visit to its territory.
3. Such an inquiry shall be conducted confidentially, and the cooperation of the State party shall be sought at all stages of the proceedings.
4. After examining the findings of such an inquiry, the Committee shall transmit without delay these findings to the State party concerned, together with any comments and recommendations.
5. The State party concerned shall, as soon as possible and within six months of receiving the findings, comments and recommendations transmitted by the Committee, submit its observations to the Committee.
6. After such proceedings have been completed with regard to an inquiry made in accordance with paragraph 2 of the present article, the Committee may, after consultation with the State party concerned, decide to include a summary account of the results of the proceedings in its report provided for in article 16 of the present Protocol.
7. Each State party may, at the time of signature or ratification of the present Protocol or accession thereto, declare that it does not recognize the competence of the Committee provided for in the present article in respect of the rights set forth in some or all of the instruments listed in paragraph 1.

8. Any State party having made a declaration in accordance with paragraph 7 of the present article may, at any time, withdraw this declaration by notification to the Secretary-General of the United Nations.

Article 14
Follow-up to the inquiry procedure

1. The Committee may, if necessary, after the end of the period of six months referred to in article 13 (5), invite the State party concerned to inform it of the measures taken and envisaged in response to an inquiry conducted under article 13 of the present Protocol.

2. The Committee may invite the State party to submit further information about any measures that the State party has taken in response to an inquiry conducted under article 13, including as deemed appropriate by the Committee, in the State party's subsequent reports under article 44 of the Convention, article 12 of the Optional Protocol to the Convention on the sale of children, child prostitution and child pornography or article 8 of the Optional Protocol to the Convention on the involvement of children in armed conflict, where applicable.

Part IV
Final provisions
Article 15
International assistance and cooperation

1. The Committee may transmit, with the consent of the State party concerned, to United Nations specialized agencies, funds and programmes and other competent bodies its views or recommendations concerning communications and inquiries that indicate a need for technical advice or assistance, together with the State party's observations and suggestions, if any, on these views or recommendations.

2. The Committee may also bring to the attention of such bodies, with the consent of the State party concerned, any matter arising out of communications considered under the present Protocol that may assist them in deciding, each within its field of competence, on the advisability of international measures likely to contribute to assisting States parties in achieving progress in the implementation of the rights recognized in the Convention and/or the Optional Protocols thereto.

Article 16
Report to the General Assembly

The Committee shall include in its report submitted every two years to the General Assembly in accordance with article 44 (5) of the Convention a summary of its activities under the present Protocol.

Article 17
Dissemination of and information on the Optional Protocol

Each State party undertakes to make widely known and to disseminate the present Protocol and to facilitate access to information about the views and recommendations of the Committee, in particular with regard to matters involving the State party, by appropriate and active means and in accessible formats to adults and children alike, including those with disabilities.

Article 18
Signature, ratification and accession

1. The present Protocol is open for signature to any State that has signed, ratified or acceded to the Convention or either of the first two Optional Protocols thereto.
2. The present Protocol is subject to ratification by any State that has ratified or acceded to the Convention or either of the first two Optional Protocols thereto. Instruments of ratification shall be deposited with the Secretary-General of the United Nations.
3. The present Protocol shall be open to accession by any State that has ratified or acceded to the Convention or either of the first two Optional Protocols thereto.
4. Accession shall be effected by the deposit of an instrument of accession with the Secretary-General.

Article 19
Entry into force

1. The present Protocol shall enter into force three months after the deposit of the tenth instrument of ratification or accession.
2. For each State ratifying the present Protocol or acceding to it after the deposit of the tenth instrument of ratification or instrument of accession, the present Protocol shall enter into force three months after the date of the deposit of its own instrument of ratification or accession.

Article 20
Violations occurring after the entry into force

1. The Committee shall have competence solely in respect of violations by the State party of any of the rights set forth in the Convention and/or the first two Optional Protocols thereto occurring after the entry into force of the present Protocol.

2. If a State becomes a party to the present Protocol after its entry into force, the obligations of that State vis-à-vis the Committee shall relate only to violations of the rights set forth in the Convention and/or the first two Optional Protocols thereto occurring after the entry into force of the present Protocol for the State concerned.

Article 21
Amendments

1. Any State party may propose an amendment to the present Protocol and submit it to the Secretary-General of the United Nations. The Secretary-General shall communicate any proposed amendments to States parties with a request to be notified whether they favour a meeting of States parties for the purpose of considering and deciding upon the proposals. In the event that, within four months of the date of such communication, at least one third of the States parties favour such a meeting, the Secretary-General shall convene the meeting under the auspices of the United Nations. Any amendment adopted by a majority of two thirds of the States parties present and voting shall be submitted by the Secretary-General to the General Assembly for approval and, thereafter, to all States parties for acceptance.

2. An amendment adopted and approved in accordance with paragraph 1 of the present article shall enter into force on the thirtieth day after the number of instruments of acceptance deposited reaches two thirds of the number of States parties at the date of adoption of the amendment. Thereafter, the amendment shall enter into force for any State party on the thirtieth day following the deposit of its own instrument of acceptance. An amendment shall be binding only on those States parties that have accepted it.

Article 22
Denunciation

1. Any State party may denounce the present Protocol at any time by written notification to the Secretary-General of the United Nations. The denunciation shall take effect one year after the date of receipt of the notification by the Secretary-General.

2. Denunciation shall be without prejudice to the continued application of the provisions of the present Protocol to any communication submitted under articles 5 or 12 or any inquiry initiated under article 13 before the effective date of denunciation.

Article 23
Depositary and notification by the Secretary-General

1. The Secretary-General of the United Nations shall be the depositary of the present Protocol.

2. The Secretary-General shall inform all States of:

(a) Signatures, ratifications and accessions under the present Protocol;

(b) The date of entry into force of the present Protocol and of any amendment thereto under article 21;

(c) Any denunciation under article 22.

Article 24
Languages

1. The present Protocol, of which the Arabic, Chinese, English, French, Russian and Spanish texts are equally authentic, shall be deposited in the archives of the United Nations.

2. The Secretary-General of the United Nations shall transmit certified copies of the present Protocol to all States.

CHAPTER V

REGIONAL LEGISLATIONS DIRECTLY PROTECTING THE RIGHTS OF CHILDREN

1. African Charter on the Rights and Welfare of the Child, 1990

The African Charter is a valuable regional convention relating to the rights of children. The African Charter was adopted by the Organization of African Unity (OAU) in Addis Ababa, Ethiopia in 1990, and entered into force in the same year (OAU Doc. CAB/LEG/24.9/49). The Charter clearly points out that for the aims of the Charter, "a child means every human being below the age of 18 years". This means that the African Charter, like other regional and international conventions, applies the age of 18 as a maximum standard for the recognition of a person as a child. By this provision, the Charter has surely accepted that the age below 18 is an integral part of childhood and should be respected by all African states. The Charter clearly states that "the abduction, the sale of, or trafficking in children for any purpose or in any form, by any person including the parents or legal guardians of the child" is strictly prohibited.

Although the aims of the Charter for the protection of children and their integrity are highly regarded, its provisions have been frequently violated by African states. In particular, children have been used as an important weapon in armed conflicts. They have also been sexually exploitated in many conflicts. Thus, the protection which guarantees the life and integrity of children was not strong at the time of its implementation. Even in peacetime, many children were subjected to slavery conditions, including economic exploitation. However, one cannot ignore the fact that the provisions of the African Charter are very useful for the progressive development and consolidation of the rights of children in Africa and their future. They have opened the door to the recognition of the rights of children in peace and war. The Charter demands that:

Preamble

The African Member States of the Organization of African Unity, Parties to the present Charter entitled 'African Charter on the Rights and Welfare of the Child',

Considering that the Charter of the Organization of African Unity recognizes the paramountcy of Human Rights and the African Charter on Human and People's Rights proclaimed and agreed that everyone is entitled to all the rights and freedoms recognized and guaranteed therein, without distinction of any kind such as race, ethnic group, colour. sex, language, religion, political or any other opinion, national and social origin, fortune, birth or other status,

Recalling the Declaration on the Rights and WeLfare of the African Child (AHG/ST.4 Rev.l) adopted by the Assembly of Heads of State and Government of the Organization of African Unity, at its Sixteenth Ordinary Session in Monrovia, Liberia. from 17 to 20 July 1979, recognized the need to take appropriate measures to promote and protect the rights and welfare of the African Child,

Noticing with concern that the situation of most African children, remains critical due to the unique factors of their socio-economic, cultural, traditional and developmental circumstances, natural disasters, armed conflicts, exploitation and hunger, and on account of the child's physical and mental immaturity he/she needs special safeguards and care,

Recognizing that the child occupies a unique and privileged position in the African society and that for the full and harmonious development of his personality. the child should grow up in a family environment in an atmosphere of happiness, love and understanding,

Recognizing that the child, due to the needs of his physical and mental development requires particular care with regard to health, physical, mental, moral and social development. and requires legal protection in conditions of freedom, dignity and security,

Taking into consideration the virtues of their cultural heritage, historical background and the values of the African civilization which should inspire and characterize their reflection on the concept of the rights and welfare of the child,

Considering that the promotion and protection of the rights and welfare of the child also implies the performance of duties on the part of everyone,

Reaffirming adherence to the principles of the rights and welfare of the child contained in the declaration, conventions and other instruments of the Organization of African Unity and in the United Nations and in particular the United Nations Convention on the Rights of the Child; and the OAU Heads of State and Government's Declaration on the Rights and Welfare of the African Child.

Have agreed as follows

PART 1: RIGHTS AND DUTIES

CHAPTER ONE: RIGHTS AND WELFARE OF THE CHILD

Article 1: Obligation of States Parties

1. Member States of the Organization of African Unity Parties to the present Charter shall recognize the rights, freedoms and duties enshrined in this Charter and shall undertake to the necessary steps, in accordance with their Constitutional processes and with the provisions of the present Charter, to adopt such legislative or other measures as may be necessary to give effect to the provisions of this Charter.

2. Nothing in this Charter shall affect any provisions that are more conductive to the realization of the rights and welfare of the child contained in the law of a State Party or in any other international Convention or agreement in force in that State.

3. Any custom, tradition, cultural or religious practice that is inconsistent with the rights, duties and obligations contained in the present Charter shall to the extent of such inconsistency be discouraged.

Article 2: Definition of a Child

For the purposes of this Charter. a child means every human being below the age of 18 years.

Article 3: Non-Discrimination

Every child shall be entitled to the enjoyment of the rights and freedoms recognized and guaranteed in this Charter irrespective of the child's or his/her parents' or legal guardians' race, ethnic group, colour, sex, language, religion, political or other opinion, national and social origin, fortune, birth or other status.

Article 4: Best Interests of the Child

1. In all actions concerning the child undertaken by any person or authority the best interests of the child shall be the primary consideration.

2. In all judicial or administrative proceedings affecting a child who is capable of communicating his/her own views, and opportunity shall be provided for the views of the child to be heard either directly or through an impartial representative as a party to the proceedings. and those views

shall be taken into consideration by the relevant authority in accordance with the provisions of appropriate law.

Article 5: Survival and Development

1. Every child has an inherent right to life. This right shall be protected by law.

2. States Parties to the present Charter shall ensure, to the maximum extent possible, the survival, protection and development of the child.

3. Death sentence shall not be pronounced for crimes committed by children.

Article 6: Name and Nationality

1. Every child shall have the right from his birth no a name.

2. Every child shall be registered immediately after birth.

3. Every child has the right to acquire a nationality.

4. States Parties to the present Charter shall undertake to ensure that their Constitutional legislation recognize the principles according to which a child shall acquire the nationality of the State in the territory of which he has been born if, at the time of the child's birth. he is not granted nationality by any other State in accordance with its laws.

Article 7: Freedom of Expression

Every child who is capable of communicating his or her own views shall be assured the rights to express his opinions freely in all matters and to disseminate his opinions subject to such restrictions as are prescribed by laws.

Article 8: Freedom of Association

Every child shall have the right to free association and freedom of peaceful assembly in conformity with the law.

Article 9: Freedom of Thought, Conscience and Religion

1. Every child shall have the right to freedom of thought conscience and religion.

2. Parents. and where applicable, legal guardians shall have a duty to provide guidance and direction in the exercise of these rights having regard to the evolving capacities, and best interests of the child.

3. States Parties shall respect the duty of parents and where applicable, legal guardians to provide guidance and direction in the enjoyment of these rights subject to the national laws and policies.

Article 10: Protection of Privacy

No child shall be subject to arbitrary or unlawful interference with his privacy, family home or correspondence, or to the attacks upon his honour or reputation, provided that parents or legal guardians shall have the right to exercise reasonable supervision over the conduct of their children. The child has the right to the protection of the law against such interference or attacks.

Article 11: Education

1. Every child shall have the right to an education.

2. The education of the child shall be directed to:

(a) the promotion and development of the child's personality, talents and mental and physical abilities to their fullest potential;

(b) fostering respect for human rights and fundamental freedoms with particular reference to those set out in the provisions of various African instruments on human and peoples' rights and international human rights declarations and conventions;

(c) the preservation and strengthening of positive African morals, traditional values and cultures;

(d) the preparation of the child for responsible life in a free society, in the spirit of understanding tolerance, dialogue, mutual respect and friendship among all peoples ethnic, tribal and religious groups;

(e) the preservation of national independence and territorial integrity;

(f) the promotion and achievements of African Unity and Solidarity;

(g) the development of respect for the environment and natural resources;

(h) the promotion of the child's understanding of primary health care.

3. States Parties to the present Charter shall take all appropriate measures with a view to achieving the full realization of this right and shall in particular:

(a) provide free and compulsory basic education:

(b) encourage the development of secondary education in its different forms and to progressively make it free and accessible to all;

(c) make the higher education accessible to all on the basis of capacity and ability by every appropriate means;

(d) take measures to encourage regular attendance at schools and the reduction of drop-out rates;

(e) take special measures in respect of female, gifted and disadvantaged children, to ensure equal access to education for all sections of the community.

4. States Parties to the present Charter shall respect the rights and duties of parents, and where applicable, of legal guardians to choose for their children's schools, other than those established by public authorities, which conform to such minimum standards may be approved by the State, to ensure the religious and moral education of the child in a manner with the evolving capacities of the child.

5. States Parties to the present Charter shall take all appropriate measures to ensure that a child who is subjected to schools or parental discipline shall be treated with humanity and with respect for the inherent dignity of the child and in conformity with the present Charter.

6. States Parties to the present Charter shall have all appropriate measures to ensure that children who become pregnant before completing their education shall have an opportunity to continue with their education on the basis of their individual ability.

7. No part of this Article shall be construed as to interfere with the liberty of individuals and bodies to establish and direct educational institutions subject to the observance of the principles set out in paragraph I of this Article and the requirement teal the education given in such institutions shall conform to such minimum standards as may be laid down by the States.

Article 12: Leisure, Recreation and Cultural Activities

1. States Parties recognize the right of the child to rest and leisure, to engage in play and recreational activities appropriate to the age of the child and to participate freely in cultural life and the arts.

2. States Parties shall respect and promote the right of the child to fully participate in cultural and artistic life and shall encourage the provision of appropriate and equal opportunities for cultural, artistic, recreational and leisure activity.

Article 13: Handicapped Children

1. Every child who is mentally or physically disabled shall have the right to special measures of protection in keeping with his physical and moral needs and under conditions which ensure his dignity, promote his self-reliance and active participation in the community.

2. States Parties to the present Charter shall ensure, subject to available resources, to a disabled child and to those responsible for his care, of assistance for which application is made and which is appropriate to the child's condition and in particular shall ensure that the disabled child has effective access to training, preparation for employment and recreation opportunities in a manner conducive to the child achieving the fullest

possible social integration, individual development and his cultural and moral development.

3. The States Parties to the present Charter shall use their available resources with a view to achieving progressively the full convenience of the mentally and physically disabled person to movement and access to public highway buildings and other places to which the disabled may legitimately want to have access to.

Article 14: Health and Health Services

1. Every child shall have the right to enjoy the best attainable state of physical, mental and spiritual health.

2. States Parties to the present Charter shall undertake to pursue the full implementation of this right and in particular shall take measures:

(a) to reduce infant and child morality rate;

(b) to ensure the provision of necessary medical assistance and health care to all children with emphasis on the development of primary health care;

(c) to ensure the provision of adequate nutrition and safe drinking water;

(d) to combat disease and malnutrition within the framework of primary health care through the application of appropriate technology;

(e) to ensure appropriate health care for expectant and nursing mothers;

(f) to develop preventive health care and family life education and provision of service;

(g) to integrate basic health service programmes in national development plans;

(h) to ensure that all sectors of the society, in particular, parents, children, community leaders and community workers are informed and supported in the use of basic knowledge of child health and nutrition, the advantages of breastfeeding, hygiene and environmental sanitation and the prevention of domestic and other accidents;

(i) to ensure the meaningful participation of non-governmental organizations, local communities and the beneficiary population in the planning and management of a basic service programme for children;

(j) to support through technical and financial means, the mobilization of local community resources in the development of primary health care for children.

Article 15: Child Labour

1. Every child shall be protected from all forms of economic exploitation and from performing any work that is likely to be hazardous or to interfere with the child's physical, mental, spiritual, moral, or social development.

2. States Parties to the present Charter take all appropriate legislative and administrative measures to ensure the full implementation of this Article which covers both the formal and informal sectors of employment and having regard to the relevant provisions of the International Labour Organization's instruments relating to children, States Parties shall in particular:

(a) provide through legislation, minimum wages for admission to every employment;

(b) provide for appropriate regulation of hours and conditions of employment;

(c) provide for appropriate penalties or other sanctions to ensure the effective enforcement of this Article;

(d) promote the dissemination of information on the hazards of child labour to all sectors of the community.

Article 16: Protection Against Child Abuse and Torture

1. States Parties to the present Charter shall take specific legislative, administrative, social and educational measures to protect the child from all forms of torture, inhuman or degrading treatment and especially physical or mental injury or abuse, neglect or maltreatment including sexual abuse, while in the care of the child.

2. Protective measures under this Article shall include effective procedures for the establishment of special monitoring units to provide necessary support for the child and for those who have the care of the child, as well as other forms of prevention and for identification, reporting referral investigation, treatment, and follow-up of instances of child abuse and neglect.

Article 17: Administration of Juvenile Justice

1. Every child accused or found guilty of having infringed penal law shall have the right to special treatment in a manner consistent with the child's sense of dignity and worth and which reinforces the child's respect for human rights and fundamental freedoms of others.

2. States Parties to the present Charter shall in particular:

(a) ensure that no child who is detained or imprisoned or otherwise deprived of his/her liberty is subjected to torture, inhuman or degrading treatment or punishment;
(b) ensure that children are separated from adults in their place of detention or imprisonment;
(c) ensure that every child accused in infringing the penal law:
(i) shall be presumed innocent until duly recognized guilty;
(ii) shall be informed promptly in a language that he understands and in detail of the charge against him, and shall be entitled to the assistance of an interpreter if he or she cannot understand the language used;
(iii) shall be afforded legal and other appropriate assistance in the preparation and presentation of his defence;
(iv) shall have the matter determined as speedily as possible by an impartial tribunal and if found guilty, be entitled to an appeal by a higher tribunal;
(d) prohibit the press and the public from trial.

3. The essential aim of treatment of every child during the trial and also if found guilty of infringing the penal law shall be his or her reformation, re-integration into his or her family and social rehabilitation.

4. There shall be a minimum age below which children shall be presumed not to have the capacity to infringe the penal law.

Article 18: Protection of the Family

1. The family shall be the natural unit and basis of society. it shall enjoy the protection and support of the State for its establishment and development.

2. States Parties to the present Charter shall take appropriate steps to ensure equality of rights and responsibilities of spouses with regard to children during marriage and in the even of its dissolution. In case of the dissolution, provision shall be made for the necessary protection of the child.

3. No child shall be deprived of maintenance by reference to the parents' marital status.

Article 19: Parent Care and Protection

1. Every child shall be entitled to the enjoyment of parental care and protection and shall, whenever possible, have the right to reside with his or her parents. No child shall be separated from his parents against his will, except when a judicial authority determines in accordance with the appropriate law, that such separation is in the best interest of the child.

2. Every child who is separated from one or both parents shall have the right to maintain personal relations and direct contact with both parents on a regular basis.

3. Where separation results from the action of a State Party, the State Party shall provide the child, or if appropriate, another member of the family with essential information concerning the whereabouts of the absent member or members of the family. States Parties shall also ensure that the submission of such a request shall not entail any adverse consequences for the person or persons in whose respect it is made.

4. Where a child is apprehended by a State Party, his parents or guardians shall, as soon as possible, be notified of such apprehension by that State Party.

Article 20: Parental Responsibilities

1. Parents or other persons responsible for the child shall have the primary responsibility of the upbringing and development the child and shall have the duty:

(a) to ensure that the best interests of the child are their basic concern at all times-

(b) to secure, within their abilities and financial capacities, conditions of living necessary to the child's development; and

(c) to ensure that domestic discipline is administered winh humanity and in a manner consistent with the inherent dignity of the child.

2. States Parties to the present Charter shall in accordance with their means and national conditions the all appropriate measures;

(a) to assist parents and other persons responsible for the child and in case of need provide material assistance and support programmes particularly with regard to nutrition, health, education, clothing and housing;

(b) to assist parents and others responsible for the child in the performance of child-rearing and ensure the development of institutions responsible for providing care of children; and

(c) to ensure that the children of working parents are provided with care services and facilities.

Article 21: Protection against Harmful Social and Cultural Practices

1. States Parties to the present Charter shall take all appropriate measures to eliminate harmful social and cultural practices affecting the welfare, dignity, normal growth and development of the child and in particular:

(a) those customs and practices prejudicial to the health or life of the child; and

(b) those customs and practices discriminatory to the child on the grounds of sex or other status.

2. Child marriage and the betrothal of girls and boys shall be prohibited and effective action, including legislation, shall be taken to specify the minimum age of marriage to be 18 years and make registration of all marriages in an official registry compulsory.

Article 22: Armed Conflicts

1. States Parties to this Charter shall undertake to respect and ensure respect for rules of international humanitarian law applicable in armed conflicts which affect the child.

2. States Parties to the present Charter shall take all necessary measures to ensure that no child shall take a direct part in hostilities and refrain in particular, from recruiting any child.

3. States Parties to the present Charter shall, in accordance with their obligations under international humanitarian law, protect the civilian population in armed conflicts and shall take all feasible measures to ensure the protection and care of children who are affected by armed conflicts. Such rules shall also apply to children in situations of internal armed conflicts, tension and strife.

Article 23: Refugee Children

1. States Parties to the present Charter shall take all appropriate measures to ensure that a child who is seeking refugee status or who is considered a refugee in accordance with applicable international or domestic law shall, whether unaccompanied or accompanied by parents, legal guardians or close relatives, receive appropriate protection and humanitarian assistance in the enjoyment of the rights set out in this Charter and other international human rights and humanitarian instruments to which the States are Parties.

2. States Parties shall undertake to cooperate with existing international organizations which protect and assist refugees in their efforts to protect and assist such a child and to trace the parents or other close relatives or an unaccompanied refugee child in order to obtain information necessary for reunification with the family.

3. Where no parents, legal guardians or close relatives can be found, the child shall be accorded the same protection as any other child permanently or temporarily deprived of his family environment for any reason.

4. The provisions of this Article apply mutatis mutandis to internally displaced children whether through natural disaster, internal armed conflicts, civil strife, breakdown of economic and social order or howsoever caused.

Article 24: Adoption

States Parties which recognize the system of adoption shall ensure that the best interest of the child shall be the paramount consideration and they shall:

(a) establish competent authorities to determine matters of adoption and ensure that the adoption is carried out in conformity with applicable laws and procedures and on the basis of all relevant and reliable information. that the adoption is permissible in view of the child's status concerning parents, relatives and guardians and that. if necessary, the appropriate persons concerned have given their informed consent to the adoption on the basis of appropriate counselling;

(b) recognize that inter-country adoption in those States who have ratified or adhered to the International Convention on the Rights of the Child or this Charter. may. as the last resort, be considered as an alternative means of a child's care, if the child cannot be placed in a foster or an adoptive family or cannot in any suitable manner be cared for in the child's country of origin;

(c) ensure that the child affected by inter-country adoption enjoys safeguards and standards equivalent to those existing in the case of national adoption;

(d) take all appropriate measures to ensure that in inter-country adoption, the placement does not result in trafficking or improper financial gain for those who try to adopt a child;

(e) promote, where appropriate, the objectives of this Article by concluding bilateral or multilateral arrangements or agreements, and endeavour, within this framework to ensure that the placement of the child in another country is carried out by competent authorities or organs;

(f) establish a machinery to monitor the well-being of the adopted child.

Article 25: Separation from Parents

1. Any child who is permanently or temporarily deprived of his family environment for any reason shall be entitled to special protection and assistance;

2. States Parties to the present Charter:

(a) shall ensure that a child who is parentless, or who is temporarily or permanently deprived of his or her family environment, or who in his or her best interest cannot be brought up or allowed to remain in that environment shall be provided with alternative family care, which could include, among others. foster placement, or placement in suitable institutions for the care of children;

(b) shall take all necessary measures to trace and re-unite children with parents or relatives where separation is caused by internal and external displacement arising from armed conflicts or natural disasters.

3. When considering alternative family care of the child and the best interests of the child, due regard shall be paid to the desirability of continuity in a child's up-bringing and to the child's ethnic, religious or linguistic background.

Article 26: Protection Against Apartheid and Discrimination

1. States Parties to the present Charter shall individually and collectively undertake to accord the highest priority to the special needs of children living under Apartheid and in States subject to military destabilization by the Apartheid regime.

2. States Parties to the present Charter shall individually and collectively undertake to accord the highest priority to the special needs of children living under regimes practising racial, ethnic. religious or other forms of discrimination as well as in States subject to military destabilization.

3. States Parties shall undertake to provide whenever possible, material assistance to such children and to direct their efforts towards the elimination of all forms of discrimination and Apartheid on the African Continent.

Article 27: Sexual Exploitation

1. States Parties to the present Charter shall undertake to protect the child from all forms of sexual exploitation and sexual abuse and shall in particular take measures to prevent:

(a) the inducement, coercion or encouragement of a child to engage in any sexual activity;

(b) the use of children in prostitution or other sexual practices;

(c) the use of children in pornographic activities, performances and materials.

Article 28: Drug Abuse

States Parties to the present Charter shall take all appropriate measures to protect the child from the use of narcotics and illicit use of psychotropic substances as defined in the relevant international treaties, and to prevent the use of children in the production and trafficking of such substances.

Article 29: Sale, Trafficking and Abduction

States Parties to the present Charter shall take appropriate measures to prevent:

(a) the abduction, the sale of, or traffick in children for any purpose or in any form, by any person including parents or legal guardians of the child;

(b) the use of children in all forms of begging.

Article 30: Children of Imprisoned Mothers

1. States Parties to the present Charter shall undertake to provide special treatment to expectant mothers and to mothers of infants and young children who have been accused or found guilty of infringing the penal law and shall in particular:

(a) ensure that a non-custodial sentence will always be first considered when sentencing such mothers;

(b) establish and promote measures alternative to institutional confinement for the treatment of such mothers;

(c) establish special alternative institutions for holding such mothers;

(d) ensure that a mother shall not be imprisoned with her child;

(e) ensure that a death sentence shall not be imposed on such mothers;

(f) the essential aim of the penitentiary system will be the reformation, the integration of the mother to the family and social rehabilitation.

Article 31: Responsibility of the Child

Every child shall have responsibilities towards his family and society, the State and other legally recognized communities and the international community. The child, subject to his age and ability, and such limitations as may be contained in the present Charter, shall have the duty;

(a) to work for the cohesion of the family, to respect his parents, superiors and elders at all times and to assist them in case of need;

(b) to serve his national community by placing his physical and intellectual abilities at its service;

(c) to preserve and strengthen social and national solidarity;

(d) to preserve and strengthen African cultural values in his relations with other members of the society, in the spirit of tolerance, dialogue and consultation and to contribute to the moral well-being of society;

(e) to preserve and strengthen the independence and the integrity of his country;

(f) to contribute to the best of his abilities. at all times and at all levels, to the promotion and achievement of African Unity.

PART 11

CHAPTER TWO: ESTABLISHMENT AND ORGANIZATION OF THE COMMITTEE ON THE RIGHTS AND WELFARE OF THE CHILD

Article 32: The Committee

An African Committee of Experts on the Rights and Welfare of the Child hereinafter called `the Committee' shall be established within the Organization of African Unity to promote and protect the rights and welfare of the child.

Article 33: Composition

1. The Committee shall consist of 11 members of high moral standing, integrity, impartiality and competence in matters of the rights and welfare of the child.

2. The members of the Committee shall serve in their personal capacity.

3. The Committee shall not include more than one national of the same State.

Article 34: Election

As soon as this Charter shall enter into force the members of the Committee shall be elected by secret ballot by the Assembly of Heads of State and Government from a list of persons nominated by the States Parties to the present Charter.

Article 35: Candidates

Each State Party to the present Charter may nominate not more than two candidates. The candidates must have one of the nationalities of the States Parties to the present Charter. When two candidates are nominated by a State, one of them shall not be a national of that State.

Article 36

1. The Secretary-General of the Organization of African Unity shall invite States Parties to the present Charter to nominate candidates at least six months before the elections.

2. The Secretary-General of the Organization of African Unity shall draw up in alphabetical order, a list of persons nominated and communicate it to the Heads of State and Government at least two months before the elections.

Article 37: Term of Office

1. The members of the Committee shall be elected for a tenn of five years and may not be re-elected, however. the term of four of the members elected at the first election shall expire after two years and the term of six others, after four years.

2. Immediately after the first election, the Chairman of the Assembly of Heads of State and Government of the Organization of African Unity shall draw lots to determine the names of those members referred to in sub-paragraph 1 of this Article.

3. The Secretary-General of the Organization of African Unity shall convene the first meeting of Committee at the Headquarters of the Organization within six months of the election of the members of the Committee, and thereafter the Committee shall be convened by its Chairman whenever necessary, at least once a year.

Article 38: Bureau

1. The Committee shall establish its own Rules of Procedure.
2. The Committee shall elect its officers for a period of two years.
3. Seven Committee members shall form the quorum.
4. In case of an equality of votes, the Chairman shall have a casting vote.
5. The working languages of the Committee shall be the official languages of the OAU.

Article 39: Vacancy

If a member of the Committee vacates his office for any reason other than the nonmal expiration of a term, the State which nominated that member shall appoint another member from among its nationals to serve for the remainder of the term - subject to the approval of the Assembly.

Article 40: Secretariat

The Secretary-General of the Organization of African Unity shall appoint a Secretary for the Committee.

Article 41: Privileges and Immunities

In discharging their duties. members of the Committee shall enjoy the privileges and immunities provided for in the General Convention on the Privileges and Immunities of the Organization of Afncan Unity.

CHAPTER THREE: MANDATE AND PROCEDURE OF THE COMMITTEE

Article 42: Mandate

The functions of the Committee shall be:

(a) To promote and protect the rights enshrined in this Charter and in particular to:

(i) collect and document information, commission inter-disciplinary assessment of situations on African problems in the fields of the rights and welfare of the child, organize meetings, encourage national and local institutions concerned with the rights and welfare of the child, and where necessary give its views and make recommendations to Governments;

(ii) formulate and lay down principles and rules aimed at protecting the rights and welfare of children in Africa;

(iii) cooperate with other African, international and regional Institutions and organizations concerned with the promotion and protection of the rights and welfare of the child.

(b) To monitor the implementation and ensure protection of the rights enshrined in this Charter.

(c) To interpret the provisions of the present Charter at the request of a State Party, an Institution of the Organization of African Unity or any other person or Institution recognized by the Organization of African Unity, or any State Party.

(d) Perform such other task as may be entrusted to it by the Assembly of Heads of State and Government, Secretary-General of the OAU and any other organs of the OAU or the United Nations.

Article 43: Reporting Procedure

1. Every State Party to the present Charter shall undertake to submit to the Committee through the Secretary-General of the Organization of African Unity, reports on the measures they have adopted which give

effect to the provisions of this Charter and on the progress made in the enjoyment of these rights:

(a) within two years of the entry into force of the Charter for the State Party concerned: and

(b) and thereafter, *every three years.*

2. Every report made under this Article shall:

(a) contain sufficient information on the implementation of the present Charter to provide the Committee with comprehensive understanding of the implementation of the Charter in the relevant country; and

(b) shall indicate factors and difficulties, if any, affecting the fulfilment of the obligations contained in the Charter.

3. A State Party which has submitted a comprehensive first report to the Committee need not, in its subsequent reports submitted in accordance with paragraph I (a) of this Article, repeat the basic information previously provided.

Article 44: Communications

1. The Committee may receive communication, from any person, group or non-governmental organization recognized by the Organization of African Unity, by a Member State, or the United Nations relating to any matter covered by this Charter.

2. Every communication to the Committee shall contain the name and address of the author and shall be treated in confidence.

Article 45: Investigations by the Committee

1. The Committee may, resort to any appropriate method of investigating any matter falling within the ambit of the present Charter, request from the States Parties any information relevant to the implementation of the Charter and may also resort to any appropriate method of investigating the measures the State Party has adopted to implement the Charter.

2. The Committee shall submit to each Ordinary Session of the Assembly of Heads of State and Government every two years, a report on its activities and on any communication made under Article [44] of this Charter.

3. The Committee shall publish its report after it has been considered by the Assembly of Heads of State and Government.

4. States Parties shall make the Committee's reports widely available to the public in their own countries.

CHAPTER FOUR: MISCELLANEOUS PROVISIONS

Article 46: Sources of Inspiration

The Committee shall draw inspiration from International Law on Human Rights, particularly from the provisions of the African Charter on Human and Peoples' Rights, the Charter of the Organization of African Unity, the Universal Declaration on Human Rights, the International Convention on the Rights of the Child, and other instruments adopted by the United Nations and by African countries in the field of human rights and from African values and traditions.

Article 47: Signature, Ratification or Adherence

1. The present Charter shall be open to signature by all the Member States of the Organization of African Unity.

2. The present Charter shall be subject to ratification or adherence by Member States of the Organization of African Unity. The instruments of ratification or adherence to the present Charter shall be deposited with the Secretary-General of the Organization of African Unity.

3. The present Charter shall come into force 30 days after the reception by the Secretary-General of the Organization of African Unity of the instruments of ratification or adherence of 15 Member States of the Organization of African Unity.

Article 48: Amendment and Revision of the Charter

1. The present Charter may be amended or revised if any State Party makes a written request to that effect to the Secretary-General of the Organization of African Unity, provided that the proposed amendment is not submitted to the Assembly of Heads of State and Government for consideration until all the States Parties have been duly notified of it and the Committee has given its opinion on the amendment.

2. An amendment shall be approved by a simple majority of the States Parties.

2. European Convention on the Exercise of Children's Rights, 1996

The European states have been the main developers of children's human rights. It is on this account that they have also actively participated in discussions on the protection of children's rights from various points of view. Their contribution can be seen in the European Convention on the

Exercise of Children's Rights, which was adopted in 1996 by the Council of Europe. It entered into force in 2000.

The key element of the European Convention is the definition of the age of children in its provisions: it states that the Convention applies "to children who have not reached the age of 18 years". This means that the Convention adopts the same policy as other international conventions governing the age of children. Based on this legal fact, the age of 18 should therefore be respected within other European bilateral or multilateral instruments. And, more importantly, no convention can violate this age, so its enforcement may thus be considered as a customary rule which has to be respected by all European states. In short, the European Convention aims at various protections which are essential for the development of the integrity and respect of children. These include social, cultural, economic, political, language and race, without regard to their background. The contracting parties to the Convention are convinced that "the rights and best interests of children should be promoted, and to that end children should have the opportunity to exercise their rights, in particular in family proceedings affecting them", by one means or another. The Convention also emphasises the proper treatment of children in front of the judicial authorities, and their inalienable rights with regard to self-protection through expressing their views. The text of the Convention states:

Preamble

The member States of the Council of Europe and the other States signatory hereto,

Considering that the aim of the Council of Europe is to achieve greater unity between its members;

Having regard to the United Nations Convention on the rights of the child and in particular Article 4 which requires States Parties to undertake all appropriate legislative, administrative and other measures for the implementation of the rights recognised in the said Convention;

Noting the contents of Recommendation 1121 (1990) of the Parliamentary Assembly on the rights of the child;

Convinced that the rights and best interests of children should be promoted and to that end children should have the opportunity to exercise their rights, in particular in family proceedings affecting them;

Recognising that children should be provided with relevant information to enable such rights and best interests to be promoted and that due weight should be given to the views of children;

Recognising the importance of the parental role in protecting and promoting the rights and best interests of children and considering that, where necessary, States should also engage in such protection and promotion;

Considering, however, that in the event of conflict it is desirable for families to try to reach agreement before bringing the matter before a judicial authority,

Have agreed as follows:

Chapter I – Scope and object of the Convention and definitions

Article 1 – Scope and object of the Convention

1. This Convention shall apply to children who have not reached the age of 18 years.

2. The object of the present Convention is, in the best interests of children, to promote their rights, to grant them procedural rights and to facilitate the exercise of these rights by ensuring that children are, themselves or through other persons or bodies, informed and allowed to participate in proceedings affecting them before a judicial authority.

3. For the purposes of this Convention proceedings before a judicial authority affecting children are family proceedings, in particular those involving the exercise of parental responsibilities such as residence and access to children.

4.Every State shall, at the time of signature or when depositing its instrument of ratification, acceptance, approval or accession, by a declaration addressed to the Secretary General of the Council of Europe, specify at least three categories of family cases before a judicial authority to which this Convention is to apply.

5. Any Party may, by further declaration, specify additional categories of family cases to which this Convention is to apply or provide information concerning the application of Article 5, paragraph 2 of Article 9, paragraph 2 of Article 10 and Article 11.

6. Nothing in this Convention shall prevent Parties from applying rules more favourable to the promotion and the exercise of children's rights.

Article 2 – Definitions

For the purposes of this Convention:

a. the term "judicial authority" means a court or an administrative authority having equivalent powers;

b. the term "holders of parental responsibilities" means parents and other persons or bodies entitled to exercise some or all parental responsibilities;

c. the term "representative" means a person, such as a lawyer, or a body appointed to act before a judicial authority on behalf of a child;

d. the term "relevant information" means information which is appropriate to the age and understanding of the child, and which will be given to enable the child to exercise his or her rights fully unless the provision of such information were contrary to the welfare of the child.

Chapter II – Procedural measures to promote the exercise of children's rights

A. Procedural rights of a child

Article 3 – Right to be informed and to express his or her views in proceedings

A child considered by internal law as having sufficient understanding, in the case of proceedings before a judicial authority affecting him or her, shall be granted, and shall be entitled to request, the following rights:

a. to receive all relevant information;

b. to be consulted and express his or her views;

c. to be informed of the possible consequences of compliance with these views and the possible consequences of any decision.

Article 4 – Right to apply for the appointment of a special representative

1. Subject to Article 9, the child shall have the right to apply, in person or through other persons or bodies, for a special representative in proceedings before a judicial authority affecting the child where internal law precludes the holders of parental responsibilities from representing the child as a result of a conflict of interest with the latter.

2. States are free to limit the right in paragraph 1 to children who are considered by internal law to have sufficient understanding.

Article 5 – Other possible procedural rights

Parties shall consider granting children additional procedural rights in relation to proceedings before a judicial authority affecting them, in particular:

a. the right to apply to be assisted by an appropriate person of their choice in order to help them express their views;

b. the right to apply themselves, or through other persons or bodies, for the appointment of a separate representative, in appropriate cases a lawyer;

c. the right to appoint their own representative;

d. the right to exercise some or all of the rights of parties to such proceedings.

B. Role of judicial authorities

Article 6 – Decision-making process

In proceedings affecting a child, the judicial authority, before taking a decision, shall:

a. consider whether it has sufficient information at its disposal in order to take a decision in the best interests of the child and, where necessary, it shall obtain further information, in particular from the holders of parental responsibilities;

b. in a case where the child is considered by internal law as having sufficient understanding:

c. ensure that the child has received all relevant information;

d. consult the child in person in appropriate cases, if necessary privately, itself or through other persons or bodies, in a manner appropriate to his or her understanding, unless this would be manifestly contrary to the best interests of the child;

e. allow the child to express his or her views;

f. give due weight to the views expressed by the child.

Article 7 – Duty to act speedily

In proceedings affecting a child the judicial authority shall act speedily to avoid any unnecessary delay and procedures shall be available to ensure that its decisions are rapidly enforced. In urgent cases the judicial authority shall have the power, where appropriate, to take decisions which are immediately enforceable.

Article 8 – Acting on own motion

In proceedings affecting a child the judicial authority shall have the power to act on its own motion in cases determined by internal law where the welfare of a child is in serious danger.

Article 9 – Appointment of a representative

1. In proceedings affecting a child where, by internal law, the holders of parental responsibilities are precluded from representing the child as a result of a conflict of interest between them and the child, the judicial

authority shall have the power to appoint a special representative for the child in those proceedings.

2. Parties shall consider providing that, in proceedings affecting a child, the judicial authority shall have the power to appoint a separate representative, in appropriate cases a lawyer, to represent the child.

C. Role of representatives

Article 10

1. In the case of proceedings before a judicial authority affecting a child the representative shall, unless this would be manifestly contrary to the best interests of the child:

a. provide all relevant information to the child, if the child is considered by internal law as having sufficient understanding;

b. provide explanations to the child if the child is considered by internal law as having sufficient understanding, concerning the possible consequences of compliance with his or her views and the possible consequences of any action by the representative;

c. determine the views of the child and present these views to the judicial authority.

2. Parties shall consider extending the provisions of paragraph 1 to the holders of parental responsibilities.

D. Extension of certain provisions

Article 11

Parties shall consider extending the provisions of Articles 3, 4 and 9 to proceedings affecting children before other bodies and to matters affecting children which are not the subject of proceedings.

E. National bodies

Article 12

1. Parties shall encourage, through bodies which perform, *inter alia*, the functions set out in paragraph 2, the promotion and the exercise of children's rights.

2. The functions are as follows:

a. to make proposals to strengthen the law relating to the exercise of children's rights;

b. to give opinions concerning draft legislation relating to the exercise of children's rights;

c. to provide general information concerning the exercise of children's rights to the media, the public and persons and bodies dealing with questions relating to children;
d. to seek the views of children and provide them with relevant information.

F. Other matters

Article 13 – Mediation or other processes to resolve disputes

In order to prevent or resolve disputes or to avoid proceedings before a judicial authority affecting children, Parties shall encourage the provision of mediation or other processes to resolve disputes and the use of such processes to reach agreement in appropriate cases to be determined by Parties.

Article 14 – Legal aid and advice

Where internal law provides for legal aid or advice for the representation of children in proceedings before a judicial authority affecting them, such provisions shall apply in relation to the matters covered by Articles 4 and 9.

Article 15 – Relations with other international instruments

This Convention shall not restrict the application of any other international instrument which deals with specific issues arising in the context of the protection of children and families, and to which a Party to this Convention is, or becomes, a Party.

Chapter III – Standing Committee

Article 16 – Establishment and functions of the Standing Committee

1. A Standing Committee is set up for the purposes of this Convention.

2. The Standing Committee shall keep under review problems relating to this Convention. It may, in particular:

a. consider any relevant questions concerning the interpretation or implementation of the Convention. The Standing Committee's conclusions concerning the implementation of the Convention may take the form of a recommendation; recommendations shall be adopted by a three-quarters majority of the votes cast;
b. propose amendments to the Convention and examine those proposed in accordance with Article 20;

c. provide advice and assistance to the national bodies having the functions under paragraph 2 of Article 12 and promote international co-operation between them.

Article 17 – Composition

1. Each Party may be represented on the Standing Committee by one or more delegates. Each Party shall have one vote.

2. Any State referred to in Article 21, which is not a Party to this Convention, may be represented in the Standing Committee by an observer. The same applies to any other State or to the European Community after having been invited to accede to the Convention in accordance with the provisions of Article 22.

3. Unless a Party has informed the Secretary General of its objection, at least one month before the meeting, the Standing Committee may invite the following to attend as observers at all its meetings or at one meeting or part of a meeting:

a. any State not referred to in paragraph 2 above;

b. the United Nations Committee on the Rights of the Child;

c. the European Community;

d. any international governmental body;

e. any international non-governmental body with one or more functions mentioned under paragraph 2 of Article 12;

f. any national governmental or non-governmental body with one or more functions mentioned under paragraph 2 of Article 12.

4. The Standing Committee may exchange information with relevant organisations dealing with the exercise of children's rights.

Article 18 – Meetings

1. At the end of the third year following the date of entry into force of this Convention and, on his or her own initiative, at any time after this date, the Secretary General of the Council of Europe shall invite the Standing Committee to meet.

2. Decisions may only be taken in the Standing Committee if at least one-half of the Parties are present.

3. Subject to Articles 16 and 20 the decisions of the Standing Committee shall be taken by a majority of the members present.

4. Subject to the provisions of this Convention the Standing Committee shall draw up its own rules of procedure and the rules of procedure of any working party it may set up to carry out all appropriate tasks under the Convention.

Article 19 – Reports of the Standing Committee

After each meeting, the Standing Committee shall forward to the Parties and the Committee of Ministers of the Council of Europe a report on its discussions and any decisions taken.

Chapter IV – Amendments to the Convention

Article 20

1. Any amendment to the articles of this Convention proposed by a Party or the Standing Committee shall be communicated to the Secretary General of the Council of Europe and forwarded by him or her, at least two months before the next meeting of the Standing Committee, to the member States of the Council of Europe, any signatory, any Party, any State invited to sign this Convention in accordance with the provisions of Article 21 and any State or the European Community invited to accede to it in accordance with the provisions of Article 22.

2. Any amendment proposed in accordance with the provisions of the preceding paragraph shall be examined by the Standing Committee which shall submit the text adopted by a three-quarters majority of the votes cast to the Committee of Ministers for approval. After its approval, this text shall be forwarded to the Parties for acceptance.

3. Any amendment shall enter into force on the first day of the month following the expiration of a period of one month after the date on which all Parties have informed the Secretary General that they have accepted it.

Chapter V – Final clauses

Article 21 – Signature, ratification and entry into force

1. This Convention shall be open for signature by the member States of the Council of Europe and the non-member States which have participated in its elaboration.

2. This Convention is subject to ratification, acceptance or approval. Instruments of ratification, acceptance or approval shall be deposited with the Secretary General of the Council of Europe.

3. This Convention shall enter into force on the first day of the month following the expiration of a period of three months after the date on which three States, including at least two member States of the Council of Europe, have expressed their consent to be bound by the Convention in accordance with the provisions of the preceding paragraph.

4. In respect of any signatory which subsequently expresses its consent to be bound by it, the Convention shall enter into force on the first day of

the month following the expiration of a period of three months after the date of the deposit of its instrument of ratification, acceptance or approval.

Article 22 – Non-member States and the European Community

1. After the entry into force of this Convention, the Committee of Ministers of the Council of Europe may, on its own initiative or following a proposal from the Standing Committee and after consultation of the Parties, invite any non-member State of the Council of Europe, which has not participated in the elaboration of the Convention, as well as the European Community to accede to this Convention by a decision taken by the majority provided for in Article 20, sub-paragraph d of the Statute of the Council of Europe, and by the unanimous vote of the representatives of the contracting States entitled to sit on the Committee of Ministers.

2. In respect of any acceding State or the European Community, the Convention shall enter into force on the first day of the month following the expiration of a period of three months after the date of deposit of the instrument of accession with the Secretary General of the Council of Europe.

Article 23 – Territorial application

1. Any State may, at the time of signature or when depositing its instrument of ratification, acceptance, approval or accession, specify the territory or territories to which this Convention shall apply.

2. Any Party may, at any later date, by a declaration addressed to the Secretary General of the Council of Europe, extend the application of this Convention to any other territory specified in the declaration and for whose international relations it is responsible or on whose behalf it is authorised to give undertakings. In respect of such territory the Convention shall enter into force on the first day of the month following the expiration of a period of three months after the date of receipt of such declaration by the Secretary General.

3. Any declaration made under the two preceding paragraphs may, in respect of any territory specified in such declaration, be withdrawn by a notification addressed to the Secretary General. The withdrawal shall become effective on the first day of the month following the expiration of a period of three months after the date of receipt of such notification by the Secretary General.

Article 24 – Reservations

No reservation may be made to the Convention.

Article 25 – Denunciation

1. Any Party may at any time denounce this Convention by means of a notification addressed to the Secretary General of the Council of Europe.

2. Such denunciation shall become effective on the first day of the month following the expiration of a period of three months after the date of receipt of notification by the Secretary General.

Article 26 – Notifications

The Secretary General of the Council of Europe shall notify the member States of the Council, any signatory, any Party and any other State or the European Community which has been invited to accede to this Convention of:

a. any signature;

b. the deposit of any instrument of ratification, acceptance, approval or accession;

c. any date of entry into force of this Convention in accordance with Articles 21 or 22;

d. any amendment adopted in accordance with Article 20 and the date on which such an amendment enters into force;

e. any declaration made under the provisions of Articles 1 and 23;

f. any denunciation made in pursuance of the provisions of Article 25;

g. any other act, notification or communication relating to this Convention.

In witness whereof, the undersigned, being duly authorised thereto, have signed this Convention.

Done at Strasbourg, the 25th January 1996, in English and French, both texts being equally authentic, in a single copy which shall be deposited in the archives of the Council of Europe. The Secretary General of the Council of Europe shall transmit certified copies to each member State of the Council of Europe, to the non-member States which have participated in the elaboration of this Convention, to the European Community and to any State invited to accede to this Convention.

CHAPTER VI

INTERNATIONAL LEGISLATIONS SHIELDING THE RIGHTS OF JUVENILE DELINQUENCY

1. Standard Minimum Rules for the Treatment of Prisoners, 1955

The general intention of criminal jurisdiction has been to protect juveniles from all kinds of prejudice and behaviour which discriminate against them in the application of criminal justice. But this intention has been unsuccessful, and there are still many serious problems that have solved. One of the most significant documents relating to the protection of juveniles by the United Nations Organization is the Standard Minimum Rules for the Treatment of Prisoners, adopted in 1955. Although, this international document is not exhaustive, and does not have the power of law-making treaties, it is significant in the recognition of certain rights of juveniles. It paved the way for the future development of the law and protection of young persons.

Document

Preliminary Observations

5. (1) The rules do not seek to regulate the management of institutions set aside for young persons such as Borstal institutions or correctional schools, but in general part I would be equally applicable in such institutions.

(2) The category of young prisoners should include at least all young persons who come within the jurisdiction of juvenile courts. As a rule, suck young persons should not be sentenced to imprisonment.

PART I
RULES OF GENERAL APPLICATION

Register

8. (d) Young persons shall be kept separate from adults.

Exercise and sport
21. (2) Young prisoners, and others of suitable age and physique, shall receive physical and recreational training during the period of exercise. To this end space, installations and equipment should be provided.

PART II
RULES APPLICABLE TO SPECIAL CATEGORIES

A.PRISONERS UNDER SENTENCE

Work
71. (5) Vocational training in useful trades shall be provided for prisoners able to profit thereby and especially for young prisoners.

Education and recreation
77. (1) Provision shall be made for the further education of all prisoners capable of profiting thereby, including religious instruction in the countries where this is possible. The education of illiterates and young prisoners shall be compulsory and special attention shall be paid to it by the administration.

C. PRISONERS UNDER ARREST OR AWAITING TRIAL

85. (2) Young untried prisoners shall be kept separate from adults and shall in principle be detained in separate institutions.

2. United Nations Standard Minimum Rules for the Administration of Juvenile Justice, ("The Beijing Rules"), 1985

Although the protection of children's rights has sometimes been regarded as a necessary condition for the implementation of justice, this protection has not been particularly strong. The United Nations Standard Minimum Rules for the Administration of Juvenile Justice is almost the first international instrument which deals directly with the question of juveniles and the protection of their rights. This instrument was adopted by General Assembly Resolution 40/33 in 1985. Its intention is to protect all juveniles when they are, for one reason or another, caught up in the justice system, and it deals with the appropriate treatment of juvenile prisoners and offenders within the territories of members of the United Nations. The United Nations Standard Minimum Rules for the Administration of

Juvenile Justice is also known as the Beijing Rules, since it was first proposed in Beijing. This instrument provides that:

PART ONE

GENERAL PRINCIPLES

1. Fundamental perspectives

1.1 Member States shall seek, in conformity with their respective general interests, to further the well-being of the juvenile and her or his family.

1.2 Member States shall endeavour to develop conditions that will ensure for the juvenile a meaningful life in the community, which, during that period in life when she or he is most susceptible to deviant behaviour, will foster a process of personal development and education that is as free from crime and delinquency as possible.

1.3 Sufficient attention shall be given to positive measures that involve the full mobilization of all possible resources, including the family, volunteers and other community groups, as well as schools and other community institutions, for the purpose of promoting the well-being of the juvenile, with a view to reducing the need for intervention under the law, and of effectively, fairly and humanely dealing with the juvenile in conflict with the law.

1.4 Juvenile justice shall be conceived as an integral part of the national development process of each country, within a comprehensive framework of social justice for all juveniles, thus, at the same time, contributing to the protection of the young and the maintenance of a peaceful order in society.

1.5 These Rules shall be implemented in the context of economic, social and cultural conditions prevailing in each Member State.

1.6 Juvenile justice services shall be systematically developed and coordinated with a view to improving and sustaining the competence of personnel involved in the services, including their methods, approaches and attitudes.

Commentary

These broad fundamental perspectives refer to comprehensive social policy in general and aim at promoting juvenile welfare to the greatest possible extent, which will minimize the necessity of intervention by the juvenile justice system, and in turn, will reduce the harm that may be caused by any intervention. Such care measures for the young, before the onset of delinquency, are basic policy requisites designed to obviate the need for the application of the Rules.

Rules 1.1 to 1.3 point to the important role that a constructive social policy for juveniles will play, inter alia, in the prevention of juvenile crime and delinquency. Rule 1.4 defines juvenile justice as an integral part of social justice for juveniles, while rule 1.6 refers to the necessity of constantly improving juvenile justice, without falling behind the development of progressive social policy for juveniles in general and bearing in mind the need for consistent improvement of staff services.
Rule 1.5 seeks to take account of existing conditions in Member States which would cause the manner of implementation of particular rules necessarily to be different from the manner adopted in other States.

2. Scope of the Rules and definitions used

2.1 The following Standard Minimum Rules shall be applied to juvenile offenders impartially, without distinction of any kind, for example as to race, colour, sex, language, religion, political or other opinions, national or social origin, property, birth or other status.

2.2 For purposes of these Rules, the following definitions shall be applied by Member States in a manner which is compatible with their respective legal systems and concepts:

(a) A juvenile is a child or young person who, under the respective legal systems, may be dealt with for an offence in a manner which is different from an adult;

(b) An offence is any behaviour (act or omission) that is punishable by law under the respective legal systems;

(c) A juvenile offender is a child or young person who is alleged to have committed or who has been found to have committed an offence.

2.3 Efforts shall be made to establish, in each national jurisdiction, a set of laws, rules and provisions specifically applicable to juvenile offenders and institutions and bodies entrusted with the functions of the administration of juvenile justice and designed:

(a) To meet the varying needs of juvenile offenders, while protecting their basic rights;

(b) To meet the needs of society;

(c) To implement the following rules thoroughly and fairly.

Commentary

The Standard Minimum Rules are deliberately formulated so as to be applicable within different legal systems and, at the same time, to set some minimum standards for the handling of juvenile offenders under any definition of a juvenile and under any system of dealing with juvenile offenders. The Rules are always to be applied impartially and without distinction of any kind.

Rule 2.1 therefore stresses the importance of the Rules always being applied impartially and without distinction of any kind. The rule follows the formulation of principle 2 of the Declaration of the Rights of the Child.

Rule 2.2 defines "juvenile" and "offence" as the components of the notion of the "juvenile offender", who is the main subject of these Standard Minimum Rules (see, however, also rules 3 and 4). It should be noted that age limits will depend on, and are explicitly made dependent on, each respective legal system, thus fully respecting the economic, social, political, cultural and legal systems of Member States. This makes for a wide variety of ages coming under the definition of "juvenile", ranging from 7 years to 18 years or above. Such a variety seems inevitable in view of the different national legal systems and does not diminish the impact of these Standard Minimum Rules.

Rule 2.3 is addressed to the necessity of specific national legislation for the optimal implementation of these Standard Minimum Rules, both legally and practically.

3. Extension of the Rules

3.1 The relevant provisions of the Rules shall be applied not only to juvenile offenders but also to juveniles who may be proceeded against for any specific behaviour that would not be punishable if committed by an adult.

3.2 Efforts shall be made to extend the principles embodied in the Rules to all juveniles who are dealt with in welfare and care proceedings.

3.3 Efforts shall also be made to extend the principles embodied in the Rules to young adult offenders.

Commentary

Rule 3 extends the protection afforded by the Standard Minimum Rules for the Administration of Juvenile Justice to cover:

(a) The so-called "status offences" prescribed in various national legal systems where the range of behaviour considered to be an offence is wider for juveniles than it is for adults (for example, truancy, school and family disobedience, public drunkenness, etc.) (rule 3.1);

(b) Juvenile welfare and care proceedings (rule 3.2);

(c) Proceedings dealing with young adult offenders, depending of course on each given age limit (rule 3.3).

The extension of the Rules to cover these three areas seems to be justified. Rule 3.1 provides minimum guarantees in those fields, and rule 3.2 is considered a desirable step in the direction of more fair, equitable and humane justice for all juveniles in conflict with the law.

4. Age of criminal responsibility

4.1 In those legal systems recognizing the concept of the age of criminal responsibility for juveniles, the beginning of that age shall not be fixed at too low an age level, bearing in mind the facts of emotional, mental and intellectual maturity.

Commentary

The minimum age of criminal responsibility differs widely owing to history and culture. The modern approach would be to consider whether a child can live up to the moral and psychological components of criminal responsibility; that is, whether a child, by virtue of her or his individual discernment and understanding, can be held responsible for essentially antisocial be ha vi our. If the age of criminal responsibility is fixed too low or if there is no lower age limit at all, the notion of responsibility would become meaningless. In general, there is a close relationship between the notion of responsibility for delinquent or criminal behaviour and other social rights and responsibilities (such as marital status, civil majority, etc.).

Efforts should therefore be made to agree on a reasonable lowest age limit that is applicable internationally.

5. Aims of juvenile justice

5.1 The juvenile justice system shall emphasize the well-being of the juvenile and shall ensure that any reaction to juvenile offenders shall always be in proportion to the circumstances of both the offenders and the offence.

Commentary

Rule 5 refers to two of the most important objectives of juvenile justice. The first objective is the promotion of the well-being of the juvenile. This is the main focus of those legal systems in which juvenile offenders are dealt with by family courts or administrative authorities, but the well-being of the juvenile should also be emphasized in legal systems that follow the criminal court model, thus contributing to the avoidance of merely punitive sanctions. (See also rule 14.)

The second objective is "the principle of proportionality". This principle is well-known as an instrument for curbing punitive sanctions, mostly expressed in terms of just deserts in relation to the gravity of the offence. The response to young offenders should be based on the consideration not only of the gravity of the offence but also of personal circumstances. The individual circumstances of the offender (for example social status, family situation, the harm caused by the offence or other factors affecting personal circumstances) should influence the proportionality of the reactions (for example by having regard to the offender's endeavour to indemnify the victim or to her or his willingness to turn to wholesome and useful life).

By the same token, reactions aiming to ensure the welfare of the young offender may go beyond necessity and therefore infringe upon the fundamental rights of the young individual, as has been observed in some juvenile justice systems. Here, too, the proportionality of the reaction to the circumstances of both the offender and the offence, including the victim, should be safeguarded.

In essence, rule 5 calls for no less and no more than a fair reaction in any given cases of juvenile delinquency and crime. The issues combined in the rule may help to stimulate development in both regards: new and innovative types of reactions are as desirable as precautions against any undue widening of the net of formal social control over juveniles.

6. Scope of discretion

6.1 In view of the varying special needs of juveniles as well as the variety of measures available, appropriate scope for discretion shall be allowed at all stages of proceedings and at the different levels of juvenile justice administration, including investigation, prosecution, adjudication and the follow-up of dispositions.

6.2 Efforts shall be made, however, to ensure sufficient accountability at all stages and levels in the exercise of any such discretion.

6.3 Those who exercise discretion shall be specially qualified or trained to exercise it judiciously and in accordance with their functions and mandates.

Commentary

Rules 6.1, 6.2 and 6.3 combine several important features of effective, fair and humane juvenile justice administration: the need to permit the exercise of discretionary power at all significant levels of processing so that those who make determinations can take the actions deemed to be most appropriate in each individual case; and the need to provide checks and balances in order to curb any abuses of discretionary power and to safeguard the rights of the young offender. Accountability and professionalism are instruments best apt to curb broad discretion. Thus, professional qualifications and expert training are emphasized here as a valuable means of ensuring the judicious exercise of discretion in matters of juvenile offenders. (See also rules 1.6 and 2.2.) The formulation of specific guidelines on the exercise of discretion and the provision of systems of review, appeal and the like in order to permit scrutiny of decisions and accountability are emphasized in this context. Such mechanisms are not specified here, as they do not easily lend themselves to incorporation into international standard minimum rules, which cannot possibly cover all differences in justice systems.

7. Rights of juveniles

7.1 Basic procedural safeguards such as the presumption of innocence, the right to be notified of the charges, the right to remain silent, the right to counsel, the right to the presence of a parent or guardian, the right to confront and cross-examine witnesses and the right to appeal to a higher authority shall be guaranteed at all stages of proceedings.

Commentary

Rule 7.1 emphasizes some important points that represent essential elements for a fair and just trial and that are internationally recognized in existing human rights instruments (See also rule 14.). The presumption of innocence, for instance, is also to be found in article 11 of the Universal Declaration of Human rights and in article 14, paragraph 2, of the International Covenant on Civil and Political Rights. Rules 14 seq. of these Standard Minimum Rules specify issues that are important for proceedings in juvenile cases, in particular, while rule 7.1 affirms the most basic procedural safeguards in a general way.

8. Protection of privacy

8.1 The juvenile's right to privacy shall be respected at all stages in order to avoid harm being caused to her or him by undue publicity or by the process of labelling.

8.2 In principle, no information that may lead to the identification of a juvenile offender shall be published.

Commentary

Rule 8 stresses the importance of the protection of the juvenile's right to privacy. Young persons are particularly susceptible to stigmatization.

Criminological research into labelling processes has provided evidence of the detrimental effects (of different kinds) resulting from the permanent identification of young persons as "delinquent" or "criminal".

Rule 8 stresses the importance of protecting the juvenile from the adverse effects that may result from the publication in the mass media of information about the case (for example the names of young offenders, alleged or convicted). The interest of the individual should be protected and upheld, at least in principle (The general contents of rule 8 are further specified in rule 2 1.).

9. Saving clause

9.1 Nothing in these Rules shall be interpreted as precluding the application of the Standard Minimum Rules for the Treatment of Prisoners adopted by the United Nations and other human rights instruments and standards recognized by the international community that relate to the care and protection of the young.

Commentary

Rule 9 is meant to avoid any misunderstanding in interpreting and implementing the present Rules in conformity with principles contained in relevant existing or emerging international human rights instruments and standards-such as the Universal Declaration of Human Rights, the International Covenant on Economic, Social and Cultural Rights and the International Covenant on Civil and Political Rights, and the Declaration of the Rights of the Child and the draft convention on the rights of the child. It should be understood that the application of the present Rules is without prejudice to any such international instruments which may contain provisions of wider application (See also rule 27.).

PART TWO
INVESTIGATION AND PROSECUTION

10. Initial contact

10.1 Upon the apprehension of a juvenile, her or his parents or guardian shall be immediately notified of such apprehension, and, where such immediate notification is not possible, the parents or guardian shall be notified within the shortest possible time thereafter.

10.2 A judge or other competent official or body shall, without delay, consider the issue of release.

10.3 Contacts between the law enforcement agencies and a juvenile offender shall be managed in such a way as to respect the legal status of the juvenile, promote the well-being of the juvenile and avoid harm to her or him, with due regard to the circumstances of the case.

Commentary
Rule 10.1 is in principle contained in rule 92 of the Standard Minimum Rules for the Treatment of Prisoners.

The question of release (rule 10.2) shall be considered without delay by a judge or other competent official. The latter refers to any person or institution in the broadest sense of the term, including community boards or police authorities having power to release an arrested person. (See also the International Covenant on Civil and Political Rights, article 9, paragraph 3.)

Rule 10.3 deals with some fundamental aspects of the procedures and behaviour on the part of the police and other law enforcement officials in cases of juvenile crime. To "avoid harm" admittedly is flexible wording and covers many features of possible interaction (for example the use of harsh language, physical violence or exposure to the environment). Involvement in juvenile justice processes in itself can be "harmful" to juveniles; the term "avoid harm" should be broadly interpreted, therefore, as doing the least harm possible to the juvenile in the first instance, as well as any additional or undue harm. This is especially important in the initial contact with law enforcement agencies, which might profoundly influence the juvenile's attitude towards the State and society. Moreover, the success of any further intervention is largely dependent on such initial contacts. Compassion and kind firmness are important in these situations.

11. Diversion

11.1 Consideration shall be given, wherever appropriate, to dealing with juvenile offenders without resorting to formal trial by the competent authority, referred to in rule 14.1 below.

11.2 The police, the prosecution or other agencies dealing with juvenile cases shall be empowered to dispose of such cases, at their discretion, without recourse to formal hearings, in accordance with the criteria laid down for that purpose in the respective legal system and also in accordance with the principles contained in these Rules.

11.3 Any diversion involving referral to appropriate community or other services shall require the consent of the juvenile, or her or his parents or guardian, provided that such decision to refer a case shall be subject to review by a competent authority, upon application.

11.4 In order to facilitate the discretionary disposition of juvenile cases, efforts shall be made to provide for community programmes, such as temporary supervision and guidance, restitution, and compensation of victims.

Commentary

Diversion, involving removal from criminal justice processing and, frequently, redirection to community support services, is commonly practised on a formal and informal basis in many legal systems. This practice serves to hinder the negative effects of subsequent proceedings in juvenile justice administration (for example the stigma of conviction and sentence). In many cases, non-intervention would be the best response. Thus, diversion at the outset and without referral to alternative (social) services may be the optimal response. This is especially the case where the offence is of a non-serious nature and where the family, the school or other informal social control institutions have already reacted, or are likely to react, in an appropriate and constructive manner.

As stated in rule 11.2, diversion may be used at any point of decision-making-by the police, the prosecution or other agencies such as the courts, tribunals, boards or councils. It may be exercised by one authority or several or all authorities, according to the rules and policies of the respective systems and in line with the present Rules. It need not necessarily be limited to petty cases, thus rendering diversion an important instrument.

Rule 11.3 stresses the important requirement of securing the consent of the young offender (or the parent or guardian) to the recommended diversionary measure(s). (Diversion to community service without such consent would contradict the Abolition of Forced Labour Convention.) However, this consent should not be left unchallengeable, since it might sometimes be given out of sheer desperation on the part of the juvenile. The rule underlines that care should be taken to minimize the potential for coercion and intimidation at all levels in the diversion process. Juveniles should not feel pressured (for example in order to avoid court appearance) or be pressured into consenting to diversion programmes. Thus, it is advocated that provision should be made for an objective appraisal of the appropriateness of dispositions involving young offenders by a "competent authority upon application". (The "competent authority,' may be different from that referred to in rule 14.)

Rule 11.4 recommends the provision of viable alternatives to juvenile justice processing in the form of community-based diversion. Programmes that involve settlement by victim restitution and those that seek to avoid future conflict with the law through temporary supervision and guidance are especially commended. The merits of individual cases would make diversion appropriate, even when more serious offences have been committed (for example first offence, the act having been committed under peer pressure, etc.).

12. Specialization within the police

12.1 In order to best fulfil their functions, police officers who frequently or exclusively deal with juveniles or who are primarily engaged in the prevention of juvenile crime shall be specially instructed and trained. In large cities, special police units should be established for that purpose.

Commentary

Rule 12 draws attention to the need for specialized training for all law enforcement officials who are involved in the administration of juvenile justice. As police are the first point of contact with the juvenile justice system, it is most important that they act in an informed and appropriate manner.

While the relationship between urbanization and crime is clearly complex, an increase in juvenile crime has been associated with the growth of large cities, particularly with rapid and unplanned growth. Specialized police units would therefore be indispensable, not only in the interest of implementing specific principles contained in the present instrument (such as rule 1.6) but more generally for improving the prevention and control of juvenile crime and the handling of juvenile offenders.

13. Detention pending trial

13.1 Detention pending trial shall be used only as a measure of last resort and for the shortest possible period of time.

13.2 Whenever possible, detention pending trial shall be replaced by alternative measures, such as close supervision, intensive care or placement with a family or in an educational setting or home.

13.3 Juveniles under detention pending trial shall be entitled to all rights and guarantees of the Standard Minimum Rules for the Treatment of Prisoners adopted by the United Nations.

13.4 Juveniles under detention pending trial shall be kept separate from adults and shall be detained in a separate institution or in a separate part of an institution also holding adults.

13.5 While in custody, juveniles shall receive care, protection and all necessary individual assistance-social, educational, vocational, psychological, medical and physical-that they may require in view of their age, sex and personality.

Commentary

The danger to juveniles of"criminal contamination" while in detention pending trial must not be underestimated. It is therefore important to stress the need for alternative measures. By doing so, rule 13.1 encourages the devising of new and innovative measures to avoid such detention in the interest of the well-being of the juvenile. Juveniles under detention pending trial are entitled to all the rights and guarantees of the Standard Minimum Rules for the Treatment of Prisoners as well as the International Covenant on Civil and Political Rights, especially article 9 and article 10, paragraphs 2 (b) and 3.

Rule 13.4 does not prevent States from taking other measures against the negative influences of adult offenders which are at least as effective as the measures mentioned in the rule.

Different forms of assistance that may become necessary have been enumerated to draw attention to the broad range of particular needs of young detainees to be addressed (for example females or males, drug addicts, alcoholics, mentally ill juveniles, young persons suffering from the trauma, for example, of arrest, etc.).

Varying physical and psychological characteristics of young detainees may warrant classification measures by which some are kept separate while in detention pending trial, thus contributing to the avoidance of victimization and rendering more appropriate assistance.

The Sixth United Nations Congress on the Prevention of Crime and the Treatment of Offenders, in its resolution 4 on juvenile justice standards, specified that the Rules, inter alia, should reflect the basic principle that pre-trial detention should be used only as a last resort, that no minors should be held in a facility where they are vulnerable to the negative influences of adult detainees and that account should always be taken of the needs particular to their stage of development.

PART THREE
ADJUDICATION AND DISPOSITION

14. Competent authority to adjudicate

14.1 Where the case of a juvenile offender has not been diverted (under rule 11), she or he shall be dealt with by the competent authority (court, tribunal, board, council, etc.) according to the principles of a fair and just trial.

14.2 The proceedings shall be conducive to the best interests of the juvenile and shall be conducted in an atmosphere of understanding, which shall allow the juvenile to participate therein and to express herself or himself freely.

Commentary
It is difficult to formulate a definition of the competent body or person that would universally describe an adjudicating authority. "Competent authority" is meant to include those who preside over courts or tribunals (composed of a single judge or of several members), including professional and lay magistrates as well as administrative boards (for example the Scottish and Scandinavian systems) or other more informal community and conflict resolution agencies of an adjudicatory nature.

The procedure for dealing with juvenile offenders shall in any case follow the minimum standards that are applied almost universally for any criminal defendant under the procedure known as "due process of law". In accordance with due process, a "fair and just trial" includes such basic safeguards as the presumption of innocence, the presentation and examination of witnesses, the common legal defences, the right to remain silent, the right to have the last word in a hearing, the right to appeal, etc. (See also rule 7.1.)

15. Legal counsel, parents and guardians

15.1 Throughout the proceedings the juvenile shall have the right to be represented by a legal adviser or to apply for free legal aid where there is provision for such aid in the country.

15.2 The parents or the guardian shall be entitled to participate in the proceedings and may be required by the competent authority to attend them in the interest of the juvenile. They may, however, be denied participation by the competent authority if there are reasons to assume that such exclusion is necessary in the interest of the juvenile.

Commentary
Rule 15.1 uses terminology similar to that found in rule 93 of the Standard Minimum Rules for the Treatment of Prisoners. Whereas legal counsel and free legal aid are needed to assure the juvenile legal assistance, the right of the parents or guardian to participate as stated in rule 15.2 should be viewed as general psychological and emotional assistance to the juvenile-a function extending throughout the procedure.
The competent authority's search for an adequate disposition of the case may pro fit, in particular, fro m the co-operation of the legal representatives of the juvenile (or, for that matter, some other personal assistant who the juvenile can and does really trust). Such concern can be

thwarted if the presence of parents or guardians at the hearings plays a negative role, for instance, if they display a hostile attitude towards the juvenile, hence, the possibility of their exclusion must be provided for.

16. Social inquiry reports

16.1 In all cases except those involving minor offences, before the competent authority renders a final disposition prior to sentencing, the background and circumstances in which the juvenile is living or the conditions under which the offence has been committed shall be properly investigated so as to facilitate judicious adjudication of the case by the competent authority.

Commentary

Social inquiry reports (social reports or pre-sentence reports) are an indispensable aid in most legal proceedings involving juveniles. The competent authority should be informed of relevant facts about the juvenile, such as social an d family background, school career, educational experiences, etc. For this purpose, some jurisdictions use special social services or personnel attached to the court or board. Other personnel, including probation officers, may serve the same function. The rule therefore requires that adequate social services should be available to deliver social inquiry reports of a qualified nature.

17. Guiding principles in adjudication and disposition

17.1 The disposition of the competent authority shall be guided by the following principles:

(a) The reaction taken shall always be in proportion not only to the circumstances and the gravity of the offence but also to the circumstances and the needs of the juvenile as well as to the needs of the society;

(b) Restrictions on the personal liberty of the juvenile shall be imposed only after careful consideration and shall be limited to the possible minimum;

(c) Deprivation of personal liberty shall not be imposed unless the juvenile is adjudicated of a serious act involving violence against another person or of persistence in committing other serious offences and unless there is no other appropriate response;

(d) The well-being of the juvenile shall be the guiding factor in the consideration of her or his case.

17.2 Capital punishment shall not be imposed for any crime committed by juveniles.

17.3 Juveniles shall not be subject to corporal punishment.

17.4 The competent authority shall have the power to discontinue the proceedings at any time.

Commentary

The main difficulty in formulating guidelines for the adjudication of young persons stems from the fact that there are unresolved conflicts of a philosophical nature, such as the following:

(a) Rehabilitation versus just desert;

(b) Assistance versus repression and punishment;

(c) Reaction according to the singular merits of an individual case versus reaction according to the protection of society in general;

(d) General deterrence versus individual incapacitation.

The conflict between these approaches is more pronounced in juvenile cases than in adult cases. With the variety of causes and reactions characterizing juvenile cases, these alternatives become intricately interwoven.

It is not the function of the Standard Minimum Rules for the Administration of Juvenile Justice to prescribe which approach is to be followed but rather to identify one that is most closely in consonance with internationally accepted principles. Therefore the essential elements as laid down in rule 17.1, in particular in subparagraphs (a) and (c), are mainly to be understood as practical guidelines that should ensure a common starting point; if heeded by the concerned authorities (see also rule 5), they could contribute considerably to ensuring that the fundamental rights of juvenile offenders are protected, especially the fundamental rights of personal development and education.

Rule 17.1 (b) implies that strictly punitive approaches are not appropriate. Whereas in adult cases, and possibly also in cases of severe offences by juveniles, just desert and retributive sanctions might be considered to have some merit, in juvenile cases such considerations should always be outweighed by the interest of safeguarding the well-being and the future of the young person.

In line with resolution 8 of the Sixth United Nations Congress, rule 17.1 (b) encourages the use of alternatives to institutionalization to the maximum extent possible, bearing in mind the need to respond to the specific requirements of the young. Thus, full use should be made of the range of existing alternative sanctions and new alternative sanctions should be developed, bearing the public safety in mind. Probation should be granted to the greatest possible extent via suspended sentences, conditional sentences, board orders and other dispositions.

Rule 17.1 (c) corresponds to one of the guiding principles in resolution 4 of the Sixth Congress which aims at avoiding incarceration in the case of juveniles unless there is no other appropriate response that will protect the public safety.

The provision prohibiting capital punishment in rule 17.2 is in accordance with article 6, paragraph 5, of the International Covenant on Civil and Political Rights.

The provision against corporal punishment is in line with article 7 of the International Covenant on Civil and Political Rights and the Declaration on the Protection of All Persons from Being Subjected to Torture and Other Cruel, Inhuman or Degrading Treatment or Punishment, as well as the Convention against Torture and Other Cruel, Inhuman or Degrading Treatment or Punishment and the draft convention on the rights of the child.

The power to discontinue the proceedings at any time (rule 17.4) is a characteristic inherent in the handling of juvenile offenders as opposed to adults. At any time, circumstances may become known to the competent authority which would make a complete cessation of the intervention appear to be the best disposition of the case.

18. Various disposition measures

18.1 A large variety of disposition measures shall be made available to the competent authority, allowing for flexibility so as to avoid institutionalization to the greatest extent possible. Such measures, some of which may be combined, include:

(a) Care, guidance and supervision orders;
(b) Probation;
(c) Community service orders;
(d) Financial penalties, compensation and restitution;
(e) Intermediate treatment and other treatment orders;
(f) Orders to participate in group counselling and similar activities;
(g) Orders concerning foster care, living communities or other educational settings;
(h) Other relevant orders.

18.2 No juvenile shall be removed from parental supervision, whether partly or entire l y, unless the circumstances of her or his case make this necessary.

Commentary

Rule 18.1 attempts to enumerate some of the important reactions and sanctions that have been practised and proved successful thus far, in different legal systems. On the whole they represent promising opinions that deserve replication and further development. The rule does not enumerate staffing requirements because of possible shortages of adequate staff in some regions; in those regions measures requiring less staff may be tried or developed. The examples given in rule 18.1 have in common, above all, a reliance on and an appeal to the community for the effective implementation of alternative dispositions. Community-based correction is a traditional measure that has taken on many aspects. On that basis, relevant authorities should be encouraged to offer community-based services.

Rule 18.2 points to the importance of the family which, according to article 10, paragraph l, of the International Covenant on Economic, Social and Cultural Rights, is "the natural and fundamental group unit of society". Within the family, the parents have not only the right but also the responsibility to care for and supervise their children. Rule 18.2, therefore, requires that the separation of children from their parents is a measure of last resort. It may be resorted to only when the facts of the case clearly warrant this grave step (for example child abuse).

19. Least possible use of institutionalization

19.1 The placement of a juvenile in an institution shall always be a disposition of last resort and for the minimum necessary period.

Commentary

Progressive criminology advocates the use of non-institutional over institutional treatment. Little or no difference has been found in terms of the success of institutionalization as compared to non-institutionalization. The many adverse influences on an individual that seem unavoidable within any institutional setting evidently cannot be outbalanced by treatment efforts. This is especially the case for juveniles, who are vulnerable to negative influences. Moreover, the negative effects, not only of loss of liberty but also of separation from the usual social environment, are certainly more acute for juveniles than for adults because of their early stage of development.

Rule 19 aims at restricting institutionalization in two regards: in quantity ("last resort") and in time ("minimum necessary period"). Rule 19 reflects one of the basic guiding principles of resolution 4 of the Sixth United Nations Congress: a juvenile offender should not be incarcerated unless there is no other appropriate response. The rule, therefore, makes the appeal that if a juvenile must be institutionalized, the loss of liberty should be restricted to the least possible degree, with special institutional arrangements for confinement and bearing in mind the differences in kinds of offenders, offences and institutions. In fact, priority should be given to "open" over "closed" institutions. Furthermore, any facility should be of a correctional or educational rather than of a prison type.

20. Avoidance of unnecessary delay
20.1 Each case shall from the outset be handled expeditiously, without any unnecessary delay.

Commentary
The speedy conduct of formal procedures in juvenile cases is a paramount concern. Otherwise whatever good may be achieved by the procedure and the disposition is at risk. As time passes, the juvenile will find it increasingly difficult, if not impossible, to relate the procedure and disposition to the offence, both intellectually and psychologically.

21. Records
21.1 Records of juvenile offenders shall be kept strictly confidential and closed to third parties. Access to such records shall be limited to persons directly concerned with the disposition of the case at hand or other duly authorized persons.

21.2 Records of juvenile offenders shall not be used in adult proceedings in subsequent cases involving the same offender.

Commentary
The rule attempts to achieve a balance between conflicting interests connected with records or files: those of the police, prosecution and other authorities in improving control versus the interests of the juvenile offender. (See also rule 8.) "Other duly authorized persons" would generally include among others, researchers.

22. Need for professionalism and training
22.1 Professional education, in-service training, refresher courses and other appropriate modes of instruction shall be utilized to establish and maintain the necessary professional competence of all personnel dealing with juvenile cases.

22.2 Juvenile justice personnel shall reflect the diversity of juveniles who come into contact with the juvenile justice system. Efforts shall be made to ensure the fair representation of women and minorities in juvenile justice agencies.

Commentary

The authorities competent for disposition may be persons with very different backgrounds (magistrates in the United Kingdom of Great Britain and Northern Ireland and in regions influenced by the common law system; legally trained judges in countries using Roman law and in regions influenced by them; and elsewhere elected or appointed laymen or jurists, members of community-based boards, etc.). For all these authorities, a minimum training in law, sociology, psychology, criminology and behavioural sciences would be required. This is considered as important as the organizational specialization and independence of the competent authority.

For social workers and probation officers, it might not be feasible to require professional specialization as a prerequisite for taking over any function dealing with juvenile offenders. Thus, professional on-the job instruction would be minimum qualifications.

Professional qualifications are an essential element in ensuring the impartial and effective administration of juvenile justice. Accordingly, it is necessary to improve the recruitment, advancement and professional training of personnel and to provide them with the necessary means to enable them to properly fulfil their functions.

All political, social, sexual, racial, religious, cultural or any other kind of discrimination in the selection, appointment and advancement of juvenile justice personnel should be avoided in order to achieve impartiality in the administration of juvenile justice. This was recommended by the Sixth Congress. Furthermore, the Sixth Congress called on Member States to ensure the fair and equal treatment of women as criminal justice personnel and recommended that special measures should be taken to recruit, train and facilitate the advancement of female personnel in juvenile justice administration.

PART FOUR
NON-INSTITUTIONAL TREATMENT

23. Effective implementation of disposition

23.1 Appropriate provisions shall be made for the implementation of orders of the competent authority, as referred to in rule 14.1 above, by that authority itself or by some other authority as circumstances may require

23.2 Such provisions shall include the power to modify the orders as the competent authority may deem necessary from time to time, provided that such modification shall be determined in accordance with the principles contained in these Rules.

Commentary

Disposition in juvenile cases, more so than in adult cases, tends to influence the offender's life for a long period of time. Thus, it is important that the competent authority or an independent body (parole board, probation office, youth welfare institutions or others) with qualifications equal to those of the competent authority that originally disposed of the case should monitor the implementation of the disposition. In some countries, a juge de l'execution des peines has been installed for this purpose.

The composition, powers and functions of the authority must be flexible; they are described in general terms in rule 23 in order to ensure wide acceptability.

24. Provision of needed assistance

24.1 Efforts shall be made to provide juveniles, at all stages of the proceedings, with necessary assistance such as lodging, education or vocational training, employment or any other assistance, helpful and practical, in order to facilitate the rehabilitative process.

Commentary

The promotion of the well-being of the juvenile is of paramount consideration. Thus, rule 24 emphasizes the importance of providing requisite facilities, services and other necessary assistance as may further the best interests of the juvenile throughout the rehabilitative process.

25. Mobilization of volunteers and other community services

25.1 Volunteers, voluntary organizations, local institutions and other community resources shall be called upon to contribute effectively to the rehabilitation of the juvenile in a community setting and, as far as possible, within the family unit.

Commentary

This rule reflects the need for a rehabilitative orientation of all work with juvenile offenders. Co-operation with the community is indispensable if the directives of the competent authority are to be carried out effectively. Volunteers and voluntary services, in particular, have proved to be valuable resources but are at present underutilized. In some instances, the co-operation of ex-offenders (including ex-addicts) can be of considerable assistance.

Rule 25 emanates from the principles laid down in rules 1.1 to 1.6 and follows the relevant provisions of the International Covenant on Civil and Political Rights.

PART FIVE
INSTITUTIONAL TREATMENT

26. Objectives of institutional treatment

26.1 The objective of training and treatment of juveniles placed in institutions is to provide care, protection, education and vocational skills, with a view to assisting them to assume socially constructive and productive roles in society.

26.2 Juveniles in institutions shall receive care, protection and all necessary assistance-social, educational, vocational, psychological, medical and physical-that they may require because of their age, sex, and personality and in the interest of their wholesome development.

26.3 Juveniles in institutions shall be kept separate from adults and shall be detained in a separate institution or in a separate part of an institution also holding adults.

26.4 Young female offenders placed in an institution deserve special attention as to their personal needs and problems. They shall by no means receive less care, protection, assistance, treatment and training than young male offenders. Their fair treatment shall be ensured.

26.5 In the interest and well-being of the institutionalized juvenile, the parents or guardians shall have a right of access.

26.6 Inter-ministerial and inter-departmental co-operation shall be fostered for the purpose of providing adequate academic or, as appropriate, vocational training to institutionalized juveniles, with a view to ensuring that they do no leave the institution at an educational disadvantage.

Commentary

The objectives of institutional treatment as stipulated in rules 26.1 and 26.2 would be acceptable to any system and culture. However, they have not yet been attained everywhere, and much more has to be done in this respect.

Medical and psychological assistance, in particular, are extremely important for institutionalized drug addicts, violent and mentally ill young persons.

The avoidance of negative influences through adult offenders and the safeguarding of the well-being of juveniles in an institutional setting, as stipulated in rule 26.3, are in line with one of the basic guiding principles of the Rules, as set out by the Sixth Congress in its resolution 4. The rule does not prevent States from taking other measures against the negative influences of adult offenders, which are at least as effective as the measures mentioned in the rule. (See also rule 13.4)

Rule 26.4 addresses the fact that female offenders normally receive less attention than their male counterparts. as pointed out by the Sixth Congress. In particular, resolution 9 of the Sixth Congress calls for the fair treatment of female offenders at every stage of criminal justice processes and for special attention to their particular problems and needs while in custody. Moreover, this rule should also be considered in the light of the Caracas Declaration of the Sixth Congress, which, inter alia, calls for equal treatment in criminal justice administration, and against the background of the Declaration on the Elimination of Discrimination against Women and the Convention on the Elimination of All Forms of Discrimination against Women.

The right of access (rule 26.5) follows from the provisions of rules 7.1, 10.1, 15.2 and 18.2. Inter-ministerial and inter-departmental co-operation (rule 26.6) are of particular importance in the interest of generally enhancing the quality of institutional treatment and training.

27. Application of the Standard Minimum Rules for the Treatment of Prisoners adopted by the United Nations

27.1 The Standard Minimum Rules for the Treatment of Prisoners and related recommendations shall be applicable as far as relevant to the treatment of juvenile offenders in institutions, including those in detention pending adjudication.

27.2 Efforts shall be made to implement the relevant principles laid down in the Standard Minimum Rules for the Treatment of Prisoners to the largest possible extent so as to meet the varying needs of juveniles specific to their age, sex and personality.

Commentary

The Standard Minimum Rules for the Treatment of Prisoners were among the first instruments of this kind to be promulgated by the United Nations. It is generally agreed that they have had a world-wide impact. Although there are still countries where implementation is more an aspiration than a fact, those Standard Minimum Rules continue to be an important influence in the humane and equitable administration of correctional institutions.

Some essential protections covering juvenile offenders in institutions are contained in the Standard Minimum Rules for the Treatment of Prisoners (accommodation, architecture, bedding, clothing, complaints and requests, contact with the outside world, food, medical care, religious service, separation of ages, staffing, work, etc.) as are provisions concerning punishment and discipline, and restraint for dangerous offenders. It would not be appropriate to modify those Standard Minimum Rules according to the particular characteristics of institutions for juvenile offenders within the scope of the Standard Minimum Rules for the Administration of Juvenile Justice.

Rule 27 focuses on the necessary requirements for juveniles in institutions (rule 27.1) as well as on the varying needs specific to their age, sex and personality (rule 27.2). Thus, the objectives and content of the rule interrelate to the relevant provisions of the Standard Minimum Rules for the Treatment of Prisoners.

28. Frequent and early recourse to conditional release

28.1 Conditional release from an institution shall be used by the appropriate authority to the greatest possible extent, and shall be granted at the earliest possible time.

28.2 Juveniles released conditionally from an institution shall be assisted and supervised by an appropriate authority and shall receive full support by the community.

Commentary

The power to order conditional release may rest with the competent authority, as mentioned in rule 14.1 or with some other authority. In view of this, it is adequate to refer here to the "appropriate,' rather than to the "competent" authority.

Circumstances permitting, conditional release shall be preferred to serving a full sentence. Upon evidence of satisfactory progress towards rehabilitation, even offenders who had been deemed dangerous at the time of their institutionalization can be conditionally released whenever feasible. Like probation , such release may be conditional on the satisfactory fulfilment of the requirements specified by the relevant authorities for a period of time established in the decision, for example relating to "good behaviour" of the offender, attendance in community programmes, residence in half-way houses, etc.

In the case of offenders conditionally released from an institution, assistance and supervision by a probation or other officer (particularly where probation has not yet been adopted) should be provided and community support should be encouraged.

29. Semi-institutional arrangements

29.1 Efforts shall be made to provide semi-institutional arrangements, such as half-way houses, educational homes, day-time training centres and other such appropriate arrangements that may assist juveniles in their proper reintegration into society.

Commentary

The importance of care following a period of institutionalization should not be underestimated. This rule emphasizes the necessity of forming a net of semi-institutional arrangements.

This rule also emphasizes the need for a diverse range of facilities and services designed to meet the different needs of young offenders re-entering the community and to provide guidance and structural support as an important step towards successful reintegration into society.

PART SIX
RESEARCH, PLANNING, POLICY FORMULATION AND EVALUATION

30. Research as a basis for planning, policy formulation and evaluation

30.1 Efforts shall be made to organize and promote necessary research as a basis for effective planning and policy formulation.

30.2 Efforts shall be made to review and appraise periodically the trends, problems and causes of juvenile delinquency and crime as well as the varying particular needs of juveniles in custody.

30.3 Efforts shall be made to establish a regular evaluative research mechanism built into the system of juvenile justice administration and to collect and analyse relevant data and information for appropriate assessment and future improvement and reform of the administration.

30.4 The delivery of services in juvenile justice administration shall be systematically planned and implemented as an integral part of national development efforts.

Commentary

The utilization of research as a basis for an informed juvenile justice policy is widely acknowledged as an important mechanism for keeping practices abreast of advances in knowledge and the continuing development and improvement of the juvenile justice system. The mutual feedback between research and policy is especially important in juvenile justice. With rapid and often drastic changes in the life-styles of the young and in the forms and dimensions of juvenile crime, the societal and justice responses to juvenile crime and delinquency quickly become outmoded and inadequate.

Rule 30 thus establishes standards for integrating research into the process of policy formulation and application in juvenile justice administration. The rule draws particular attention to the need for regular review and evaluation of existing programmes and measures and for planning within the broader context of overall development objectives.

A constant appraisal of the needs of juveniles, as well as the trends and problems of delinquency, is a prerequisite for improving the methods of formulating appropriate policies and establishing adequate interventions, at both formal and informal levels. In this context, research by independent persons and bodies should be facilitated by responsible agencies, and it may be valuable to obtain and to take into account the views of juveniles themselves, not only those who come into contact with the system.

The process of planning must particularly emphasize a more effective and equitable system for the delivery of necessary services. Towards that end, there should be a comprehensive and regular assessment of the wide-ranging, particular needs and problems of juveniles and an identification of clear-cut priori ties. In that connection, there should also be a co-ordination in the use of existing resources, including alternatives and community support that would be suitable in setting up specific procedures designed to implement and monitor established programmes.

3. Body of Principles for the Protection of All Persons under Any Form of Detention or Imprisonment, 1988

One of the more significant forms of protection of minors, children and juveniles in the matter of criminal procedure is contained within the provisions of the Body of Principles for the Protection of All Persons under Any Form of Detention or Imprisonment. This instrument was adopted by General Assembly Resolution 43/173, on 9 December 1988. The instrument was subsequently completed by another one, the Basic Principles for the Treatment of Prisoners (Resolution 45/111, 14 December 1990). Although the Body of Principles brings together many rules about the protection of children, minors and juveniles, these rules have been variously violated by many states. Some violations have been very grave, and therefore relatively harmful to the philosophy of the international human rights law. And serious violations have not only occurred in Europe, but to a great extent in Asia, and specifically in some

Middle East countries. Even so, the provisions of this Body of Principles constitute significant support for fair justice for all individuals, including juveniles or children. The relevant provisions provide that:

Scope of the Body of Principles
These principles apply for the protection of all persons under any form of detention or imprisonment.

Use of Terms
For the purposes of the Body of Principles:

(a) "Arrest" means the act of apprehending a person for the alleged commission of an offence or by the action of an authority;

(b) "Detained person" means any person deprived of personal liberty except as a result of conviction for an offence;

(c) "Imprisoned person" means any person deprived of personal liberty as a result of conviction for an offence;

(d) "Detention" means the condition of detained persons as defined above;

(e) "Imprisonment" means the condition of imprisoned persons as defined above;

(f) The words "a judicial or other authority" means a judicial or other authority under the law whose status and tenure should afford the strongest possible guarantees of competence, impartiality and independence.

Principle 1

All persons under any form of detention or imprisonment shall be treated in a humane manner and with respect for the inherent dignity of the human person.

Principle 2

Arrest, detention or imprisonment shall only be carried out strictly in accordance with the provisions of the law and by competent officials or persons authorized for that purpose.

Principle 5

1. These principles shall be applied to all persons within the territory of any given State, without distinction of any kind, such as race, colour, sex, language, religion or religious belief, political or other opinion, national, ethnic or social origin, property, birth or other status.

2. Measures applied under the law and designed solely to protect the rights and special status of women, especially pregnant women and

nursing mothers, children and juveniles, aged, sick or handicapped persons shall not be deemed to be discriminatory. The need for, and the application of, such measures shall always be subject to review by a judicial or other authority.

Principle 16

1. Promptly after arrest and after each transfer from one place of detention or imprisonment to another, a detained or imprisoned person shall be entitled to notify or to require the competent authority to notify members of his family or other appropriate persons of his choice of his arrest, detention or imprisonment or of the transfer and of the place where he is kept in custody.

2. If a detained or imprisoned person is a foreigner, he shall also be promptly informed of his right to communicate by appropriate means with a consular post or the diplomatic mission of the State of which he is a national or which is otherwise entitled to receive such communication in accordance with international law or with the representative of the competent international organization, if he is a refugee or is otherwise under the protection of an intergovernmental organization.

3. If a detained or imprisoned person is a juvenile or is incapable of understanding his entitlement, the competent authority shall on its own initiative undertake the notification referred to in the present principle. Special attention shall be given to notifying parents or guardians.

4. Any notification referred to in the present principle shall be made or permitted to be made without delay. The competent authority may however delay a notification for a reasonable period where exceptional needs of the investigation so require.

Principle 31

The appropriate authorities shall endeavour to ensure, according to domestic law, assistance when needed to dependent and, in particular, minor members of the families of detained or imprisoned persons and shall devote a particular measure of care to the appropriate custody of children left with out supervision.

4. United Nations Guidelines for the Prevention of Juvenile Delinquency ("The Riyadh Guidelines"), 1990

One of the important instruments governing the appropriate treatment of juveniles is the 1990United Nations Guidelines for the Prevention of

Juvenile Delinquency (the Riyadh Guidelines), General Assembly Resolution 45/112. This instrument, like many other direct or indirect instruments relating to the rights of children, does not have the legally binding effect of a treaty, and its legal validity therefore has to be considered under other conditions or rules of international law such as the general principles of law, customary international law, or the real value of the resolutions of the General Assembly. The intention of this instrument is to decrease, as much as possible, the concept of criminality of juveniles and to find ways for preventing juvenile delinquency. For this reason, it formulates that:

I. FUNDAMENTAL PRINCIPLES

1. The prevention of juvenile delinquency is an essential part of crime prevention in society. By engaging in lawful, socially useful activities and adopting a humanistic orientation towards society and outlook on life, young persons can develop non-criminogenic attitudes.

2. The successful prevention of juvenile delinquency requires efforts on the part of the entire society to ensure the harmonious development of adolescents, with respect for and promotion of their personality from early childhood.

3. For the purposes of the interpretation of the present Guidelines, a child-centred orientation should be pursued. Young persons should have an active role and partnership within society and should not be considered as mere objects of socialization or control.

4. In the implementation of the present Guidelines, in accordance with national legal systems, the well-being of young persons from their early childhood should be the focus of any preventive programme.

5. The need for and importance of progressive delinquency prevention policies and the systematic study and the elaboration of measures should be recognized. These should avoid criminalizing and penalizing a child for behaviour that does not cause serious damage to the development of the child or harm to others. Such policies and measures should involve:

(a) The provision of opportunities, in particular educational opportunities, to meet the varying needs of young persons and to serve as a supportive framework for safeguarding the personal development of all young persons, particularly those who are demonstrably endangered or at social risk and are in need of special care and protection;

(b) Specialized philosophies and approaches for delinquency prevention, on the basis of laws, processes, institutions, facilities and a service delivery network aimed at reducing the motivation, need and opportunity for, or conditions giving rise to, the commission of infractions;

(c) Official intervention to be pursued primarily in the overall interest of the young person and guided by fairness and equity;

(d) Safeguarding the well-being, development, rights and interests of all young persons;

(e) Consideration that youthful behaviour or conduct that does not conform to overall social norms and values is often part of the maturation and growth process and tends to disappear spontaneously in most individuals with the transition to adulthood;

(f) Awareness that, in the predominant opinion of experts, labelling a young person as "deviant", "delinquent" or "pre-delinquent" often contributes to the development of a consistent pattern of undesirable behaviour by young persons.

6. Community-based services and programmes should be developed for the prevention of juvenile delinquency, particularly where no agencies have yet been established. Formal agencies of social control should only be utilized as a means of last resort.

II. SCOPE OF THE GUIDELINES

7. The present Guidelines should be interpreted and implemented within the broad framework of the Universal Declaration of Human Rights, the International Covenant on Economic, Social and Cultural Rights, the International Covenant on Civil and Political Rights, the Declaration of the Rights of the Child and the Convention on the Rights of the Child, and in the context of the United Nations Standard Minimum Rules for the Administration of Juvenile Justice (The Beijing Rules), as well as other instruments and norms relating to the rights, interests and well-being of all children and young persons.

8. The present Guidelines should also be implemented in the context of the economic, social and cultural conditions prevailing in each Member State.

III. GENERAL PREVENTION

9. Comprehensive prevention plans should be instituted at every level of Government and include the following:

(a) In-depth analyses of the problem and inventories of programmes, services, facilities and resources available;

(b) Well-defined responsibilities for the qualified agencies, institutions and personnel involved in preventive efforts;

(c) Mechanisms for the appropriate co-ordination of prevention efforts between governmental and non-governmental agencies;
(d) Policies, programmes and strategies based on prognostic studies to be continuously monitored and carefully evaluated in the course of implementation;
(e) Methods for effectively reducing the opportunity to commit delinquent acts;
(f) Community involvement through a wide range of services and programmes;
(g) Close interdisciplinary co-operation between national, State, provincial and local governments, with the involvement of the private sector representative citizens of the community to be served, and labour, child-care, health education, social, law enforcement and judicial agencies in taking concerted action to prevent juvenile delinquency and youth crime;
(h) Youth participation in delinquency prevention policies and processes, including recourse to community resources, youth self-help, and victim compensation and assistance programmes;
(i) Specialized personnel at all levels.

IV. SOCIALIZATION PROCESSES

10. Emphasis should be placed on preventive policies facilitating the successful socialization and integration of all children and young persons, in particular through the family, the community, peer groups, schools, vocational training and the world of work, as well as through voluntary organizations. Due respect should be given to the proper personal development of children and young persons, and they should be accepted as full and equal partners in socialization and integration processes.

A. Family

11. Every society should place a high priority on the needs and well-being of the family and of all its members.

12. Since the family is the central unit responsible for the primary socialization of children, governmental and social efforts to preserve the integrity of the family, including the extended family, should be pursued. The society has a responsibility to assist the family in providing care and protection and in ensuring the physical and mental well-being of children. Adequate arrangements including day-care should be provided.

13. Governments should establish policies that are conducive to the bringing up of children in stable and settled family environments. Families

in need of assistance in the resolution of conditions of instability or conflict should be provided with requisite services.

14. Where a stable and settled family environment is lacking and when community efforts to assist parents in this regard have failed and the extended family cannot fulfil this role, alternative placements, including foster care and adoption, should be considered. Such placements should replicate, to the extent possible, a stable and settled family environment, while, at the same time, establishing a sense of permanency for children, thus avoiding problems associated with "foster drift".

15. Special attention should be given to children of families affected by problems brought about by rapid and uneven economic, social and cultural change, in particular the children of indigenous, migrant and refugee families. As such changes may disrupt the social capacity of the family to secure the traditional rearing and nurturing of children, often as a result of role and culture conflict, innovative and socially constructive modalities for the socialization of children have to be designed.

16. Measures should be taken and programmes developed to provide families with the opportunity to learn about parental roles and obligations as regards child development and child care, promoting positive parent-child relationships, sensitizing parents to the problems of children and young persons and encouraging their involvement in family and community-based activities.

17. Governments should take measures to promote family cohesion and harmony and to discourage the separation of children from their parents, unless circumstances affecting the welfare and future of the child leave no viable alternative.

18. It is important to emphasize the socialization function of the family and extended family; it is also equally important to recognize the future role, responsibilities, participation and partnership of young persons in society.

19. In ensuring the right of the child to proper socialization, Governments and other agencies should rely on existing social and legal agencies, but, whenever traditional institutions and customs are no longer effective, they should also provide and allow for innovative measures.

B. Education

20. Governments are under an obligation to make public education accessible to all young persons.

21. Education systems should, in addition to their academic and vocational training activities, devote particular attention to the following:

(a) Teaching of basic values and developing respect for the child's own cultural identity and patterns, for the social values of the country in which the child is living, for civilizations different from the child's own and for human rights and fundamental freedoms;
(b) Promotion and development of the personality, talents and mental and physical abilities of young people to their fullest potential;
(c) Involvement of young persons as active and effective participants in, rather than mere objects of, the educational process;
(d) Undertaking activities that foster a sense of identity with and of belonging to the school and the community;
(e) Encouragement of young persons to understand and respect diverse views and opinions, as well as cultural and other differences;
(f) Provision of information and guidance regarding vocational training, employment opportunities and career development;
(g) Provision of positive emotional support to young persons and the avoidance of psychological maltreatment;
(h) Avoidance of harsh disciplinary measures, particularly corporal punishment.

22. Educational systems should seek to work together with parents, community organizations and agencies concerned with the activities of young persons.

23. Young persons and their families should be informed about the law and their rights and responsibilities under the law, as well as the universal value system, including United Nations instruments.

24. Educational systems should extend particular care and attention to young persons who are at social risk. Specialized prevention programmes and educational materials, curricula, approaches and tools should be developed and fully utilized.

25. Special attention should be given to comprehensive policies and strategies for the prevention of alcohol, drug and other substance abuse by young persons. Teachers and other professionals should be equipped and trained to prevent and deal with these problems. Information on the use and abuse of drugs, including alcohol, should be made available to the student body.

26. Schools should serve as resource and referral centres for the provision of medical, counselling and other services to young persons, particularly those with special needs and suffering from abuse, neglect, victimization and exploitation.

27. Through a variety of educational programmes, teachers and other adults and the student body should be sensitized to the problems, needs and perceptions of young persons, particularly those belonging to

underprivileged, disadvantaged, ethnic or other minority and low-income groups.

28. School systems should attempt to meet and promote the highest professional and educational standards with respect to curricula, teaching and learning methods and approaches, and the recruitment and training of qualified teachers. Regular monitoring and assessment of performance by the appropriate professional organizations and authorities should be ensured.

29. School systems should plan, develop and implement extracurricular activities of interest to young persons, in co-operation with community groups.

30. Special assistance should be given to children and young persons who find it difficult to comply with attendance codes, and to "drop-outs".

31. Schools should promote policies and rules that are fair and just; students should be represented in bodies formulating school policy, including policy on discipline, and decision-making.

C. Community

32. Community-based services and programmes which respond to the special needs, problems, interests and concerns of young persons and which offer appropriate counselling and guidance to young persons and their families should be developed, or strengthened where they exist.

33. Communities should provide, or strengthen where they exist, a wide range of community-based support measures for young persons, including community development centres, recreational facilities and services to respond to the special problems of children who are at social risk. In providing these helping measures, respect for individual rights should be ensured.

34. Special facilities should be set up to provide adequate shelter for young persons who are no longer able to live at home or who do not have homes to live in.

35. A range of services and helping measures should be provided to deal with the difficulties experienced by young persons in the transition to adulthood. Such services should include special programmes for young drug abusers which emphasize care, counselling, assistance and therapy-oriented interventions.

36. Voluntary organizations providing services for young persons should be given financial and other support by Governments and other institutions.

37. Youth organizations should be created or strengthened at the local level and given full participatory status in the management of community

affairs. These organizations should encourage youth to organize collective and voluntary projects, particularly projects aimed at helping young persons in need of assistance.

38. Government agencies should take special responsibility and provide necessary services for homeless or street children; information about local facilities, accommodation, employment and other forms and sources of help should be made readily available to young persons.

39. A wide range of recreational facilities and services of particular interest to young persons should be established and made easily accessible to them.

D. Mass media

40. The mass media should be encouraged to ensure that young persons have access to information and material from a diversity of national and international sources.

41. The mass media should be encouraged to portray the positive contribution of young persons to society.

42. The mass media should be encouraged to disseminate information on the existence of services, facilities and opportunities for young persons in society.

43. The mass media generally, and the television and film media in particular, should be encouraged to minimize the level of pornography, drugs and violence portrayed and to display violence and exploitation disfavourably, as well as to avoid demeaning and degrading presentations, especially of children, women and interpersonal relations, and to promote egalitarian principles and roles.

44. The mass media should be aware of its extensive social role and responsibility, as well as its influence, in communications relating to youthful drug and alcohol abuse. It should use its power for drug abuse prevention by relaying consistent messages through a balanced approach. Effective drug awareness campaigns at all levels should be promoted.

V. SOCIAL POLICY

45. Government agencies should give high priority to plans and programmes for young persons and should provide sufficient funds and other resources for the effective delivery of services, facilities and staff for adequate medical and mental health care, nutrition, housing and other relevant services, including drug and alcohol abuse prevention and treatment, ensuring that such resources reach and actually benefit young persons.

46. The institutionalization of young persons should be a measure of last resort and for the minimum necessary period, and the best interests of the young person should be of paramount importance. Criteria authorizing formal intervention of this type should be strictly defined and limited to the following situations: (a) where the child or young person has suffered harm that has been inflicted by the parents or guardians; (b) where the child or young person has been sexually, physically or emotionally abused by the parents or guardians; (c) where the child or young person has been neglected, abandoned or exploited by the parents or guardians; (d) where the child or young person is threatened by physical or moral danger due to the behaviour of the parents or guardians; and (e) where a serious physical or psychological danger to the child or young person has manifested itself in his or her own behaviour and neither the parents, the guardians, the juvenile himself or herself nor non-residential community services can meet the danger by means other than institutionalization.

47. Government agencies should provide young persons with the opportunity of continuing in full-time education, funded by the State where parents or guardians are unable to support the young persons, and of receiving work experience.

48. Programmes to prevent delinquency should be planned and developed on the basis of reliable, scientific research findings, and periodically monitored, evaluated and adjusted accordingly.

49. Scientific information should be disseminated to the professional community and to the public at large about the sort of behaviour or situation which indicates or may result in physical and psychological victimization, harm and abuse, as well as exploitation, of young persons.

50. Generally, participation in plans and programmes should be voluntary. Young persons themselves should be involved in their formulation, development and implementation.

51. Government should begin or continue to explore, develop and implement policies, measures and strategies within and outside the criminal justice system to prevent domestic violence against and affecting young persons and to ensure fair treatment to these victims of domestic violence.

VI. LEGISLATION AND JUVENILE JUSTICE ADMINISTRATION

52. Governments should enact and enforce specific laws and procedures to promote and protect the rights and well-being of all young persons.

53. Legislation preventing the victimization, abuse, exploitation and the use for criminal activities of children and young persons should be enacted and enforced.

54. No child or young person should be subjected to harsh or degrading correction or punishment measures at home, in schools or in any other institutions.

55. Legislation and enforcement aimed at restricting and controlling accessibility of weapons of any sort to children and young persons should be pursued.

56. In order to prevent further stigmatization, victimization and criminalization of young persons, legislation should be enacted to ensure that any conduct not considered an offence or not penalized if committed by an adult is not considered an offence and not penalized if committed by a young person.

57. Consideration should be given to the establishment of an office of ombudsman or similar independent organ, which would ensure that the status, rights and interests of young persons are upheld and that proper referral to available services is made. The ombudsman or other organ designated would also supervise the implementation of the Riyadh Guidelines, the Beijing Rules and the Rules for the Protection of Juveniles Deprived of their Liberty. The ombudsman or other organ would, at regular intervals, publish a report on the progress made and on the difficulties encountered in the implementation of the instrument. Child advocacy services should also be established.

58. Law enforcement and other relevant personnel, of both sexes, should be trained to respond to the special needs of young persons and should be familiar with and use, to the maximum extent possible, programmes and referral possibilities for the diversion of young persons from the justice system.

59. Legislation should be enacted and strictly enforced to protect children and young persons from drug abuse and drug traffickers.

VII. RESEARCH, POLICY DEVELOPMENT AND CO-ORDINATION

60. Efforts should be made and appropriate mechanisms established to promote, on both a multidisciplinary and an interdisciplinary basis, interaction and co-ordination between economic, social, education and health agencies and services, the justice system, youth, community and development agencies and other relevant institutions.

61. The exchange of information, experience and expertise gained through projects, programmes, practices and initiatives relating to youth

crime, delinquency prevention and juvenile justice should be intensified at the national, regional and international levels.

62. Regional and international co-operation on matters of youth crime, delinquency prevention and juvenile justice involving practitioners, experts and decision makers should be further developed and strengthened.

63. Technical and scientific co-operation on practical and policy-related matters, particularly in training, pilot and demonstration projects, and on specific issues concerning the prevention of youth crime and juvenile delinquency should be strongly supported by all Governments, the United Nations system and other concerned organizations.

64. Collaboration should be encouraged in undertaking scientific research with respect to effective modalities for youth crime and juvenile delinquency prevention and the findings of such research should be widely disseminated and evaluated.

65. Appropriate United Nations bodies, institutes, agencies and offices should pursue close collaboration and co-ordination on various questions related to children juvenile justice and youth crime and juvenile delinquency prevention.

66. On the basis of the present Guidelines, the United Nations Secretariat, in co-operation with interested institutions, should play an active role in the conduct of research, scientific collaboration, the formulation of policy options and the review and monitoring of their implementation, and should serve as a source of reliable information on effective modalities for delinquency prevention.

5. United Nations Rules for the Protection of Juveniles Deprived of their Liberty, 1990

The need to increase the rights of juveniles within the legislation of states has been one of the most important aspects of instruments that discuss human rights. This is particularly important in the case of those covered by the Convention, and who have been deprived of their civil liberties. The United Nations Rules for the Protection of Juveniles Deprived of their Liberty was thus adopted in 1990 by General Assembly Resolution 45/113. The purpose of this instrument is to protect juveniles accused of committing crimes. This instrument also emphasises the equal application of its rules with regard to juveniles. It states that states should implement the rules impartially, without discrimination of any kind as to colour, race, sex, religion, language, political or other opinion, cultural beliefs or practices, property, ethnic or social origin, birth or family status and disability. Of more importance is its clear statement about the age under which a person is recognized as juvenile, which says that "a juvenile is every person under the age of 18". This means that states should not bring in other arguments concerning the age limit for juveniles. However, states are free to accept a higher limit than 18. Although the significance of this instrument cannot be denied, its provisions are not respected in the actual practice of states parties. They have been repeatedly violated by members of the United Nations, and these violations have created a substantive doubt about the implementation of the principles of the human rights law. The United Nations Rules provides that:

I. Fundamental Perspectives

1. The juvenile justice system should uphold the rights and safety and promote the physical and mental well-being of juveniles. Imprisonment should be used as a last resort.

2. Juveniles should only be deprived of their liberty in accordance with the principles and procedures set forth in these Rules and in the United Nations Standard Minimum Rules for the Administration of Juvenile Justice (The Beijing Rules). Deprivation of the liberty of a juvenile should be a disposition of last resort and for the minimum necessary period and should be limited to exceptional cases. The length of the sanction should be determined by the judicial authority, without precluding the possibility of his or her early release.

3. The Rules are intended to establish minimum standards accepted by the United Nations for the protection of juveniles deprived of their liberty in all forms, consistent with human rights and fundamental freedoms, and with a view to counteracting the detrimental effects of all types of detention and to fostering integration in society.

4. The Rules should be applied impartially, without discrimination of any kind as to race, colour, sex, age, language, religion, nationality, political or other opinion, cultural beliefs or practices, property, birth or family status, ethnic or social origin, and disability. The religious and cultural beliefs, practices and moral concepts of the juvenile should be respected.

5. The Rules are designed to serve as convenient standards of reference and to provide encouragement and guidance to professionals involved in the management of the juvenile justice system.

6. The Rules should be made readily available to juvenile justice personnel in their national languages. Juveniles who are not fluent in the language spoken by the personnel of the detention facility should have the right

to the services of an interpreter free of charge whenever necessary, in particular during medical examinations and disciplinary proceedings.

7. Where appropriate, States should incorporate the Rules into their legislation or amend it accordingly and provide effective remedies for their breach, including compensation when injuries are inflicted on juveniles. States should also monitor the application of the Rules.

8. The competent authorities should constantly seek to increase the awareness of the public that the care of detained juveniles and preparation for their return to society is a social service of great importance, and to this end active steps should be taken to foster open contacts between the juveniles and the local community.

9. Nothing in the Rules should be interpreted as precluding the application of the relevant United Nations and human rights instruments and standards, recognized by the international community, that are more conducive to ensuring the rights, care and protection of juveniles, children and all young persons.

10. In the event that the practical application of particular Rules contained in sections II to V, inclusive, presents any conflict with the Rules contained in the present section, compliance with the latter shall be regarded as the predominant requirement.

II. Scope and Application of the Rules

11. For the purposes of the Rules, the following definitions should apply:

(a) A juvenile is every person under the age of 18. The age limit below which it should not be permitted to deprive a child of his or her liberty should be determined by law;

(b) The deprivation of liberty means any form of detention or imprisonment or the placement of a person in a public or private custodial setting, from which this person is not permitted to leave at will, by order of any judicial, administrative or other public authority.

12. The deprivation of liberty should be effected in conditions and circumstances which ensure respect for the human rights of juveniles. Juveniles detained in facilities should be guaranteed the benefit of meaningful activities and programmes which would serve to promote and sustain their health and self-respect, to foster their sense of responsibility and encourage those attitudes and skills that will assist them in developing their potential as members of society.

13. Juveniles deprived of their liberty shall not for any reason related to their status be denied the civil, economic, political, social or cultural

rights to which they are entitled under national or international law, and which are compatible with the deprivation of liberty.

14. The protection of the individual rights of juveniles with special regard to the legality of the execution of the detention measures shall be ensured by the competent authority, while the objectives of social integration should be secured by regular inspections and other means of control carried out, according to international standards, national laws and regulations, by a duly constituted body authorized to visit the juveniles and not belonging to the detention facility.

15. The Rules apply to all types and forms of detention facilities in which juveniles are deprived of their liberty. Sections I, II, IV and V of the Rules apply to all detention facilities and institutional settings in which juveniles are detained, and section III applies specifically to juveniles under arrest or awaiting trial.

16. The Rules shall be implemented in the context of the economic, social and cultural conditions prevailing in each Member State.

III. Juveniles under Arrest or Awaiting Trail

17. Juveniles who are detained under arrest or awaiting trial ("untried") are presumed innocent and shall be treated as such. Detention before trial shall be avoided to the extent possible and limited to exceptional circumstances. Therefore, all efforts shall be made to apply alternative measures. When preventive detention is nevertheless used, juvenile courts and investigative bodies shall give the highest priority to the most expeditious processing of such cases to ensure the shortest possible duration of detention. Untried detainees should be separated from convicted juveniles.

18. The conditions under which an untried juvenile is detained should be consistent with the rules set out below, with additional specific provisions as are necessary and appropriate, given the requirements of the presumption of innocence, the duration of the detention and the legal status and circumstances of the juvenile. These provisions would include, but not necessarily be restricted to, the following:

(a) Juveniles should have the right of legal counsel and be enabled to apply for free legal aid, where such aid is available, and to communicate regularly with their legal advisers. Privacy and confidentiality shall be ensured for such communications;

(b) Juveniles should be provided, where possible, with opportunities to pursue work, with remuneration, and continue education or training, but should not be required to do so. Work, education or training should not cause the continuation of the detention;

(c) Juveniles should receive and retain materials for their leisure and recreation as are compatible with the interests of the administration of justice.

IV. The Management of Juvenile Facilities

A. Records

19. All reports, including legal records, medical records and records of disciplinary proceedings, and all other documents relating to the form, content and details of treatment, should be placed in a confidential individual file, which should be kept up to date, accessible only to authorized persons and classified in such a way as to be easily understood. Where possible, every juvenile should have the right to contest any fact or opinion contained in his or her file so as to permit rectification of inaccurate, unfounded or unfair statements. In order to exercise this right, there should be procedures that allow an appropriate third party to have access to and to consult the file on request. Upon release, the records of juveniles shall be sealed, and, at an appropriate time, expunged.

20. No juvenile should be received in any detention facility without a valid commitment order of a judicial, administrative or other public authority. The details of this order should be immediately entered in the register. No juvenile should be detained in any facility where there is no such register.

B. Admission, registration, movement and transfer

21. In every place where juveniles are detained, a complete and secure record of the following information should be kept concerning each juvenile received:

(a) Information on the identity of the juvenile;

(b) The fact of and reasons for commitment and the authority therefor;

(c) The day and hour of admission, transfer and release;

(d) Details of the notifications to parents and guardians on every admission, transfer or release of the juvenile in their care at the time of commitment;

(e) Details of known physical and mental health problems, including drug and alcohol abuse.

22. The information on admission, place, transfer and release should be provided without delay to the parents and guardians or closest relative of the juvenile concerned.

23. As soon as possible after reception, full reports and relevant information on the personal situation and circumstances of each juvenile should be drawn up and submitted to the administration.

24. On admission, all juveniles shall be given a copy of the rules governing the detention facility and a written description of their rights and obligations in a language they can understand, together with the address of the authorities competent to receive complaints, as well as the address of public or private agencies and organizations which provide legal assistance. For those juveniles who are illiterate or who cannot understand the language in the written form, the information should be conveyed in a manner enabling full comprehension.

25. All juveniles should be helped to understand the regulations governing the internal organization of the facility, the goals and methodology of the care provided, the disciplinary requirements and procedures, other authorized methods of seeking information and of making complaints and all such other matters as are necessary to enable them to understand fully their rights and obligations during detention.

26. The transport of juveniles should be carried out at the expense of the administration in conveyances with adequate ventilation and light, in conditions that should in no way subject them to hardship or indignity. Juveniles should not be transferred from one facility to another arbitrarily.

C. Classification and placement

27. As soon as possible after the moment of admission, each juvenile should be interviewed, and a psychological and social report identifying any factors relevant to the specific type and level of care and programme required by the juvenile should be prepared. This report, together with the report prepared by a medical officer who has examined the juvenile upon admission, should be forwarded to the director for purposes of determining the most appropriate placement for the juvenile within the facility and the specific type and level of care and programme required and to be pursued. When special rehabilitative treatment is required, and the length of stay in the facility permits, trained personnel of the facility should prepare a written, individualized treatment plan specifying treatment objectives and time-frame and the means, stages and delays with which the objectives should be approached.

28. The detention of juveniles should only take place under conditions that take full account of their particular needs, status and special requirements according to their age, personality, sex and type of offence, as well as mental and physical health, and which ensure their protection from harmful influences and risk situations. The principal criterion for the

separation of different categories of juveniles deprived of their liberty should be the provision of the type of care best suited to the particular needs of the individuals concerned and the protection of their physical, mental and moral integrity and well-being.

29. In all detention facilities juveniles should be separated from adults, unless they are members of the same family. Under controlled conditions, juveniles may be brought together with carefully selected adults as part of a special programme that has been shown to be beneficial for the juveniles concerned.

30. Open detention facilities for juveniles should be established. Open detention facilities are those with no or minimal security measures. The population in such detention facilities should be as small as possible. The number of juveniles detained in closed facilities should be small enough to enable individualized treatment. Detention facilities for juveniles should be decentralized and of such size as to facilitate access and contact between the juveniles and their families. Small-scale detention facilities should be established and integrated into the social, economic and cultural environment of the community.

D. Physical environment and accommodation

31. Juveniles deprived of their liberty have the right to facilities and services that meet all the requirements of health and human dignity.

32. The design of detention facilities for juveniles and the physical environment should be in keeping with the rehabilitative aim of residential treatment, with due regard to the need of the juvenile for privacy, sensory stimuli, opportunities for association with peers and participation in sports, physical exercise and leisure-time activities. The design and structure of juvenile detention facilities should be such as to minimize the risk of fire and to ensure safe evacuation from the premises. There should be an effective alarm system in case of fire, as well as formal and drilled procedures to ensure the safety of the juveniles. Detention facilities should not be located in areas where there are known health or other hazards or risks.

33. Sleeping accommodation should normally consist of small group dormitories or individual bedrooms, while bearing in mind local standards. During sleeping hours there should be regular, unobtrusive supervision of all sleeping areas, including individual rooms and group dormitories, in order to ensure the protection of each juvenile. Every juvenile should, in accordance with local or national standards, be provided with separate and sufficient bedding, which should be clean when issued, kept in good order and changed often enough to ensure cleanliness.

34. Sanitary installations should be so located and of a sufficient standard to enable every juvenile to comply, as required, with their physical needs in privacy and in a clean and decent manner.

35. The possession of personal effects is a basic element of the right to privacy and essential to the psychological well-being of the juvenile. The right of every juvenile to possess personal effects and to have adequate storage facilities for them should be fully recognized and respected. Personal effects that the juvenile does not choose to retain or that are confiscated should be placed in safe custody. An inventory thereof should be signed by the juvenile. Steps should be taken to keep them in good condition. All such articles and money should be returned to the juvenile on release, except in so far as he or she has been authorized to spend money or send such property out of the facility. If a juvenile receives or is found in possession of any medicine, the medical officer should decide what use should be made of it.

36. To the extent possible juveniles should have the right to use their own clothing. Detention facilities should ensure that each juvenile has personal clothing suitable for the climate and adequate to ensure good health, and which should in no manner be degrading or humiliating. Juveniles removed from or leaving a facility for any purpose should be allowed to wear their own clothing.

37. Every detention facility shall ensure that every juvenile receives food that is suitably prepared and presented at normal meal times and of a quality and quantity to satisfy the standards of dietetics, hygiene and health and, as far as possible, religious and cultural requirements. Clean drinking water should be available to every juvenile at any time.

E. Education, vocational training and work

38. Every juvenile of compulsory school age has the right to education suited to his or her needs and abilities and designed to prepare him or her for return to society. Such education should be provided outside the detention facility in community schools wherever possible and, in any case, by qualified teachers through programmes integrated with the education system of the country so that, after release, juveniles may continue their education without difficulty. Special attention should be given by the administration of the detention facilities to the education of juveniles of foreign origin or with particular cultural or ethnic needs. Juveniles who are illiterate or have cognitive or learning difficulties should have the right to special education.

39. Juveniles above compulsory school age who wish to continue their education should be permitted and encouraged to do so, and every effort

should be made to provide them with access to appropriate educational programmes.

40. Diplomas or educational certificates awarded to juveniles while in detention should not indicate in any way that the juvenile has been institutionalized.

41. Every detention facility should provide access to a library that is adequately stocked with both instructional and recreational books and periodicals suitable for the juveniles, who should be encouraged and enabled to make full use of it.

42. Every juvenile should have the right to receive vocational training in occupations likely to prepare him or her for future employment.

43. With due regard to proper vocational selection and to the requirements of institutional administration, juveniles should be able to choose the type of work they wish to perform.

44. All protective national and international standards applicable to child labour and young workers should apply to juveniles deprived of their liberty.

45. Wherever possible, juveniles should be provided with the opportunity to perform remunerated labour, if possible within the local community, as a complement to the vocational training provided in order to enhance the possibility of finding suitable employment when they return to their communities. The type of work should be such as to provide appropriate training that will be of benefit to the juveniles following release. The organization and methods of work offered in detention facilities should resemble as closely as possible those of similar work in the community, so as to prepare juveniles for the conditions of normal occupational life.

46. Every juvenile who performs work should have the right to an equitable remuneration. The interests of the juveniles and of their vocational training should not be subordinated to the purpose of making a profit for the detention facility or a third party. Part of the earnings of a juvenile should normally be set aside to constitute a savings fund to be handed over to the juvenile on release. The juvenile should have the right to use the remainder of those earnings to purchase articles for his or her own use or to indemnify the victim injured by his or her offence or to send it to his or her family or other persons outside the detention facility.

F. Recreation

47. Every juvenile should have the right to a suitable amount of time for daily free exercise, in the open air whenever weather permits, during which time appropriate recreational and physical training should normally be provided. Adequate space, installations and equipment should be

provided for these activities. Every juvenile should have additional time for daily leisure activities, part of which should be devoted, if the juvenile so wishes, to arts and crafts skill development. The detention facility should ensure that each juvenile is physically able to participate in the available programmes of physical education. Remedial physical education and therapy should be offered, under medical supervision, to juveniles needing it. G. Religion

48. Every juvenile should be allowed to satisfy the needs of his or her religious and spiritual life, in particular by attending the services or meetings provided in the detention facility or by conducting his or her own services and having possession of the necessary books or items of religious observance and instruction of his or her denomination. If a detention facility contains a sufficient number of juveniles of a given religion, one or more qualified representatives of that religion should be appointed or approved and allowed to hold regular services and to pay pastoral visits in private to juveniles at their request. Every juvenile should have the right to receive visits from a qualified representative of any religion of his or her choice, as well as the right not to participate in religious services and freely to decline religious education, counselling or indoctrination.

H. Medical care

49. Every juvenile shall receive adequate medical care, both preventive and remedial, including dental, ophthalmological and mental health care, as well as pharmaceutical products and special diets as medically indicated. All such medical care should, where possible, be provided to detained juveniles through the appropriate health facilities and services of the community in which the detention facility is located, in order to prevent stigmatization of the juvenile and promote self-respect and integration into the community.

50. Every juvenile has a right to be examined by a physician immediately upon admission to a detention facility, for the purpose of recording any evidence of prior ill-treatment and identifying any physical or mental condition requiring medical attention.

51. The medical services provided to juveniles should seek to detect and should treat any physical or mental illness, substance abuse or other condition that may hinder the integration of the juvenile into society. Every detention facility for juveniles should have immediate access to adequate medical facilities and equipment appropriate to the number and requirements of its residents and staff trained in preventive health care and the handling of medical emergencies. Every juvenile who is ill, who

complains of illness or who demonstrates symptoms of physical or mental difficulties, should be examined promptly by a medical officer.

52. Any medical officer who has reason to believe that the physical or mental health of a juvenile has been or will be injuriously affected by continued detention, a hunger strike or any condition of detention should report this fact immediately to the director of the detention facility in question and to the independent authority responsible for safeguarding the well-being of the juvenile.

53. A juvenile who is suffering from mental illness should be treated in a specialized institution under independent medical management. Steps should be taken, by arrangement with appropriate agencies, to ensure any necessary continuation of mental health care after release.

54. Juvenile detention facilities should adopt specialized drug abuse prevention and rehabilitation programmes administered by qualified personnel. These programmes should be adapted to the age, sex and other requirements of the juveniles concerned, and detoxification facilities and services staffed by trained personnel should be available to drug- or alcohol-dependent juveniles.

55. Medicines should be administered only for necessary treatment on medical grounds and, when possible, after having obtained the informed consent of the juvenile concerned. In particular, they must not be administered with a view to eliciting information or a confession, as a punishment or as a means of restraint. Juveniles shall never be testers in the experimental use of drugs and treatment. The administration of any drug should always be authorized and carried out by qualified medical personnel.

I. Notification of illness, injury and death

56. The family or guardian of a juvenile and any other person designated by the juvenile have the right to be informed of the state of health of the juvenile on request and in the event of any important changes in the health of the juvenile. The director of the detention facility should notify immediately the family or guardian of the juvenile concerned, or other designated person, in case of death, illness requiring transfer of the juvenile to an outside medical facility, or a condition requiring clinical care within the detention facility for more than 48 hours. Notification should also be given to the consular authorities of the State of which a foreign juvenile is a citizen.

57. Upon the death of a juvenile during the period of deprivation of liberty, the nearest relative should have the right to inspect the death certificate, see the body and determine the method of disposal of the body.

Upon the death of a juvenile in detention, there should be an independent inquiry into the causes of death, the report of which should be made accessible to the nearest relative. This inquiry should also be made when the death of a juvenile occurs within six months from the date of his or her release from the detention facility and there is reason to believe that the death is related to the period of detention.

58. A juvenile should be informed at the earliest possible time of the death, serious illness or injury of any immediate family member and should be provided with the opportunity to attend the funeral of the deceased or go to the bedside of a critically ill relative. J. Contacts with the wider community

59. Every means should be provided to ensure that juveniles have adequate communication with the outside world, which is an integral part of the right to fair and humane treatment and is essential to the preparation of juveniles for their return to society. Juveniles should be allowed to communicate with their families, friends and other persons or representatives of reputable outside organizations, to leave detention facilities for a visit to their home and family and to receive special permission to leave the detention facility for educational, vocational or other important reasons. Should the juvenile be serving a sentence, the time spent outside a detention facility should be counted as part of the period of sentence.

60. Every juvenile should have the right to receive regular and frequent visits, in principle once a week and not less than once a month, in circumstances that respect the need of the juvenile for privacy, contact and unrestricted communication with the family and the defence counsel.

61. Every juvenile should have the right to communicate in writing or by telephone at least twice a week with the person of his or her choice, unless legally restricted, and should be assisted as necessary in order effectively to enjoy this right. Every juvenile should have the right to receive correspondence.

62. Juveniles should have the opportunity to keep themselves informed regularly of the news by reading newspapers, periodicals and other publications, through access to radio and television programmes and motion pictures, and through the visits of the representatives of any lawful club or organization in which the juvenile is interested.

K. Limitations of physical restraint and the use of force

63. Recourse to instruments of restraint and to force for any purpose should be prohibited, except as set forth in rule 64 below.

64. Instruments of restraint and force can only be used in exceptional cases, where all other control methods have been exhausted and failed, and

only as explicitly authorized and specified by law and regulation. They should not cause humiliation or degradation, and should be used restrictively and only for the shortest possible period of time. By order of the director of the administration, such instruments might be resorted to in order to prevent the juvenile from inflicting self-injury, injuries to others or serious destruction of property. In such instances, the director should at once consult medical and other relevant personnel and report to the higher administrative authority.

65. The carrying and use of weapons by personnel should be prohibited in any facility where juveniles are detained.

L. Disciplinary procedures

66. Any disciplinary measures and procedures should maintain the interest of safety and an ordered community life and should be consistent with the upholding of the inherent dignity of the juvenile and the fundamental objective of institutional care, namely, instilling a sense of justice, self-respect and respect for the basic rights of every person.

67. All disciplinary measures constituting cruel, inhuman or degrading treatment shall be strictly prohibited, including corporal punishment, placement in a dark cell, closed or solitary confinement or any other punishment that may compromise the physical or mental health of the juvenile concerned. The reduction of diet and the restriction or denial of contact with family members should be prohibited for any purpose. Labour should always be viewed as an educational tool and a means of promoting the self-respect of the juvenile in preparing him or her for return to the community and should not be imposed as a disciplinary sanction. No juvenile should be sanctioned more than once for the same disciplinary infraction. Collective sanctions should be prohibited.

68. Legislation or regulations adopted by the competent administrative authority should establish norms concerning the following, taking full account of the fundamental characteristics, needs and rights of juveniles:

(a) Conduct constituting a disciplinary offence;

(b) Type and duration of disciplinary sanctions that may be inflicted;

(c) The authority competent to impose such sanctions;

(d) The authority competent to consider appeals.

69. A report of misconduct should be presented promptly to the competent authority, which should decide on it without undue delay. The competent authority should conduct a thorough examination of the case.

70. No juvenile should be disciplinarily sanctioned except in strict accordance with the terms of the law and regulations in force. No juvenile should be sanctioned unless he or she has been informed of the alleged

infraction in a manner appropriate to the full understanding of the juvenile, and given a proper opportunity of presenting his or her defence, including the right of appeal to a competent impartial authority. Complete records should be kept of all disciplinary proceedings.

71. No juveniles should be responsible for disciplinary functions except in the supervision of specified social, educational or sports activities or in self-government programmes.

M. Inspection and complaints

72. Qualified inspectors or an equivalent duly constituted authority not belonging to the administration of the facility should be empowered to conduct inspections on a regular basis and to undertake unannounced inspections on their own initiative, and should enjoy full guarantees of independence in the exercise of this function. Inspectors should have unrestricted access to all persons employed by or working in any facility where juveniles are or may be deprived of their liberty, to all juveniles and to all records of such facilities.

73. Qualified medical officers attached to the inspecting authority or the public health service should participate in the inspections, evaluating compliance with the rules concerning the physical environment, hygiene, accommodation, food, exercise and medical services, as well as any other aspect or conditions of institutional life that affect the physical and mental health of juveniles. Every juvenile should have the right to talk in confidence to any inspecting officer.

74. After completing the inspection, the inspector should be required to submit a report on the findings. The report should include an evaluation of the compliance of the detention facilities with the present rules and relevant provisions of national law, and recommendations regarding any steps considered necessary to ensure compliance with them. Any facts discovered by an inspector that appear to indicate that a violation of legal provisions concerning the rights of juveniles or the operation of a juvenile detention facility has occurred should be communicated to the competent authorities for investigation and prosecution.

75. Every juvenile should have the opportunity of making requests or complaints to the director of the detention facility and to his or her authorized representative.

76. Every juvenile should have the right to make a request or complaint, without censorship as to substance, to the central administration, the judicial authority or other proper authorities through approved channels, and to be informed of the response without delay.

77. Efforts should be made to establish an independent office (ombudsman) to receive and investigate complaints made by juveniles deprived of their liberty and to assist in the achievement of equitable settlements.

78. Every juvenile should have the right to request assistance from family members, legal counsellors, humanitarian groups or others where possible, in order to make a complaint. Illiterate juveniles should be provided with assistance should they need to use the services of public or private agencies and organizations which provide legal counsel or which are competent to receive complaints.

N. Return to the community

79. All juveniles should benefit from arrangements designed to assist them in returning to society, family life, education or employment after release. Procedures, including early release, and special courses should be devised to this end.

80. Competent authorities should provide or ensure services to assist juveniles in re-establishing themselves in society and to lessen prejudice against such juveniles. These services should ensure', to the extent possible, that the juvenile is provided with suitable residence, employment, clothing, and sufficient means to maintain himself or herself upon release in order to facilitate successful reintegration. The representatives of agencies providing such services should be consulted and should have access to juveniles while detained, with a view to assisting them in their return to the community.

V. Personnel

81. Personnel should be qualified and include a sufficient number of specialists such as educators, vocational instructors, counsellors, social workers, psychiatrists and psychologists. These and other specialist staff should normally be employed on a permanent basis. This should not preclude part-time or volunteer workers when the level of support and training they can provide is appropriate and beneficial. Detention facilities should make use of all remedial, educational, moral, spiritual, and other resources and forms of assistance that are appropriate and available in the community, according to the individual needs and problems of detained juveniles.

82. The administration should provide for the careful selection and recruitment of every grade and type of personnel, since the proper management of detention facilities depends on their integrity, humanity,

ability and professional capacity to deal with juveniles, as well as personal suitability for the work.

83. To secure the foregoing ends, personnel should be appointed as professional officers with adequate remuneration to attract and retain suitable women and men. The personnel of juvenile detention facilities should be continually encouraged to fulfil their duties and obligations in a humane, committed, professional, fair and efficient manner, to conduct themselves at all times in such a way as to deserve and gain the respect of the juveniles, and to provide juveniles with a positive role model and perspective.

84. The administration should introduce forms of organization and management that facilitate communications between different categories of staff in each detention facility so as to enhance cooperation between the various services engaged in the care of juveniles, as well as between staff and the administration, with a view to ensuring that staff directly in contact with juveniles are able to function in conditions favourable to the efficient fulfilment of their duties.

85. The personnel should receive such training as will enable them to carry out their responsibilities effectively, in particular training in child psychology, child welfare and international standards and norms of human rights and the rights of the child, including the present Rules. The personnel should maintain and improve their knowledge and professional capacity by attending courses of in-service training, to be organized at suitable intervals throughout their career.

86. The director of a facility should be adequately qualified for his or her task, with administrative ability and suitable training and experience, and should carry out his or her duties on a full-time basis.

87. In the performance of their duties, personnel of detention facilities should respect and protect the human dignity and fundamental human rights of all juveniles, in particular, as follows:

(a) No member of the detention facility or institutional personnel may inflict, instigate or tolerate any act of torture or any form of harsh, cruel, inhuman or degrading treatment, punishment, correction or discipline under any pretext or circumstance whatsoever;

(b) All personnel should rigorously oppose and combat any act of corruption, reporting it without delay to the competent authorities;

(c) All personnel should respect the present Rules. Personnel who have reason to believe that a serious violation of the present Rules has occurred or is about to occur should report the matter to their superior authorities or organs vested with reviewing or remedial power;

(d) All personnel should ensure the full protection of the physical and mental health of juveniles, including protection from physical, sexual and emotional abuse and exploitation, and should take immediate action to secure medical attention whenever required;
(e) All personnel should respect the right of the juvenile to privacy, and, in particular, should safeguard all confidential matters concerning juveniles or their families learned as a result of their professional capacity;
(f) All personnel should seek to minimize any differences between life inside and outside the detention facility which tend to lessen due respect for the dignity of juveniles as human beings.

CHAPTER VII

INTERNATIONAL LEGISLATIONS PROHIBITING ABUSE OF CHILDREN

1. Vienna Declaration and Program of Action: World Conference on Human Rights, 1993

One of the most effective contributions on the rights of minors, children and juveniles was carried out under the Vienna Declaration and Programme of Action: World Conference on Human Rights in 1993. The Declaration was the result of an important World Conference which examined many aspects of international human rights. The Conference was, in fact, arranged for several reasons, among which were: *a)* to strengthen the provisions of the human rights law; *b)* to improve the application of the international human rights principles between different legislations; *c)* to create equal rights between all individuals in the world; *d)* to decrease the violations of the human rights law under the jurisdiction of different states; *e)* to enforce the norms of the Universal Declaration of Human Rights; *f)* to protect the rights of different persons under particular procedures within the machinery of states; and *g)* to create cooperation between different states for the effective enforcement of the human rights principles concerning those who are the victims of violations of the human rights norms by their own governments. The Declaration has many of principles on the protection of the rights of children, listed in the following sections:

18. The human rights of women and of the girl-child are an inalienable, integral and indivisible part of universal human rights. The full and equal participation of women in political, civil, economic, social and cultural life, at the national, regional and international levels, and the eradication of all forms of discrimination on grounds of sex are priority objectives of the international community.

Gender-based violence and all forms of sexual harassment and exploitation, including those resulting from cultural prejudice and international trafficking, are incompatible with the dignity and worth of the human person, and must be eliminated. This can be achieved by legal measures and through national action and international cooperation in such fields as economic and social development, education, safe maternity and health care, and social support.

The human rights of women should form an integral part of the United Nations human rights activities, including the promotion of all human rights instruments relating to women.

The World Conference on Human Rights urges Governments, institutions, intergovernmental and non-governmental organizations to intensify their efforts for the protection and promotion of human rights of women and the girl-child.

21. The World Conference on Human Rights, welcoming the early ratification of the Convention on the Rights of the Child by a large number of States and noting the recognition of the human rights of children in the World Declaration on the Survival, Protection and Development of Children and Plan of Action adopted by the World Summit for Children, urges universal ratification of the Convention by 1995 and its effective implementation by States parties through the adoption of all the necessary legislative, administrative and other measures and the allocation to the maximum extent of the available resources. In all actions concerning children, non-discrimination and the best interest of the child should be primary considerations and the views of the child given due weight. National and international mechanisms and programmes should be strengthened for the defence and protection of children, in particular, the girl-child, abandoned children, street children, economically and sexually exploited children, including through child pornography, child prostitution or sale of organs, children victims of diseases including acquired immunodeficiency syndrome, refugee and displaced children, children in detention, children in armed conflict, as well as children victims of famine and drought and other emergencies. International cooperation and solidarity should be promoted to support the implementation of the Convention and the rights of the child should be a priority in the United Nations system-wide action on human rights.

The World Conference on Human Rights also stresses that the child for the full and harmonious development of his or her personality should grow up in a family environment which accordingly merits broader protection.

23. The World Conference on Human Rights reaffirms that everyone, without distinction of any kind, is entitled to the right to seek and to enjoy

in other countries asylum from persecution, as well as the right to return to one's own country. In this respect it stresses the importance of the Universal Declaration of Human Rights, the 1951 Convention relating to the Status of Refugees, its 1967 Protocol and regional instruments. It expresses its appreciation to States that continue to admit and host large numbers of refugees in their territories, and to the Office of the United Nations High Commissioner for Refugees for its dedication to its task. It also expresses its appreciation to the United Nations Relief and Works Agency for Palestine Refugees in the Near East.

The World Conference on Human Rights recognizes that gross violations of human rights, including in armed conflicts, are among the multiple and complex factors leading to displacement of people.

The World Conference on Human Rights recognizes that, in view of the complexities of the global refugee crisis and in accordance with the Charter of the United Nations, relevant international instruments and international solidarity and in the spirit of burden-sharing, a comprehensive approach by the international community is needed in coordination and cooperation with the countries concerned and relevant organizations, bearing in mind the mandate of the United Nations High Commissioner for Refugees. This should include the development of strategies to address the root causes and effects of movements of refugees and other displaced persons, the strengthening of emergency preparedness and response mechanisms, the provision of effective protection and assistance, bearing in mind the special needs of women and children, as well as the achievement of durable solutions, primarily through the preferred solution of dignified and safe voluntary repatriation, including solutions such as those adopted by the international refugee conferences. The World Conference on Human Rights underlines the responsibilities of States, particularly as they relate to the countries of origin.

In the light of the comprehensive approach, the World Conference on Human Rights emphasizes the importance of giving special attention including through intergovernmental and humanitarian organizations and finding lasting solutions to questions related to internally displaced persons including their voluntary and safe return and rehabilitation.

In accordance with the Charter of the United Nations and the principles of humanitarian law, the World Conference on Human Rights further emphasizes the importance of and the need for humanitarian assistance to victims of all natural and man-made disasters.

29. The World Conference on Human Rights expresses grave concern about continuing human rights violations in all parts of the world in

disregard of standards as contained in international human rights instruments and international humanitarian law and about the lack of sufficient and effective remedies for the victims.

The World Conference on Human Rights is deeply concerned about violations of human rights during armed conflicts, affecting the civilian population, especially women, children, the elderly and the disabled. The Conference therefore calls upon States and all parties to armed conflicts strictly to observe international humanitarian law, as set forth in the Geneva Conventions of 1949 and other rules and principles of international law, as well as minimum standards for protection of human rights, as laid down in international conventions.

The World Conference on Human Rights reaffirms the right of the victims to be assisted by humanitarian organizations, as set forth in the Geneva Conventions of 1949 and other relevant instruments of international humanitarian law, and calls for the safe and timely access for such assistance.

…..

B. EQUALITY, DIGNITY AND TOLERANCE

4. The rights of the child

45. The World Conference on Human Rights reiterates the principle of "First Call for Children" and, in this respect, underlines the importance of major national and international efforts, especially those of the United Nations Children's Fund, for promoting respect for the rights of the child to survival, protection, development and participation.

46. Measures should be taken to achieve universal ratification of the Convention on the Rights of the Child by 1995 and the universal signing of the World Declaration on the Survival, Protection and Development of Children and Plan of Action adopted by the World Summit for Children, as well as their effective implementation. The World Conference on Human Rights urges States to withdraw reservations to the Convention on the Rights of the Child contrary to the object and purpose of the Convention or otherwise contrary to international treaty law.

47. The World Conference on Human Rights urges all nations to undertake measures to the maximum extent of their available resources, with the support of international cooperation, to achieve the goals in the World Summit Plan of Action. The Conference calls on States to integrate the Convention on the Rights of the Child into their national action plans. By means of these national action plans and through international efforts, particular priority should be placed on reducing infant and maternal

mortality rates, reducing malnutrition and illiteracy rates and providing access to safe drinking water and to basic education. Whenever so called for, national plans of action should be devised to combat devastating emergencies resulting from natural disasters and armed conflicts and the equally grave problem of children in extreme poverty.

48. The World Conference on Human Rights urges all States, with the support of international cooperation, to address the acute problem of children under especially difficult circumstances. Exploitation and abuse of children should be actively combated, including by addressing their root causes. Effective measures are required against female infanticide, harmful child labour, sale of children and organs, child prostitution, child pornography, as well as other forms of sexual abuse.

49. The World Conference on Human Rights supports all measures by the United Nations and its specialized agencies to ensure the effective protection and promotion of human rights of the girl child. The World Conference on Human Rights urges States to repeal existing laws and regulations and remove customs and practices which discriminate against and cause harm to the girl child.

50. The World Conference on Human Rights strongly supports the proposal that the Secretary-General initiate a study into means of improving the protection of children in armed conflicts. Humanitarian norms should be implemented and measures taken in order to protect and facilitate assistance to children in war zones. Measures should include protection for children against indiscriminate use of all weapons of war, especially anti-personnel mines. The need for aftercare and rehabilitation of children traumatized by war must be addressed urgently. The Conference calls on the Committee on the Rights of the Child to study the question of raising the armed forces.

51. The World Conference on Human Rights recommends that matters relating to human rights and the situation of children be regularly reviewed and monitored by all relevant organs and mechanisms of the United Nations system and by the supervisory bodies of the specialized agencies in accordance with their mandates.

52. The World Conference on Human Rights recognizes the important role played by non-governmental organizations in the effective implementation of all human rights instruments and, in particular, the Convention on the Rights of the Child.

53. The World Conference on Human Rights recommends that the Committee on the Rights of the Child, with the assistance of the Centre for Human Rights, be enabled expeditiously and effectively to meet its

mandate, especially in view of the unprecedented extent of ratification and subsequent submission of country reports.

2. Declaration on the Elimination of Violence against Women, 1993

Although the United Nations has been very active in putting an end to violations against women, immoral and illegal activities against women and female children have been continuously carried out in times of peace and war. In order to prevent and minimize these violations against women and female children, the Declaration on the Elimination of Violence against Women was adopted in 1993 by United Nations General Assembly Resolution 48/104. Its intention is to emphasise that violence against women constitutes a crime, and violates their rights and freedoms. The relevant parts of the Declaration state:

Recognizing that violence against women is a manifestation of historically unequal power relations between men and women, which have led to domination over and discrimination against women by men and to the prevention of the full advancement of women, and that violence against women is one of the crucial social mechanisms by which women are forced into a subordinate position compared with men,

Concerned that some groups of women, such as women belonging to minority groups, indigenous women, refugee women, migrant women, women living in rural or remote communities, destitute women, women in institutions or in detention, female children, women with disabilities, elderly women and women in situations of armed conflict, are especially vulnerable to violence,

Article 2

Violence against women shall be understood to encompass, but not be limited to, the following:

(a) Physical, sexual and psychological violence occurring in the family, including battering, sexual abuse of female children in the household, dowry-related violence, marital rape, female genital mutilation and other traditional practices harmful to women, non-spousal violence and violence related to exploitation;

(b) Physical, sexual and psychological violence occurring within the general community, including rape, sexual abuse, sexual harassment and intimidation at work, in educational institutions and elsewhere, trafficking in women and forced prostitution;

(c) Physical, sexual and psychological violence perpetrated or condoned by the State, wherever it occurs.

Article 4

States should condemn violence against women and should not invoke any custom, tradition or religious consideration to avoid their obligations with respect to its elimination. States should pursue by all appropriate means and without delay a policy of eliminating violence against women and, to this end, should:

.....

(g) Work to ensure, to the maximum extent feasible in the light of their available resources and, where needed, within the framework of international cooperation, that women subjected to violence and, where appropriate, their children have specialized assistance, such as rehabilitation, assistance in child care and maintenance, treatment, counselling, and health and social services, facilities and programmes, as well as support structures, and should take all other appropriate measures to promote their safety and physical and psychological rehabilitation;

3. Convention concerning the Prohibition and Immediate Action for the Elimination of the Worst Forms of Child Labour, 1999

The Convention concerning the Prohibition and Immediate Action for the Elimination of the Worst Forms of Child Labour was adopted by the International Labour Organization (ILO) in 1999, and came into force in 2000. It is one of the key conventions adopted under the authority of the ILO. The Convention aims to prevent all types of child slavery under the legal, political or cultural practice of different states. Other intentions of the Convention are the prohibition of the use of children for financial purposes in connection with pornography, prostitution and debt bondage. Under its provisions, the ILO International Programme on the Elimination of Child Labour is responsible for assisting in the implementation of the intentions of the Convention within the territory of states parties.

One of the most important principles of the Convention relates to the age limit of children. It reads that "For the purposes of this Convention, the term *child* shall apply to all persons under the age of 18". This stipulation of the Convention overlaps the key provision of the Optional Protocols to the Convention on the Rights of the Child concerning the age limit of children. They imply the establishment of a general rule of international law concerning the age of children and its compulsory respect in any future instruments regarding the protection of children. Although the provisions of the 1999 Convention of ILO concerning the rights of children are important achievements, they have not been respected by many states and they are therefore frequently violated. The unfortunate fact is that even states that fully respect the provisions of the relevant convention concerning the prohibition of child slavery within their legislation have not been very particular about the purchasing materials manufactured by those children, who work under conditions of near-slavery, contrary to the norms of the human rights law. The Convention states:

The General Conference of the International Labour Organization,

Having been convened at Geneva by the Governing Body of the International Labour Office, and having met in its 87th Session on 1 June 1999, and

Considering the need to adopt new instruments for the prohibition and elimination of the worst forms of child labour, as the main priority for national and international action, including international cooperation and assistance, to complement the Convention and the Recommendation concerning Minimum Age for Admission to Employment, 1973, which remain fundamental instruments on child labour, and

Considering that the effective elimination of the worst forms of child labour requires immediate and comprehensive action, taking into account the importance of free basic education and the need to remove the children concerned from all such work and to provide for their rehabilitation and social integration while addressing the needs of their families, and

Recalling the resolution concerning the elimination of child labour adopted by the International Labour Conference at its 83rd Session in 1996, and

Recognizing that child labour is to a great extent caused by poverty and that the long-term solution lies in sustained economic growth leading to social progress, in particular poverty alleviation and universal education, and

Recalling the Convention on the Rights of the Child adopted by the United Nations General Assembly on 20 November 1989, and

Recalling the ILO Declaration on Fundamental Principles and Rights at Work and its Follow-up, adopted by the International Labour Conference at its 86th Session in 1998, and

Recalling that some of the worst forms of child labour are covered by other international instruments, in particular the Forced Labour Convention, 1930, and the United Nations Supplementary Convention on the Abolition of Slavery, the Slave Trade, and Institutions and Practices Similar to Slavery, 1956, and

Having decided upon the adoption of certain proposals with regard to child labour, which is the fourth item on the agenda of the session, and

Having determined that these proposals shall take the form of an international Convention;

Adopts this seventeenth day of June of the year one thousand nine hundred and ninety-nine the following Convention, which may be cited as the Worst Forms of Child Labour Convention, 1999.

Article 1

Each Member which ratifies this Convention shall take immediate and effective measures to secure the prohibition and elimination of the worst forms of child labour as a matter of urgency.

Article 2

For the purposes of this Convention, the term *child* shall apply to all persons under the age of 18.

Article 3

For the purposes of this Convention, the term *the worst forms of child labour* comprises:

(a) all forms of slavery or practices similar to slavery, such as the sale and trafficking of children, debt bondage and serfdom and forced or compulsory labour, including forced or compulsory recruitment of children for use in armed conflict;

(b) the use, procuring or offering of a child for prostitution, for the production of pornography or for pornographic performances;

(c) the use, procuring or offering of a child for illicit activities, in particular for the production and trafficking of drugs as defined in the relevant international treaties;

(d) work which, by its nature or the circumstances in which it is carried out, is likely to harm the health, safety or morals of children.

Article 4

1. The types of work referred to under Article 3(d) shall be determined by national laws or regulations or by the competent authority, after consultation with the organizations of employers and workers concerned, taking into consideration relevant international standards, in particular Paragraphs 3 and 4 of the Worst Forms of Child Labour Recommendation, 1999.

2. The competent authority, after consultation with the organizations of employers and workers concerned, shall identify where the types of work so determined exist.

3. The list of the types of work determined under paragraph 1 of this Article shall be periodically examined and revised as necessary, in consultation with the organizations of employers and workers concerned.

Article 5

Each Member shall, after consultation with employers' and workers' organizations, establish or designate appropriate mechanisms to monitor the implementation of the provisions giving effect to this Convention.

Article 6

1. Each Member shall design and implement programmes of action to eliminate as a priority the worst forms of child labour.

2. Such programmes of action shall be designed and implemented in consultation with relevant government institutions and employers' and workers' organizations, taking into consideration the views of other concerned groups as appropriate.

Article 7

1. Each Member shall take all necessary measures to ensure the effective implementation and enforcement of the provisions giving effect to this Convention including the provision and application of penal sanctions or, as appropriate, other sanctions.

2. Each Member shall, taking into account the importance of education in eliminating child labour, take effective and time-bound measures to:

(a) prevent the engagement of children in the worst forms of child labour;

(b) provide the necessary and appropriate direct assistance for the removal of children from the worst forms of child labour and for their rehabilitation and social integration;

(c) ensure access to free basic education, and, wherever possible and appropriate, vocational training, for all children removed from the worst forms of child labour;

(d) identify and reach out to children at special risk; and

(e) take account of the special situation of girls.

3. Each Member shall designate the competent authority responsible for the implementation of the provisions giving effect to this Convention.

Article 8

Members shall take appropriate steps to assist one another in giving effect to the provisions of this Convention through enhanced international cooperation and/or assistance including support for social and economic development, poverty eradication programmes and universal education.

Article 9

The formal ratifications of this Convention shall be communicated to the Director-General of the International Labour Office for registration.

Article 10

1. This Convention shall be binding only upon those Members of the International Labour Organization whose ratifications have been registered with the Director-General of the International Labour Office.

2. It shall come into force 12 months after the date on which the ratifications of two Members have been registered with the Director-General.

3. Thereafter, this Convention shall come into force for any Member 12 months after the date on which its ratification has been registered.

Article 11

1. A Member which has ratified this Convention may denounce it after the expiration of ten years from the date on which the Convention first comes into force, by an act communicated to the Director-General of the International Labour Office for registration. Such denunciation shall not take effect until one year after the date on which it is registered.

2. Each Member which has ratified this Convention and which does not, within the year following the expiration of the period of ten years mentioned in the preceding paragraph, exercise the right of denunciation provided for in this Article, will be bound for another period of ten years and, thereafter, may denounce this Convention at the expiration of each period of ten years under the terms provided for in this Article.

Article 12

1. The Director-General of the International Labour Office shall notify all Members of the International Labour Organization of the registration of all ratifications and acts of denunciation communicated by the Members of the Organization.

2. When notifying the Members of the Organization of the registration of the second ratification, the Director-General shall draw the attention of

the Members of the Organization to the date upon which the Convention shall come into force.

Article 13

The Director-General of the International Labour Office shall communicate to the Secretary-General of the United Nations, for registration in accordance with article 102 of the Charter of the United Nations, full particulars of all ratifications and acts of denunciation registered by the Director-General in accordance with the provisions of the preceding Articles.

Article 14

At such times as it may consider necessary, the Governing Body of the International Labour Office shall present to the General Conference a report on the working of this Convention and shall examine the desirability of placing on the agenda of the Conference the question of its revision in whole or in part.

Article 15

1. Should the Conference adopt a new Convention revising this Convention in whole or in part, then, unless the new Convention otherwise provides—

(a) the ratification by a Member of the new revising Convention shall ipso jure involve the immediate denunciation of this Convention, notwithstanding the provisions of Article 11 above, if and when the new revising Convention shall have come into force;

(b) as from the date when the new revising Convention comes into force, this Convention shall cease to be open to ratification by the Members.

2. This Convention shall in any case remain in force in its actual form and content for those Members which have ratified it but have not ratified the revising Convention.

Article 16

The English and French versions of the text of this Convention are equally authoritative.

4. Optional Protocol to the Convention on the Rights of the Child on the Sale of Children, Child Prostitution and Child Pornography, 2000

Whilst one cannot deny that the Convention on the Rights of the Child is one of the milestones of the United Nations with regard to the rights of children and their international protection from unjustified actions or decisions, the provisions of the Convention could not deal with all aspects of the protection of the rights of the child. For instance, the Convention could not deal with the question of child trafficking and sexual exploitation of children, and this was a serious omission. To create effective protection of the rights of the child within the international community as a whole, the Optional Protocol to the Convention on the Rights of the Child on the Sale of Children, Child Prostitution and Child Pornography was formulated and adopted for signature, ratification and accession in 2000 by General Assembly Resolution A/RES/54/263. . The Protocol entered into force in 2002.

The Optional Protocol has many of different purposes. Some of these are to prevent unlawful acts against children, to emphasise that the sexual exploitation of children is against human morality, to re-criminalize the sexual exploitation of children, to oblige all states of the international community to act against any unlawful measures against children, to underline that all types of child pornography are prohibited, to emphasize that the provisions of the Convention on the Rights of the Child have to be respected and implemented by all states, to create different measures for prevention, prosecution and punishment, to establish certain effective possibilities for cooperation and assistance between different states, and also to extradite those who have been engaged in child trafficking. The Convention on the Rights of the Child, the Optional Protocol on the Involvement of Children in Armed Conflict and the Optional Protocol to the Convention on the Rights of the Child on the sale of Children, Child Prostitution and Child Pornography are three integrated instruments for the protection of children from all types of illegal, unjustified, immoral, hazardous and irrational measures. In other words, they together constitute a valuable juridical body for the protection of the sovereignty of children, juveniles, youth or minors. The Optional Protocol states:

The States Parties to the present Protocol,

Considering that, in order further to achieve the purposes of the Convention on the Rights of the Child and the implementation of its provisions, especially articles 1, 11, 21, 32, 33, 34, 35 and 36, it would be appropriate to extend the measures that States Parties should undertake in order to guarantee the protection of the child from the sale of children, child prostitution and child pornography,

Considering also that the Convention on the Rights of the Child recognizes the right of the child to be protected from economic exploitation and from performing any work that is likely to be hazardous or to interfere with the child's education, or to be harmful to the child's health or physical, mental, spiritual, moral or social development,

Gravely concerned at the significant and increasing international traffic in children for the purpose of the sale of children, child prostitution and child pornography,

Deeply concerned at the widespread and continuing practice of sex tourism, to which children are especially vulnerable, as it directly promotes the sale of children, child prostitution and child pornography,

Recognizing that a number of particularly vulnerable groups, including girl children, are at greater risk of sexual exploitation and that girl children are disproportionately represented among the sexually exploited,

Concerned about the growing availability of child pornography on the Internet and other evolving technologies, and recalling the International Conference on Combating Child Pornography on the Internet, held in Vienna in 1999, in particular its conclusion calling for the worldwide criminalization of the production, distribution, exportation, transmission, importation, intentional possession and advertising of child pornography, and stressing the importance of closer cooperation and partnership between Governments and the Internet industry,

Believing that the elimination of the sale of children, child prostitution and child pornography will be facilitated by adopting a holistic approach, addressing the contributing factors, including underdevelopment, poverty, economic disparities, inequitable socio-economic structure, dysfunctioning families, lack of education, urban-rural migration, gender discrimination, irresponsible adult sexual behaviour, harmful traditional practices, armed conflicts and trafficking in children,

Believing also that efforts to raise public awareness are needed to reduce consumer demand for the sale of children, child prostitution and child pornography, and believing further in the importance of strengthening global partnership among all actors and of improving law enforcement at the national level,

Noting the provisions of international legal instruments relevant to the protection of children, including the Hague Convention on Protection of Children and Cooperation in Respect of Intercountry Adoption, the Hague

Convention on the Civil Aspects of International Child Abduction, the Hague Convention on Jurisdiction, Applicable Law,

Recognition, Enforcement and Cooperation in Respect of Parental Responsibility and Measures for the Protection of Children, and International Labour Organization Convention No. 182 on the Prohibition and Immediate Action for the Elimination of the Worst Forms of Child Labour,

Encouraged by the overwhelming support for the Convention on the Rights of the Child, demonstrating the widespread commitment that exists for the promotion and protection of the rights of the child,

Recognizing the importance of the implementation of the provisions of the Programme of Action for the Prevention of the Sale of Children, Child Prostitution and Child Pornography and the Declaration and Agenda for Action adopted at the World Congress against Commercial Sexual Exploitation of Children, held in Stockholm from 27 to 31 August 1996, and the other relevant decisions and recommendations of pertinent international bodies, taking due account of the importance of the traditions and cultural values of each people for the protection and harmonious development of the child,

Have agreed as follows:

Article 1

States Parties shall prohibit the sale of children, child prostitution and child pornography as provided for by the present Protocol.

Article 2

For the purposes of the present Protocol:

(a) Sale of children means any act or transaction whereby a child is transferred by any person or group of persons to another for remuneration or any other consideration;

(b) Child prostitution means the use of a child in sexual activities for remuneration or any other form of consideration;

(c) Child pornography means any representation, by whatever means, of a child engaged in real or simulated explicit sexual activities or any representation of the sexual parts of a child for primarily sexual purposes.

Article 3

1. Each State Party shall ensure that, as a minimum, the following acts and activities are fully covered under its criminal or penal law, whether such offences are committed domestically or transnationally or on an individual or organized basis:

(a) In the context of sale of children as defined in article 2:

(i) Offering, delivering or accepting, by whatever means, a child for the purpose of:

a. Sexual exploitation of the child;

b. Transfer of organs of the child for profit;

c. Engagement of the child in forced labour;

(ii) Improperly inducing consent, as an intermediary, for the adoption of a child in violation of applicable international legal instruments on adoption;

(b) Offering, obtaining, procuring or providing a child for child prostitution, as defined in article 2;

(c) Producing, distributing, disseminating, importing, exporting, offering, selling or possessing for the above purposes child pornography as defined in article 2.

2. Subject to the provisions of the national law of a State Party, the same shall apply to an attempt to commit any of the said acts and to complicity or participation in any of the said acts.

3. Each State Party shall make such offences punishable by appropriate penalties that take into account their grave nature.

4. Subject to the provisions of its national law, each State Party shall take measures, where appropriate, to establish the liability of legal persons for offences established in paragraph 1 of the present article. Subject to the legal principles of the State Party, such liability of legal persons may be criminal, civil or administrative.

5. States Parties shall take all appropriate legal and administrative measures to ensure that all persons involved in the adoption of a child act in conformity with applicable international legal instruments.

Article 4

1. Each State Party shall take such measures as may be necessary to establish its jurisdiction over the offences referred to in article 3, paragraph 1, when the offences are committed in its territory or on board a ship or aircraft registered in that State.

2. Each State Party may take such measures as may be necessary to establish its jurisdiction over the offences referred to in article 3, paragraph 1, in the following cases:

(a) When the alleged offender is a national of that State or a person who has his habitual residence in its territory;

(b) When the victim is a national of that State.

3. Each State Party shall also take such measures as may be necessary to establish its jurisdiction over the aforementioned offences when the

alleged offender is present in its territory and it does not extradite him or her to another State Party on the ground that the offence has been committed by one of its nationals.

4. The present Protocol does not exclude any criminal jurisdiction exercised in accordance with internal law.

Article 5

1. The offences referred to in article 3, paragraph 1, shall be deemed to be included as extraditable offences in any extradition treaty existing between States Parties and shall be included as extraditable offences in every extradition treaty subsequently concluded between them, in accordance with the conditions set forth in such treaties.

2. If a State Party that makes extradition conditional on the existence of a treaty receives a request for extradition from another State Party with which it has no extradition treaty, it may consider the present Protocol to be a legal basis for extradition in respect of such offences. Extradition shall be subject to the conditions provided by the law of the requested State.

3. States Parties that do not make extradition conditional on the existence of a treaty shall recognize such offences as extraditable offences between themselves subject to the conditions provided by the law of the requested State.

4. Such offences shall be treated, for the purpose of extradition between States Parties, as if they had been committed not only in the place in which they occurred but also in the territories of the States required to establish their jurisdiction in accordance with article 4.

5. If an extradition request is made with respect to an offence described in article 3, paragraph 1, and the requested State Party does not or will not extradite on the basis of the nationality of the offender, that State shall take suitable measures to submit the case to its competent authorities for the purpose of prosecution.

Article 6

1. States Parties shall afford one another the greatest measure of assistance in connection with investigations or criminal or extradition proceedings brought in respect of the offences set forth in article 3, paragraph 1, including assistance in obtaining evidence at their disposal necessary for the proceedings.

2. States Parties shall carry out their obligations under paragraph 1 of the present article in conformity with any treaties or other arrangements on mutual legal assistance that may exist between them. In the absence of

such treaties or arrangements, States Parties shall afford one another assistance in accordance with their domestic law.

Article 7

States Parties shall, subject to the provisions of their national law:

(a) Take measures to provide for the seizure and confiscation, as appropriate, of:

(i) Goods, such as materials, assets and other instrumentalities used to commit or facilitate offences under the present protocol;

(ii) Proceeds derived from such offences;

(b) Execute requests from another State Party for seizure or confiscation of goods or proceeds referred to in subparagraph (a) (i) and (ii);

(c) Take measures aimed at closing, on a temporary or definitive basis, premises used to commit such offences.

Article 8

1. States Parties shall adopt appropriate measures to protect the rights and interests of child victims of the practices prohibited under the present Protocol at all stages of the criminal justice process, in particular by:

(a) Recognizing the vulnerability of child victims and adapting procedures to recognize their special needs, including their special needs as witnesses;

(b) Informing child victims of their rights, their role and the scope, timing and progress of the proceedings and of the disposition of their cases;

(c) Allowing the views, needs and concerns of child victims to be presented and considered in proceedings where their personal interests are affected, in a manner consistent with the procedural rules of national law;

(d) Providing appropriate support services to child victims throughout the legal process;

(e) Protecting, as appropriate, the privacy and identity of child victims and taking measures in accordance with national law to avoid the inappropriate dissemination of information that could lead to the identification of child victims;

(f) Providing, in appropriate cases, for the safety of child victims, as well as that of their families and witnesses on their behalf, from intimidation and retaliation;

(g) Avoiding unnecessary delay in the disposition of cases and the execution of orders or decrees granting compensation to child victims.

2. States Parties shall ensure that uncertainty as to the actual age of the victim shall not prevent the initiation of criminal investigations, including investigations aimed at establishing the age of the victim.

3. States Parties shall ensure that, in the treatment by the criminal justice system of children who are victims of the offences described in the present Protocol, the best interest of the child shall be a primary consideration.

4. States Parties shall take measures to ensure appropriate training, in particular legal and psychological training, for the persons who work with victims of the offences prohibited under the present Protocol.

5. States Parties shall, in appropriate cases, adopt measures in order to protect the safety and integrity of those persons and/or organizations involved in the prevention and/or protection and rehabilitation of victims of such offences.

6. Nothing in the present article shall be construed to be prejudicial to or inconsistent with the rights of the accused to a fair and impartial trial.

Article 9

1. States Parties shall adopt or strengthen, implement and disseminate laws, administrative measures, social policies and programmes to prevent the offences referred to in the present Protocol. Particular attention shall be given to protect children who are especially vulnerable to such practices.

2. States Parties shall promote awareness in the public at large, including children, through information by all appropriate means, education and training, about the preventive measures and harmful effects of the offences referred to in the present Protocol. In fulfilling their obligations under this article, States Parties shall encourage the participation of the community and, in particular, children and child victims, in such information and education and training programmes, including at the international level.

3. States Parties shall take all feasible measures with the aim of ensuring all appropriate assistance to victims of such offences, including their full social reintegration and their full physical and psychological recovery.

4. States Parties shall ensure that all child victims of the offences described in the present Protocol have access to adequate procedures to seek, without discrimination, compensation for damages from those legally responsible.

5. States Parties shall take appropriate measures aimed at effectively prohibiting the production and dissemination of material advertising the offences described in the present Protocol.

Article 10

1. States Parties shall take all necessary steps to strengthen international cooperation by multilateral, regional and bilateral arrangements for the prevention, detection, investigation, prosecution and punishment of those responsible for acts involving the sale of children, child prostitution, child pornography and child sex tourism. States Parties shall also promote international cooperation and coordination between their authorities, national and international non-governmental organizations and international organizations.

2. States Parties shall promote international cooperation to assist child victims in their physical and psychological recovery, social reintegration and repatriation.

3. States Parties shall promote the strengthening of international cooperation in order to address the root causes, such as poverty and underdevelopment, contributing to the vulnerability of children to the sale of children, child prostitution, child pornography and child sex tourism.

4. States Parties in a position to do so shall provide financial, technical or other assistance through existing multilateral, regional, bilateral or other programmes.

Article 11

Nothing in the present Protocol shall affect any provisions that are more conducive to the realization of the rights of the child and that may be contained in:

(a) The law of a State Party;

(b) International law in force for that State.

Article 12

1. Each State Party shall, within two years following the entry into force of the present Protocol for that State Party, submit a report to the Committee on the Rights of the Child providing comprehensive information on the measures it has taken to implement the provisions of the Protocol.

2. Following the submission of the comprehensive report, each State Party shall include in the reports they submit to the Committee on the Rights of the Child, in accordance with article 44 of the Convention, any further information with respect to the implementation of the present Protocol. Other States Parties to the Protocol shall submit a report every five years.

3. The Committee on the Rights of the Child may request from States Parties further information relevant to the implementation of the present Protocol.

Article 13

1. The present Protocol is open for signature by any State that is a party to the Convention or has signed it.

2. The present Protocol is subject to ratification and is open to accession by any State that is a party to the Convention or has signed it. Instruments of ratification or accession shall be deposited with the Secretary- General of the United Nations.

Article 14

1. The present Protocol shall enter into force three months after the deposit of the tenth instrument of ratification or accession.

2. For each State ratifying the present Protocol or acceding to it after its entry into force, the Protocol shall enter into force one month after the date of the deposit of its own instrument of ratification or accession.

Article 15

1. Any State Party may denounce the present Protocol at any time by written notification to the Secretary- General of the United Nations, who shall thereafter inform the other States Parties to the Convention and all States that have signed the Convention. The denunciation shall take effect one year after the date of receipt of the notification by the Secretary-General.

2. Such a denunciation shall not have the effect of releasing the State Party from its obligations under the present Protocol in regard to any offence that occurs prior to the date on which the denunciation becomes effective. Nor shall such a denunciation prejudice in any way the continued consideration of any matter that is already under consideration by the Committee on the Rights of the Child prior to the date on which the denunciation becomes effective.

Article 16

1. Any State Party may propose an amendment and file it with the Secretary-General of the United Nations. The Secretary-General shall thereupon communicate the proposed amendment to States Parties with a request that they indicate whether they favour a conference of States Parties for the purpose of considering and voting upon the proposals. In the event that, within four months from the date of such communication, at

least one third of the States Parties favour such a conference, the Secretary-General shall convene the conference under the auspices of the United Nations. Any amendment adopted by a majority of States Parties present and voting at the conference shall be submitted to the General Assembly of the United Nations for approval.

2. An amendment adopted in accordance with paragraph 1 of the present article shall enter into force when it has been approved by the General Assembly and accepted by a two-thirds majority of States Parties.

3. When an amendment enters into force, it shall be binding on those States Parties that have accepted it, other States Parties still being bound by the provisions of the present Protocol and any earlier amendments they have accepted.

Article 17

1. The present Protocol, of which the Arabic, Chinese, English, French, Russian and Spanish texts are equally authentic, shall be deposited in the archives of the United Nations.

2. The Secretary-General of the United Nations shall transmit certified copies of the present Protocol to all States Parties to the Convention and all States that have signed the Convention.

5. Optional Protocol to the Convention on the Rights of the Child on the Involvement of Children in Armed Conflict, 2000

The Optional Protocol to the Convention on the Rights of the Child on the Involvement of Children in Armed Conflict from 2000 is the second protocol to the Convention on the Rights of the Child. It was drafted to take into effective legislation certain provisions which could not be entered into the provisions of the original convention because of the ideological, military, economic and political conflicts between different states. The intention of the protocol is therefore to underline that certain acts against children are prohibited, and that states parties should take the necessary measures for the prohibition of those acts within their respective legislation without regard to their national interests. Internationally, the Optional Protocol is considered to be one of the key treaties in international human rights law and the international humanitarian law of armed conflicts which aims to protect the legal statute of children. The Protocol was adopted by General Assembly Resolution A/RES/54/263 in May 2000, and it came into force in 2002.

One of the more controversial articles of the Protocol is its provision regarding the age of children, which is why some states have refused to ratify it. The Protocol states that "States Parties shall take all feasible measures to ensure that members of their armed forces who have not attained the age of 18 years do not take a direct part in hostilities". This age limit also prevents the sexual exploitation of children. It may be stated that the policy of the Protocol, together with the original convention on the rights of the child, constitute an integral part of the international legal system which will greatly help in the development of sovereignty and consequently the integrity of children under different legislation. The provisions of the Protocol are:

The States Parties to the present Protocol,

Encouraged by the overwhelming support for the Convention on the Rights of the Child, demonstrating the widespread commitment that exists to strive for the promotion and protection of the rights of the child,

Reaffirming that the rights of children require special protection, and calling for continuous improvement of the situation of children without distinction, as well as for their development and education in conditions of peace and security,

Disturbed by the harmful and widespread impact of armed conflict on children and the long-term consequences it has for durable peace, security and development,

Condemning the targeting of children in situations of armed conflict and direct attacks on objects protected under international law, including places that generally have a significant presence of children, such as schools and hospitals,

Noting the adoption of the Rome Statute of the International Criminal Court, in particular, the inclusion therein as a war crime, of conscripting or enlisting children under the age of 15 years or using them to participate actively in hostilities in both international and non-international armed conflicts,

Considering therefore that to strengthen further the implementation of rights recognized in the Convention on the Rights of the Child there is a need to increase the protection of children from involvement in armed conflict,

Noting that article 1 of the Convention on the Rights of the Child specifies that, for the purposes of that Convention, a child means every human being below the age of 18 years unless, under the law applicable to the child, majority is attained earlier,

Convinced that an optional protocol to the Convention that raises the age of possible recruitment of persons into armed forces and their participation in hostilities will contribute effectively to the implementation of the principle that the best interests of the child are to be a primary consideration in all actions concerning children,

Noting that the twenty-sixth International Conference of the Red Cross and Red Crescent in December 1995 recommended, inter alia, that parties to conflict take every feasible step to ensure that children below the age of 18 years do not take part in hostilities,

Welcoming the unanimous adoption, in June 1999, of International Labour Organization Convention No. 182 on the Prohibition and Immediate Action for the Elimination of the Worst Forms of Child Labour, which prohibits, inter alia, forced or compulsory recruitment of children for use in armed conflict,

Condemning with the gravest concern the recruitment, training and use within and across national borders of children in hostilities by armed groups distinct from the armed forces of a State, and recognizing the responsibility of those who recruit, train and use children in this regard,

Recalling the obligation of each party to an armed conflict to abide by the provisions of international humanitarian law,

Stressing that the present Protocol is without prejudice to the purposes and principles contained in the Charter of the United Nations, including Article 51, and relevant norms of humanitarian law,

Bearing in mind that conditions of peace and security based on full respect of the purposes and principles contained in the Charter and observance of applicable human rights instruments are indispensable for the full protection of children, in particular during armed conflicts and foreign occupation,

Recognizing the special needs of those children who are particularly vulnerable to recruitment or use in hostilities contrary to the present Protocol owing to their economic or social status or gender,

Mindful of the necessity of taking into consideration the economic, social and political root causes of the involvement of children in armed conflicts,

Convinced of the need to strengthen international cooperation in the implementation of the present Protocol, as well as the physical and psychosocial rehabilitation and social reintegration of children who are victims of armed conflict,

Encouraging the participation of the community and, in particular, children and child victims in the dissemination of informational and educational programmes concerning the implementation of the Protocol,

Have agreed as follows:

Article 1

States Parties shall take all feasible measures to ensure that members of their armed forces who have not attained the age of 18 years do not take a direct part in hostilities.

Article 2

States Parties shall ensure that persons who have not attained the age of 18 years are not compulsorily recruited into their armed forces.

Article 3

1. States Parties shall raise the minimum age for the voluntary recruitment of persons into their national armed forces from that set out in article 38, paragraph 3, of the Convention on the Rights of the Child, taking account of the principles contained in that article and recognizing that under the Convention persons under the age of 18 years are entitled to special protection.

2. Each State Party shall deposit a binding declaration upon ratification of or accession to the present Protocol that sets forth the minimum age at which it will permit voluntary recruitment into its national armed forces and a description of the safeguards it has adopted to ensure that such recruitment is not forced or coerced.

3. States Parties that permit voluntary recruitment into their national armed forces under the age of 18 years shall maintain safeguards to ensure, as a minimum, that:

(a) Such recruitment is genuinely voluntary;

(b) Such recruitment is carried out with the informed consent of the person's parents or legal guardians;

(c) Such persons are fully informed of the duties involved in such military service;

(d) Such persons provide reliable proof of age prior to acceptance into national military service.

4. Each State Party may strengthen its declaration at any time by notification to that effect addressed to the Secretary-General of the United Nations, who shall inform all States Parties. Such notification shall take effect on the date on which it is received by the Secretary-General.

5. The requirement to raise the age in paragraph 1 of the present article does not apply to schools operated by or under the control of the armed forces of the States Parties, in keeping with articles 28 and 29 of the Convention on the Rights of the Child.

Article 4

1. Armed groups that are distinct from the armed forces of a State should not, under any circumstances, recruit or use in hostilities persons under the age of 18 years.

2. States Parties shall take all feasible measures to prevent such recruitment and use, including the adoption of legal measures necessary to prohibit and criminalize such practices.

3. The application of the present article shall not affect the legal status of any party to an armed conflict.

Article 5

Nothing in the present Protocol shall be construed as precluding provisions in the law of a State Party or in international instruments and international humanitarian law that are more conducive to the realization of the rights of the child.

Article 6

1. Each State Party shall take all necessary legal, administrative and other measures to ensure the effective implementation and enforcement of the provisions of the present Protocol within its jurisdiction.

2. States Parties undertake to make the principles and provisions of the present Protocol widely known and promoted by appropriate means, to adults and children alike.

3. States Parties shall take all feasible measures to ensure that persons within their jurisdiction recruited or used in hostilities contrary to the present Protocol are demobilized or otherwise released from service. States Parties shall, when necessary, accord to such persons all appropriate assistance for their physical and psychological recovery and their social reintegration.

Article 7

1. States Parties shall cooperate in the implementation of the present Protocol, including in the prevention of any activity contrary thereto and in the rehabilitation and social reintegration of persons who are victims of acts contrary thereto, including through technical cooperation and financial assistance. Such assistance and cooperation will be undertaken in consultation with the States Parties concerned and the relevant international organizations.

2. States Parties in a position to do so shall provide such assistance through existing multilateral, bilateral or other programmes or, inter alia,

through a voluntary fund established in accordance with the rules of the General Assembly.

Article 8

1. Each State Party shall, within two years following the entry into force of the present Protocol for that State Party, submit a report to the Committee on the Rights of the Child providing comprehensive information on the measures it has taken to implement the provisions of the Protocol, including the measures taken to implement the provisions on participation and recruitment.

2. Following the submission of the comprehensive report, each State Party shall include in the reports it submits to the Committee on the Rights of the Child, in accordance with article 44 of the Convention, any further information with respect to the implementation of the Protocol. Other States Parties to the Protocol shall submit a report every five years.

3. The Committee on the Rights of the Child may request from States Parties further information relevant to the implementation of the present Protocol.

Article 9

1. The present Protocol is open for signature by any State that is a party to the Convention or has signed it.

2. The present Protocol is subject to ratification and is open to accession by any State. Instruments of ratification or accession shall be deposited with the Secretary-General of the United Nations.

3. The Secretary-General, in his capacity as depositary of the Convention and the Protocol, shall inform all States Parties to the Convention and all States that have signed the Convention of each instrument of declaration pursuant to article 3.

Article 10

1. The present Protocol shall enter into force three months after the deposit of the tenth instrument of ratification or accession.

2. For each State ratifying the present Protocol or acceding to it after its entry into force, the Protocol shall enter into force one month after the date of the deposit of its own instrument of ratification or accession.

Article 11

1. Any State Party may denounce the present Protocol at any time by written notification to the Secretary- General of the United Nations, who shall thereafter inform the other States Parties to the Convention and all

States that have signed the Convention. The denunciation shall take effect one year after the date of receipt of the notification by the Secretary-General. If, however, on the expiry of that year the denouncing State Party is engaged in armed conflict, the denunciation shall not take effect before the end of the armed conflict.

2. Such a denunciation shall not have the effect of releasing the State Party from its obligations under the present Protocol in regard to any act that occurs prior to the date on which the denunciation becomes effective. Nor shall such a denunciation prejudice in any way the continued consideration of any matter that is already under consideration by the Committee on the Rights of the Child prior to the date on which the denunciation becomes effective.

Article 12

1. Any State Party may propose an amendment and file it with the Secretary-General of the United Nations. The Secretary-General shall thereupon communicate the proposed amendment to States Parties with a request that they indicate whether they favour a conference of States Parties for the purpose of considering and voting upon the proposals. In the event that, within four months from the date of such communication, at least one third of the States Parties favour such a conference, the Secretary-General shall convene the conference under the auspices of the United Nations. Any amendment adopted by a majority of States Parties present and voting at the conference shall be submitted to the General Assembly of the United Nations for approval.

2. An amendment adopted in accordance with paragraph 1 of the present article shall enter into force when it has been approved by the General Assembly and accepted by a two-thirds majority of States Parties.

3. When an amendment enters into force, it shall be binding on those States Parties that have accepted it, other States Parties still being bound by the provisions of the present Protocol and any earlier amendments they have accepted.

Article 13

1. The present Protocol, of which the Arabic, Chinese, English, French, Russian and Spanish texts are equally authentic, shall be deposited in the archives of the United Nations.

2. The Secretary-General of the United Nations shall transmit certified copies of the present Protocol to all States Parties to the Convention and all States that have signed the Convention.

6. Protocol to Prevent, Suppress and Punish Trafficking in Persons, Especially Women and Children, Supplementing the United Nations Convention against Transnational Organized Crime, 2001

Trafficking in persons, in particular the trafficking of women and children for sexual purposes has often been one of the serious issues within the legal body of international human rights law.[1] This issue was again raised by 148 countries in Palermo, Italy, at a United Nations Conference in 2000. The conference finally formulated one convention and two protocols protecting the rights of women, children and men. The Protocol to Prevent, Suppress and Punish Trafficking in Persons, Especially Women and Children, supplementing the United Nations Convention Against Transnational Organized Crime, is a valuable international treaty to address the crime of trafficking in persons, especially women and children. The Protocol was adopted in 2001. The provisions of the Protocol aim to develop the wording of the original convention in a much more practical way.[2] The intention of the Protocol is to prevent trafficking in women and children internationally, and to establish the basic outlines for judicial cooperation and exchanges of all types of information concerning trafficking between the parties to the agreement. For this purpose, the Protocol aims to harmonize the provisions of the national legislation of different states and to create effective legislation against the trafficking in women and children. Although the provisions of the Protocol clearly referred to the prohibition of sex trafficking, the policy of the Protocol has not been so strong. This is because many states dispute the difference between prostitution and trafficking, and seek to legalize trafficking as sex work. In addition, the value of the Protocol is mostly more conventional than practical since sex trafficking in women and children has been continuing between different countries, and sexual exploitation of children is frequent. This can be seen in the reports of many international bodies or in internet communication.

The Protocol states:

[1] Kerstin Nordlöf,. Economic Raison d'être of Trafficking in Children in Rätten i Kris (2012)

[2] G.A. Res. 25, annex I, U.N. GAOR, 55th Sess., Supp. No. 49, at 44, U.N. Doc. A/45/49 (Vol. I) (2001).

Preamble

The States Parties to this Protocol,

Declaring that effective action to prevent and combat trafficking in persons, especially women and children, requires a comprehensive international approach in the countries of origin, transit and destination that includes measures to prevent such trafficking, to punish the traffickers and to protect the victims of such trafficking, including by protecting their internationally recognized human rights,

Taking into account the fact that, despite the existence of a variety of international instruments containing rules and practical measures to combat the exploitation of persons, especially women and children, there is no universal instrument that addresses all aspects of trafficking in persons,

Concerned that, in the absence of such an instrument, persons who are vulnerable to trafficking will not be sufficiently protected,

Recalling General Assembly resolution 53/111 of 9 December 1998, in which the Assembly decided to establish an open-ended intergovernmental ad hoc committee for the purpose of elaborating a comprehensive international convention against transnational organized crime and of discussing the elaboration of, inter alia, an international instrument addressing trafficking in women and children,

Convinced that supplementing the United Nations Convention against Transnational Organized Crime with an international instrument for the prevention, suppression and punishment of trafficking in persons, especially women and children, will be useful in preventing and combating that crime,

Have agreed as follows:

I. General provisions

Article 1

Relation with the United Nations Convention against Transnational Organized Crime

1. This Protocol supplements the United Nations Convention against Transnational Organized Crime. It shall be interpreted together with the Convention.

2. The provisions of the Convention shall apply, mutatis mutandis, to this Protocol unless otherwise provided herein.

3. The offences established in accordance with article 5 of this Protocol shall be regarded as offences established in accordance with the Convention.

Article 2

Statement of purpose

The purposes of this Protocol are:

(a) To prevent and combat trafficking in persons, paying particular attention to women and children;

(b) To protect and assist the victims of such trafficking, with full respect for their human rights; and

(c) To promote cooperation among States Parties in order to meet those objectives.

Article 3

Use of terms

For the purposes of this Protocol:

(a) "Trafficking in persons" shall mean the recruitment, transportation, transfer, harbouring or receipt of persons, by means of the threat or use of force or other forms of coercion, of abduction, of fraud, of deception, of the abuse of power or of a position of vulnerability or of the giving or receiving of payments or benefits to achieve the consent of a person having control over another person, for the purpose of exploitation. Exploitation shall include, at a minimum, the exploitation of the prostitution of others or other forms of sexual exploitation, forced labour or services, slavery or practices similar to slavery, servitude or the removal of organs;

(b) The consent of a victim of trafficking in persons to the intended exploitation set forth in subparagraph (a) of this article shall be irrelevant where any of the means set forth in subparagraph (a) have been used;

(c) The recruitment, transportation, transfer, harbouring or receipt of a child for the purpose of exploitation shall be considered "trafficking in persons" even if this does not involve any of the means set forth in subparagraph (a) of this article;

(d) "Child" shall mean any person under eighteen years of age.

Article 4

Scope of application

This Protocol shall apply, except as otherwise stated herein, to the prevention, investigation and prosecution of the offences established in accordance with article 5 of this Protocol, where those offences are transnational in nature and involve an organized criminal group, as well as to the protection of victims of such offences.

Article 5

Criminalization

1. Each State Party shall adopt such legislative and other measures as may be necessary to establish as criminal offences the conduct set forth in article 3 of this Protocol, when committed intentionally.

2. Each State Party shall also adopt such legislative and other measures as may be necessary to establish as criminal offences:

(a) Subject to the basic concepts of its legal system, attempting to commit an offence established in accordance with paragraph 1 of this article;

(b) Participating as an accomplice in an offence established in accordance with paragraph 1 of this article; and

(c) Organizing or directing other persons to commit an offence established in accordance with paragraph 1 of this article.

II. Protection of victims of trafficking in persons

Article 6

Assistance to and protection of victims of trafficking in persons

1. In appropriate cases and to the extent possible under its domestic law, each State Party shall protect the privacy and identity of victims of trafficking in persons, including, inter alia, by making legal proceedings relating to such trafficking confidential.

2. Each State Party shall ensure that its domestic legal or administrative system contains measures that provide to victims of trafficking in persons, in appropriate cases:

(a) Information on relevant court and administrative proceedings;

(b) Assistance to enable their views and concerns to be presented and considered at appropriate stages of criminal proceedings against offenders, in a manner not prejudicial to the rights of the defence.

3. Each State Party shall consider implementing measures to provide for the physical, psychological and social recovery of victims of trafficking in persons, including, in appropriate cases, in cooperation with non-governmental organizations, other relevant organizations and other elements of civil society, and, in particular, the provision of:

(a) Appropriate housing;

(b) Counselling and information, in particular as regards their legal rights, in a language that the victims of trafficking in persons can understand;

(c) Medical, psychological and material assistance; and

(d) Employment, educational and training opportunities.

4. Each State Party shall take into account, in applying the provisions of this article, the age, gender and special needs of victims of trafficking in persons, in particular the special needs of children, including appropriate housing, education and care.

5. Each State Party shall endeavour to provide for the physical safety of victims of trafficking in persons while they are within its territory.

6. Each State Party shall ensure that its domestic legal system contains measures that offer victims of trafficking in persons the possibility of obtaining compensation for damage suffered.

Article 7

Status of victims of trafficking in persons in receiving States

1. In addition to taking measures pursuant to article 6 of this Protocol, each State Party shall consider adopting legislative or other appropriate measures that permit victims of trafficking in persons to remain in its territory, temporarily or permanently, in appropriate cases.

2. In implementing the provision contained in paragraph 1 of this article, each State Party shall give appropriate consideration to humanitarian and compassionate factors.

Article 8

Repatriation of victims of trafficking in persons

1. The State Party of which a victim of trafficking in persons is a national or in which the person had the right of permanent residence at the time of entry into the territory of the receiving State Party shall facilitate and accept, with due regard for the safety of that person, the return of that person without undue or unreasonable delay.

2. When a State Party returns a victim of trafficking in persons to a State Party of which that person is a national or in which he or she had, at the time of entry into the territory of the receiving State Party, the right of permanent residence, such return shall be with due regard for the safety of that person and for the status of any legal proceedings related to the fact that the person is a victim of trafficking and shall preferably be voluntary.

3. At the request of a receiving State Party, a requested State Party shall, without undue or unreasonable delay, verify whether a person who is a victim of trafficking in persons is its national or had the right of permanent residence in its territory at the time of entry into the territory of the receiving State Party.

4. In order to facilitate the return of a victim of trafficking in persons who is without proper documentation, the State Party of which that person is a national or in which he or she had the right of permanent residence at

the time of entry into the territory of the receiving State Party shall agree to issue, at the request of the receiving State Party, such travel documents or other authorization as may be necessary to enable the person to travel to and re-enter its territory.

5. This article shall be without prejudice to any right afforded to victims of trafficking in persons by any domestic law of the receiving State Party.

6. This article shall be without prejudice to any applicable bilateral or multilateral agreement or arrangement that governs, in whole or in part, the return of victims of trafficking in persons.

III. Prevention, cooperation and other measures

Article 9

Prevention of trafficking in persons

1. States Parties shall establish comprehensive policies, programmes and other measures:

(a) To prevent and combat trafficking in persons; and

(b) To protect victims of trafficking in persons, especially women and children, from revictimization.

2. States Parties shall endeavour to undertake measures such as research, information and mass media campaigns and social and economic initiatives to prevent and combat trafficking in persons.

3. Policies, programmes and other measures established in accordance with this article shall, as appropriate, include cooperation with non-governmental organizations, other relevant organizations and other elements of civil society.

4. States Parties shall take or strengthen measures, including through bilateral or multilateral cooperation, to alleviate the factors that make persons, especially women and children, vulnerable to trafficking, such as poverty, underdevelopment and lack of equal opportunity.

5. States Parties shall adopt or strengthen legislative or other measures, such as educational, social or cultural measures, including through bilateral and multilateral cooperation, to discourage the demand that fosters all forms of exploitation of persons, especially women and children, that leads to trafficking.

Article 10

Information exchange and training

1. Law enforcement, immigration or other relevant authorities of States Parties shall, as appropriate, cooperate with one another by

exchanging information, in accordance with their domestic law, to enable them to determine:

(a) Whether individuals crossing or attempting to cross an international border with travel documents belonging to other persons or without travel documents are perpetrators or victims of trafficking in persons;

(b) The types of travel document that individuals have used or attempted to use to cross an international border for the purpose of trafficking in persons; and

(c) The means and methods used by organized criminal groups for the purpose of trafficking in persons, including the recruitment and transportation of victims, routes and links between and among individuals and groups engaged in such rafficking, and possible measures for detecting them.

2. States Parties shall provide or strengthen training for law enforcement, immigration and other relevant officials in the prevention of trafficking in persons. The training should focus on methods used in preventing such trafficking, prosecuting the traffickers and protecting the rights of the victims, including protecting the victims from the traffickers. The training should also take into account the need to consider human rights and child- and gender-sensitive issues and it should encourage cooperation with non-governmental organizations, other relevant organizations and other elements of civil society.

3. A State Party that receives information shall comply with any request by the State Party that transmitted the information that places restrictions on its use.

Article 11

Border measures

1. Without prejudice to international commitments in relation to the free movement of people, States Parties shall strengthen, to the extent possible, such border controls as may be necessary to prevent and detect trafficking in persons.

2. Each State Party shall adopt legislative or other appropriate measures to prevent, to the extent possible, means of transport operated by commercial carriers from being used in the commission of offences established in accordance with article 5 of this Protocol.

3. Where appropriate, and without prejudice to applicable international conventions, such measures shall include establishing the obligation of commercial carriers, including any transportation company or the owner or operator of any means of transport, to ascertain that all passengers are in

possession of the travel documents required for entry into the receiving State.

4. Each State Party shall take the necessary measures, in accordance with its domestic law, to provide for sanctions in cases of violation of the obligation set forth in paragraph 3 of this article.

5. Each State Party shall consider taking measures that permit, in accordance with its domestic law, the denial of entry or revocation of visas of persons implicated in the commission of offences established in accordance with this Protocol.

6. Without prejudice to article 27 of the Convention, States Parties shall consider strengthening cooperation among border control agencies by, inter alia, establishing and maintaining direct channels of communication.

Article 12

Security and control of documents

Each State Party shall take such measures as may be necessary, within available means:

(a) To ensure that travel or identity documents issued by it are of such quality that they cannot easily be misused and cannot readily be falsified or unlawfully altered, replicated or issued; and

(b) To ensure the integrity and security of travel or identity documents issued by or on behalf of the State Party and to prevent their unlawful creation, issuance and use.

Article 13

Legitimacy and validity of documents

At the request of another State Party, a State Party shall, in accordance with its domestic law, verify within a reasonable time the legitimacy and validity of travel or identity documents issued or purported to have been issued in its name and suspected of being used for trafficking in persons.

IV. Final provisions

Article 14

Saving clause

1. Nothing in this Protocol shall affect the rights, obligations and responsibilities of States and individuals under international law, including international humanitarian law and international human rights law and, in particular, where applicable, the 1951 Convention and the 1967 Protocol relating to the Status of Refugees and the principle of non-refoulement as contained therein.

2. The measures set forth in this Protocol shall be interpreted and applied in a way that is not discriminatory to persons on the ground that they are victims of trafficking in persons. The interpretation and application of those measures shall be consistent with internationally recognized principles of non-discrimination.

Article 15

Settlement of disputes

1. States Parties shall endeavour to settle disputes concerning the interpretation or application of this Protocol through negotiation.

2. Any dispute between two or more States Parties concerning the interpretation or application of this Protocol that cannot be settled through negotiation within a reasonable time shall, at the request of one of those States Parties, be submitted to arbitration. If, six months after the date of the request for arbitration, those States Parties are unable to agree on the organization of the arbitration, any one of those States Parties may refer the dispute to the International Court of Justice by request in accordance with the Statute of the Court.

3. Each State Party may, at the time of signature, ratification, acceptance or approval of or accession to this Protocol, declare that it does not consider itself bound by paragraph 2 of this article. The other States Parties shall not be bound by paragraph 2 of this article with respect to any State Party that has made such a reservation.

4. Any State Party that has made a reservation in accordance with paragraph 3 of this article may at any time withdraw that reservation by notification to the Secretary-General of the United Nations.

Article 16

Signature, ratification, acceptance, approval and accession

1. This Protocol shall be open to all States for signature from 12 to 15 December 2000 in Palermo, Italy, and thereafter at United Nations Headquarters in New York until 12 December 2002.

2. This Protocol shall also be open for signature by regional economic integration organizations provided that at least one member State of such organization has signed this Protocol in accordance with paragraph 1 of this article.

3. This Protocol is subject to ratification, acceptance or approval. Instruments of ratification, acceptance or approval shall be deposited with the Secretary-General of the United Nations. A regional economic integration organization may deposit its instrument of ratification, acceptance or approval if at least one of its member States has done

likewise. In that instrument of ratification, acceptance or approval, such organization shall declare the extent of its competence with respect to the matters governed by this Protocol. Such organization shall also inform the depositary of any relevant modification in the extent of its competence.

4. This Protocol is open for accession by any State or any regional economic integration organization of which at least one member State is a Party to this Protocol. Instruments of accession shall be deposited with the Secretary-General of the United Nations. At the time of its accession, a regional economic integration organization shall declare the extent of its competence with respect to matters governed by this Protocol. Such organization shall also inform the depositary of any relevant modification in the extent of its competence.

Article 17

Entry into force

1. This Protocol shall enter into force on the ninetieth day after the date of deposit of the fortieth instrument of ratification, acceptance, approval or accession, except that it shall not enter into force before the entry into force of the Convention. For the purpose of this paragraph, any instrument deposited by a regional economic integration organization shall not be counted as additional to those deposited by member States of such organization.

2. For each State or regional economic integration organization ratifying, accepting, approving or acceding to this Protocol after the deposit of the fortieth instrument of such action, this Protocol shall enter into force on the thirtieth day after the date of deposit by such State or organization of the relevant instrument or on the date this Protocol enters into force pursuant to paragraph 1 of this article, whichever is the later.

Article 18

Amendment

1. After the expiry of five years from the entry into force of this Protocol, a State Party to the Protocol may propose an amendment and file it with the Secretary-General of the United Nations, who shall thereupon communicate the proposed amendment to the States Parties and to the Conference of the Parties to the Convention for the purpose of considering and deciding on the proposal. The States Parties to this Protocol meeting at the Conference of the Parties shall make every effort to achieve consensus on each amendment. If all efforts at consensus have been exhausted and no agreement has been reached, the amendment shall, as a last resort, require for its adoption a two-thirds majority vote of the States Parties to this

Protocol present and voting at the meeting of the Conference of the Parties.

2. Regional economic integration organizations, in matters within their competence, shall exercise their right to vote under this article with a number of votes equal to the number of their member States that are Parties to this Protocol. Such organizations shall not exercise their right to vote if their member States exercise theirs and vice versa.

3. An amendment adopted in accordance with paragraph 1 of this article is subject to ratification, acceptance or approval by States Parties.

4. An amendment adopted in accordance with paragraph 1 of this article shall enter into force in respect of a State Party ninety days after the date of the deposit with the Secretary-General of the United Nations of an instrument of ratification, acceptance or approval of such amendment.

5. When an amendment enters into force, it shall be binding on those States Parties which have expressed their consent to be bound by it. Other States Parties shall still be bound by the provisions of this Protocol and any earlier amendments that they have ratified, accepted or approved.

Article 19

Denunciation

1. A State Party may denounce this Protocol by written notification to the Secretary-General of the United Nations. Such denunciation shall become effective one year after the date of receipt of the notification by the Secretary-General.

2. A regional economic integration organization shall cease to be a Party to this Protocol when all of its member States have denounced it.

Article 20

Depositary and languages

1. The Secretary-General of the United Nations is designated depositary of this Protocol.

2. The original of this Protocol, of which the Arabic, Chinese, English, French, Russian and Spanish texts are equally authentic, shall be deposited with the Secretary-General of the United Nations.

IN WITNESS WHEREOF, the undersigned plenipotentiaries, being duly authorized thereto by their respective Governments, have signed this Protocol.

7. Guidelines on Justice in Matters Involving Child Victims and Witnesses of Crime, 2005

One of the significant instruments protecting rights of children is the work of the UN Economic and Social Council entitled Guidelines on Justice in Matters involving Children Victims and Witnesses of Crime. [3] It may be asserted that the Guidelines on Justice is partly the development of the provisions of the Declaration of Basic Principles of Justice for Victims of Crime and Abuse of Power[4] as are also necessary in the interests of the children. Although the Declaration does not explicitly refer to the rights of children, it would be a mistake to state that the Declaration ignore children as victims of crime. From a regional aspect, the Council Framework Decision of 15 March 2001 on the standing of victims in criminal proceedings emphasises the importance of ensuring victims of crime a high level of physical, psychological, social and juridical protection. This protection is regardless of the member state in which they are present. It has particularly pointed out that "Victims' needs should be considered and addressed in a comprehensive, coordinated manner, avoiding partial or inconsistent solutions which may give rise to secondary victimisation."[5] In particular, vulnerable victims should be treated with appropriate measures. Therefore, the Decision demands to grant programs to help crime victims which includes before, during and after criminal investigations and proceedings.

The Guidelines on Justice in Matters involving Children Victims and Witnesses of Crime was created to make sure that children who have been harmed by crime or witnessed criminal behavior are fully protected and defended when they tell, during the criminal proceedings, what have occurred to them. The chief intention of the instrument is to protect various rights of children under criminal justice process and encourage all children not hesitate to tell the truth. The instrument has particularly stated that it applies to person under 18 years. According to it, the term "child victims and witnesses" implies "children and adolescents, under the age of 18, who are victims of crime or witnesses to crime regardless of their role in the offence or in the prosecution of the alleged offender or groups of offenders." The instrument also encourages all professionals and other

---

[3] UN Economic and Social Council (ECOSOC), *UN Economic and Social Council 2005/20: Guidelines on Justice in Matters Involving Child Victims and Witnesses of Crime*, 22 July 2005, E/RES/2005/20, available at: http://www.unhcr.org/refworld/docid/468922c92.html [accessed 14 May 2012].

[4] Adopted by General Assembly resolution 40/34 of 29 November 1985.

[5] Para.5, (2001/220/JHA), www.crimecouncil.gov.ie/Victims_of_crime.html.

responsible persons to respect certain cross-cutting principles regarding protection of the rights of children. These are such as dignity, non-discrimination, best interests of the child, protection, and right to participation. As a whole, the provisions of the instrument recognise certain definite duties and responsibilities for national or international authorities who deal, in one way or another, with the rights of children. Therefore the instrument aims to guarantee physical, psychological and moral integrity of children and their individual needs, age, capacity including intellectual maturity.

Resolution 2005/20 Guidelines on Justice in Matters Involving Child Victims and Witnesses of Crime

The Economic and Social Council,

Recalling its resolution 1996/16 of 23 July 1996, in which it requested the Secretary-General to continue to promote the use and application of United Nations standards and norms in crime prevention and criminal justice,

Recalling also its resolution 2004/27 of 21 July 2004 on guidelines on justice for child victims and witnesses of crime, in which it requested the Secretary-General to convene an intergovernmental expert group in order to develop guidelines on justice in matters involving child victims and witnesses of crime,

Recalling further General Assembly resolution 40/34 of 29 November 1985, by which the Assembly adopted the Declaration of Basic Principles of Justice for Victims of Crime and Abuse of Power, annexed to the resolution,

Recalling the provisions of the Convention on the Rights of the Child, adopted by the General Assembly by its resolution 44/25 of 20 November 1989, in particular articles 3 and 39 thereof, as well as the provisions of the Optional Protocol to the Convention on the Rights of the Child on the sale of children, child prostitution and child pornography, adopted by the Assembly by its resolution 54/263 of 25 May 2000, in particular article 8 thereof,

Recognizing that justice for child victims and witnesses of crime must be assured while safeguarding the rights of accused persons,

Recognizing also that children who are victims and witnesses are particularly vulnerable and need special protection, assistance and support appropriate to their age, level of maturity and unique needs in order to prevent further hardship and trauma that may result from their participation in the criminal justice process,

Mindful of the serious physical, psychological and emotional consequences of crime and victimization for child victims and witnesses, in particular in cases involving sexual exploitation,

Mindful also of the fact that the participation of child victims and witnesses in the criminal justice process is necessary for effective prosecutions, in particular where the child victim may be the only witness,

Recognizing the efforts of the International Bureau for Children's Rights in laying the groundwork for the development of guidelines on justice in matters involving child victims and witnesses of crime,

Noting with appreciation the work of the Intergovernmental Expert Group Meeting to Develop Guidelines on Justice in Matters involving Child Victims and Witnesses of Crime, held in Vienna on 15 and 16 March 2005, for which extrabudgetary resources were provided by the Government of Canada, and taking note of the report of the

Intergovernmental Expert Group,[6]

Taking note of the report of the Eleventh United Nations Congress on Crime Prevention and Criminal Justice, held in Bangkok from 18 to 25 April 2005, regarding the item entitled "Making standards work: fifty years of standard-setting in crime prevention and criminal justice",

Welcoming the Bangkok Declaration on Synergies and Responses: Strategic Alliances in Crime Prevention and Criminal Justice,[7] adopted at the high-level segment of the Eleventh United Nations Congress on Crime Prevention and Criminal Justice, in particular paragraphs 17 and 33 thereof, in which the importance of providing support and services to witnesses and victims of crime is recognized,

1. *Adopts* the Guidelines on Justice in Matters involving Child Victims and Witnesses of Crime, annexed to the present resolution, as a useful framework that could assist Member States in enhancing the protection of child victims and witnesses in the criminal justice system;

2. *Invites* Member States to draw, where appropriate, on the Guidelines in the development of legislation, procedures, policies and practices for children who are victims of crime or witnesses in criminal proceedings;

---

[6] E/CN.15/2005/14/Add.1.

[7] A/CONF.203/18, chap. I, resolution 1.

3. *Calls upon* Member States that have developed legislation, procedures, policies or practices for child victims and witnesses to make information available to other States, upon request and where appropriate, and to assist them in developing and implementing training or other activities in relation to the use of the Guidelines;

4. *Calls upon* the United Nations Office on Drugs and Crime to provide technical assistance, within available extrabudgetary resources, not excluding the use of existing resources from the regular budget of the United Nations Office on Drugs and Crime,[8] as well as advisory services, to Member States, upon request, to assist them in the use of the Guidelines;

5. *Requests* the Secretary-General to ensure the widest possible dissemination of the Guidelines among Member States, the institutes of the United Nations Crime Prevention and Criminal Justice Programme network and other international, regional and non-governmental organizations and institutions;

6. *Recommends* that Member States bring the Guidelines to the attention of relevant governmental and non-governmental organizations and institutions;

7. *Invites* the institutes of the United Nations Crime Prevention and Criminal Justice Programme network to provide training in relation to the Guidelines and to consolidate and disseminate information on successful models at the national level;

8. *Requests* the Secretary-General to report to the Commission on Crime Prevention and Criminal Justice at its seventeenth session on the implementation of the present resolution.

Annex

Guidelines on Justice in Matters involving Child Victims and Witnesses of Crime

I. Objectives

1. The present Guidelines on Justice for Child Victims and Witnesses of Crime set forth good practice based on the consensus of contemporary knowledge and relevant international and regional norms, standards and principles.

[8] This new language does not provide a basis for an increase in the regular budget or requests for supplemental increases.

2. The Guidelines should be implemented in accordance with relevant national legislation and judicial procedures as well as take into consideration legal, social, economic, cultural and geographical conditions. However, States should constantly endeavour to overcome practical difficulties in the application of the Guidelines.

3. The Guidelines provide a practical framework to achieve the following objectives:

(a) To assist in the review of national and domestic laws, procedures and practices so that these ensure full respect for the rights of child victims and witnesses of crime and contribute to the implementation of the Convention on the Rights of the Child,[9] by parties to that Convention;

(b) To assist Governments, international organizations, public agencies, non-governmental and community-based organizations and other interested parties in designing and implementing legislation, policy, programmes and practices that address key issues related to child victims and witnesses of crime;

(c) To guide professionals and, where appropriate, volunteers working with child victims and witnesses of crime in their day-to-day practice in the adult and juvenile justice process at the national, regional and international levels, consistent with the Declaration of Basic Principles of Justice for Victims of Crime and Abuse of Power;[10]

(d) To assist and support those caring for children in dealing sensitively with child victims and witnesses of crime.

4. In implementing the Guidelines, each jurisdiction should ensure that adequate training, selection and procedures are put in place to protect and meet the special needs of child victims and witnesses of crime, where the nature of the victimization affects categories of children differently, such as sexual assault of children, especially girls.

5. The Guidelines cover a field in which knowledge and practice are growing and improving. They are neither intended to be exhaustive nor to preclude further development, provided it is in harmony with their underlying objectives and principles.

6. The Guidelines could also be applied to processes in informal and customary systems of justice such as restorative justice and in non-

---

[9] General Assembly resolution 44/25, annex.
[10] General Assembly resolution 40/34, annex.

criminal fields of law including, but not limited to, custody, divorce, adoption, child protection, mental health, citizenship, immigration and refugee law.

II. Special considerations

7. The Guidelines were developed:

(a) Cognizant that millions of children throughout the world suffer harm as a result of crime and abuse of power and that the rights of those children have not been adequately recognized and that they may suffer additional hardship when assisting in the justice process;

(b) Recognizing that children are vulnerable and require special protection appropriate to their age, level of maturity and individual special needs;

(c) Recognizing that girls are particularly vulnerable and may face discrimination at all stages of the justice system;

(d) Reaffirming that every effort must be made to prevent victimization of children, including through implementation of the Guidelines for the Prevention of Crime;[11]

(e) Cognizant that children who are victims and witnesses may suffer additional hardship if mistakenly viewed as offenders when they are in fact victims and witnesses;

(f) Recalling that the Convention on the Rights of the Child sets forth requirements and principles to secure effective recognition of the rights of children and that the Declaration of Basic Principles of Justice for Victims of Crime and Abuse of Power sets forth principles to provide victims with the right to information, participation, protection, reparation and assistance;

(g) Recalling international and regional initiatives that implement the principles of the Declaration of Basic Principles of Justice for Victims of Crime and Abuse of Power, including the *Handbook on Justice for Victims* and the *Guide for Policy Makers on the Declaration of Basic Principles*, both issued by the United Nations Office for Drug Control and Crime Prevention in 1999;

(h) Recognizing the efforts of the International Bureau for Children's Rights in laying the groundwork for the development of guidelines on justice for child victims and witnesses of crime;

---

[11] Resolution 2002/13, annex.

(i) Considering that improved responses to child victims and witnesses of crime can make children and their families more willing to disclose instances of victimization and more supportive of the justice process;

(j) Recalling that justice for child victims and witnesses of crime must be assured while safeguarding the rights of accused and convicted offenders;

(k) Bearing in mind the variety of legal systems and traditions, and noting that crime is increasingly transnational in nature and that there is a need to ensure that child victims and witnesses of crime receive equivalent protection in all countries.

III. Principles

8. As stated in international instruments and in particular the Convention on the Rights of the Child as reflected in the work of the Committee on the Rights of the Child, and in order to ensure justice for child victims and witnesses of crime, professionals and others responsible for the well-being of those children must respect the following cross-cutting principles:

(a) *Dignity*. Every child is a unique and valuable human being and as such his or her individual dignity, special needs, interests and privacy should be respected and protected;

(b) *Non-discrimination*. Every child has the right to be treated fairly and equally, regardless of his or her or the parent's or legal guardian's race, ethnicity, colour, gender, language, religion, political or other opinion, national, ethnic or social origin, property, disability and birth or other status;

(c) *Best interests of the child*. While the rights of accused and convicted offenders should be safeguarded, every child has the right to have his or her best interests given primary consideration. This includes the right to protection and to a chance for harmonious development:

(i) *Protection*. Every child has the right to life and survival and to be shielded from any form of hardship, abuse or neglect, including physical, psychological, mental and emotional abuse and neglect;

(ii) *Harmonious development*. Every child has the right to a chance for harmonious development and to a standard of living adequate for physical, mental, spiritual, moral and social growth. In the case of a child who has been traumatized, every step should be taken to enable the child to enjoy healthy development;

(d) *Right to participation.* Every child has, subject to national procedural law, the right to express his or her views, opinions and beliefs freely, in his or her own words, and to contribute especially to the decisions affecting his or her life, including those taken in any judicial processes, and to have those views taken into consideration according to his or her abilities, age, intellectual maturity and evolving capacity.

IV. Definitions

9. Throughout these Guidelines, the following definitions apply:

(a) "Child victims and witnesses" denotes children and adolescents, under the age of 18, who are victims of crime or witnesses to crime regardless of their role in the offence or in the prosecution of the alleged offender or groups of offenders;

(b) "Professionals" refers to persons who, within the context of their work, are in contact with child victims and witnesses of crime or are responsible for addressing the needs of children in the justice system and for whom these Guidelines are applicable. This includes, but is not limited to, the following: child and victim advocates and support persons; child protection service practitioners; child welfare agency staff; prosecutors and, where appropriate, defence lawyers; diplomatic and consular staff; domestic violence programme staff; judges; court staff; law enforcement officials; medical and mental health professionals; and social workers;

(c) "Justice process" encompasses detection of the crime, making of the complaint, investigation, prosecution and trial and post-trial procedures, regardless of whether the case is handled in a national, international or regional criminal justice system for adults or juveniles, or in a customary or informal system of justice;

(d) "Child-sensitive" denotes an approach that balances the child's right to protection and that takes into account the child's individual needs and views.

V. The right to be treated with dignity and compassion

10. Child victims and witnesses should be treated in a caring and sensitive manner throughout the justice process, taking into account their personal situation and immediate needs, age, gender, disability and level of maturity and fully respecting their physical, mental and moral integrity.

11. Every child should be treated as an individual with his or her individual needs, wishes and feelings.

12. Interference in the child's private life should be limited to the minimum needed at the same time as high standards of evidence collection are maintained in order to ensure fair and equitable outcomes of the justice process.

13. In order to avoid further hardship to the child, interviews, examinations and other forms of investigation should be conducted by trained professionals who proceed in a sensitive, respectful and thorough manner.

14. All interactions described in these Guidelines should be conducted in a child-sensitive manner in a suitable environment that accommodates the special needs of the child, according to his or her abilities, age, intellectual maturity and evolving capacity. They should also take place in a language that the child uses and understands.

VI. The right to be protected from discrimination

15. Child victims and witnesses should have access to a justice process that protects them from discrimination based on the child's, parent's or legal guardian's race, colour, gender, language, religion, political or other opinion, ational, ethnic or social origin, property, disability and birth or other status.

16. The justice process and support services available to child victims and witnesses and their families should be sensitive to the child's age, wishes, understanding, gender, sexual orientation, ethnic, cultural, religious, linguistic and social background, caste, socio-economic condition and immigration or refugee status, as well as to the special needs of the child, including health, abilities and capacities. Professionals should be trained and educated about such differences.

17. In certain cases, special services and protection will need to be instituted to take account of gender and the different nature of specific offences against children, such as sexual assault involving children.

18. Age should not be a barrier to a child's right to participate fully in the justice process. Every child should be treated as a capable witness, subject to examination, and his or her testimony should not be presumed invalid or untrustworthy by reason of the child's age alone as long as his or her age and maturity allow the giving of intelligible and credible testimony, with or without communication aids and other assistance.

VII. The right to be informed

19. Child victims and witnesses, their parents or guardians and legal representatives, from their first contact with the justice process and throughout that process, should be promptly and adequately informed, to the extent feasible and appropriate, of, inter alia:

(a) The availability of health, psychological, social and other relevant services as well as the means of accessing such services along with legal or other advice or representation, compensation and emergency financial support, where applicable;

(b) The procedures for the adult and juvenile criminal justice process, including the role of child victims and witnesses, the importance, timing and manner of testimony, and ways in which "questioning" will be conducted during the investigation and trial;

(c) The existing support mechanisms for the child when making a complaint and participating in the investigation and court proceedings;

(d) The specific places and times of hearings and other relevant events;

(e) The availability of protective measures;

(f) The existing mechanisms for review of decisions affecting child victims and witnesses;

(g) The relevant rights for child victims and witnesses pursuant to the Convention on the Rights of the Child and the Declaration of Basic Principles of Justice for Victims of Crime and Abuse of Power.

20. In addition, child victims, their parents or guardians and legal representatives should be promptly and adequately informed, to the extent feasible and appropriate, of:

(a) The progress and disposition of the specific case, including the apprehension, arrest and custodial status of the accused and any pending changes to that status, the prosecutorial decision and relevant post-trial developments and the outcome of the case;

(b) The existing opportunities to obtain reparation from the offender or from the State through the justice process, through alternative civil proceedings or through other processes.

VIII. The right to be heard and to express views and concerns

21. Professionals should make every effort to enable child victims and witnesses to express their views and concerns related to their involvement in the justice process, including by:

(a) Ensuring that child victims and where appropriate witnesses are consulted on the matters set forth in paragraph 19 above;

(b) Ensuring that child victims and witnesses are enabled to express freely and in their own manner their views and concerns regarding their involvement in the justice process, their concerns regarding safety in relation to the accused, the manner in which they prefer to provide testimony and their feelings about the conclusions of the process;

(c) Giving due regard to the child's views and concerns and, if they are unable to accommodate them, explain the reasons to the child.

IX. The right to effective assistance

22. Child victims and witnesses and, where appropriate, family members should have access to assistance provided by professionals who have received relevant training as set out in paragraphs 40 to 42 below. This may include assistance and support services such as financial, legal, counselling, health, social and educational services, physical and psychological recovery services and other services necessary for the child's reintegration. All such assistance should address the child's needs and enable him or her to participate effectively at all stages of the justice process.

23. In assisting child victims and witnesses, professionals should make every effort to coordinate support so that the child is not subjected to excessive interventions.

24. Child victims and witnesses should receive assistance from support persons, such as child victim/witness specialists, commencing at the initial report and continuing until such services are no longer required.

25. Professionals should develop and implement measures to make it easier for children to testify or give evidence to improve communication and understanding at the pre-trial and trial stages. These measures may include:

(a) Child victim and witness specialists to address the child's special needs;

(b) Support persons, including specialists and appropriate family members to accompany the child during testimony;

(c) Where appropriate, to appoint guardians to protect the child's legal interests.

X. The right to privacy

26. Child victims and witnesses should have their privacy protected as a matter of primary importance.

27. Information relating to a child's involvement in the justice process should be protected. This can be achieved through maintaining confidentiality and restricting disclosure of information that may lead to identification of a child who is a victim or witness in the justice process.

28. Measures should be taken to protect children from undue exposure to the public by, for example, excluding the public and the media from the courtroom during the child's testimony, where permitted by national law.

XI. The right to be protected from hardship during the justice process

29. Professionals should take measures to prevent hardship during the detection, investigation and prosecution process in order to ensure that the best interests and dignity of child victims and witnesses are respected.

30. Professionals should approach child victims and witnesses with sensitivity, so that they:

(a) Provide support for child victims and witnesses, including accompanying the child throughout his or her involvement in the justice process, when it is in his or her best interests;

(b) Provide certainty about the process, including providing child victims and witnesses with clear expectations as to what to expect in the process, with as much certainty as possible. The child's participation in hearings and trials should be planned ahead of time and every effort should be made to ensure continuity in the relationships between children and the professionals in contact with them throughout the process;

(c) Ensure that trials take place as soon as practical, unless delays are in the child's best interest. Investigation of crimes involving child victims and witnesses should also be expedited and there should be procedures, laws or court rules that provide for cases involving child victims and witnesses to be expedited;

(d) Use child-sensitive procedures, including interview rooms designed for children, interdisciplinary services for child victims integrated in the same location, modified court environments that take child witnesses into consideration, recesses during a child's testimony, hearings scheduled at times of day appropriate to the age and maturity of the child, an appropriate notification system to ensure the child goes to court only when necessary and other appropriate measures to facilitate the child's testimony.

31. Professionals should also implement measures:

(a) To limit the number of interviews: special procedures for collection of evidence from child victims and witnesses should be implemented in order to reduce the number of interviews, statements, hearings and, specifically, unnecessary contact with the justice process, such as through use of video recording;

(b) To ensure that child victims and witnesses are protected, if compatible with the legal system and with due respect for the rights of the defence, from being cross-examined by the alleged perpetrator: as necessary, child victims and witnesses should be interviewed, and examined in court, out of sight of the alleged perpetrator, and separate courthouse waiting rooms and private interview areas should be provided;

(c) To ensure that child victims and witnesses are questioned in a child-sensitive manner and allow for the exercise of supervision by judges, facilitate testimony and reduce potential intimidation, for example by using testimonial aids or appointing psychological experts.

XII. The right to safety

32. Where the safety of a child victim or witness may be at risk, appropriate measures should be taken to require the reporting of those safety risks to appropriate authorities and to protect the child from such risk before, during and after the justice process.

33. Professionals who come into contact with children should be required to notify appropriate authorities if they suspect that a child victim or witness has been harmed, is being harmed or is likely to be harmed.

34. Professionals should be trained in recognizing and preventing intimidation, threats and harm to child victims and witnesses. Where child victims and witnesses may be the subject of intimidation, threats or harm, appropriate conditions should be put in place to ensure the safety of the child. Such safeguards could include:

(a) Avoiding direct contact between child victims and witnesses and the alleged perpetrators at any point in the justice process;

(b) Using court-ordered restraining orders supported by a registry system;

(c) Ordering pre-trial detention of the accused and setting special "no contact" bail conditions;

(d) Placing the accused under house arrest;

(e) Wherever possible and appropriate, giving child victims and witnesses protection by the police or other relevant agencies and safeguarding their whereabouts from disclosure.

XIII. The right to reparation

35. Child victims should, wherever possible, receive reparation in order to achieve full redress, reintegration and recovery. Procedures for obtaining and enforcing reparation should be readily accessible and child-sensitive.

36. Provided the proceedings are child-sensitive and respect these Guidelines, combined criminal and reparations proceedings should be encouraged, together with informal and community justice procedures such as restorative justice.

37. Reparation may include restitution from the offender ordered in the criminal court, aid from victim compensation programmes administered by the State and damages ordered to be paid in civil proceedings. Where possible, costs of social and educational reintegration, medical treatment, mental health care and legal services should be addressed. Procedures should be instituted to ensure enforcement of reparation orders and payment of reparation before fines.

XIV. The right to special preventive measures

38. In addition to preventive measures that should be in place for all children, special strategies are required for child victims and witnesses who are particularly vulnerable to recurring victimization or offending.

39. Professionals should develop and implement comprehensive and specially tailored strategies and interventions in cases where there are risks that child victims may be victimized further. These strategies and interventions should take into account the nature of the victimization, including victimization related to abuse in the home, sexual exploitation, abuse in institutional settings and trafficking. The strategies may include those based on government, neighbourhood and citizen initiatives.

XV. Implementation

40. Adequate training, education and information should be made available to professionals, working with child victims and witnesses with a view to improving and sustaining specialized methods, approaches and attitudes in order to protect and deal effectively and sensitively with child victims and witnesses.

41. Professionals should be trained to effectively protect and meet the needs of child victims and witnesses, including in specialized units and services.

42. This training should include:

(a) Relevant human rights norms, standards and principles, including the rights of the child;

(b) Principles and ethical duties of their office;

(c) Signs and symptoms that indicate crimes against children;

(d) Crisis assessment skills and techniques, especially for making referrals, with an emphasis placed on the need for confidentiality;

(e) Impact, consequences, including negative physical and psychological effects, and trauma of crimes against children;

(f) Special measures and techniques to assist child victims and witnesses in the justice process;

(g) Cross-cultural and age-related linguistic, religious, social and gender issues;

(h) Appropriate adult-child communication skills;

(i) Interviewing and assessment techniques that minimize any trauma to the child while maximizing the quality of information received from the child;

(j) Skills to deal with child victims and witnesses in a sensitive, understanding, constructive and reassuring manner;

(k) Methods to protect and present evidence and to question child witnesses;

(l) Roles of, and methods used by, professionals working with child victims and witnesses.

43. Professionals should make every effort to adopt an interdisciplinary and cooperative approach in aiding children by familiarizing themselves

with the wide array of available services, such as victim support, advocacy, economic assistance, counselling, education, health, legal and social services. This approach may include protocols for the different stages of the justice process to encourage cooperation among entities that provide services to child victims and witnesses, as well as other forms of multidisciplinary work that includes police, prosecutor, medical, social services and psychological personnel working in the same location.

44. International cooperation should be enhanced between States and all sectors of society, both at the national and international levels, including mutual assistance for the purpose of facilitating collection and exchange of information and the detection, investigation and prosecution of transnational crimes involving child victims and witnesses.

45. Professionals should consider utilizing the present Guidelines as a basis for developing laws and written policies, standards and protocols aimed at assisting child victims and witnesses involved in the justice process.

46. Professionals should be enabled to periodically review and evaluate their role, together with other agencies in the justice process, in ensuring the protection of the rights of the child and the effective implementation of the present Guidelines.

36th plenary meeting 22 July 2005

8. The Statutes of International Criminal Courts

The system of international criminal law is one of the most important and essential parts of public international law. It offers particular protection for individuals, groups, organization and states from unlawful regional, national and international criminal behaviour. The system sets forth certain international standards designed to protect all children in peace or war. This policy of the system can be examined not only within the content of numerous international treaties, but also within the provisions of the statutes of international criminal tribunals/courts, such as the International Criminal Tribunal for the former Yugoslavia (ICTY), United Nations Security Council Resolution 827 (1993); the International Criminal Tribunal for Rwanda (ICTR), United Nations Security Council Resolution 955 (1994); the Special Court for the Sierra Leone (SCSL), Treaty between United Nations and government of Sierra Leone (2000), and the permanent International Criminal Court (ICC), (1998). They deal *inter alia* with war crimes, crimes against humanity and genocide. All these courts have aimed to protect children's rights within the procedures of criminal jurisdictions.

The most valuable principles protecting children's rights are formulated in the Statutes of the SCSL and the ICC. The provisions of both courts are the manifestation of a modern developed system protecting children's rights in the procedures of criminal courts. In particular, they should be considered as an integral part of customary international criminal law and general principles of law that have to be regulated, if they are not already implemented, into domestic systems. The ICC has no jurisdiction over a person under 18. The Statute of the ICC emphasises that protection of the victims and witnesses are a necessary corollary for an effective and successful jurisdiction. According to Article 68 of the Statute:

> The Court shall take appropriate measures to protect the safety, physical and psychological well-being, dignity and privacy of victims and witnesses. In so doing, the Court shall have regard to all relevant factors, including age, gender … and health, and the nature of the crime, in particular, but not limited to, where the crime involves sexual or gender violence or violence against children.

Similarly, the Rules of Procedure and Evidence of the Statute in Rule 7 (3) provide that:

> 3. In performing its functions, the Unit shall give due regard to the particular needs of children, elderly persons and persons with disabilities. In order to facilitate the participation and protection of children as witnesses, the Unit may assign, as appropriate, and with the agreement of the parents or the legal guardian, a child-support person to assist a child through all stages of the proceedings.

The Victims and Witnesses Unit of the ICC is responsible for including persons with expertise in the area of children, and traumatized children in particular. Article 6 (e) of the Elements of Crimes for the protection of children provides that:

Article 6 (e)

Genocide by forcibly transferring children

Elements

1. The perpetrator forcibly transferred one or more persons.[12]

---

[12] The term 'forcibly' is not restricted to physical force, but may include threat of force or coercion, such as that caused by fear of violence, duress, detention,

2. Such person or persons belonged to a particular national, ethnical, racial or religious group.

3. The perpetrator intended to destroy, in whole or in part, that national, ethnical, racial or religious group, as such.

4. The transfer was from that group to another group.

5. The person or persons were under the age of 18 years.

6. The perpetrator knew, or should have known, that the person or persons were under the age of 18 years.

7. The conduct took place in the context of a manifest pattern of similar conduct directed against that group or was conduct that could itself effect such destruction.

The SCSL has particularly very tight rules regarding the protection of children's rights in the proceedings of criminal jurisdiction. The Court deals with crimes against humanity, violations of Article 3 common to the Geneva Conventions and war crimes listed in the Additional Protocol II of the Geneva Conventions, other serious violations of international humanitarian law, and finally crimes under Sierra Leonean law. Its rules are so formulated that they should not violate the rights of minors including their social, physical or personality. It should be stressed that the procedures of the Court have had a definite function in the development and consolidation of children's rights in the proceedings of criminal justice. The Court has particularly stated that *conscripting* or *enlisting children* under the age of 15 to be active in armed conflicts, or using them to actively participate in hostilities, constitutes serious *war crimes* in international criminal law.[13] The Court constitutes the first international

---

psychological oppression or abuse of power, against such person or persons or another person, or by taking advantage of a coercive environment.

[13] Unfortunately, crimes against children were not only committed during national armed conflicts in Sierra Leone, but also, by the United Nations armed forces In one of its resolutions, the Security Council emphasises that "12. *Expresses its serious concern* at the violence, particularly sexual violence, suffered by women and children during the conflict in Sierra Leone, and emphasizes the importance of addressing these issues effectively; 14. *Expresses its serious concern* at allegations that some United Nations personnel may have been involved in sexual abuse of women and children in camps for refugees and internally displaced people in the region, supports the Secretary-General's policy of zero tolerance for such abuse, looks forward to the Secretary-General's report on the outcome of the investigation into these allegations, and requests him to make recommendations on how to prevent any such crimes in future, while calling on States concerned to take the necessary measures to bring to justice their own nationals responsible for such

court permitted to have criminal jurisdiction over juveniles between the ages of 15–18. Nevertheless, the Statute of the Court promotes “young age and the desirability of promoting his or her rehabilitation, reintegration into and assumption of a constructive role in society”. The Court accordingly recognized child participation in a conflict as sufficient grounds for classifying him/her as a child victim or witness despite the age-limit.[14]

Some of the most significant provisions of the Court formulated into its Statute or the Rules of Procedures and Evidence are:

Article 5

Crimes under Sierra Leonean law

The Special Court shall have the power to prosecute persons who have committed the following crimes under Sierra Leonean law:

a. Offences relating to the abuse of girls under the Prevention of Cruelty to Children Act, 1926 (Cap. 31):

i. Abusing a girl under 13 years of age, contrary to section 6;

ii. Abusing a girl between 13 and 14 years of age, contrary to section 7;

iii. Abduction of a girl for immoral purposes, contrary to section 12.

b. Offences relating to the wanton destruction of property under the Malicious Damage Act, 1861:

i. Setting fire to dwelling - houses, any person being therein, contrary to section 2;

ii. Setting fire to public buildings, contrary to sections 5 and 6;

iii. Setting fire to other buildings, contrary to section 6.

Article 7

Jurisdiction over persons of 15 years of age

1. The Special Court shall have no jurisdiction over any person who was under the age of 15 at the time of the alleged commission of the crime. Should any person who was at the time of the alleged commission of the crime between 15 and 18 years of age come before the Court, he or she shall be treated with dignity and a sense of worth, taking into account his or her young age and the desirability of promoting his or her rehabilitation, reintegration into and assumption of a constructive role in

crimes.” Resolution 1400 (2002), adopted by the Security Council at its 4500th meeting, on 28 March 2002.

[14] Farhad Malekian and Kerstin Nordlöf, International Criminal Status of Children, Encyclopaedia of Criminology & Criminal Justice, 5 volumes (Jay S. Albanese, editor), to be published by Wiley-Blackwell (2012).

society, and in accordance with international human rights standards, in particular the rights of the child.

2. In the disposition of a case against a juvenile offender, the Special Court shall order any of the following: care guidance and supervision orders, community service orders, counselling, foster care, correctional, educational and vocational training programmes, approved schools and, as appropriate, any programmes of disarmament, demobilization and reintegration or programmes of child protection agencies.

Article 15

The Prosecutor

1. The Prosecutor shall be responsible for the investigation and prosecution of persons who bear the greatest responsibility for serious violations of international humanitarian law and crimes under Sierra Leonean law committed in the territory of Sierra Leone since 30 November 1996. The Prosecutor shall act independently as a separate organ of the Special Court. He or she shall not seek or receive instructions from any Government or from any other source.

2. The Office of the Prosecutor shall have the power to question suspects, victims and witnesses, to collect evidence and to conduct on-site investigations. In carrying out these tasks, the Prosecutor shall, as appropriate, be assisted by the Sierra Leonean authorities concerned.

3. The Prosecutor shall be appointed by the Secretary-General for a three-year term and shall be eligible for re-appointment. He or she shall be of high moral character and possess the highest level of professional competence, and have extensive experience in the conduct of investigations and prosecutions of criminal cases.

4. The Prosecutor shall be assisted by a Sierra Leonean Deputy Prosecutor, and by such other Sierra Leonean and international staff as may be required to perform the functions assigned to him or her effectively and efficiently. Given the nature of the crimes committed and the particular sensitivities of girls, young women and children victims of rape, sexual assault, abduction and slavery of all kinds, due consideration should be given in the appointment of staff to the employment of prosecutors and investigators experienced in gender-related crimes and juvenile justice.

5. In the prosecution of juvenile offenders, the Prosecutor shall ensure that the child-rehabilitation programme is not placed at risk and that, where appropriate, resort should be had to alternative truth and reconciliation mechanisms, to the extent of their availability.

The Rules of Procedures and Evidence
Rule 34

Witnesses and Victims Section *(amended 29 May 2004)*

....

(iii) Ensure that they receive relevant support, counselling and other appropriate assistance, including medical assistance, physical and psychological rehabilitation, especially in cases of rape, sexual assault and crimes against children.

(B) The Section personnel shall include experts in trauma, including trauma related to crimes of sexual violence and violence against children. Where appropriate the Section shall cooperate with non-governmental and intergovernmental organizations.

Rule 90

Testimony of Witnesses *(amended 7 March 2003 and amended 14 May 2007)*

(C) A child shall be permitted to testify if the Chamber is of the opinion that he is sufficiently mature to be able to report the facts of which he had knowledge, that he understands the duty to tell the truth, and is not subject to undue influence. However, he shall not be compelled to testify by solemn declaration.

CHAPTER VIII

REGIONAL LEGISLATIONS PROHIBITING ABUSE OF CHILDREN

1. Inter-American Convention on the Prevention, Punishment and Eradication of Violence Against Women, 1994

The Inter-American Convention on the Prevention, Punishment and Eradication of Violence Against Women is of fundamental importance to international human rights law, and also constitutes an integral part of international criminal law. It was adopted by the General Assembly on 9 June 1994, and came into force on 5 March 1995.It stipulates measures that have to be taken by the State Parties in order to eradicate violence against women. The articles particularly dealing with children read:

CHAPTER III
DUTIES OF THE STATES
Article 8

The States Parties agree to undertake progressively specific measures, including programs:

a) to promote awareness and observance of the right of women to be free from violence, and the right of women to have their human rights respected and protected;

b) to modify social and cultural patterns of conduct of men and women, including the development of formal and informal educational programs appropriate to every level of the educational process, to counteract prejudices, customs and all other practices which are based on the idea of the inferiority or superiority of either of the sexes or on the stereotyped roles for men and women which legitimize or exacerbate violence against women;

c) to promote the education and training of all those involved in the administration of justice, police and other law enforcement officers as well as other personnel responsible for implementing policies for the prevention, punishment and eradication of violence against women;

d) to provide appropriate specialized services for women who have been subjected to violence, through public and private sector agencies, including shelters, counseling services for ail family members where appropriate, and care and custody of the affected children;

e) to promote and support governmental and private sector education designed to raise the awareness of the public with respect to the problems of and remedies for violence against women;

f) to provide women who are subjected to violence access to effective readjustment and training programs to enable them to fully participate in public, private and social life;

g) to encourage the communications media to develop appropriate media guidelines in order to contribute to the eradication of violence against women in all its forms, and to enhance respect for the dignity of women;

h) to ensure research and the gathering of statistics and other relevant information relating to the causes, consequences and frequency of violence against women, in order to assess the effectiveness of measures to prevent, punish and eradicate violence against women and to formulate and implement the necessary changes; and

i) to foster international cooperation for the exchange of ideas and experiences and the execution of programs aimed at protecting women who are subjected to violence.

Article 9

With respect to the adoption of the measures in this Chapter, the States Parties shall take special account of the vulnerability of women to violence by reason of, among others, their race or ethnic background or their status as migrants, refugees or displaced persons. Similar consideration shall be given to women subjected to violence while pregnant or who are disabled, of minor age, elderly, socioeconomically disadvantaged, affected by armed conflict or deprived of their freedom.

2. The Framework Decisions of the European Union on Combating Trafficking in Human Beings 2002

The Council Framework Decision of 19 July 2002 on combating trafficking in human beings has an important role in the implementation of international human rights law in Europe. The Decision aims to effectively combat and eradicate trafficking between European states. It has especially focused on sex trafficking in women and the sexual exploitation of children. In general, the Decisions mean to emphasise that European states should contribute in different ways to the protection of women and children's rights, their integrity and social equality. According to the Decision, trafficking constitutes serious abuse and a deception of vulnerable persons who have limited social opportunities. It therefore encourages states to introduce severe sanctions on perpetrators. The Decisions have thus recognized prevention of trafficking in human beings as an integral part of combating organized crime.

The Decisions provide:

Official Journal L 203, 01/08/2002 P. 0001 - 0004

Council Framework Decision of 19 July 2002 on combating trafficking in human beings (2002/629/JHA)

THE COUNCIL OF THE EUROPEAN UNION,

Having regard to the Treaty on European Union, and in particular Article 29, Article 31(e) and Article 34(2)(b) thereof,

Having regard to the proposal of the Commission (1),

Having regard to the opinion of the European Parliament (2),

Whereas:

(1) The Action Plan of the Council and the Commission on how best to implement the provisions of the Treaty of Amsterdam on an area of freedom, security and justice(3), the Tampere European Council on 15 and 16 October 1999, the Santa Maria da Feira European Council on 19 and 20 June 2000, as listed in the Scoreboard, and the European Parliament in its Resolution of 19 May 2000 on the communication from the Commission "for further actions in the fight against trafficking in women" indicate or call for legislative action against trafficking in human beings, including common definitions, incriminations and sanctions.

(2) Council Joint Action 97/154/JHA of 24 February 1997 concerning action to combat trafficking in human beings and sexual exploitation of children (4) needs to be followed by further legislative action addressing the divergence of legal approaches in the Member States and contributing to the development of an efficient judicial and law enforcement cooperation against trafficking in human beings.

(3) Trafficking in human beings comprises serious violations of fundamental human rights and human dignity and involves ruthless practices such as the abuse and deception of vulnerable persons, as well as the use of violence, threats, debt bondage and coercion.

(4) The UN protocol to prevent, suppress and punish trafficking in persons, especially women and children, supplementing the UN Convention

against transnational organised crimes, represents a decisive step towards international cooperation in this field.

(5) Children are more vulnerable and are therefore at greater risk of falling victim to trafficking.

(6) The important work performed by international organisations, in particular the UN, must be complemented by that of the European Union.

(7) It is necessary that the serious criminal offence of trafficking in human beings be addressed not only through individual action by each Member State but by a comprehensive approach in which the definition of constituent elements of criminal law common to all Member States, including effective, proportionate and dissuasive sanctions, forms an integral part. In accordance with the principles of subsidiarity and proportionality, this Framework Decision confines itself to the minimum required in order to achieve those objectives at European level and does not go beyond what is necessary for that purpose.

(8) It is necessary to introduce sanctions on perpetrators sufficiently severe to allow for trafficking in human beings to be included within the scope of instruments already adopted for the purpose of combating organised crime such as Council Joint Action 98/699/JHA of 3 December 1998 on money laundering, the identification, tracing, freezing, seizing and confiscation of the instrumentalities and the proceeds from crime(5) and Council Joint Action 98/733/JHA of 21 December 1998 on making it a criminal offence to participate in a criminal organisation in the Member States of the European Union(6).

(9) This Framework Decision should contribute to the fight against and prevention of trafficking in human beings by complementing the instruments adopted in this area such as Council Joint Action 96/700/JHA of 29 November 1996 establishing an incentive and exchange programme for persons responsible for combating trade in human beings and sexual exploitation of children (STOP)(7), Council Joint Action 96/748/JHA of 16 December 1996 extending the mandate given to the Europol Drugs Unit(8), Decision No 293/2000/EC of the European Parliament and of the Council of 24 January 2000 adopting a programme of Community action (the Daphne programme) (2000 to 2003) on preventive measures to fight violence against children, young persons and women(9), Council Joint Action 98/428/JHA of 29 June 1998 on the creation of a European Judicial Network(10), Council Joint Action 96/277/JHA of 22 April 1996 concerning a framework for the exchange of liaison magistrates to improve judicial cooperation between the Member States of the European Union(11) and Council Joint Action 98/427/JHA of 29 June 1998 on good practice in mutual legal assistance in criminal matters(12).

(10) Council Joint Action 97/154/JHA should accordingly cease to apply in so far as it concerns trafficking in human beings,
HAS ADOPTED THIS FRAMEWORK DECISION:

Article 1

Offences concerning trafficking in human beings for the purposes of labour exploitation or sexual exploitation

1. Each Member State shall take the necessary measures to ensure that the following acts are punishable: the recruitment, transportation, transfer, harbouring, subsequent reception of a person, including exchange or transfer of control over that person, where:

(a) use is made of coercion, force or threat, including abduction, or

(b) use is made of deceit or fraud, or

(c) there is an abuse of authority or of a position of vulnerability, which is such that the person has no real and acceptable alternative but to submit to the abuse involved, or

(d) payments or benefits are given or received to achieve the consent of a person having control over another person for the purpose of exploitation of that person's labour or services, including at least forced or compulsory labour or services, slavery or practices similar to slavery or servitude, or for the purpose of the exploitation of the prostitution of others or other forms of sexual exploitation, including in pornography.

2. The consent of a victim of trafficking in human beings to the exploitation, intended or actual, shall be irrelevant where any of the means set forth in paragraph 1 have been used.

3. When the conduct referred to in paragraph 1 involves a child, it shall be a punishable trafficking offence even if none of the means set forth in paragraph 1 have been used.

4. For the purpose of this Framework Decision, "child" shall mean any person below 18 years of age.

Article 2

Instigation, aiding, abetting and attempt

Each Member State shall take the necessary measures to ensure that the instigation of, aiding, abetting or attempt to commit an offence referred to in Article 1 is punishable.

Article 3

Penalties

1. Each Member State shall take the necessary measures to ensure that an offence referred to in Articles 1 and 2 is punishable by effective,

proportionate and dissuasive criminal penalties, which may entail extradition.

2. Each Member State shall take the necessary measures to ensure that an offence referred to in Article 1 is punishable by terms of imprisonment with a maximum penalty that is not less than eight years where it has been committed in any of the following circumstances:

(a) the offence has deliberately or by gross negligence endangered the life of the victim;

(b) the offence has been committed against a victim who was particularly vulnerable. A victim shall be considered to have been particularly vulnerable at least when the victim was under the age of sexual majority under national law and the offence has been committed for the purpose of the exploitation of the prostitution of others or other forms of sexual exploitation, including pornography;

(c) the offence has been committed by use of serious violence or has caused particularly serious harm to the victim;

(d) the offence has been committed within the framework of a criminal organisation as defined in Joint Action 98/733/JHA, apart from the penalty level referred to therein.

Article 4

Liability of legal persons

1. Each Member State shall take the necessary measures to ensure that legal persons can be held liable for an offence referred to in Articles 1 and 2, committed for their benefit by any person, acting either individually or as part of an organ of the legal person, who has a leading position within the legal person, based on:

(a) a power of representation of the legal person, or

(b) an authority to take decisions on behalf of the legal person, or

(c) an authority to exercise control within the legal person.

2. Apart from the cases already provided for in paragraph 1, each Member State shall take the necessary measures to ensure that legal persons can be held liable where the lack of supervision or control by a person referred to in paragraph 1 have rendered possible the commission of an offence referred to in Articles 1 and 2 for the benefit of that legal person by a person under its authority.

3. Liability of legal persons under paragraphs 1 and 2 shall not exclude criminal proceedings against natural persons who are perpetrators, instigators or accessories in an offence referred to in Articles 1 and 2.

4. For the purpose of this Framework Decision, legal person shall mean any entity having such status under the applicable law, except for

States or other public bodies in the exercise of State authority and for public international organisations.

Article 5

Sanctions on legal persons

Each Member State shall take the necessary measures to ensure that a legal person held liable pursuant to Article 4 is punishable by effective, proportionate and dissuasive sanctions, which shall include criminal or non-criminal fines and may include other sanctions, such as:

(a) exclusion from entitlement to public benefits or aid, or

(b) temporary or permanent disqualification from the practice of commercial activities, or

(c) placing under judicial supervision, or

(d) a judicial winding-up order, or

(e) temporary or permanent closure of establishments which have been used for committing the offence.

Article 6

Jurisdiction and prosecution

1. Each Member State shall take the necessary measures to establish its jurisdiction over an offence referred to in Articles 1 and 2 where:

(a) the offence is committed in whole or in part within its territory, or

(b) the offender is one of its nationals, or

(c) the offence is committed for the benefit of a legal person established in the territory of that Member State.

2. A Member State may decide that it will not apply or that it will apply only in specific cases or circumstances, the jurisdiction rules set out in paragraphs 1(b) and 1(c) as far as the offence is committed outside its territory.

3. A Member State which, under its laws, does not extradite its own nationals shall take the necessary measures to establish its jurisdiction over and to prosecute, where appropriate, an offence referred to in Articles 1 and 2 when it is committed by its own nationals outside its territory.

4. Member States shall inform the General Secretariat of the Council and the Commission accordingly where they decide to apply paragraph 2, where appropriate with an indication of the specific cases or circumstances in which the decision applies.

Article 7

Protection of and assistance to victims

1. Member States shall establish that investigations into or prosecution of offences covered by this Framework Decision shall not be dependent on the report or accusation made by a person subjected to the offence, at least in cases where Article 6(1)(a) applies.

2. Children who are victims of an offence referred to in Article 1 should be considered as particularly vulnerable victims pursuant to Article 2(2), Article 8(4) and Article 14(1) of Council Framework Decision 2001/220/JHA of 15 March 2001 on the standing of victims in criminal proceedings(13).

3. Where the victim is a child, each Member State shall take the measures possible to ensure appropriate assistance for his or her family. In particular, each Member State shall, where appropriate and possible, apply Article 4 of Framework Decision 2001/220/JHA to the family referred to.

Article 8

Territorial scope

This Framework Decision shall apply to Gibraltar.

Article 9

Application of Joint Action 97/154/JHA

Joint Action 97/154/JHA shall cease to apply in so far as it concerns trafficking in human beings.

Article 10

Implementation

1. Member States shall take the necessary measures to comply with this Framework Decision before 1 August 2004.

2. By the date referred to in paragraph 1, Member States shall transmit to the General Secretariat of the Council and to the Commission the text of the provisions transposing into their national law the obligations imposed on them under this Framework Decision. The Council will, by 1 August 2005 at the latest, on the basis of a report established on the basis of this information and a written report transmitted by the Commission, assess the extent to which Member States have taken the necessary measures in order to comply with this Framework Decision.

Article 11

Entry into force

This Framework Decision shall enter into force on the day of its publication in the Official Journal.

Done at Brussels, 19 July 2002.

3. The European Convention on Action against Trafficking in Human Beings, 2005

Another regional convention protecting children's rights and prohibiting the abuse of children is the Council of Europe's Convention on Action against Trafficking in Human Beings, Warsaw 2005. The Convention was formulated to fill the gap between regional and international instruments concerning the prohibition of trafficking in human beings. Two of the chief reasons for the adoption of the Convention are the rapid growth of trafficking in human beings in Europe and the absence of an effective policy to protect the rights of individuals who are the victims of trafficking. The Convention also aims to promote action against trafficking between the European states. It has therefore the intention to protect children's rights by all means and has consequently emphasised that its provisions should apply to "all forms of trafficking in human beings, whether national or transnational, whether or not connected with organised crime". This policy brings all victims of trafficking under a single umbrella.

Some of the significant parts of the Convention relating to the protection of children can be examined here:

Preamble

The member States of the Council of Europe and the other Signatories hereto,

Considering that the aim of the Council of Europe is to achieve a greater unity between its members;

Considering that trafficking in human beings constitutes a violation of human rights and an offence to the dignity and the integrity of the human being;

Considering that trafficking in human beings may result in slavery for victims;

Considering that respect for victims' rights, protection of victims and action to combat trafficking in human beings must be the paramount objectives;

Considering that all actions or initiatives against trafficking in human beings must be non-discriminatory, take gender equality into account as well as a child-rights approach;

Recalling the declarations by the Ministers for Foreign Affairs of the Member States at the 112th (14-15 May 2003) and the 114th (12-13 May 2004) Sessions of the Committee of Ministers calling for reinforced action by the Council of Europe on trafficking in human beings;

Bearing in mind the Convention for the Protection of Human Rights and Fundamental Freedoms (1950) and its protocols;

Bearing in mind the following recommendations of the Committee of Ministers to member states of the Council of Europe: Recommendation No. R (91) 11 on sexual exploitation, pornography and prostitution of, and trafficking in, children and young adults; Recommendation No. R (97) 13 concerning intimidation of witnesses and the rights of the defence; Recommendation No. R (2000) 11 on action against trafficking in human beings for the purpose of sexual exploitation and Recommendation Rec (2001) 16 on the protection of children against sexual exploitation; Recommendation Rec (2002) 5 on the protection of women against violence;

Bearing in mind the following recommendations of the Parliamentary Assembly of the Council of Europe: Recommendation 1325 (1997) on traffic in women and forced prostitution in Council of Europe member states; Recommendation 1450 (2000) on violence against women in Europe; Recommendation 1545 (2002) on a campaign against trafficking in women; Recommendation 1610 (2003) on migration connected with trafficking in women and prostitution; Recommendation 1611 (2003) on trafficking in organs in Europe; Recommendation 1663 (2004) Domestic slavery: servitude, au pairs and mail-order brides;

Bearing in mind the European Union Council Framework Decision of 19 July 2002 on combating trafficking in human beings the European Union Council Framework Decision of 15 March 2001 on the standing of victims in criminal proceedings and the European Union Council Directive of 29 April 2004 on the residence permit issued to third-country nationals who are victims of trafficking in human beings or who have been the subject of an action to facilitate illegal immigration, who cooperate with the competent authorities;

Taking due account of the United Nations Convention against Transnational Organized Crime and the Protocol thereto to Prevent, Suppress and Punish Trafficking in Persons, Especially Women and Children with a view to improving the protection which they afford and developing the standards established by them;

Taking due account of the other international legal instruments relevant in the field of action against trafficking in human beings;

Taking into account the need to prepare a comprehensive international legal instrument focusing on the human rights of victims of trafficking and setting up a specific monitoring mechanism,

Have agreed as follows:

Chapter I – Purposes, scope, non-discrimination principle and definitions

Article 1 – Purposes of the Convention

1. The purposes of this Convention are:

a to prevent and combat trafficking in human beings, while guaranteeing gender equality

b to protect the human rights of the victims of trafficking, design a comprehensive framework for the protection and assistance of victims and witnesses, while guaranteeing gender equality, as well as to ensure effective investigation and prosecution;

c to promote international cooperation on action against trafficking in human beings.

2. In order to ensure effective implementation of its provisions by the Parties, this Convention sets up a specific monitoring mechanism.

Article 2 – Scope

This Convention shall apply to all forms of trafficking in human beings, whether national or transnational, whether or not connected with organised crime.

Article 3 – Non-discrimination principle

The implementation of the provisions of this Convention by Parties, in particular the enjoyment of measures to protect and promote the rights of victims, shall be secured without discrimination on any ground such as sex, race, colour, language, religion, political or other opinion, national or social origin, association with a national minority, property, birth or other status.

Article 4 – Definitions

For the purposes of this Convention :

a "Trafficking in human beings" shall mean the recruitment, transportation, transfer, harbouring or receipt of persons, by means of the threat or use of force or other forms of coercion, of abduction, of fraud, of deception, of the abuse of power or of a position of vulnerability or of the giving or receiving of payments or benefits to achieve the consent of a person having control over another person, for the purpose of exploitation. Exploitation shall include, at a minimum, the exploitation of the prostitution of others or other forms of sexual exploitation, forced labour or services, slavery or practices similar to slavery, servitude or the removal of organs;

b The consent of a victim of “trafficking in human beings” to the intended exploitation set forth in subparagraph (a) of this article shall be irrelevant where any of the means set forth in subparagraph (a) have been used;

c The recruitment, transportation, transfer, harbouring or receipt of a child for the purpose of exploitation shall be considered "trafficking in human beings" even if this does not involve any of the means set forth in subparagraph (a) of this article;

d "Child" shall mean any person under eighteen years of age;

e "Victim" shall mean any natural person who is subject to trafficking in human beings as defined in this article.

Chapter II – Prevention, co-operation and other measures

Article 5 – Prevention of trafficking in human beings

1. Each Party shall take measures to establish or strengthen national co-ordination between the various bodies responsible for preventing and combating trafficking in human beings.

2. Each Party shall establish and/or strengthen effective policies and programmes to prevent trafficking in human beings, by such means as: research, information, awareness raising and education campaigns, social and economic initiatives and training programmes, in particular for persons vulnerable to trafficking and for professionals concerned with trafficking in human beings.

3. Each Party shall promote a Human Rights-based approach and shall use gender mainstreaming and a child-sensitive approach in the development, implementation and assessment of all the policies and programmes referred to in paragraph 2.

4. Each Party shall take appropriate measures, as may be necessary, to enable migration to take place legally, in particular through dissemination of accurate information by relevant offices, on the conditions enabling the legal entry in and stay on its territory.

5. Each Party shall take specific measures to reduce children’s vulnerability to trafficking, notably by creating a protective environment for them.

6. Measures established in accordance with this article shall involve, where appropriate, non-governmental organisations, other relevant organisations and other elements of civil society committed to the prevention of trafficking in human beings and victim protection or assistance.

Article 6 – Measures to discourage the demand

To discourage the demand that fosters all forms of exploitation of persons, especially women and children, that leads to trafficking, each Party shall adopt or strengthen legislative, administrative, educational, social, cultural or other measures including:

a research on best practices, methods and strategies;

b raising awareness of the responsibility and important role of media and civil society in identifying the demand as one of the root causes of trafficking in human beings;

c target information campaigns involving, as appropriate, inter alia, public authorities and policy makers;

d preventive measures, including educational programmes for boys and girls during their schooling, which stress the unacceptable nature of discrimination based on sex, and its disastrous consequences, the importance of gender equality and the dignity and integrity of every human being.

Article 7 – Border measures

1. Without prejudice to international commitments in relation to the free movement of persons, Parties shall strengthen, to the extent possible, such border controls as may be necessary to prevent and detect trafficking in human beings.

2. Each Party shall adopt legislative or other appropriate measures to prevent, to the extent possible, means of transport operated by commercial carriers from being used in the commission of offences established in accordance with this Convention.

3. Where appropriate, and without prejudice to applicable international conventions, such measures shall include establishing the obligation of commercial carriers, including any transportation company or the owner or operator of any means of transport, to ascertain that all passengers are in possession of the travel documents required for entry into the receiving State.

4. Each Party shall take the necessary measures, in accordance with its internal law, to provide for sanctions in cases of violation of the obligation set forth in paragraph 3 of this article.

5. Each Party shall adopt such legislative or other measures as may be necessary to permit, in accordance with its internal law, the denial of entry or revocation of visas of persons implicated in the commission of offences established in accordance with this Convention.

6. Parties shall strengthen co-operation among border control agencies by, *inter alia*, establishing and maintaining direct channels of communication.

Article 8 – Security and control of documents

Each Party shall adopt such measures as may be necessary:

a To ensure that travel or identity documents issued by it are of such quality that they cannot easily be misused and cannot readily be falsified or unlawfully altered, replicated or issued; and

b To ensure the integrity and security of travel or identity documents issued by or on behalf of the Party and to prevent their unlawful creation and issuance.

Article 9 – Legitimacy and validity of documents

At the request of another Party, a Party shall, in accordance with its internal law, verify within a reasonable time the legitimacy and validity of travel or identity documents issued or purported to have been issued in its name and suspected of being used for trafficking in human beings.

Chapter III – Measures to protect and promote the rights of victims, guaranteeing gender equality

Article 10 – Identification of the victims

1. Each Party shall provide its competent authorities with persons who are trained and qualified in preventing and combating trafficking in human beings, in identifying and helping victims, including children, and shall ensure that the different authorities collaborate with each other as well as with relevant support organisations, so that victims can be identified in a procedure duly taking into account the special situation of women and child victims and, in appropriate cases, issued with residence permits under the conditions provided for in Article 14 of the present Convention.

2. Each Party shall adopt such legislative or other measures as may be necessary to identify victims as appropriate in collaboration with other Parties and relevant support organisations. Each Party shall ensure that, if the competent authorities have reasonable grounds to believe that a person has been victim of trafficking in human beings, that person shall not be removed from its territory until the identification process as victim of an offence provided for in Article 18 of this Convention has been completed

by the competent authorities and shall likewise ensure that that person receives the assistance provided for in Article 12, paragraphs 1 and 2.

3. When the age of the victim is uncertain and there are reasons to believe that the victim is a child, he or she shall be presumed to be a child and shall be accorded special protection measures pending verification of his/her age.

4. As soon as an unaccompanied child is identified as a victim, each Party shall:

a provide for representation of the child by a legal guardian, organisation or authority which shall act in the best interests of that child;

b take the necessary steps to establish his/her identity and nationality;

c make every effort to locate his/her family when this is in the best interests of the child.

Article 11 – Protection of private life

1. Each Party shall protect the private life and identity of victims. Personal data regarding them shall be stored and used in conformity with the conditions provided for by the Convention for the Protection of Individuals with regard to Automatic Processing of Personal Data (ETS No. 108).

2. Each Party shall adopt measures to ensure, in particular, that the identity, or details allowing the identification, of a child victim of trafficking are not made publicly known, through the media or by any other means, except, in exceptional circumstances, in order to facilitate the tracing of family members or otherwise secure the well-being and protection of the child.

3. Each Party shall consider adopting, in accordance with Article 10 of the Convention for the Protection of Human Rights and Fundamental Freedoms as interpreted by the European Court of Human Rights, measures aimed at encouraging the media to protect the private life and identity of victims through self-regulation or through regulatory or co-regulatory measures.

Article 12 – Assistance to victims

1. Each Party shall adopt such legislative or other measures as may be necessary to assist victims in their physical, psychological and social recovery. Such assistance shall include at least:

a standards of living capable of ensuring their subsistence, through such measures as: appropriate and secure accommodation, psychological and material assistance;

b access to emergency medical treatment;

c translation and interpretation services, when appropriate;

d counselling and information, in particular as regards their legal rights and the services available to them, in a language that they can understand;

e assistance to enable their rights and interests to be presented and considered at appropriate stages of criminal proceedings against offenders;

f access to education for children.

2. Each Party shall take due account of the victim's safety and protection needs.

3. In addition, each Party shall provide necessary medical or other assistance to victims lawfully resident within its territory who do not have adequate resources and need such help.

4. Each Party shall adopt the rules under which victims lawfully resident within its territory shall be authorised to have access to the labour market, to vocational training and education.

5. Each Party shall take measures, where appropriate and under the conditions provided for by its internal law, to co-operate with non-governmental organisations, other relevant organisations or other elements of civil society engaged in assistance to victims.

6. Each Party shall adopt such legislative or other measures as may be necessary to ensure that assistance to a victim is not made conditional on his or her willingness to act as a witness.

7. For the implementation of the provisions set out in this article, each Party shall ensure that services are provided on a consensual and informed basis, taking due account of the special needs of persons in a vulnerable position and the rights of children in terms of accommodation, education and appropriate health care.

Article 13 – Recovery and reflection period

1. Each Party shall provide in its internal law a recovery and reflection period of at least 30 days, when there are reasonable grounds to believe that the person concerned is a victim. Such a period shall be sufficient for the person concerned to recover and escape the influence of traffickers and/or to take an informed decision on cooperating with the competent authorities. During this period it shall not be possible to enforce any expulsion order against him or her. This provision is without prejudice to the activities carried out by the competent authorities in all phases of the relevant national proceedings, and in particular when investigating and

prosecuting the offences concerned. During this period, the Parties shall authorise the persons concerned to stay in their territory.

2. During this period, the persons referred to in paragraph 1 of this Article shall be entitled to the measures contained in Article 12, paragraphs 1 and 2.

3. The Parties are not bound to observe this period if grounds of public order prevent it or if it is found that victim status is being claimed improperly.

Article 14 – Residence permit

1. Each Party shall issue a renewable residence permit to victims, in one or other of the two following situations or in both:

a the competent authority considers that their stay is necessary owing to their personal situation;

b the competent authority considers that their stay is necessary for the purpose of their co-operation with the competent authorities in investigation or criminal proceedings.

2. The residence permit for child victims, when legally necessary, shall be issued in accordance with the best interests of the child and, where appropriate, renewed under the same conditions.

3. The non-renewal or withdrawal of a residence permit is subject to the conditions provided for by the internal law of the Party.

4. If a victim submits an application for another kind of residence permit, the Party concerned shall take into account that he or she holds, or has held, a residence permit in conformity with paragraph 1.

5. Having regard to the obligations of Parties to which Article 40 of this Convention refers, each Party shall ensure that granting of a permit according to this provision shall be without prejudice to the right to seek and enjoy asylum.

Article 15 – Compensation and legal redress

1. Each Party shall ensure that victims have access, as from their first contact with the competent authorities, to information on relevant judicial and administrative proceedings in a language which they can understand.

2. Each Party shall provide, in its internal law, for the right to legal assistance and to free legal aid for victims under the conditions provided by its internal law.

3. Each Party shall provide, in its internal law, for the right of victims to compensation from the perpetrators.

4. Each Party shall adopt such legislative or other measures as may be necessary to guarantee compensation for victims in accordance with the

conditions under its internal law, for instance through the establishment of a fund for victim compensation or measures or programmes aimed at social assistance and social integration of victims, which could be funded by the assets resulting from the application of measures provided in Article 23.

Article 16 – Repatriation and return of victims

1. The Party of which a victim is a national or in which that person had the right of permanent residence at the time of entry into the territory of the receiving Party shall, with due regard for his or her rights, safety and dignity, facilitate and accept, his or her return without undue or unreasonable delay.

2. When a Party returns a victim to another State, such return shall be with due regard for the rights, safety and dignity of that person and for the status of any legal proceedings related to the fact that the person is a victim, and shall preferably be voluntary.

3. At the request of a receiving Party, a requested Party shall verify whether a person is its national or had the right of permanent residence in its territory at the time of entry into the territory of the receiving Party.

4. In order to facilitate the return of a victim who is without proper documentation, the Party of which that person is a national or in which he or she had the right of permanent residence at the time of entry into the territory of the receiving Party shall agree to issue, at the request of the receiving Party, such travel documents or other authorisation as may be necessary to enable the person to travel to and re-enter its territory.

5. Each Party shall adopt such legislative or other measures as may be necessary to establish repatriation programmes, involving relevant national or international institutions and non governmental organisations. These programmes aim at avoiding re-victimisation. Each Party should make its best effort to favour the reintegration of victims into the society of the State of return, including reintegration into the education system and the labour market, in particular through the acquisition and improvement of their professional skills. With regard to children, these programmes should include enjoyment of the right to education and measures to secure adequate care or receipt by the family or appropriate care structures.

6. Each Party shall adopt such legislative or other measures as may be necessary to make available to victims, where appropriate in co-operation with any other Party concerned, contact information of structures that can assist them in the country where they are returned or repatriated, such as law enforcement offices, non-governmental organisations, legal professions able to provide counselling and social welfare agencies.

7. Child victims shall not be returned to a State, if there is indication, following a risk and security assessment, that such return would not be in the best interests of the child.

Article 17 – Gender equality

Each Party shall, in applying measures referred to in this chapter, aim to promote gender equality and use gender mainstreaming in the development, implementation and assessment of the measures.

Chapter IV – Substantive criminal law

Article 18 – Criminalisation of trafficking in human beings

Each Party shall adopt such legislative and other measures as may be necessary to establish as criminal offences the conduct contained in article 4 of this Convention, when committed intentionally.

Article 19 – Criminalisation of the use of services of a victim

Each Party shall consider adopting such legislative and other measures as may be necessary to establish as criminal offences under its internal law, the use of services which are the object of exploitation as referred to in Article 4 paragraph a of this Convention, with the knowledge that the person is a victim of trafficking in human beings.

Article 20 – Criminalisation of acts relating to travel or identity documents

Each Party shall adopt such legislative and other measures as may be necessary to establish as criminal offences the following conducts, when committed intentionally and for the purpose of enabling the trafficking in human beings:

a forging a travel or identity document;

b procuring or providing such a document;

c retaining, removing, concealing, damaging or destroying a travel or identity document of another person.

Article 21 – Attempt and aiding or abetting

1. Each Party shall adopt such legislative and other measures as may be necessary to establish as criminal offences when committed intentionally, aiding or abetting the commission of any of the offences established in accordance with Articles 18 and 20 of the present Convention.
2. Each Party shall adopt such legislative and other measures as may be necessary to establish as criminal offences when committed intentionally,

an attempt to commit the offences established in accordance with Articles 18 and 20, paragraph a, of this Convention.

Article 22 – Corporate liability

1. Each Party shall adopt such legislative and other measures as may be necessary to ensure that a legal person can be held liable for a criminal offence established in accordance with this Convention, committed for its benefit by any natural person, acting either individually or as part of an organ of the legal person, who has a leading position within the legal person, based on:

a a power of representation of the legal person;
b an authority to take decisions on behalf of the legal person;
c an authority to exercise control within the legal person.

2. Apart from the cases already provided for in paragraph 1, each Party shall take the measures necessary to ensure that a legal person can be held liable where the lack of supervision or control by a natural person referred to in paragraph 1 has made possible the commission of a criminal offence established in accordance with this Convention for the benefit of that legal person by a natural person acting under its authority.

3. Subject to the legal principles of the Party, the liability of a legal person may be criminal, civil or administrative.

4. Such liability shall be without prejudice to the criminal liability of the natural persons who have committed the offence.

Article 23 – Sanctions and measures

1. Each Party shall adopt such legislative and other measures as may be necessary to ensure that the criminal offences established in accordance with Articles 18 to 21 are punishable by effective, proportionate and dissuasive sanctions. These sanctions shall include, for criminal offences established in accordance with Article 18 when committed by natural persons, penalties involving deprivation of liberty which can give rise to extradition.

2. Each Party shall ensure that legal persons held liable in accordance with Article 22 shall be subject to effective, proportionate and dissuasive criminal or non-criminal sanctions or measures, including monetary sanctions.

3. Each Party shall adopt such legislative and other measures as may be necessary to enable it to confiscate or otherwise deprive the instrumentalities and proceeds of criminal offences established in accordance with Articles 18 and 20, paragraph a, of this Convention, or property the value of which corresponds to such proceeds.

4. Each Party shall adopt such legislative or other measures as may be necessary to enable the temporary or permanent closure of any establishment which was used to carry out trafficking in human beings, without prejudice to the rights of *bona fide* third parties or to deny the perpetrator, temporary or permanently, the exercise of the activity in the course of which this offence was committed.

Article 24 – Aggravating circumstances

Each Party shall ensure that the following circumstances are regarded as aggravating circumstances in the determination of the penalty for offences established in accordance with Article 18 of this Convention:

a the offence deliberately or by gross negligence endangered the life of the victim;

b the offence was committed against a child;

c the offence was committed by a public official in the performance of her/his duties;

d the offence was committed within the framework of a criminal organisation.

Article 25 – Previous convictions

Each Party shall adopt such legislative and other measures providing for the possibility to take into account final sentences passed by another Party in relation to offences established in accordance with this Convention when determining the penalty.

Article 26 – Non-punishment provision

Each Party shall, in accordance with the basic principles of its legal system, provide for the possibility of not imposing penalties on victims for their involvement in unlawful activities, to the extent that they have been compelled to do so.

Chapter V – Investigation, prosecution and procedural law

Article 27 – *Ex parte* and *ex officio* applications

1. Each Party shall ensure that investigations into or prosecution of offences established in accordance with this Convention shall not be dependent upon the report or accusation made by a victim, at least when the offence was committed in whole or in part on its territory.

2. Each Party shall ensure that victims of an offence in the territory of a Party other than the one where they reside may make a complaint before the competent authorities of their State of residence. The competent authority to which the complaint is made, insofar as it does not itself have

competence in this respect, shall transmit it without delay to the competent authority of the Party in the territory in which the offence was committed. The complaint shall be dealt with in accordance with the internal law of the Party in which the offence was committed.

3. Each Party shall ensure, by means of legislative or other measures, in accordance with the conditions provided for by its internal law, to any group, foundation, association or non-governmental organisations which aims at fighting trafficking in human beings or protection of human rights, the possibility to assist and/or support the victim with his or her consent during criminal proceedings concerning the offence established in accordance with Article 18 of this Convention.

Article 28 – Protection of victims, witnesses and collaborators with the judicial authorities

1. Each Party shall adopt such legislative or other measures as may be necessary to provide effective and appropriate protection from potential retaliation or intimidation in particular during and after investigation and prosecution of perpetrators, for:

a Victims;

b As appropriate, those who report the criminal offences established in accordance with Article 18 of this Convention or otherwise co-operate with the investigating or prosecuting authorities;

c witnesses who give testimony concerning criminal offences established in accordance with Article 18 of this Convention;

d when necessary, members of the family of persons referred to in subparagraphs a and c.

2. Each Party shall adopt such legislative or other measures as may be necessary to ensure and to offer various kinds of protection. This may include physical protection, relocation, identity change and assistance in obtaining jobs.

3. A child victim shall be afforded special protection measures taking into account the best interests of the child.

4. Each Party shall adopt such legislative or other measures as may be necessary to provide, when necessary, appropriate protection from potential retaliation or intimidation in particular during and after investigation and prosecution of perpetrators, for members of groups, foundations, associations or non-governmental organisations which carry out the activities set out in Article 27, paragraph 3.

5. Each Party shall consider entering into agreements or arrangements with other States for the implementation of this article.

Article 29 – Specialised authorities and co-ordinating bodies

1. Each Party shall adopt such measures as may be necessary to ensure that persons or entities are specialised in the fight against trafficking and the protection of victims. Such persons or entities shall have the necessary independence in accordance with the fundamental principles of the legal system of the Party, in order for them to be able to carry out their functions effectively and free from any undue pressure. Such persons or the staffs of such entities shall have adequate training and financial resources for their tasks.

2. Each Party shall adopt such measures as may be necessary to ensure co-ordination of the policies and actions of their governments' departments and other public agencies against trafficking in human beings, where appropriate, through setting up co-ordinating bodies.

3. Each Party shall provide or strengthen training for relevant officials in the prevention of and fight against trafficking in human beings, including Human Rights training. The training may be agency-specific and shall, as appropriate, focus on: methods used in preventing such trafficking, prosecuting the traffickers and protecting the rights of the victims, including protecting the victims from the traffickers.

4. Each Party shall consider appointing National Rapporteurs or other mechanisms for monitoring the anti-trafficking activities of State institutions and the implementation of national legislation requirements.

Article 30 – Court proceedings

In accordance with the Convention for the Protection of Human Rights and Fundamental Freedoms, in particular Article 6, each Party shall adopt such legislative or other measures as may be necessary to ensure in the course of judicial proceedings:

a the protection of victims' private life and, where appropriate, identity;

b victims' safety and protection from intimidation, in accordance with the conditions under its internal law and, in the case of child victims, by taking special care of children's needs and ensuring their right to special protection measures.

Article 31 – Jurisdiction

1. Each Party shall adopt such legislative and other measures as may be necessary to establish jurisdiction over any offence established in accordance with this Convention, when the offence is committed:

a in its territory; or

b on board a ship flying the flag of that Party; or

c on board an aircraft registered under the laws of that Party; or d by one of its nationals or by a stateless person who has his or her habitual residence in its territory, if the offence is punishable under criminal law where it was committed or if the offence is committed outside the territorial jurisdiction of any State;

e against one of its nationals.

2. Each Party may, at the time of signature or when depositing its instrument of ratification, acceptance, approval or accession, by a declaration addressed to the Secretary General of the Council of Europe, declare that it reserves the right not to apply or to apply only in specific cases or conditions the jurisdiction rules laid down in paragraphs 1 (d) and (e) of this article or any part thereof.

3. Each Party shall adopt such measures as may be necessary to establish jurisdiction over the offences referred to in this Convention, in cases where an alleged offender is present in its territory and it does not extradite him/her to another Party, solely on the basis of his/her nationality, after a request for extradition.

4. When more than one Party claims jurisdiction over an alleged offence established in accordance with this Convention, the Parties involved shall, where appropriate, consult with a view to determining the most appropriate jurisdiction for prosecution.

5. Without prejudice to the general norms of international law, this Convention does not exclude any criminal jurisdiction exercised by a Party in accordance with internal law.

Chapter VI – International co-operation and co-operation with civil society

Article 32 – General principles and measures for international co-operation

The Parties shall co-operate with each other, in accordance with the provisions of this Convention, and through application of relevant applicable international and regional instruments, arrangements agreed on the basis of uniform or reciprocal legislation and internal laws, to the widest extent possible, for the purpose of:

- preventing and combating trafficking in human beings;
- protecting and providing assistance to victims;
- investigations or proceedings concerning criminal offences established in accordance with this Convention.

Article 33 – Measures relating to endangered or missing persons

1. When a Party, on the basis of the information at its disposal has reasonable grounds to believe that the life, the freedom or the physical

integrity of a person referred to in Article 28, paragraph 1, is in immediate danger on the territory of another Party, the Party that has the information shall, in such a case of emergency, transmit it without delay to the latter so as to take the appropriate protection measures.

2. The Parties to this Convention may consider reinforcing their co-operation in the search for missing people, in particular for missing children, if the information available leads them to believe that she/he is a victim of trafficking in human beings. To this end, the Parties may conclude bilateral or multilateral treaties with each other.

Article 34 – Information

1. The requested Party shall promptly inform the requesting Party of the final result of the action taken under this chapter. The requested Party shall also promptly inform the requesting Party of any circumstances which render impossible the carrying out of the action sought or are likely to delay it significantly.

2. A Party may, within the limits of its internal law, without prior request, forward to another Party information obtained within the framework of its own investigations when it considers that the disclosure of such information might assist the receiving Party in initiating or carrying out investigations or proceedings concerning criminal offences established in accordance with this Convention or might lead to a request for co-operation by that Party under this chapter.

3. Prior to providing such information, the providing Party may request that it be kept confidential or used subject to conditions. If the receiving Party cannot comply with such request, it shall notify the providing Party, which shall then determine whether the information should nevertheless be provided. If the receiving Party accepts the information subject to the conditions, it shall be bound by them.

4. All information requested concerning Articles 13, 14 and 16, necessary to provide the rights conferred by these articles, shall be transmitted at the request of the Party concerned without delay with due respect to Article 11 of the present Convention.

Article 35 – Co-operation with civil society

Each Party shall encourage state authorities and public officials, to co-operate with non-governmental organisations, other relevant organisations and members of civil society, in establishing strategic partnerships with the aim of achieving the purpose of this Convention.

Chapter VII – Monitoring mechanism

Article 36 – Group of experts on action against trafficking in human beings

1. The Group of experts on action against trafficking in human beings (hereinafter referred to as "GRETA"), shall monitor the implementation of this Convention by the Parties.

2. GRETA shall be composed of a minimum of 10 members and a maximum of 15 members, taking into account a gender and geographical balance, as well as a multidisciplinary expertise. They shall be elected by the Committee of the Parties for a term of office of 4 years, renewable once, chosen from amongst nationals of the States Parties to this Convention.

3. The election of the members of GRETA shall be based on the following principles:

a they shall be chosen from among persons of high moral character, known for their recognised competence in the fields of Human Rights, assistance and protection of victims and of action against trafficking in human beings or having professional experience in the areas covered by this Convention;

b they shall sit in their individual capacity and shall be independent and impartial in the exercise of their functions and shall be available to carry out their duties in an effective manner;

c no two members of GRETA may be nationals of the same State;

d they should represent the main legal systems.

4. The election procedure of the members of GRETA shall be determined by the Committee of Ministers, after consulting with and obtaining the unanimous consent of the Parties to the Convention, within a period of one year following the entry into force of this Convention. GRETA shall adopt its own rules of procedure.

Article 37 – Committee of the Parties

1. The Committee of the Parties shall be composed of the representatives on the Committee of Ministers of the Council of Europe of the member States Parties to the Convention and representatives of the Parties to the Convention, which are not members of the Council of Europe.

2. The Committee of the Parties shall be convened by the Secretary General of the Council of Europe. Its first meeting shall be held within a period of one year following the entry into force of this Convention in order to elect the members of GRETA. It shall subsequently meet

whenever one-third of the Parties, the President of GRETA or the Secretary General so requests.

3. The Committee of the Parties shall adopt its own rules of procedure.

Article 38 – Procedure

1. The evaluation procedure shall concern the Parties to the Convention and be divided in rounds, the length of which is determined by GRETA. At the beginning of each round GRETA shall select the specific provisions on which the evaluation procedure shall be based.

2. GRETA shall define the most appropriate means to carry out this evaluation. GRETA may in particular adopt a questionnaire for each evaluation round, which may serve as a basis for the evaluation of the implementation by the Parties of the present Convention. Such a questionnaire shall be addressed to all Parties. Parties shall respond to this questionnaire, as well as to any other request of information from GRETA.

3. GRETA may request information from civil society.

4. GRETA may subsidiarily organise, in co-operation with the national authorities and the "contact person" appointed by the latter, and, if necessary, with the assistance of independent national experts, country visits. During these visits, GRETA may be assisted by specialists in specific fields.

5. GRETA shall prepare a draft report containing its analysis concerning the implementation of the provisions on which the evaluation is based, as well as its suggestions and proposals concerning the way in which the Party concerned may deal with the problems which have been identified. The draft report shall be transmitted for comments to the Party which undergoes the evaluation. Its comments are taken into account by GRETA when establishing its report.

6. On this basis, GRETA shall adopt its report and conclusions concerning the measures taken by the Party concerned to implement the provisions of the present Convention. This report and conclusions shall be sent to the Party concerned and to the Committee of the Parties. The report and conclusions of GRETA shall be made public as from their adoption, together with eventual comments by the Party concerned.

7. Without prejudice to the procedure of paragraphs 1 to 6 of this article, the Committee of the Parties may adopt, on the basis of the report and conclusions of GRETA, recommendations addressed to this Party (a) concerning the measures to be taken to implement the conclusions of GRETA, if necessary setting a date for submitting information on their implementation, and (b) aiming at promoting co-operation with that Party for the proper implementation of the present Convention.

Chapter VIII – Relationship with other international instruments

Article 39 – Relationship with the Protocol to prevent, suppress and punish trafficking in persons, especially women and children, supplementing the United Nations Convention against transnational organised crime

This Convention shall not affect the rights and obligations derived from the provisions of the Protocol to prevent, suppress and punish trafficking in persons, especially women and children, supplementing the United Nations Convention against transnational organised crime, and is intended to enhance the protection afforded by it and develop the standards contained therein.

Article 40 – Relationship with other international instruments

1. This Convention shall not affect the rights and obligations derived from other international instruments to which Parties to the present Convention are Parties or shall become Parties and which contain provisions on matters governed by this Convention and which ensure greater protection and assistance for victims of trafficking.

2. The Parties to the Convention may conclude bilateral or multilateral agreements with one another on the matters dealt with in this Convention, for purposes of supplementing or strengthening its provisions or facilitating the application of the principles embodied in it.

3. Parties which are members of the European Union shall, in their mutual relations, apply Community and European Union rules in so far as there are Community or European Union rules governing the particular subject concerned and applicable to the specific case, without prejudice to the object and purpose of the present Convention and without prejudice to its full application with other Parties.

4. Nothing in this Convention shall affect the rights, obligations and responsibilities of States and individuals under international law, including international humanitarian law and international human rights law and, in particular, where applicable, the 1951 Convention and the 1967 Protocol relating to the Status of Refugees and the principle of *non-refoulement* as contained therein.

4. Council of Europe Convention on the Protection of Children against Sexual Exploitation and Sexual Abuse, 2007

Serious violations of the rights of children across the world, and in particular the use of children for sexual purposes and exploitation, as well as protecting the rights of child victims were some of the key reasons for the formulation of the Council of Europe's Convention on the Protection of Children against Sexual Exploitation and Sexual Abuse in 2007. The Convention was adopted and opened for signature on the occasion of the 28th Conference of European Ministers of Justice in Lanzarote, Spain. Many states have signed and ratified the Convention and, as a result, the Convention became binding on 1 July 2010. The Convention has a very high legal validity and should be considered one of the most authoritative international treaties aiming at the prevention of the sexual abuse of children at a national, regional or international level. It obliges the contracting parties to work separately and collectively to prevent all forms of sexual use of children. The Convention in fact constitutes the first international agreement to deal exclusively with all forms of child sexual abuse including pedeopornography, prostitution, corruption, grooming of children through exposure to sexual activities and contacts. It also deals with sex tourism.

One of the better provisions of the Convention concerns the age of the child. Under it, a child is a person under the age of 18. This limit indirectly encourages the modification of the provisions of any other convention that considers a child is someone under 15 to offer more secure protection of children's rights and the prevention of any form of sexual abuses. This point is particularly significant in the case of children who are used in armed conflicts—particularly females. Above all, the Convention recognizes the duties and responsibilities of each contracting party to take necessary and constructive measures to inform persons who work, in one way or another, with children's education, health, social protection, judicial and any other law enforcement sectors, about children's rights. It is one of the special duties of the contracting parties to be sure that persons working with children have properly understood the meaning of the sexual exploitation or sexual abuse of children.

A problematic position of the Convention is that it does not make clear whether consumption of alcohol by teachers, for instance, , and their participation in high school children's parties or activities and sexual abuse of students is criminalized. Although the Convention places a duty on each party to inform those who work in children's education that all forms of sexual abuse of children is criminal, the relevant provision is strongly subject to legal debate. One of the serious issues is that high school children may be worried about their future results, and thus not report or object to the abuser. This is the case in many countries, such as Sweden, for example. The hope is that the provisions of the Convention are sufficiently understood by individuals and not misinterpreted.

However, it is true that the Council of Europe has launched a pan-European campaign to increase public knowledge and encourage children to overcome their fears and break their silence concerning sexual abuse, and report them to legal authorities.

The Convention provides that:

Preamble

The member States of the Council of Europe and the other signatories hereto;

Considering that the aim of the Council of Europe is to achieve a greater unity between its members;

Considering that every child has the right to such measures of protection as are required by his or her status as a minor, on the part of his or her family, society and the State;

Observing that the sexual exploitation of children, in particular child pornography and prostitution, and all forms of sexual abuse of children, including acts which are committed abroad, are destructive to children's health and psycho-social development;

Observing that the sexual exploitation and sexual abuse of children have grown to worrying proportions at both national and international level, in particular as regards the increased use by both children and perpetrators of information and communication technologies (ICTs), and that preventing and combating such sexual exploitation and sexual abuse of children require international co-operation;

Considering that the well-being and best interests of children are fundamental values shared by all member States and must be promoted without any discrimination;

Recalling the Action Plan adopted at the 3rd Summit of Heads of State and Governments of the Council of Europe (Warsaw, 16-17 May 2005), calling for the elaboration of measures to stop sexual exploitation of children;

Recalling in particular the Committee of Ministers Recommendation No. R (91) 11 concerning sexual exploitation, pornography and prostitution of, and trafficking in, children and young adults, Recommendation Rec(2001)16 on the protection of children against sexual exploitation, and the Convention on Cybercrime (ETS No. 185), especially Article 9 thereof, as well as the Council of Europe Convention on Action against Trafficking in Human Beings (CETS No. 197);

Bearing in mind the Convention for the Protection of Human Rights and Fundamental Freedoms (1950, ETS No. 5), the revised European

Social Charter (1996, ETS No. 163), and the European Convention on the Exercise of Children's Rights (1996, ETS No. 160);

Also bearing in mind the United Nations Convention on the Rights of the Child, especially Article 34 thereof, the Optional Protocol on the sale of children, child prostitution and child pornography, the Protocol to Prevent, Suppress and Punish Trafficking in Persons, Especially Women and Children, supplementing the United Nations Convention against Transnational Organized Crime, as well as the International Labour Organization Convention concerning the Prohibition and Immediate Action for the Elimination of the Worst Forms of Child Labour;

Bearing in mind the Council of the European Union Framework Decision on combating the sexual exploitation of children and child pornography (2004/68/JHA), the Council of the European Union Framework Decision on the standing of victims in criminal proceedings (2001/220/JHA), and the Council of the European Union Framework Decision on combating trafficking in human beings (2002/629/JHA);

Taking due account of other relevant international instruments and programmes in this field, in particular the Stockholm Declaration and Agenda for Action, adopted at the 1st World Congress against Commercial Sexual Exploitation of Children (27-31 August 1996), the Yokohama Global Commitment adopted at the 2nd World Congress against Commercial Sexual Exploitation of Children (17-20 December 2001), the Budapest Commitment and Plan of Action, adopted at the preparatory Conference for the 2nd World Congress against Commercial Sexual Exploitation of Children (20-21 November 2001), the United Nations General Assembly Resolution S-27/2 "A world fit for children" and the three-year programme "Building a Europe for and with children", adopted following the 3rd Summit and launched by the Monaco Conference (4-5 April 2006);

Determined to contribute effectively to the common goal of protecting children against sexual exploitation and sexual abuse, whoever the perpetrator may be, and of providing assistance to victims;

Taking into account the need to prepare a comprehensive international instrument focusing on the preventive, protective and criminal law aspects of the fight against all forms of sexual exploitation and sexual abuse of children and setting up a specific monitoring mechanism,

Have agreed as follows:

Chapter I – Purposes, non-discrimination principle and definitions

Article 1 – Purposes

1. The purposes of this Convention are to:

a prevent and combat sexual exploitation and sexual abuse of children;

b protect the rights of child victims of sexual exploitation and sexual abuse;

c promote national and international co-operation against sexual exploitation and sexual abuse of children.

2. In order to ensure effective implementation of its provisions by the Parties, this Convention sets up a specific monitoring mechanism.

Article 2 – Non-discrimination principle

The implementation of the provisions of this Convention by the Parties, in particular the enjoyment of measures to protect the rights of victims, shall be secured without discrimination on any ground such as sex, race, colour, language, religion, political or other opinion, national or social origin, association with a national minority, property, birth, sexual orientation, state of health, disability or other status.

Article 3 – Definitions

For the purposes of this Convention:

a "child" shall mean any person under the age of 18 years;
b "sexual exploitation and sexual abuse of children" shall include the behaviour as referred to in Articles 18 to 23 of this Convention;
c "victim" shall mean any child subject to sexual exploitation or sexual abuse.

Chapter II – Preventive measures

Article 4 – Principles

Each Party shall take the necessary legislative or other measures to prevent all forms of sexual exploitation and sexual abuse of children and to protect children.

Article 5 – Recruitment, training and awareness raising of persons working in contact with children

1. Each Party shall take the necessary legislative or other measures to encourage awareness of the protection and rights of children among persons who have regular contacts with children in the education, health, social protection, judicial and law-enforcement sectors and in areas relating to sport, culture and leisure activities.

2. Each Party shall take the necessary legislative or other measures to ensure that the persons referred to in paragraph 1 have an adequate knowledge of sexual exploitation and sexual abuse of children, of the means to identify them and of the possibility mentioned in Article 12, paragraph 1.

3. Each Party shall take the necessary legislative or other measures, in conformity with its internal law, to ensure that the conditions to accede to those professions whose exercise implies regular contacts with children ensure that the candidates to these professions have not been convicted of acts of sexual exploitation or sexual abuse of children.

Article 6 – Education for children

Each Party shall take the necessary legislative or other measures to ensure that children, during primary and secondary education, receive information on the risks of sexual exploitation and sexual abuse, as well as on the means to protect themselves, adapted to their evolving capacity. This information, provided in collaboration with parents, where appropriate, shall be given within a more general context of information on sexuality and shall pay special attention to situations of risk, especially those involving the use of new information and communication technologies.

Article 7 – Preventive intervention programmes or measures

Each Party shall ensure that persons who fear that they might commit any of the offences established in accordance with this Convention may have access, where appropriate, to effective intervention programmes or measures designed to evaluate and prevent the risk of offences being committed.

Article 8 – Measures for the general public

1. Each Party shall promote or conduct awareness raising campaigns addressed to the general public providing information on the phenomenon of sexual exploitation and sexual abuse of children and on the preventive measures which can be taken.

2. Each Party shall take the necessary legislative or other measures to prevent or prohibit the dissemination of materials advertising the offences established in accordance with this Convention.

Article 9 – Participation of children, the Private sector, the media and civil society

1. Each Party shall encourage the participation of children, according to their evolving capacity, in the development and the implementation of

state policies, programmes or others initiatives concerning the fight against sexual exploitation and sexual abuse of children.

2. Each Party shall encourage the private sector, in particular the information and communication technology sector, the tourism and travel industry and the banking and finance sectors, as well as civil society, to participate in the elaboration and implementation of policies to prevent sexual exploitation and sexual abuse of children and to implement internal norms through self-regulation or co-regulation.

3. Each Party shall encourage the media to provide appropriate information concerning all aspects of sexual exploitation and sexual abuse of children, with due respect for the independence of the media and freedom of the press.

4. Each Party shall encourage the financing, including, where appropriate, by the creation of funds, of the projects and programmes carried out by civil society aiming at preventing and protecting children from sexual exploitation and sexual abuse.

Chapter III – Specialised authorities and co-ordinating bodies

Article 10 – National measures of co-ordination and collaboration

1. Each Party shall take the necessary measures to ensure the co-ordination on a national or local level between the different agencies in charge of the protection from, the prevention of and the fight against sexual exploitation and sexual abuse of children, notably the education sector, the health sector, the social services and the law-enforcement and judicial authorities.

2. Each Party shall take the necessary legislative or other measures to set up or designate:

a independent competent national or local institutions for the promotion and protection of the rights of the child, ensuring that they are provided with specific resources and responsibilities;

b mechanisms for data collection or focal points, at the national or local levels and in collaboration with civil society, for the purpose of observing and evaluating the phenomenon of sexual exploitation and sexual abuse of children, with due respect for the requirements of personal data protection.

3. Each Party shall encourage co-operation between the competent state authorities, civil society and the private sector, in order to better prevent and combat sexual exploitation and sexual abuse of children.

Chapter IV – Protective measures and assistance to victims

Article 11 – Principles

1. Each Party shall establish effective social programmes and set up multidisciplinary structures to provide the necessary support for victims, their close relatives and for any person who is responsible for their care.

2. Each Party shall take the necessary legislative or other measures to ensure that when the age of the victim is uncertain and there are reasons to believe that the victim is a child, the protection and assistance measures provided for children shall be accorded to him or her pending verification of his or her age.

Article 12 – Reporting suspicion of sexual exploitation or sexual abuse

1. Each Party shall take the necessary legislative or other measures to ensure that the confidentiality rules imposed by internal law on certain professionals called upon to work in contact with children do not constitute an obstacle to the possibility, for those professionals, of their reporting to the services responsible for child protection any situation where they have reasonable grounds for believing that a child is the victim of sexual exploitation or sexual abuse.

2. Each Party shall take the necessary legislative or other measures to encourage any person who knows about or suspects, in good faith, sexual exploitation or sexual abuse of children to report these facts to the competent services.

Article 13 – Helplines

Each Party shall take the necessary legislative or other measures to encourage and support the setting up of information services, such as telephone or Internet helplines, to provide advice to callers, even confidentially or with due regard for their anonymity.

Article 14 – Assistance to victims

1. Each Party shall take the necessary legislative or other measures to assist victims, in the short and long term, in their physical and psycho-social recovery. Measures taken pursuant to this paragraph shall take due account of the child's views, needs and concerns.

2. Each Party shall take measures, under the conditions provided for by its internal law, to co-operate with non-governmental organisations, other relevant organisations or other elements of civil society engaged in assistance to victims.

3. When the parents or persons who have care of the child are involved in his or her sexual exploitation or sexual abuse, the intervention procedures taken in application of Article 11, paragraph 1, shall include:

– the possibility of removing the alleged perpetrator;

– the possibility of removing the victim from his or her family environment. The conditions and duration of such removal shall be determined in accordance with the best interests of the child.

4. Each Party shall take the necessary legislative or other measures to ensure that the persons who are close to the victim may benefit, where appropriate, from therapeutic assistance, notably emergency psychological care.

Chapter V – Intervention programmes or measures

Article 15 – General principles

1. Each Party shall ensure or promote, in accordance with its internal law, effective intervention programmes or measures for the persons referred to in Article 16, paragraphs 1 and 2, with a view to preventing and minimising the risks of repeated offences of a sexual nature against children. Such programmes or measures shall be accessible at any time during the proceedings, inside and outside prison, according to the conditions laid down in internal law.

2. Each Party shall ensure or promote, in accordance with its internal law, the development of partnerships or other forms of co-operation between the competent authorities, in particular health-care services and the social services, and the judicial authorities and other bodies responsible for following the persons referred to in Article 16, paragraphs 1 and 2.

3. Each Party shall provide, in accordance with its internal law, for an assessment of the dangerousness and possible risks of repetition of the offences established in accordance with this Convention, by the persons referred to in Article 16, paragraphs 1 and 2, with the aim of identifying appropriate programmes or measures.

4. Each Party shall provide, in accordance with its internal law, for an assessment of the effectiveness of the programmes and measures implemented.

Article 16 – Recipients of intervention programmes and measures

1. Each Party shall ensure, in accordance with its internal law, that persons subject to criminal proceedings for any of the offences established in accordance with this Convention may have access to the programmes or measures mentioned in Article 15, paragraph 1, under conditions which are neither detrimental nor contrary to the rights of the defence and to the requirements of a fair and impartial trial, and particularly with due respect for the rules governing the principle of the presumption of innocence.

2. Each Party shall ensure, in accordance with its internal law, that persons convicted of any of the offences established in accordance with this Convention may have access to the programmes or measures mentioned in Article 15, paragraph 1.

3. Each Party shall ensure, in accordance with its internal law, that intervention programmes or measures are developed or adapted to meet the developmental needs of children who sexually offend, including those who are below the age of criminal responsibility, with the aim of addressing their sexual behavioural problems.

Article 17 – Information and consent

1. Each Party shall ensure, in accordance with its internal law, that the persons referred to in Article 16 to whom intervention programmes or measures have been proposed are fully informed of the reasons for the proposal and consent to the programme or measure in full knowledge of the facts.

2. Each Party shall ensure, in accordance with its internal law, that persons to whom intervention programmes or measures have been proposed may refuse them and, in the case of convicted persons, that they are made aware of the possible consequences a refusal might have.

Chapter VI – Substantive criminal law

Article 18 – Sexual abuse

1. Each Party shall take the necessary legislative or other measures to ensure that the following intentional conduct is criminalised:

a engaging in sexual activities with a child who, according to the relevant provisions of national law, has not reached the legal age for sexual activities;

b engaging in sexual activities with a child where:

– use is made of coercion, force or threats; or

– abuse is made of a recognised position of trust, authority or influence over the child, including within the family; or

– abuse is made of a particularly vulnerable situation of the child, notably because of a mental or physical disability or a situation of dependence.

2. For the purpose of paragraph 1 above, each Party shall decide the age below which it is prohibited to engage in sexual activities with a child.

3. The provisions of paragraph 1.a are not intended to govern consensual sexual activities between minors.

Article 19 – Offences concerning child prostitution

1. Each Party shall take the necessary legislative or other measures to ensure that the following intentional conduct is criminalised:

a recruiting a child into prostitution or causing a child to participate in prostitution;

b coercing a child into prostitution or profiting from or otherwise exploiting a child for such purposes;

c having recourse to child prostitution.

2. For the purpose of the present article, the term "child prostitution" shall mean the fact of using a child for sexual activities where money or any other form of remuneration or consideration is given or promised as payment, regardless if this payment, promise or consideration is made to the child or to a third person.

Article 20 – Offences concerning child pornography

1. Each Party shall take the necessary legislative or other measures to ensure that the following intentional conduct, when committed without right, is criminalised:

a producing child pornography;

b offering or making available child pornography;

c distributing or transmitting child pornography;

d procuring child pornography for oneself or for another person;

e possessing child pornography;

f knowingly obtaining access, through information and communication technologies, to child pornography.

2. For the purpose of the present article, the term "child pornography" shall mean any material that visually depicts a child engaged in real or simulated sexually explicit conduct or any depiction of a child's sexual organs for primarily sexual purposes.

3. Each Party may reserve the right not to apply, in whole or in part, paragraph 1.a and e to the production and possession of pornographic material:

– consisting exclusively of simulated representations or realistic images of a non-existent child;

– involving children who have reached the age set in application of Article 18, paragraph 2, where these images are produced and possessed by them with their consent and solely for their own private use.

4. Each Party may reserve the right not to apply, in whole or in part, paragraph 1.f.

Article 21 – Offences concerning the participation of a child in pornographic performances

1. Each Party shall take the necessary legislative or other measures to ensure that the following intentional conduct is criminalised:

a recruiting a child into participating in pornographic performances or causing a child to participate in such performances;

b coercing a child into participating in pornographic performances or profiting from or otherwise exploiting a child for such purposes;

c knowingly attending pornographic performances involving the participation of children.

2. Each Party may reserve the right to limit the application of paragraph 1.c to cases where children have been recruited or coerced in conformity with paragraph 1.a or b.

Article 22 – Corruption of children

Each Party shall take the necessary legislative or other measures to criminalise the intentional causing, for sexual purposes, of a child who has not reached the age set in application of Article 18, paragraph 2, to witness sexual abuse or sexual activities, even without having to participate.

Article 23 – Solicitation of children for sexual purposes

Each Party shall take the necessary legislative or other measures to criminalise the intentional proposal, through information and communication technologies, of an adult to meet a child who has not reached the age set in application of Article 18, paragraph 2, for the purpose of committing any of the offences established in accordance with Article 18, paragraph 1.a, or Article 20, paragraph 1.a, against him or her, where this proposal has been followed by material acts leading to such a meeting.

Article 24 – Aiding or abetting and attempt

1. Each Party shall take the necessary legislative or other measures to establish as criminal offences, when committed intentionally, aiding or abetting the commission of any of the offences established in accordance with this Convention.

2. Each Party shall take the necessary legislative or other measures to establish as criminal offences, when committed intentionally, attempts to commit the offences established in accordance with this Convention.

3. Each Party may reserve the right not to apply, in whole or in part, paragraph 2 to offences established in accordance with Article 20, paragraph 1.b, d, e and f, Article 21, paragraph 1.c, Article 22 and Article 23.

Article 25 – Jurisdiction

1. Each Party shall take the necessary legislative or other measures to establish jurisdiction over any offence established in accordance with this Convention, when the offence is committed:

a in its territory; or
b on board a ship flying the flag of that Party; or
c on board an aircraft registered under the laws of that Party; or
d by one of its nationals; or
e by a person who has his or her habitual residence in its territory.

2. Each Party shall endeavour to take the necessary legislative or other measures to establish jurisdiction over any offence established in accordance with this Convention where the offence is committed against one of its nationals or a person who has his or her habitual residence in its territory.

3. Each Party may, at the time of signature or when depositing its instrument of ratification, acceptance, approval or accession, by a declaration addressed to the Secretary General of the Council of Europe, declare that it reserves the right not to apply or to apply only in specific cases or conditions the jurisdiction rules laid down in paragraph 1.e of this article.

4. For the prosecution of the offences established in accordance with Articles 18, 19, 20, paragraph 1.a, and 21, paragraph 1.a and b, of this Convention, each Party shall take the necessary legislative or other measures to ensure that its jurisdiction as regards paragraph 1.d is not subordinated to the condition that the acts are criminalised at the place where they were performed.

5. Each Party may, at the time of signature or when depositing its instrument of ratification, acceptance, approval or accession, by a declaration addressed to the Secretary General of the Council of Europe, declare that it reserves the right to limit the application of paragraph 4 of this article, with regard to offences established in accordance with Article 18, paragraph 1.b, second and third indents, to cases where its national has his or her habitual residence in its territory.

6. For the prosecution of the offences established in accordance with Articles 18, 19, 20, paragraph 1.a, and 21 of this Convention, each Party shall take the necessary legislative or other measures to ensure that its jurisdiction as regards paragraphs 1.d and e is not subordinated to the condition that the prosecution can only be initiated following a report from the victim or a denunciation from the State of the place where the offence was committed.

7. Each Party shall take the necessary legislative or other measures to establish jurisdiction over the offences established in accordance with this Convention, in cases where an alleged offender is present on its territory and it does not extradite him or her to another Party, solely on the basis of his or her nationality.

8. When more than one Party claims jurisdiction over an alleged offence established in accordance with this Convention, the Parties involved shall, where appropriate, consult with a view to determining the most appropriate jurisdiction for prosecution.

9. Without prejudice to the general rules of international law, this Convention does not exclude any criminal jurisdiction exercised by a Party in accordance with its internal law.

Article 26 – Corporate liability

1. Each Party shall take the necessary legislative or other measures to ensure that a legal person can be held liable for an offence established in accordance with this Convention, committed for its benefit by any natural person, acting either individually or as part of an organ of the legal person, who has a leading position within the legal person, based on:

a power of representation of the legal person;

b an authority to take decisions on behalf of the legal person;

c an authority to exercise control within the legal person.

2. Apart from the cases already provided for in paragraph 1, each Party shall take the necessary legislative or other measures to ensure that a legal person can be held liable where the lack of supervision or control by a natural person referred to in paragraph 1 has made possible the commission of an offence established in accordance with this Convention for the benefit of that legal person by a natural person acting under its authority.

3. Subject to the legal principles of the Party, the liability of a legal person may be criminal, civil or administrative.

4. Such liability shall be without prejudice to the criminal liability of the natural persons who have committed the offence.

Article 27 – Sanctions and measures

1. Each Party shall take the necessary legislative or other measures to ensure that the offences established in accordance with this Convention are punishable by effective, proportionate and dissuasive sanctions, taking into account their seriousness. These sanctions shall include penalties involving deprivation of liberty which can give rise to extradition.

2. Each Party shall take the necessary legislative or other measures to ensure that legal persons held liable in accordance with Article 26 shall be subject to effective, proportionate and dissuasive sanctions which shall include monetary criminal or non-criminal fines and may include other measures, in particular:

a exclusion from entitlement to public benefits or aid;

b temporary or permanent disqualification from the practice of commercial activities;

c placing under judicial supervision;

d judicial winding-up order.

3. Each Party shall take the necessary legislative or other measures to:

a provide for the seizure and confiscation of:

– goods, documents and other instrumentalities used to commit the offences, established in accordance with this Convention or to facilitate their commission;

– proceeds derived from such offences or property the value of which corresponds to such proceeds;

b enable the temporary or permanent closure of any establishment used to carry out any of the offences established in accordance with this Convention, without prejudice to the rights of *bona fide* third parties, or to deny the perpetrator, temporarily or permanently, the exercise of the professional or voluntary activity involving contact with children in the course of which the offence was committed.

4. Each Party may adopt other measures in relation to perpetrators, such as withdrawal of parental rights or monitoring or supervision of convicted persons.

5. Each Party may establish that the proceeds of crime or property confiscated in accordance with this article can be allocated to a special fund in order to finance prevention and assistance programmes for victims of any of the offences established in accordance with this Convention.

Article 28 – Aggravating circumstances

Each Party shall take the necessary legislative or other measures to ensure that the following circumstances, in so far as they do not already form part of the constituent elements of the offence, may, in conformity with the relevant provisions of internal law, be taken into consideration as aggravating circumstances in the determination of the sanctions in relation to the offences established in accordance with this Convention:

a the offence seriously damaged the physical or mental health of the victim;

b the offence was preceded or accompanied by acts of torture or serious violence;

c the offence was committed against a particularly vulnerable victim;

d the offence was committed by a member of the family, a person cohabiting with the child or a person having abused his or her authority;

e the offence was committed by several people acting together;

f the offence was committed within the framework of a criminal organisation;

g the perpetrator has previously been convicted of offences of the same nature.

Article 29 – Previous convictions

Each Party shall take the necessary legislative or other measures to provide for the possibility to take into account final sentences passed by another Party in relation to the offences established in accordance with this Convention when determining the sanctions.

Chapter VII – Investigation, prosecution and procedural law

Article 30 – Principles

1. Each Party shall take the necessary legislative or other measures to ensure that investigations and criminal proceedings are carried out in the best interests and respecting the rights of the child.

2. Each Party shall adopt a protective approach towards victims, ensuring that the investigations and criminal proceedings do not aggravate the trauma experienced by the child and that the criminal justice response is followed by assistance, where appropriate.

3. Each Party shall ensure that the investigations and criminal proceedings are treated as priority and carried out without any unjustified delay.

4. Each Party shall ensure that the measures applicable under the current chapter are not prejudicial to the rights of the defence and the requirements of a fair and impartial trial, in conformity with Article 6 of the Convention for the Protection of Human Rights and Fundamental Freedoms.

5. Each Party shall take the necessary legislative or other measures, in conformity with the fundamental principles of its internal law:

– to ensure an effective investigation and prosecution of offences established in accordance with this Convention, allowing, where appropriate, for the possibility of covert operations;

– to enable units or investigative services to identify the victims of the offences established in accordance with Article 20, in particular by analysing child pornography material, such as photographs and audiovisual recordings transmitted or made available through the use of information and communication technologies.

Article 31 – General measures of protection

1. Each Party shall take the necessary legislative or other measures to protect the rights and interests of victims, including their special needs as witnesses, at all stages of investigations and criminal proceedings, in particular by:

a informing them of their rights and the services at their disposal and, unless they do not wish to receive such information, the follow-up given to their complaint, the charges, the general progress of the investigation or proceedings, and their role therein as well as the outcome of their cases;

b ensuring, at least in cases where the victims and their families might be in danger, that they may be informed, if necessary, when the person prosecuted or convicted is released temporarily or definitively;

c enabling them, in a manner consistent with the procedural rules of internal law, to be heard, to supply evidence and to choose the means of having their views, needs and concerns presented, directly or through an intermediary, and considered;

d providing them with appropriate support services so that their rights and interests are duly presented and taken into account;

e protecting their privacy, their identity and their image and by taking measures in accordance with internal law to prevent the public dissemination of any information that could lead to their identification;

f providing for their safety, as well as that of their families and witnesses on their behalf, from intimidation, retaliation and repeat victimisation;

g ensuring that contact between victims and perpetrators within court and law enforcement agency premises is avoided, unless the competent authorities establish otherwise in the best interests of the child or when the investigations or proceedings require such contact.

2. Each Party shall ensure that victims have access, as from their first contact with the competent authorities, to information on relevant judicial and administrative proceedings.

3. Each Party shall ensure that victims have access, provided free of charge where warranted, to legal aid when it is possible for them to have the status of parties to criminal proceedings.

4. Each Party shall provide for the possibility for the judicial authorities to appoint a special representative for the victim when, by internal law, he or she may have the status of a party to the criminal

proceedings and where the holders of parental responsibility are precluded from representing the child in such proceedings as a result of a conflict of interest between them and the victim.

5. Each Party shall provide, by means of legislative or other measures, in accordance with the conditions provided for by its internal law, the possibility for groups, foundations, associations or governmental or non-governmental organisations, to assist and/or support the victims with their consent during criminal proceedings concerning the offences established in accordance with this Convention.

6. Each Party shall ensure that the information given to victims in conformity with the provisions of this article is provided in a manner adapted to their age and maturity and in a language that they can understand.

Article 32 – Initiation of proceedings

Each Party shall take the necessary legislative or other measures to ensure that investigations or prosecution of offences established in accordance with this Convention shall not be dependent upon the report or accusation made by a victim, and that the proceedings may continue even if the victim has withdrawn his or her statements.

Article 33 – Statute of limitation

Each Party shall take the necessary legislative or other measures to ensure that the statute of limitation for initiating proceedings with regard to the offences established in accordance with Articles 18, 19, paragraph 1.a and b, and 21, paragraph 1.a and b, shall continue for a period of time sufficient to allow the efficient starting of proceedings after the victim has reached the age of majority and which is commensurate with the gravity of the crime in question.

Article 34 – Investigations

1. Each Party shall adopt such measures as may be necessary to ensure that persons, units or services in charge of investigations are specialised in the field of combating sexual exploitation and sexual abuse of children or that persons are trained for this purpose. Such units or services shall have adequate financial resources.

2. Each Party shall take the necessary legislative or other measures to ensure that uncertainty as to the actual age of the victim shall not prevent the initiation of criminal investigations.

Article 35 – Interviews with the child

1. Each Party shall take the necessary legislative or other measures to ensure that:

a interviews with the child take place without unjustified delay after the facts have been reported to the competent authorities;

b interviews with the child take place, where necessary, in premises designed or adapted for this purpose;

c interviews with the child are carried out by professionals trained for this purpose;

d the same persons, if possible and where appropriate, conduct all interviews with the child;

e the number of interviews is as limited as possible and in so far as strictly necessary for the purpose of criminal proceedings;

f the child may be accompanied by his or her legal representative or, where appropriate, an adult of his or her choice, unless a reasoned decision has been made to the contrary in respect of that person.

2. Each Party shall take the necessary legislative or other measures to ensure that all interviews with the victim or, where appropriate, those with a child witness, may be videotaped and that these videotaped interviews may be accepted as evidence during the court proceedings, according to the rules provided by its internal law.

3. When the age of the victim is uncertain and there are reasons to believe that the victim is a child, the measures established in paragraphs 1 and 2 shall be applied pending verification of his or her age.

Article 36 – Criminal court proceedings

1. Each Party shall take the necessary legislative or other measures, with due respect for the rules governing the autonomy of legal professions, to ensure that training on children's rights and sexual exploitation and sexual abuse of children is available for the benefit of all persons involved in the proceedings, in particular judges, prosecutors and lawyers.

2. Each Party shall take the necessary legislative or other measures to ensure, according to the rules provided by its internal law, that:

a the judge may order the hearing to take place without the presence of the public;

b the victim may be heard in the courtroom without being present, notably through the use of appropriate communication technologies.

Chapter VIII – Recording and storing of data

Article 37 – Recording and storing of national data on convicted sexual offenders

1. For the purposes of prevention and prosecution of the offences established in accordance with this Convention, each Party shall take the necessary legislative or other measures to collect and store, in accordance with the relevant provisions on the protection of personal data and other appropriate rules and guarantees as prescribed by domestic law, data relating to the identity and to the genetic profile (DNA) of persons convicted of the offences established in accordance with this Convention.

2. Each Party shall, at the time of signature or when depositing its instrument of ratification, acceptance, approval or accession, communicate to the Secretary General of the Council of Europe the name and address of a single national authority in charge for the purposes of paragraph 1.

3. Each Party shall take the necessary legislative or other measures to ensure that the information referred to in paragraph 1 can be transmitted to the competent authority of another Party, in conformity with the conditions established in its internal law and the relevant international instruments.

Chapter IX – International co-operation

Article 38 – General principles and measures for international co-operation

1. The Parties shall co-operate with each other, in accordance with the provisions of this Convention, and through the application of relevant applicable international and regional instruments, arrangements agreed on the basis of uniform or reciprocal legislation and internal laws, to the widest extent possible, for the purpose of:

a preventing and combating sexual exploitation and sexual abuse of children;

b protecting and providing assistance to victims;

c investigations or proceedings concerning the offences established in accordance with this Convention.

2. Each Party shall take the necessary legislative or other measures to ensure that victims of an offence established in accordance with this Convention in the territory of a Party other than the one where they reside may make a complaint before the competent authorities of their State of residence.

3. If a Party that makes mutual legal assistance in criminal matters or extradition conditional on the existence of a treaty receives a request for legal assistance or extradition from a Party with which it has not

concluded such a treaty, it may consider this Convention the legal basis for mutual legal assistance in criminal matters or extradition in respect of the offences established in accordance with this Convention.

4. Each Party shall endeavour to integrate, where appropriate, prevention and the fight against sexual exploitation and sexual abuse of children in assistance programmes for development provided for the benefit of third states.

Chapter X – Monitoring mechanism

Article 39 – Committee of the Parties

1. The Committee of the Parties shall be composed of representatives of the Parties to the Convention.

2. The Committee of the Parties shall be convened by the Secretary General of the Council of Europe. Its first meeting shall be held within a period of one year following the entry into force of this Convention for the tenth signatory having ratified it. It shall subsequently meet whenever at least one third of the Parties or the Secretary General so requests.

3. The Committee of the Parties shall adopt its own rules of procedure.

Article 40 – Other representatives

1. The Parliamentary Assembly of the Council of Europe, the Commissioner for Human Rights, the European Committee on Crime Problems (CDPC), as well as other relevant Council of Europe intergovernmental committees, shall each appoint a representative to the Committee of the Parties.

2. The Committee of Ministers may invite other Council of Europe bodies to appoint a representative to the Committee of the Parties after consulting the latter.

3. Representatives of civil society, and in particular non-governmental organisations, may be admitted as observers to the Committee of the Parties following the procedure established by the relevant rules of the Council of Europe.

4. Representatives appointed under paragraphs 1 to 3 above shall participate in meetings of the Committee of the Parties without the right to vote.

Article 41 – Functions of the Committee of the Parties

1. The Committee of the Parties shall monitor the implementation of this Convention. The rules of procedure of the Committee of the Parties shall determine the procedure for evaluating the implementation of this Convention.

2. The Committee of the Parties shall facilitate the collection, analysis and exchange of information, experience and good practice between States to improve their capacity to prevent and combat sexual exploitation and sexual abuse of children.

3. The Committee of the Parties shall also, where appropriate:

a facilitate the effective use and implementation of this Convention, including the identification of any problems and the effects of any declaration or reservation made under this Convention;

b express an opinion on any question concerning the application of this Convention and facilitate the exchange of information on significant legal, policy or technological developments.

4. The Committee of the Parties shall be assisted by the Secretariat of the Council of Europe in carrying out its functions pursuant to this article.

5. The European Committee on Crime Problems (CDPC) shall be kept periodically informed regarding the activities mentioned in paragraphs 1, 2 and 3 of this article.

Chapter XI – Relationship with other international instruments

Article 42 – Relationship with the United Nations Convention on the Rights of the Child and its Optional Protocol on the sale of children, child prostitution and child pornography

This Convention shall not affect the rights and obligations arising from the provisions of the United Nations Convention on the Rights of the Child and its Optional Protocol on the sale of children, child prostitution and child pornography, and is intended to enhance the protection afforded by them and develop and complement the standards contained therein.

Article 43 – Relationship with other international instruments

1. This Convention shall not affect the rights and obligations arising from the provisions of other international instruments to which Parties to the present Convention are Parties or shall become Parties and which contain provisions on matters governed by this Convention and which ensure greater protection and assistance for child victims of sexual exploitation or sexual abuse.

2. The Parties to the Convention may conclude bilateral or multilateral agreements with one another on the matters dealt with in this Convention, for purposes of supplementing or strengthening its provisions or facilitating the application of the principles embodied in it.

3. Parties which are members of the European Union shall, in their mutual relations, apply Community and European Union rules in so far as there are Community or European Union rules governing the particular

subject concerned and applicable to the specific case, without prejudice to the object and purpose of the present Convention and without prejudice to its full application with other Parties.

Chapter XII – Amendments to the Convention

Article 44 – Amendments

1. Any proposal for an amendment to this Convention presented by a Party shall be communicated to the Secretary General of the Council of Europe and forwarded by him or her to the member States of the Council of Europe, any signatory, any State Party, the European Community, any State invited to sign this Convention in accordance with the provisions of Article 45, paragraph 1, and any State invited to accede to this Convention in accordance with the provisions of Article 46, paragraph 1.

2. Any amendment proposed by a Party shall be communicated to the European Committee on Crime Problems (CDPC), which shall submit to the Committee of Ministers its opinion on that proposed amendment.

3. The Committee of Ministers shall consider the proposed amendment and the opinion submitted by the CDPC and, following consultation with the non-member States Parties to this Convention, may adopt the amendment.

4. The text of any amendment adopted by the Committee of Ministers in accordance with paragraph 3 of this article shall be forwarded to the Parties for acceptance.

5. Any amendment adopted in accordance with paragraph 3 of this article shall enter into force on the first day of the month following the expiration of a period of one month after the date on which all Parties have informed the Secretary General that they have accepted it.

Chapter XIII – Final clauses

Article 45 – Signature and entry into force

1. This Convention shall be open for signature by the member States of the Council of Europe, the non-member States which have participated in its elaboration as well as the European Community.

2. This Convention is subject to ratification, acceptance or approval. Instruments of ratification, acceptance or approval shall be deposited with the Secretary General of the Council of Europe.

3. This Convention shall enter into force on the first day of the month following the expiration of a period of three months after the date on which 5 signatories, including at least 3 member States of the Council of Europe, have expressed their consent to be bound by the Convention in accordance with the provisions of the preceding paragraph.

4. In respect of any State referred to in paragraph 1 or the European Community, which subsequently expresses its consent to be bound by it, the Convention shall enter into force on the first day of the month following the expiration of a period of three months after the date of the deposit of its instrument of ratification, acceptance or approval.

Article 46 – Accession to the Convention

1. After the entry into force of this Convention, the Committee of Ministers of the Council of Europe may, after consultation of the Parties to this Convention and obtaining their unanimous consent, invite any non-member State of the Council of Europe, which has not participated in the elaboration of the Convention, to accede to this Convention by a decision taken by the majority provided for in Article 20.d of the Statute of the Council of Europe, and by unanimous vote of the representatives of the Contracting States entitled to sit on the Committee of Ministers.

2. In respect of any acceding State, the Convention shall enter into force on the first day of the month following the expiration of a period of three months after the date of deposit of the instrument of accession with the Secretary General of the Council of Europe.

Article 47 – Territorial application

1. Any State or the European Community may, at the time of signature or when depositing its instrument of ratification, acceptance, approval or accession, specify the territory or territories to which this Convention shall apply.

2. Any Party may, at any later date, by a declaration addressed to the Secretary General of the Council of Europe, extend the application of this Convention to any other territory specified in the declaration and for whose international relations it is responsible or on whose behalf it is authorised to give undertakings. In respect of such territory, the Convention shall enter into force on the first day of the month following the expiration of a period of three months after the date of receipt of such declaration by the Secretary General.

3. Any declaration made under the two preceding paragraphs may, in respect of any territory specified in such declaration, be withdrawn by a notification addressed to the Secretary General of the Council of Europe. The withdrawal shall become effective on the first day of the month following the expiration of a period of three months after the date of receipt of such notification by the Secretary General.

Article 48 – Reservations

No reservation may be made in respect of any provision of this Convention, with the exception of the reservations expressly established. Any reservation may be withdrawn at any time.

Article 49 – Denunciation

1. Any Party may, at any time, denounce this Convention by means of a notification addressed to the Secretary General of the Council of Europe.
2. Such denunciation shall become effective on the first day of the month following the expiration of a period of three months after the date of receipt of the notification by the Secretary General.

Article 50 – Notification

1. The Secretary General of the Council of Europe shall notify the member States of the Council of Europe, any State signatory, any State Party, the European Community, any State invited to sign this Convention in accordance with the provisions of Article 45 and any State invited to accede to this Convention in accordance with the provisions of Article 46 of:

a any signature;

b the deposit of any instrument of ratification, acceptance, approval or accession;

c any date of entry into force of this Convention in accordance with Articles 45 and 46;

d any amendment adopted in accordance with Article 44 and the date on which such an amendment enters into force;

e any reservation made under Article 48;

f any denunciation made in pursuance of the provisions of Article 49;

g any other act, notification or communication relating to this Convention.

In witness whereof the undersigned, being duly authorised thereto, have signed this Convention.

Done at Lanzarote, this 25th day of October 2007, in English and in French, both texts being equally authentic, in a single copy which shall be deposited in the archives of the Council of Europe. The Secretary General of the Council of Europe shall transmit certified copies to each member State of the Council of Europe, to the non-member States which have participated in the elaboration of this Convention, to the European Community and to any State invited to accede to this Convention.

CHAPTER IX

INTERNATIONAL LEGISLATIONS ELIMINATING DISCRIMINATION OF CHILDREN

1. Convention on Consent to Marriage, Minimum Age for Marriage and Registration of Marriages, 1962

For good or ill, legal civilization does not accord with technical civilization. However, it's astonishing that violations of basic human rights still frequently recur. This is especially obvious where the rights of women and children in the case of consent to marriage are concerned. As a matter of fact, many societies have seriously disregarded the consent both of women to marriage, and girls who have not still attained legal age and have therefore been forced to marry. The Convention on Consent to Marriage, Minimum Age for Marriage and Registration of Marriages which was adopted by the General Assembly in 1962 aims to prevent all forced marriages. It came into force two years after its adoption. The Convention has been significant to the protection of the right of children not to be married under the conditions of sale, slavery, force, threat, degradation or debt bondage. The intention is also to prevent the development of the exploitation of women and children. The Convention has established legal rules which go against certain traditional practices of societies which have been imposed and forcibly carried out by family members on females, and particularly by men. The provisions of the Convention also modify the position of females who are forced to get married because of the misunderstanding and misinterpretation of religious requirements.

Document

The Contracting States,

Desiring, in conformity with the Charter of the United Nations, to promote universal respect for, and observance of, human rights and fundamental freedoms for all, without distinction as to race, sex, language or religion,

Recalling that article 16 of the Universal Declaration of Human Rights states that:

(1) Men and women of full age, without any limitation due to race, nationality or religion, have the right to marry and to found a family. They are entitled to equal rights as to marriage, during marriage and at its dissolution.

(2) Marriage shall be entered into only with the free and full consent of the intending spouses,

Recalling further that the General Assembly of the United Nations declared, by resolution 843 (IX) of 17 December 1954, that certain customs, ancient laws and practices relating to marriage and the family were inconsistent with the principles set forth in the Charter of the United Nations and in the Universal Declaration of Human Rights,

Reaffirming that all States, including those which have or assume responsibility for the administration of Non-Self-Governing and Trust Territories until their achievement of independence, should take all appropriate measures with a view to abolishing such customs, ancient laws and practices by ensuring, inter alia, complete freedom in the choice of a spouse, eliminating completely child marriages and the betrothal of young girls before the age of puberty, establishing appropriate penalties where necessary and establishing a civil or other register in which all marriages will be recorded,

Hereby agree as hereinafter provided:

Article 1

1. No marriage shall be legally entered into without the full and free consent of both parties, such consent to be expressed by them in person after due publicity and in the presence of the authority competent to solemnize the marriage and of witnesses, as prescribed by law.

2. Notwithstanding anything in paragraph 1 above, it shall not be necessary for one of the parties to be present when the competent authority is satisfied that the circumstances are exceptional and that the party has, before a competent authority and in such manner as may be prescribed by law, expressed and not withdrawn consent.

Article 2

States Parties to the present Convention shall take legislative action to specify a minimum age for marriage. No marriage shall be legally entered into by any person under this age, except where a competent authority has granted a dispensation as to age, for serious reasons, in the interest of the intending spouses.

Article 3

All marriages shall be registered in an appropriate official register by the competent authority.

Article 4

1. The present Convention shall, until 31 December 1963, be open for signature on behalf of all States Members of the United Nations or members of any of the specialized agencies, and of any other State invited by the General Assembly of the United Nations to become a Party to the Convention.

2. The present Convention is subject to ratification. The instruments of ratification shall be deposited with the Secretary-General of the United Nations.

Article 5

1. The present Convention shall be open for accession to all States referred to in article 4, paragraph 1.

2. Accession shall be effected by the deposit of an instrument of accession with the Secretary-General of the United Nations.

Article 6

1. The present Convention shall come into force on the ninetieth day following the date of deposit of the eighth instrument of ratification or accession.

2. For each State ratifying or acceding to the Convention after the deposit of the eighth instrument of ratification or accession, the Convention shall enter into force on the ninetieth day after deposit by such State of its instrument of ratification or accession.

Article 7

1. Any Contracting State may denounce the present Convention by written notification to the Secretary-General of the United Nations. Denunciation shall take effect one year after the date of receipt of the notification by the Secretary-General.

2. The present Convention shall cease to be in force as from the date when the denunciation which reduces the number of Parties to less than eight becomes effective.

Article 8

Any dispute which may arise between any two or more Contracting States concerning the interpretation or application of the present Convention which is not settled by negotiation shall, at the request of all the parties to the dispute, be referred to the International Court of Justice for decision, unless the parties agree to another mode of settlement.

Article 9

The Secretary-General of the United Nations shall notify all States Members of the United Nations and the non-member States contemplated in article 4, paragraph 1, of the present Convention of the following:

(a) Signatures and instruments of ratification received in accordance with article 4;

(b) Instruments of accession received in accordance with article 5;

(c) The date upon which the Convention enters into force in accordance with article 6;

(d) Notifications of denunciation received in accordance with article 7, paragraph l;

(e) Abrogation in accordance with article 7, paragraph 2.

Article 10

1. The present Convention, of which the Chinese, English, French, Russian and Spanish texts shall be equally authentic, shall be deposited in the archives of the United Nations.

2. The Secretary-General of the United Nations shall transmit a certified copy of the Convention to all States Members of the United Nations and to the non-member States contemplated in article 4, paragraph 1.

2. Declaration on the Elimination of Discrimination against Women, 1967

Discrimination has a long history. In fact, discrimination of men by men has been one of the greatest social problems between most civilizations. In particular, the issue was identified within the extensive work of the United Nations, and has been the subject of various discussions in the General Assembly. A clear example of this was the discrimination, or apartheid, in South Africa, the United States, Australia, France, Russia and many other countries. However, these types of discrimination should not be confused with the discrimination of women or female children within most societies. The difference between the former and the latter is that the former is commonly known to be the practice of one race against another, while the latter is the practice of one race against its own females. Nevertheless, we do not deny that discrimination can also be exercised among the same race, a clear example being the discrimination against different religious groups in the Islamic Republic of Iran.

The Commission on Human Rights was very active in the question of discrimination against women and children between 1949 and 1959. Its works are the Convention on the Political Rights of Women of 1952, the Convention on the Nationality of Married Women of 1957, the Convention on Consent to Marriage, Minimum Age for Marriage and Registration of Marriages of 1962, and the Recommendation on Consent to Marriage, Minimum Age for Marriage and Registration of Marriages of 1965. The intention of all these conventions is to shield the rights of women in different societies. In order to emphasise the important function of the previous convention, the Commission adopted the Declaration on the Elimination of Discrimination against Women which was proclaimed by the General Assembly Resolution 2263(XXII) in 1967.

Although the words of the Declaration are essential for the creation of equal balance between men and women, the Declaration has also been one of the most controversial instruments in the history of legislation protecting the rights of females, because of the provisions of Articles 6 and 10. It is for this reason that subsequent instruments protecting female rights do not have any provisions about the function of the Declaration. The intentions of the Declaration are, in fact, outlawed or unmentionable within the boundaries of human rights law. It must nevertheless be asserted that the words of the Declaration have to be respected by all states if the principle of equality between men and women is to be taken seriously. The relevant parts of the declaration concerning the protection of children state:

Considering that discrimination against women is incompatible with human dignity and with the welfare of the family and of society, prevents their participation, on equal terms with men, in the political, social, economic and cultural life of their countries and is an obstacle to the full development of the potentialities of women in the service of their countries and of humanity,

Bearing in mind the great contribution made by women to social, political, economic and cultural life and the part they play in the family and particularly in the rearing of children,

Article 6

1. Without prejudice to the safeguarding of the unity and the harmony of the family, which remains the basic unit of any society, all appropriate measures, particularly legislative measures, shall be taken to ensure to women, married or unmarried, equal rights with men in the field of civil law, and in particular:

(a) The right to acquire, administer, enjoy, dispose of and inherit property, including property acquired during marriage;

(b) The right to equality in legal capacity and the exercise thereof;

(c) The same rights as men with regard to the law on the movement of persons.

2. All appropriate measures shall be taken to ensure the principle of equality of status of the husband and wife, and in particular:

(a) Women shall have the same right as men to free choice of a spouse and to enter into marriage only with their free and full consent;

(b) Women shall have equal rights with men during marriage and at its dissolution. In all cases the interest of the children shall be paramount;

(c) Parents shall have equal rights and duties in matters relating to their children. In all cases the interest of the children shall be paramount.

3. Child marriage and the betrothal of young girls before puberty shall be prohibited, and effective action, including legislation, shall be taken to specify a minimum age for marriage and to make the registration of marriages in an official registry compulsory.

Article 10

1. All appropriate measures shall be taken to ensure to women, married or unmarried, equal rights with men in the field of economic and social life, and in particular:

(a) The right, without discrimination on grounds of marital status or any other grounds, to receive vocational training, to work, to free choice of profession and employment, and to professional and vocational advancement;

(b) The right to equal remuneration with men and to equality of treatment in respect of work of equal value;

(c) The right to leave with pay, retirement privileges and provision for security in respect of unemployment, sickness, old age or other incapacity to work;

(d) The right to receive family allowances on equal terms with men.

2. In order to prevent discrimination against women on account of marriage or maternity and to ensure their effective right to work, measures shall be taken to prevent their dismissal in the event of marriage or

maternity and to provide paid maternity leave, with the guarantee of returning to former employment, and to provide the necessary social services, including child-care facilities.

3. Measures taken to protect women in certain types of work, for reasons inherent in their physical nature, shall not be regarded as discriminatory.

3. Convention on the Elimination of All Forms of Discrimination against Women, 1979

Since the previous conventions for the protection of females were not effective, the Convention on the Elimination of All Forms of Discrimination against Women was adopted in 1979 under the supervision of General Assembly Resolution 34/180, in order to fill this gap. The Convention came into force in 1981. One of the more significant aims of the Convention is to put an end to all forms of discrimination against women which are carried out in different societies. These include all aspects of social, economic, cultural, educational and political relations. In short, the Convention opens an important door to the recognition of the integrity of women and female children who are the subjects of daily discrimination in their given societies. It aims to integrate the rights of females into the legislations of states parties. The whole character of the Convention is considered to be an international Bill of Rights for the protection of women from various forms of degradation and inhuman treatment. The provisions of the Convention are also useful for the prevention of sexual violence against women in times of armed conflict. But one cannot deny that the provisions of the Convention are frequently violated by many of those states which have already ratified its framework. The relevant parts of the Convention relating to the protection of children state:

Bearing in mind the great contribution of women to the welfare of the family and to the development of society, so far not fully recognized, the social significance of maternity and the role of both parents in the family and in the upbringing of children, and aware that the role of women in procreation should not be a basis for discrimination but that the upbringing of children requires a sharing of responsibility between men and women and society as a whole,

Aware that a change in the traditional role of men as well as the role of women in society and in the family is needed to achieve full equality between men and women,

Article 5

States Parties shall take all appropriate measures:

(a) To modify the social and cultural patterns of conduct of men and women, with a view to achieving the elimination of prejudices and customary and all other practices which are based on the idea of the inferiority or the superiority of either of the sexes or on stereotyped roles for men and women;

(b) To ensure that family education includes a proper understanding of maternity as a social function and the recognition of the common responsibility of men and women in the upbringing and development of their children, it being understood that the interest of the children is the primordial consideration in all cases.

Article 9

1. States Parties shall grant women equal rights with men to acquire, change or retain their nationality. They shall ensure in particular that neither marriage to an alien nor change of nationality by the husband during marriage shall automatically change the nationality of the wife, render her stateless or force upon her the nationality of the husband.

2. States Parties shall grant women equal rights with men with respect to the nationality of their children.

Article 11

1. States Parties shall take all appropriate measures to eliminate discrimination against women in the field of employment in order to ensure, on a basis of equality of men and women, the same rights, in particular:

(a) The right to work as an inalienable right of all human beings;

(b) The right to the same employment opportunities, including the application of the same criteria for selection in matters of employment;

(c) The right to free choice of profession and employment, the right to promotion, job security and all benefits and conditions of service and the right to receive vocational training and retraining, including apprenticeships, advanced vocational training and recurrent training;

(d) The right to equal remuneration, including benefits, and to equal treatment in respect of work of equal value, as well as equality of treatment in the evaluation of the quality of work;

(e) The right to social security, particularly in cases of retirement, unemployment, sickness, invalidity and old age and other incapacity to work, as well as the right to paid leave;

(f) The right to protection of health and to safety in working conditions, including the safeguarding of the function of reproduction.

2. In order to prevent discrimination against women on the grounds of marriage or maternity and to ensure their effective right to work, States Parties shall take appropriate measures:

(a) To prohibit, subject to the imposition of sanctions, dismissal on the grounds of pregnancy or of maternity leave and discrimination in dismissals on the basis of marital status;

(b) To introduce maternity leave with pay or with comparable social benefits without loss of former employment, seniority or social allowances;

(c) To encourage the provision of the necessary supporting social services to enable parents to combine family obligations with work responsibilities and participation in public life, in particular through promoting the establishment and development of a network of child-care facilities;

(d) To provide special protection to women during pregnancy in types of work proved to be harmful to them.

3. Protective legislation relating to matters covered in this article shall be reviewed periodically in the light of scientific and technological knowledge and shall be revised, repealed or extended as necessary.

Article 16

1. States Parties shall take all appropriate measures to eliminate discrimination against women in all matters relating to marriage and family relations and in particular shall ensure, on a basis of equality of men and women:

(a) The same right to enter into marriage;

(b) The same right freely to choose a spouse and to enter into marriage only with their free and full consent;

(c) The same rights and responsibilities during marriage and at its dissolution;

(d) The same rights and responsibilities as parents, irrespective of their marital status, in matters relating to their children; in all cases the interests of the children shall be paramount;

(e) The same rights to decide freely and responsibly on the number and spacing of their children and to have access to the information, education and means to enable them to exercise these rights;

(f) The same rights and responsibilities with regard to guardianship, wardship, trusteeship and adoption of children, or similar institutions where these concepts exist in national legislation; in all cases the interests of the children shall be paramount;

(g) The same personal rights as husband and wife, including the right to choose a family name, a profession and an occupation;

(h) The same rights for both spouses in respect of the ownership, acquisition, management, administration, enjoyment and disposition of property, whether free of charge or for a valuable consideration.

2. The betrothal and the marriage of a child shall have no legal effect, and all necessary action, including legislation, shall be taken to specify a minimum age for marriage and to make the registration of marriages in an official registry compulsory.

4. Beijing Declaration and Platform for Action, Fourth World Conference on Women: Action for Equality, Development and Peace, 1995

The Beijing Declaration and Platform for Action, Fourth World Conference on Women: Action for Equality, Development and Peace, 1995 is one of the best known international conferences ever arranged for the protection of the rights of women under the rule of law within the system of international human rights law. A key reason for this Conference was the serious violations against women and girls within the territories of the former Yugoslavia, based on armed conflicts. In fact, the continuous reports of rape, torture, humiliation and various sexual insults of women and children made the aims of the Conference extensive and controversial. The outcome was a significant declaration which was also confirmed in 1995 by General Assembly Resolution 50/203. The resolution requires states to "an active and visible policy of mainstreaming a gender perspective at all levels, including in the design, monitoring and evaluation of all policies, as appropriate, in order to ensure the effective implementation of the Platform". The Declaration also emphasised the need to take necessary measures for the protection of females, thus issues such as women and poverty should be taken seriously. It encouraged all states to improve, and not ignore, women's health. It also spoke about the fundamental principles of human rights and their application in the case of all females. In addition, it asked all states to create opportunities for education and training in a variety of businesses for the promotion of the rights of women. It condemned oral, physical and sexual abuse, and the rape of female children. It must be asserted that the Declaration is a new international instrument in the field of international criminal law and international humanitarian law for the protection of women. Some of the relevant parts of the Declaration are:

BEIJING DECLARATION

1. We, the Governments, participating in the Fourth World Conference on Women,

2. Gathered here in Beijing, in September 1995, the year of the fiftieth anniversary of the founding of the United Nations,

3. Determined to advance the goals of equality, development and peace for all women everywhere in the interest of all humanity,

4. Acknowledging the voices of all women everywhere and taking note of the diversity of women and their roles and circumstances, honouring the women who paved the way and inspired by the hope present in the world's youth,

5. Recognize that the status of women has advanced in some important respects in the past decade but that progress has been uneven, inequalities between women and men have persisted and major obstacles remain, with serious consequences for the well-being of all people,

6. Also recognize that this situation is exacerbated by the increasing poverty that is affecting the lives of the majority of the world's people, in particular women and children, with origins in both the national and international domains,

7. Dedicate ourselves unreservedly to addressing these constraints and obstacles and thus enhancing further the advancement and empowerment of women all over the world, and agree that this requires urgent action in the spirit of determination, hope, cooperation and solidarity, now and to carry us forward into the next century.

We reaffirm our commitment to:

8. The equal rights and inherent human dignity of women and men and other purposes and principles enshrined in the Charter of the United Nations, to the Universal Declaration of Human Rights and other international human rights instruments, in particular the Convention on the Elimination of All Forms of Discrimination against Women and the Convention on the Rights of the Child, as well as the Declaration on the Elimination of Violence against Women and the Declaration on the Right to Development;

9. Ensure the full implementation of the human rights of women and of the girl child as an inalienable, integral and indivisible part of all human rights and fundamental freedoms;

10. Build on consensus and progress made at previous United Nations conferences and summits - on women in Nairobi in 1985, on children in New York in 1990, on environment and development in Rio de Janeiro in 1992, on human rights in Vienna in 1993, on population and development

in Cairo in 1994 and on social development in Copenhagen in 1995 with the objectives of achieving equality, development and peace;

11. Achieve the full and effective implementation of the Nairobi Forward-looking Strategies for the Advancement of Women;

12. The empowerment and advancement of women, including the right to freedom of thought, conscience, religion and belief, thus contributing to the moral, ethical, spiritual and intellectual needs of women and men, individually or in community with others and thereby guaranteeing them the possibility of realizing their full potential in society and shaping their lives in accordance with their own aspirations.

We are determined to:

22. Intensify efforts and actions to achieve the goals of the Nairobi Forward-looking Strategies for the Advancement of Women by the end of this century;

23. Ensure the full enjoyment by women and the girl child of all human rights and fundamental freedoms, and take effective action against violations of these rights and freedoms;

24. Take all necessary measures to eliminate all forms of discrimination against women and the girl child and remove all obstacles to gender equality and the advancement and empowerment of women;

Mission Statement

1. The Platform for Action is an agenda for women's empowerment. It aims at accelerating the implementation of the Nairobi Forward-looking Strategies for the Advancement of Women and at removing all the obstacles to women's active participation in all spheres of public and private life through a full and equal share in economic, social, cultural and political decision-making. This means that the principle of shared power and responsibility should be established between women and men at home, in the workplace and in the wider national and international communities. Equality between women and men is a matter of human rights and a condition for social justice and is also a necessary and fundamental prerequisite for equality, development and peace. A transformed partnership based on equality between women and men is a condition for people-centred sustainable development. A sustained and long-term commitment is essential, so that women and men can work together for themselves, for their children and for society to meet the challenges of the twenty-first century.

2. The Platform for Action reaffirms the fundamental principle set forth in the Vienna Declaration and Programme of Action, adopted by the World Conference on Human Rights, that the human rights of women and

of the girl child are an inalienable, integral and indivisible part of universal human rights. As an agenda for action, the Platform seeks to promote and protect the full enjoyment of all human rights and the fundamental freedoms of all women throughout their life cycle.

GLOBAL FRAMEWORK

8. The Platform for Action recognizes the importance of the agreements reached at the World Summit for Children, the United Nations Conference on Environment and Development, the World Conference on Human Rights, the International Conference on Population and Development and the World Summit for Social Development, which set out specific approaches and commitments to fostering sustainable development and international cooperation and to strengthening the role of the United Nations to that end. Similarly, the Global Conference on the Sustainable Development of Small Island Developing States, the International Conference on Nutrition, the International Conference on Primary Health Care and the World Conference on Education for All have addressed the various facets of development and human rights, within their specific perspectives, paying significant attention to the role of women and girls. In addition, the International Year for the World's Indigenous People, the International Year of the Family, the United Nations Year for Tolerance, the Geneva Declaration for Rural Women, and the Declaration on the Elimination of Violence against Women have also emphasized the issues of women's empowerment and equality.

10. Since the World Conference to Review and Appraise the Achievements of the United Nations Decade for Women: Equality, Development and Peace, held at Nairobi in 1985, and the adoption of the Nairobi Forward-looking Strategies for the Advancement of Women, the world has experienced profound political, economic, social and cultural changes, which have had both positive and negative effects on women. The World Conference on Human Rights recognized that the human rights of women and the girl child are an inalienable, integral and indivisible part of universal human rights. The full and equal participation of women in political, civil, economic, social and cultural life at the national, regional and international levels, and the eradication of all forms of discrimination on the grounds of sex are priority objectives of the international community. The World Conference on Human Rights reaffirmed the solemn commitment of all States to fulfil their obligations to promote universal respect for, and observance and protection of, all human rights and fundamental freedoms for all in accordance with the Charter of the

United Nations, other instruments related to human rights and international law. The universal nature of these rights and freedoms is beyond question.

12. The maintenance of peace and security at the global, regional and local levels, together with the prevention of policies of aggression and ethnic cleansing and the resolution of armed conflict, is crucial for the protection of the human rights of women and girl children, as well as for the elimination of all forms of violence against them and of their use as a weapon of war.

18. Recent international economic developments have had in many cases a disproportionate impact on women and children, the majority of whom live in developing countries. For those States that have carried a large burden of foreign debt, structural adjustment programmes and measures, though beneficial in the long term, have led to a reduction in social expenditures, thereby adversely affecting women, particularly in Africa and the least developed countries. This is exacerbated when responsibilities for basic social services have shifted from Governments to women.

20. Macro and micro-economic policies and programmes, including structural adjustment, have not always been designed to take account of their impact on women and girl children, especially those living in poverty. Poverty has increased in both absolute and relative terms, and the number of women living in poverty has increased in most regions. There are many urban women living in poverty; however, the plight of women living in rural and remote areas deserves special attention given the stagnation of development in such areas. In developing countries, even those in which national indicators have shown improvement, the majority of rural women continue to live in conditions of economic underdevelopment and social marginalization.

27. Since 1975, knowledge of the status of women and men, respectively, has increased and is contributing to further actions aimed at promoting equality between women and men. In several countries, there have been important changes in the relationships between women and men, especially where there have been major advances in education for women and significant increases in their participation in the paid labour force. The boundaries of the gender division of labour between productive and reproductive roles are gradually being crossed as women have started to enter formerly male-dominated areas of work and men have started to accept greater responsibility for domestic tasks, including child care. However, changes in women's roles have been greater and much more rapid than changes in men's roles. In many countries, the differences between women's and men's achievements and activities are still not

recognized as the consequences of socially constructed gender roles rather than immutable biological differences.

29. Women play a critical role in the family. The family is the basic unit of society and as such should be strengthened. It is entitled to receive comprehensive protection and support. In different cultural, political and social systems, various forms of the family exist. The rights, capabilities and responsibilities of family members must be respected. Women make a great contribution to the welfare of the family and to the development of society, which is still not recognized or considered in its full importance. The social significance of maternity, motherhood and the role of parents in the family and in the upbringing of children should be acknowledged. The upbringing of children requires shared responsibility of parents, women and men and society as a whole. Maternity, motherhood, parenting and the role of women in procreation must not be a basis for discrimination nor restrict the full participation of women in society. Recognition should also be given to the important role often played by women in many countries in caring for other members of their family.

30. While the rate of growth of world population is on the decline, world population is at an all-time high in absolute numbers, with current increments approaching 86 million persons annually. Two other major demographic trends have had profound repercussions on the dependency ratio within families. In many developing countries, 45 to 50 per cent of the population is less than 15 years old, while in industrialized nations both the number and proportion of elderly people are increasing. According to United Nations projections, 72 per cent of the population over 60 years of age will be living in developing countries by the year 2025, and more than half of that population will be women. Care of children, the sick and the elderly is a responsibility that falls disproportionately on women, owing to lack of equality and the unbalanced distribution of remunerated and unremunerated work between women and men.

37. According to World Health Organization (WHO) estimates, by the beginning of 1995 the number of cumulative cases of acquired immunodeficiency syndrome (AIDS) was 4.5 million. An estimated 19.5 million men, women and children have been infected with the human immunodeficiency virus (HIV) since it was first diagnosed and it is projected that another 20 million will be infected by the end of the decade. Among new cases, women are twice as likely to be infected as men. In the early stage of the AIDS pandemic, women were not infected in large numbers; however, about 8 million women are now infected. Young women and adolescents are particularly vulnerable. It is estimated that by

the year 2000 more than 13 million women will be infected and 4 million women will have died from AIDS-related conditions. In addition, about 250 million new cases of sexually transmitted diseases are estimated to occur every year. The rate of transmission of sexually transmitted diseases, including HIV/AIDS, is increasing at an alarming rate among women and girls, especially in developing countries.

38. Since 1975, significant knowledge and information have been generated about the status of women and the conditions in which they live. Throughout their entire life cycle, women's daily existence and long-term aspirations are restricted by discriminatory attitudes, unjust social and economic structures, and a lack of resources in most countries that prevent their full and equal participation. In a number of countries, the practice of prenatal sex selection, higher rates of mortality among very young girls and lower rates of school enrolment for girls as compared with boys suggest that son preference is curtailing the access of girl children to food, education and health care and even life itself. Discrimination against women begins at the earliest stages of life and must therefore be addressed from then onwards.

39. The girl child of today is the woman of tomorrow. The skills, ideas and energy of the girl child are vital for full attainment of the goals of equality, development and peace. For the girl child to develop her full potential she needs to be nurtured in an enabling environment, where her spiritual, intellectual and material needs for survival, protection and development are met and her equal rights safeguarded. If women are to be equal partners with men, in every aspect of life and development, now is the time to recognize the human dignity and worth of the girl child and to ensure the full enjoyment of her human rights and fundamental freedoms, including the rights assured by the Convention on the Rights of the Child, universal ratification of which is strongly urged. Yet there exists world-wide evidence that discrimination and violence against girls begin at the earliest stages of life and continue unabated throughout their lives. They often have less access to nutrition, physical and mental health care and education and enjoy fewer rights, opportunities and benefits of childhood and adolescence than do boys. They are often subjected to various forms of sexual and economic exploitation, paedophilia, forced prostitution and possibly the sale of their organs and tissues, violence and harmful practices such as female infanticide and prenatal sex selection, incest, female genital mutilation and early marriage, including child marriage.

40. Half the world's population is under the age of 25 and most of the world's youth - more than 85 per cent - live in developing countries. Policy makers must recognize the implications of these demographic factors.

Special measures must be taken to ensure that young women have the life skills necessary for active and effective participation in all levels of social, cultural, political and economic leadership. It will be critical for the international community to demonstrate a new commitment to the future - a commitment to inspiring a new generation of women and men to work together for a more just society. This new generation of leaders must accept and promote a world in which every child is free from injustice, oppression and inequality and free to develop her/his own potential. The principle of equality of women and men must therefore be integral to the socialization process.

CRITICAL AREAS OF CONCERN

44. To this end, Governments, the international community and civil society, including non-governmental organizations and the private sector, are called upon to take strategic action in the following critical areas of concern:

- The persistent and increasing burden of poverty on women
- Inequalities and inadequacies in and unequal access to education and training
- Inequalities and inadequacies in and unequal access to health care and related services
- Violence against women
- The effects of armed or other kinds of conflict on women, including those living under foreign occupation
- Inequality in economic structures and policies, in all forms of productive activities and in access to resources
- Inequality between men and women in the sharing of power and decision-making at all levels
- Insufficient mechanisms at all levels to promote the advancement of women
- Lack of respect for and inadequate promotion and protection of the human rights of women
- Stereotyping of women and inequality in women's access to and participation in all communication systems, especially in the media
- Gender inequalities in the management of natural resources and in the safeguarding of the environment
- Persistent discrimination against and violation of the rights of the girl child

CHAPTER X

INTERNATIONAL LEGISLATIONS SHELTERING DISABLED CHILDREN

1. Declaration on the Rights of Disabled Persons, 1975

The Declaration on the Rights of Disabled Persons is one of the great achievements in international human rights law. It was formulated to protect the rights of all persons including children who are, for one reason or another, incapacitated for health reasons. The Declaration was proclaimed in 1975by General Assembly Resolution 3447 (XXX). The intentions of the Declaration have also been followed by other international legal instruments under the United Nations authority. It reads:

The General Assembly,

Mindful of the pledge made by Member States, under the Charter of the United Nations to take joint and separate action in co-operation with the Organization to promote higher standards of living, full employment and conditions of economic and social progress and development,

Reaffirming its faith in human rights and fundamental freedoms and in the principles of peace, of the dignity and worth of the human person and of social justice proclaimed in the Charter,

Recalling the principles of the Universal Declaration of Human Rights, the International Covenants on Human Rights, the Declaration of the Rights of the Child and the Declaration on the Rights of Mentally Retarded Persons, as well as the standards already set for social progress in the constitutions, conventions, recommendations and resolutions of the International Labour Organisation, the United Nations Educational, Scientific and Cultural Organization, the World Health Organization, the United Nations Children's Fund and other organizations concerned,

Recalling also Economic and Social Council resolution 1921 (LVIII) of 6 May 1975 on the prevention of disability and the rehabilitation of disabled persons,

Emphasizing that the Declaration on Social Progress and Development has proclaimed the necessity of protecting the rights and assuring the welfare and rehabilitation of the physically and mentally disadvantaged,

Bearing in mind the necessity of preventing physical and mental disabilities and of assisting disabled persons to develop their abilities in the most varied fields of activities and of promoting their integration as far as possible in normal life,

Aware that certain countries, at their present stage of development, can devote only limited efforts to this end,

Proclaims this Declaration on the Rights of Disabled Persons and calls for national and international action to ensure that it will be used as a common basis and frame of reference for the protection of these rights:

1. The term "disabled person" means any person unable to ensure by himself or herself, wholly or partly, the necessities of a normal individual and/or social life, as a result of deficiency, either congenital or not, in his or her physical or mental capabilities.

2. Disabled persons shall enjoy all the rights set forth in this Declaration. These rights shall be granted to all disabled persons without any exception whatsoever and without distinction or discrimination on the basis of race, colour, sex, language, religion, political or other opinions, national or social origin, state of wealth, birth or any other situation applying either to the disabled person himself or herself or to his or her family.

3. Disabled persons have the inherent right to respect for their human dignity. Disabled persons, whatever the origin, nature and seriousness of their handicaps and disabilities, have the same fundamental rights as their fellow-citizens of the same age, which implies first and foremost the right to enjoy a decent life, as normal and full as possible.

4. Disabled persons have the same civil and political rights as other human beings; paragraph 7 of the Declaration on the Rights of Mentally Retarded Persons applies to any possible limitation or suppression of those rights for mentally disabled persons.

5. Disabled persons are entitled to the measures designed to enable them to become as self-reliant as possible.

6. Disabled persons have the right to medical, psychological and functional treatment, including prosthetic and orthetic appliances, to medical and social rehabilitation, education, vocational training and rehabilitation, aid, counselling, placement services and other services which will enable them to develop their capabilities and skills to the

maximum and will hasten the processes of their social integration or reintegration.

7. Disabled persons have the right to economic and social security and to a decent level of living. They have the right, according to their capabilities, to secure and retain employment or to engage in a useful, productive and remunerative occupation and to join trade unions.

8. Disabled persons are entitled to have their special needs taken into consideration at all stages of economic and social planning.

9. Disabled persons have the right to live with their families or with foster parents and to participate in all social, creative or recreational activities. No disabled person shall be subjected, as far as his or her residence is concerned, to differential treatment other than that required by his or her condition or by the improvement which he or she may derive there from. If the stay of a disabled person in a specialized establishment is indispensable, the environment and living conditions therein shall be as close as possible to those of the normal life of a person of his or her age.

10. Disabled persons shall be protected against all exploitation, all regulations and all treatment of a discriminatory, abusive or degrading nature.

11. Disabled persons shall be able to avail themselves of qualified legal aid when such aid proves indispensable for the protection of their persons and property. If judicial proceedings are instituted against them, the legal procedure applied shall take their physical and mental condition fully into account.

12. Organizations of disabled persons may be usefully consulted in all matters regarding the rights of disabled persons.

13. Disabled persons, their families and communities shall be fully informed, by all appropriate means, of the rights contained in this Declaration.

2. Principles for the Protection of Persons with Mental Illness and the Improvement of Mental Health Care, 1991

Another instrument which has had a direct and indirect effect in the protection of the rights of children is the Principles for the Protection of Persons with Mental Illness and the Improvement of Mental Health Care which was adopted by General Assembly Resolution 46/119 in 1991. A consideration of this instrument shows that it plays a very strong role in the protection of mentally ill persons, and in the improvement of their situation in different countries. A clear example of this need for protection is the large number of children in Russia who are suffering from serious mental illness, but receive practically no protection.

Application

These Principles shall be applied without discrimination of any kind such as on grounds of disability, race, colour, sex, language, religion, political or other opinion, national, ethnic or social origin, legal or social status, age, property or birth.

Definitions

In these Principles:

"Counsel" means a legal or other qualified representative;

"Independent authority" means a competent and independent authority prescribed by domestic law;

"Mental health care" includes analysis and diagnosis of a person's mental condition, and treatment, care and rehabilitation for a mental illness or suspected mental illness;

"Mental health facility" means any establishment, or any unit of an establishment, which as its primary function provides mental health care;

"Mental health practitioner" means a medical doctor, clinical psychologist, nurse, social worker or other appropriately trained and qualified person with specific skills relevant to mental health care;

"Patient" means a person receiving mental health care and includes all persons who are admitted to a mental health facility;

"Personal representative" means a person charged by law with the duty of representing a patient's interests in any specified respect or of exercising specified rights on the patient's behalf, and includes the parent or legal guardian of a minor unless otherwise provided by domestic law;

"The review body" means the body established in accordance with Principle 17 to review the involuntary admission or retention of a patient in a mental health facility.

General limitation clause

The exercise of the rights set forth in these Principles may be subject only to such limitations as are prescribed by law and are necessary to protect the health or safety of the person concerned or of others, or otherwise to protect public safety, order, health or morals or the fundamental rights and freedoms of others.

Principle 1

Fundamental freedoms and basic rights

1. All persons have the right to the best available mental health care, which shall be part of the health and social care system.

2. All persons with a mental illness, or who are being treated as such persons, shall be treated with humanity and respect for the inherent dignity of the human person.

3. All persons with a mental illness, or who are being treated as such persons, have the right to protection from economic, sexual and other forms of exploitation, physical or other abuse and degrading treatment.

4. There shall be no discrimination on the grounds of mental illness. "Discrimination" means any distinction, exclusion or preference that has the effect of nullifying or impairing equal enjoyment of rights. Special measures solely to protect the rights, or secure the advancement, of persons with mental illness shall not be deemed to be discriminatory. Discrimination does not include any distinction, exclusion or preference undertaken in accordance with the provisions of these Principles and necessary to protect the human rights of a person with a mental illness or of other individuals.

5. Every person with a mental illness shall have the right to exercise all civil, political, economic, social and cultural rights as recognized in the Universal Declaration of Human Rights, the International Covenant on Economic, Social and Cultural Rights, the International Covenant on Civil and Political Rights, and in other relevant instruments, such as the Declaration on the Rights of Disabled Persons and the Body of Principles for the Protection of All Persons under Any Form of Detention or Imprisonment.

6. Any decision that, by reason of his or her mental illness, a person lacks legal capacity, and any decision that, in consequence of such incapacity, a personal representative shall be appointed, shall be made only after a fair hearing by an independent and impartial tribunal established by domestic law. The person whose capacity is at issue shall be entitled to be represented by a counsel. If the person whose capacity is at issue does not himself or herself secure such representation, it shall be made available without payment by that person to the extent that he or she does not have sufficient means to pay for it. The counsel shall not in the same proceedings represent a mental health facility or its personnel and shall not also represent a member of the family of the person whose capacity is at issue unless the tribunal is satisfied that there is no conflict of interest. Decisions regarding capacity and the need for a personal representative shall be reviewed at reasonable intervals prescribed by

domestic law. The person whose capacity is at issue, his or her personal representative, if any, and any other interested person shall have the right to appeal to a higher court against any such decision.

7. Where a court or other competent tribunal finds that a person with mental illness is unable to manage his or her own affairs, measures shall be taken, so far as is necessary and appropriate to that person's condition, to ensure the protection of his or her interest.

Principle 2

Protection of minors

Special care should be given within the purposes of these Principles and within the context of domestic law relating to the protection of minors to protect the rights of minors, including, if necessary, the appointment of a personal representative other than a family member.

Principle 3

Life in the community

Every person with a mental illness shall have the right to live and work, as far as possible, in the community.

Principle 4

Determination of mental illness

1. A determination that a person has a mental illness shall be made in accordance with internationally accepted medical standards.

2. A determination of mental illness shall never be made on the basis of political, economic or social status, or membership of a cultural, racial or religious group, or any other reason not directly relevant to mental health status.

3. Family or professional conflict, or non-conformity with moral, social, cultural or political values or religious beliefs prevailing in a person's community, shall never be a determining factor in diagnosing mental illness.

4. A background of past treatment or hospitalization as a patient shall not of itself justify any present or future determination of mental illness.

5. No person or authority shall classify a person as having, or otherwise indicate that a person has, a mental illness except for purposes directly relating to mental illness or the consequences of mental illness.

Principle 5

Medical examination

No person shall be compelled to undergo medical examination with a view to determining whether or not he or she has a mental illness except in accordance with a procedure authorized by domestic law.

Principle 6

Confidentiality

The right of confidentiality of information concerning all persons to whom these Principles apply shall be respected.

Principle 7

Role of community and culture

1. Every patient shall have the right to be treated and cared for, as far as possible, in the community in which he or she lives.

2. Where treatment takes place in a mental health facility, a patient shall have the right, whenever possible, to be treated near his or her home or the home of his or her relatives or friends and shall have the right to return to the community as soon as possible.

3. Every patient shall have the right to treatment suited to his or her cultural background.

Principle 8

Standards of care

1. Every patient shall have the right to receive such health and social care as is appropriate to his or her health needs, and is entitled to care and treatment in accordance with the same standards as other ill persons.

2. Every patient shall be protected from harm, including unjustified medication, abuse by other patients, staff or others or other acts causing mental distress or physical discomfort.

Principle 9

Treatment

1. Every patient shall have the right to be treated in the least restrictive environment and with the least restrictive or intrusive treatment appropriate to the patient's health needs and the need to protect the physical safety of others.

2. The treatment and care of every patient shall be based on an individually prescribed plan, discussed with the patient, reviewed regularly, revised as necessary and provided by qualified professional staff.

3. Mental health care shall always be provided in accordance with applicable standards of ethics for mental health practitioners, including internationally accepted standards such as the Principles of Medical Ethics adopted by the United Nations General Assembly. Mental health knowledge and skills shall never be abused.

4. The treatment of every patient shall be directed towards preserving and enhancing personal autonomy.

Principle 10

Medication

1. Medication shall meet the best health needs of the patient, shall be given to a patient only for therapeutic or diagnostic purposes and shall never be administered as a punishment or for the convenience of others. Subject to the provisions of paragraph 15 of Principle 11, mental health practitioners shall only administer medication of known or demonstrated efficacy.

2. All medication shall be prescribed by a mental health practitioner authorized by law and shall be recorded in the patient's records.

Principle 11

Consent to treatment

1. No treatment shall be given to a patient without his or her informed consent, except as provided for in paragraphs 6, 7, 8, 13 and 15 below.

2. Informed consent is consent obtained freely, without threats or improper inducements, after appropriate disclosure to the patient of adequate and understandable information in a form and language understood by the patient on:

(a) The diagnostic assessment;

(b) The purpose, method, Likely duration and expected benefit of the proposed treatment;

(c) Alternative modes of treatment, including those less intrusive; and

(d) Possible pain or discomfort, risks and side-effects of the proposed treatment.

3. A patient may request the presence of a person or persons of the patient's choosing during the procedure for granting consent.

4. A patient has the right to refuse or stop treatment, except as provided for in paragraphs 6, 7, 8, 13 and 15 below. The consequences of refusing or stopping treatment must be explained to the patient.

5. A patient shall never be invited or induced to waive the right to informed consent. If the patient should seek to do so, it shall be explained to the patient that the treatment cannot be given without informed consent.

6. Except as provided in paragraphs 7, 8, 12, 13, 14 and 15 below, a proposed plan of treatment may be given to a patient without a patient's informed consent if the following conditions are satisfied:

(a) The patient is, at the relevant time, held as an involuntary patient;

(b) An independent authority, having in its possession all relevant information, including the information specified in paragraph 2 above, is satisfied that, at the relevant time, the patient lacks the capacity to give or withhold informed consent to the proposed plan of treatment or, if domestic legislation so provides, that, having regard to the patient's own safety or the safety of others, the patient unreasonably withholds such consent; and

(c) The independent authority is satisfied that the proposed plan of treatment is in the best interest of the patient's health needs.

7. Paragraph 6 above does not apply to a patient with a personal representative empowered by law to consent to treatment for the patient; but, except as provided in paragraphs 12, 13, 14 and 15 below, treatment may be given to such a patient without his or her informed consent if the personal representative, having been given the information described in paragraph 2 above, consents on the patient's behalf.

8. Except as provided in paragraphs 12, 13, 14 and 15 below, treatment may also be given to any patient without the patient's informed consent if a qualified mental health practitioner authorized by law determines that it is urgently necessary in order to prevent immediate or imminent harm to the patient or to other persons. Such treatment shall not be prolonged beyond the period that is strictly necessary for this purpose.

9. Where any treatment is authorized without the patient's informed consent, every effort shall nevertheless be made to inform the patient about the nature of the treatment and any possible alternatives and to involve the patient as far as practicable in the development of the treatment plan.

10. All treatment shall be immediately recorded in the patient's medical records, with an indication of whether involuntary or voluntary.

11. Physical restraint or involuntary seclusion of a patient shall not be employed except in accordance with the officially approved procedures of the mental health facility and only when it is the only means available to prevent immediate or imminent harm to the patient or others. It shall not be prolonged beyond the period which is strictly necessary for this purpose. All instances of physical restraint or involuntary seclusion, the reasons for them and their nature and extent shall be recorded in the patient's medical record. A patient who is restrained or secluded shall be kept under humane conditions and be under the care and close and regular

supervision of qualified members of the staff. A personal representative, if any and if relevant, shall be given prompt notice of any physical restraint or involuntary seclusion of the patient.

12. Sterilization shall never be carried out as a treatment for mental illness.

13. A major medical or surgical procedure may be carried out on a person with mental illness only where it is permitted by domestic law, where it is considered that it would best serve the health needs of the patient and where the patient gives informed consent, except that, where the patient is unable to give informed consent, the procedure shall be authorized only after independent review.

14. Psychosurgery and other intrusive and irreversible treatments for mental illness shall never be carried out on a patient who is an involuntary patient in a mental health facility and, to the extent that domestic law permits them to be carried out, they may be carried out on any other patient only where the patient has given informed consent and an independent external body has satisfied itself that there is genuine informed consent and that the treatment best serves the health needs of the patient.

15. Clinical trials and experimental treatment shall never be carried out on any patient without informed consent, except that a patient who is unable to give informed consent may be admitted to a clinical trial or given experimental treatment, but only with the approval of a competent, independent review body specifically constituted for this purpose.

16. In the cases specified in paragraphs 6, 7, 8, 13, 14 and 15 above, the patient or his or her personal representative, or any interested person, shall have the right to appeal to a judicial or other independent authority concerning any treatment given to him or her.

Principle 12

Notice of rights

1. A patient in a mental health facility shall be informed as soon as possible after admission, in a form and a language which the patient understands, of all his or her rights in accordance with these Principles and under domestic law, which information shall include an explanation of those rights and how to exercise them.

2. If and for so long as a patient is unable to understand such information, the rights of the patient shall be communicated to the personal representative, if any and if appropriate, and to the person or persons best able to represent the patient's interests and willing to do so.

3. A patient who has the necessary capacity has the right to nominate a person who should be informed on his or her behalf, as well as a person to represent his or her interests to the authorities of the facility.

Principle 13

Rights and conditions in mental health facilities

1. Every patient in a mental health facility shall, in particular, have the right to full respect for his or her:

(a) Recognition everywhere as a person before the law;

(b) Privacy;

(c) Freedom of communication, which includes freedom to communicate with other persons in the facility; freedom to send and receive uncensored private communications; freedom to receive, in private, visits from a counsel or personal representative and, at all reasonable times, from other visitors; and freedom of access to postal and telephone services and to newspapers, radio and television;

(d) Freedom of religion or belief.

2. The environment and living conditions in mental health facilities shall be as close as possible to those of the normal life of persons of similar age and in particular shall include:

(a) Facilities for recreational and leisure activities;

(b) Facilities for education;

(c) Facilities to purchase or receive items for daily living, recreation and communication;

(d) Facilities, and encouragement to use such facilities, for a patient's engagement in active occupation suited to his or her social and cultural background, and for appropriate vocational rehabilitation measures to promote reintegration in the community. These measures should include vocational guidance, vocational training and placement services to enable patients to secure or retain employment in the community.

3. In no circumstances shall a patient be subject to forced labour. Within the limits compatible with the needs of the patient and with the requirements of institutional administration, a patient shall be able to choose the type of work he or she wishes to perform.

4. The labour of a patient in a mental health facility shall not be exploited. Every such patient shall have the right to receive the same remuneration for any work which he or she does as would, according to domestic law or custom, be paid for such work to a non-patient. Every such patient shall, in any event, have the right to receive a fair share of any

remuneration which is paid to the mental health facility for his or her work.

Principle 14

Resources for mental health facilities

1. A mental health facility shall have access to the same level of resources as any other health establishment, and in particular:

(a) Qualified medical and other appropriate professional staff in sufficient numbers and with adequate space to provide each patient with privacy and a programme of appropriate and active therapy;

(b) Diagnostic and therapeutic equipment for the patient;

(c) Appropriate professional care; and

(d) Adequate, regular and comprehensive treatment, including supplies of medication.

2. Every mental health facility shall be inspected by the competent authorities with sufficient frequency to ensure that the conditions, treatment and care of patients comply with these Principles.

Principle 15

Admission principles

1. Where a person needs treatment in a mental health facility, every effort shall be made to avoid involuntary admission.

2. Access to a mental health facility shall be administered in the same way as access to any other facility for any other illness.

3. Every patient not admitted involuntarily shall have the right to leave the mental health facility at any time unless the criteria for his or her retention as an involuntary patient, as set forth in Principle 16, apply, and he or she shall be informed of that right.

Principle 16

Involuntary admission

1. A person may (a) be admitted involuntarily to a mental health facility as a patient; or (b) having already been admitted voluntarily as a patient, be retained as an involuntary patient in the mental health facility if, and only if, a qualified mental health practitioner authorized by law for that purpose determines, in accordance with Principle 4, that person has a mental illness and considers:

(a) That, because of that mental illness, there is a serious likelihood of immediate or imminent harm to that person or to other persons; or

(b) That, in the case of a person whose mental illness is severe and whose judgement is impaired, failure to admit or retain that person is likely to lead to a serious deterioration in his or her condition or will prevent the giving of appropriate treatment that can only be given by admission to a mental health facility in accordance with the principle of the least restrictive alternative.

In the case referred to in subparagraph (b), a second such mental health practitioner, independent of the first, should be consulted where possible. If such consultation takes place, the involuntary admission or retention may not take place unless the second mental health practitioner concurs.

2. Involuntary admission or retention shall initially be for a short period as specified by domestic law for observation and preliminary treatment pending review of the admission or retention by the review body. The grounds of the admission shall be communicated to the patient without delay and the fact of the admission and the grounds for it shall also be communicated promptly and in detail to the review body, to the patient's personal representative, if any, and, unless the patient objects, to the patient's family.

3. A mental health facility may receive involuntarily admitted patients only if the facility has been designated to do so by a competent authority prescribed by domestic law.

Principle 17

Review body

1. The review body shall be a judicial or other independent and impartial body established by domestic law and functioning in accordance with procedures laid down by domestic law. It shall, in formulating its decisions, have the assistance of one or more qualified and independent mental health practitioners and take their advice into account.

2. The review body's initial review, as required by paragraph 2 of Principle 16, of a decision to admit or retain a person as an involuntary patient shall take place as soon as possible after that decision and shall be conducted in accordance with simple and expeditious procedures as specified by domestic law.

3. The review body shall periodically review the cases of involuntary patients at reasonable intervals as specified by domestic law.

4. An involuntary patient may apply to the review body for release or voluntary status, at reasonable intervals as specified by domestic law.

5. At each review, the review body shall consider whether the criteria for involuntary admission set out in paragraph 1 of Principle 16 are still satisfied, and, if not, the patient shall be discharged as an involuntary patient.

6. If at any time the mental health practitioner responsible for the case is satisfied that the conditions for the retention of a person as an involuntary patient are no longer satisfied, he or she shall order the discharge of that person as such a patient.

7. A patient or his personal representative or any interested person shall have the right to appeal to a higher court against a decision that the patient be admitted to, or be retained in, a mental health facility.

Principle 18

Procedural safeguards

1. The patient shall be entitled to choose and appoint a counsel to represent the patient as such, including representation in any complaint procedure or appeal. If the patient does not secure such services, a counsel shall be made available without payment by the patient to the extent that the patient lacks sufficient means to pay.

2. The patient shall also be entitled to the assistance, if necessary, of the services of an interpreter. Where such services are necessary and the patient does not secure them, they shall be made available without payment by the patient to the extent that the patient lacks sufficient means to pay.

3. The patient and the patient's counsel may request and produce at any hearing an independent mental health report and any other reports and oral, written and other evidence that are relevant and admissible.

4. Copies of the patient's records and any reports and documents to be submitted shall be given to the patient and to the patient's counsel, except in special cases where it is determined that a specific disclosure to the patient would cause serious harm to the patient's health or put at risk the safety of others. As domestic law may provide, any document not given to the patient should, when this can be done in confidence, be given to the patient's personal representative and counsel. When any part of a document is withheld from a patient, the patient or the patient's counsel, if any, shall receive notice of the withholding and the reasons for it and shall be subject to judicial review.

5. The patient and the patient's personal representative and counsel shall be entitled to attend, participate and be heard personally in any hearing.

6. If the patient or the patient's personal representative or counsel requests that a particular person be present at a hearing, that person shall be admitted unless it is determined that the person's presence could cause serious harm to the patient's health or put at risk the safety of others.

7. Any decision whether the hearing or any part of it shall be in public or in private and may be publicly reported shall give full consideration to the patient's own wishes, to the need to respect the privacy of the patient and of other persons and to the need to prevent serious harm to the patient's health or to avoid putting at risk the safety of others.

8. The decision arising out of the hearing and the reasons for it shall be expressed in writing. Copies shall be given to the patient and his or her personal representative and counsel. In deciding whether the decision shall be published in whole or in part, full consideration shall be given to the patient's own wishes, to the need to respect his or her privacy and that of other persons, to the public interest in the open administration of justice and to the need to prevent serious harm to the patient's health or to avoid putting at risk the safety of others.

Principle 19

Access to information

1. A patient (which term in this Principle includes a former patient) shall be entitled to have access to the information concerning the patient in his or her health and personal records maintained by a mental health facility. This right may be subject to restrictions in order to prevent serious harm to the patient's health and avoid putting at risk the safety of others. As domestic law may provide, any such information not given to the patient should, when this can be done in confidence, be given to the patient's personal representative and counsel. When any of the information is withheld from a patient, the patient or the patient's counsel, if any, shall receive notice of the withholding and the reasons for it and it shall be subject to judicial review.

2. Any written comments by the patient or the patient's personal representative or counsel shall, on request, be inserted in the patient's file.

Principle 20

Criminal offenders

1. This Principle applies to persons serving sentences of imprisonment for criminal offences, or who are otherwise detained in the course of criminal proceedings or investigations against them, and who are determined to have a mental illness or who it is believed may have such an illness.

2. All such persons should receive the best available mental health care as provided in Principle 1. These Principles shall apply to them to the fullest extent possible, with only such limited modifications and exceptions as are necessary in the circumstances. No such modifications

and exceptions shall prejudice the persons' rights under the instruments noted in paragraph 5 of Principle 1.

3. Domestic law may authorize a court or other competent authority, acting on the basis of competent and independent medical advice, to order that such persons be admitted to a mental health facility.

4. Treatment of persons determined to have a mental illness shall in all circumstances be consistent with Principle 11.

Principle 21

Complaints

Every patient and former patient shall have the right to make a complaint through procedures as specified by domestic law.

Principle 22

Monitoring and remedies

States shall ensure that appropriate mechanisms are in force to promote compliance with these Principles, for the inspection of mental health facilities, for the submission, investigation and resolution of complaints and for the institution of appropriate disciplinary or judicial proceedings for professional misconduct or violation of the rights of a patient.

Principle 23

Implementation

1. States should implement these Principles through appropriate legislative, judicial, administrative, educational and other measures, which they shall review periodically.

2. States shall make these Principles widely known by appropriate and active means.

Principle 24

Scope of principles relating to mental health facilities

These Principles apply to all persons who are admitted to a mental health facility.

Principle 25

Saving of existing rights

There shall be no restriction upon or derogation from any existing rights of patients, including rights recognized in applicable international or domestic law, on the pretext that these Principles do not recognize such rights or that they recognize them to a lesser extent.

3. Standard Rules on the Equalization of Opportunities for Persons with Disabilities, 1993

Disabilities of many persons and especially children have been some of the reasons to discriminate between them and other members of society. It has thus been very difficult to protect the rights of individuals and children within different sections of society. The principles of human rights have not also been actively applied to the protection of the rights of those with disabilities. The Standard Rules on the Equalization of Opportunities for Persons with Disabilities were therefore formulated in order to prevent any kind of discrimination against the disabled. The Standard Rules were adopted in 1993 by General Assembly Resolution 48/96. With reference to children, it partly states:

Background and current needs

1. There are persons with disabilities in all parts of the world and at all levels in every society. The number of persons with disabilities in the world is large and is growing.

2. Both the causes and the consequences of disability vary throughout the world. Those variations are the result of different socio-economic circumstances and of the different provisions that States make for the well-being of their citizens.

3. Present disability policy is the result of developments over the past 200 years. In many ways it reflects the general living conditions and social and economic policies of different times. In the disability field, however, there are also many specific circumstances that have influenced the living conditions of persons with disabilities. Ignorance, neglect, superstition and fear are social factors that throughout the history of disability have isolated persons with disabilities and delayed their development.

4. Over the years disability policy developed from elementary care at institutions to education for children with disabilities and rehabilitation for persons who became disabled during adult life. Through education and rehabilitation, persons with disabilities became more active and a driving force in the further development of disability policy. Organizations of persons with disabilities, their families and advocates were formed, which advocated better conditions for persons with disabilities. After the Second World War the concepts of integration and normalization were introduced, which reflected a growing awareness of the capabilities of persons with disabilities.

5. Towards the end of the 1960s organizations of persons with disabilities in some countries started to formulate a new concept of

disability. That new concept indicated the close connection between the limitation experienced by individuals with disabilities, the design and structure of their environments and the attitude of the general population. At the same time the problems of disability in developing countries were more and more highlighted. In some of those countries the percentage of the population with disabilities was estimated to be very high and, for the most part, persons with disabilities were extremely poor.

Towards standard rules

10. Guided by the deliberations in the General Assembly, the Economic and Social Council, at its first regular session of 1990, finally agreed to concentrate on the elaboration of an international instrument of a different kind. By its resolution 1990/26 of 24 May 1990, the Council authorized the Commission for Social Development to consider, at its thirty-second session, the establishment of an ad hoc open-ended working group of government experts, funded by voluntary contributions, to elaborate standard rules on the equalization of opportunities for disabled children, youth and adults, in close collaboration with the specialized agencies, other intergovernmental bodies and non-governmental organizations, especially organizations of disabled persons. The Council also requested the Commission to finalize the text of those rules for consideration in 1993 and for submission to the General Assembly at its forty-eighth session.

11. The subsequent discussions in the Third Committee of the General Assembly at the forty-fifth session showed that there was wide support for the new initiative to elaborate standard rules on the equalization of opportunities for persons with disabilities.

12. At the thirty-second session of the Commission for Social Development, the initiative for standard rules received the support of a large number of representatives and discussions led to the adoption of resolution 32/2 of 20 February 1991, in which the Commission decided to establish an ad hoc open-ended working group in accordance with Economic and Social Council resolution 1990/26.

Purpose and content of the Standard Rules on the Equalization of Opportunities for Persons with Disabilities

13. The Standard Rules on the Equalization of Opportunities for Persons with Disabilities have been developed on the basis of the experience gained during the United Nations Decade of Disabled Persons (1983-1992). The International Bill of Human Rights, comprising the Universal Declaration of Human Rights, the International Covenant on

Economic, Social and Cultural Rights and the International Covenant on Civil and Political Rights, the Convention on the Rights of the Child and the Convention on the Elimination of All Forms of Discrimination against Women, as well as the World Programme of Action concerning Disabled Persons, constitute the political and moral foundation for the Rules.

14. Although the Rules are not compulsory, they can become international customary rules when they are applied by a great number of States with the intention of respecting a rule in international law. They imply a strong moral and political commitment on behalf of States to take action for the equalization of opportunities for persons with disabilities. Important principles for responsibility, action and cooperation are indicated. Areas of decisive importance for the quality of life and for the achievement of full participation and equality are pointed out. The Rules offer an instrument for policy-making and action to persons with disabilities and their organizations. They provide a basis for technical and economic cooperation among States, the United Nations and other international organizations.

15. The purpose of the Rules is to ensure that girls, boys, women and men with disabilities, as members of their societies, may exercise the same rights and obligations as others. In all societies of the world there are still obstacles preventing persons with disabilities from exercising their rights and freedoms and making it difficult for them to participate fully in the activities of their societies. It is the responsibility of States to take appropriate action to remove such obstacles. Persons with disabilities and their organizations should play an active role as partners in this process. The equalization of opportunities for persons with disabilities is an essential contribution in the general and worldwide effort to mobilize human resources. Special attention may need to be directed towards groups such as women, children, the elderly, the poor, migrant workers, persons with dual or multiple disabilities, indigenous people and ethnic minorities. In addition, there are a large number of refugees with disabilities who have special needs requiring attention.

Preamble

States,

Mindful of the pledge made, under the Charter of the United Nations, to take joint and separate action in cooperation with the Organization to promote higher standards of living, full employment, and conditions of economic and social progress and development,

Reaffirming the commitment to human rights and fundamental freedoms, social justice and the dignity and worth of the human person proclaimed in the Charter,

Recalling in particular the international standards on human rights, which have been laid down in the Universal Declaration of Human Rights, the International Covenant on Economic, Social and Cultural Rights and the International Covenant on Civil and Political Rights,

Underlining that those instruments proclaim that the rights recognized therein should be ensured equally to all individuals without discrimination,

Recalling the Convention on the Rights of the Child, which prohibits discrimination on the basis of disability and requires special measures to ensure the rights of children with disabilities, and the International Convention on the Protection of the Rights of All Migrant Workers and Members of Their Families, which provides for some protective measures against disability,

Recalling also the provisions in the Convention on the Elimination of All Forms of Discrimination against Women to ensure the rights of girls and women with disabilities,

Having regard to the Declaration on the Rights of Disabled Persons, the Declaration on the Rights of Mentally Retarded Persons, the Declaration on Social Progress and Development, the Principles for the Protection of Persons with Mental Illness and for the Improvement of Mental Health Care and other relevant instruments adopted by the General Assembly,

Also having regard to the relevant conventions and recommendations adopted by the International Labour Organisation, with particular reference to participation in employment without discrimination for persons with disabilities,

*Mindfu*l of the relevant recommendations and work of the United Nations Educational, Scientific and Cultural Organization, in particular the World Declaration on Education for All, the World Health Organization, the United Nations Children's Fund and other concerned organizations,

Having regard to the commitment made by States concerning the protection of the environment,

Mindful of the devastation caused by armed conflict and deploring the use of scarce resources in the production of weapons,

Recognizing that the World Programme of Action concerning Disabled Persons and the definition therein of equalization of opportunities represent earnest ambitions on the part of the international community to render those various international instruments and recommendations of practical and concrete significance,

Acknowledging that the objective of the United Nations Decade of Disabled Persons (1983-1992) to implement the World Programme of Action is still valid and requires urgent and continued action,

Recalling that the World Programme of Action is based on concepts that are equally valid in developing and industrialized countries,

Convinced that intensified efforts are needed to achieve the full and equal enjoyment of human rights and participation in society by persons with disabilities,

Re-emphasizing that persons with disabilities, and their parents, guardians, advocates and organizations, must be active partners with States in the planning and implementation of all measures affecting their civil, political, economic, social and cultural rights,

In pursuance of Economic and Social Council resolution 1990/26, and basing themselves on the specific measures required for the attainment by persons with disabilities of equality with others, enumerated in detail in the World Programme of Action,

Have adopted the Standard Rules on the Equalization of Opportunities for Persons with Disabilities outlined below, in order:

(a) To stress that all action in the field of disability presupposes adequate knowledge and experience of the conditions and special needs of persons with disabilities;

(b) To emphasize that the process through which every aspect of societal organization is made accessible to all is a basic objective of socio-economic development;

(c) To outline crucial aspects of social policies in the field of disability, including, as appropriate, the active encouragement of technical and economic cooperation;

(d) To provide models for the political decision-making process required for the attainment of equal opportunities, bearing in mind the widely differing technical and economic levels, the fact that the process must reflect keen understanding of the cultural context within which it takes place and the crucial role of persons with disabilities in it;

(e) To propose national mechanisms for close collaboration among States, the organs of the United Nations system, other intergovernmental bodies and organizations of persons with disabilities;

(f) To propose an effective machinery for monitoring the process by which States seek to attain the equalization of opportunities for persons with disabilities.

I. Preconditions for equal participation

Rule 1 Awareness-raising

States should take action to raise awareness in society about persons with disabilities, their rights, their needs, their potential and their contribution.

1. States should ensure that responsible authorities distribute up-to-date information on available programmes and services to persons with disabilities, their families, professionals in the field and the general public. Information to persons with disabilities should be presented in accessible form.

2. States should initiate and support information campaigns concerning persons with disabilities and disability policies, conveying the message that persons with disabilities are citizens with the same rights and obligations as others, thus justifying measures to remove all obstacles to full participation.

3. States should encourage the portrayal of persons with disabilities by the mass media in a positive way; organizations of persons with disabilities should be consulted on this matter.

4. States should ensure that public education programmes reflect in all their aspects the principle of full participation and equality.

5. States should invite persons with disabilities and their families and organizations to participate in public education programmes concerning disability matters.

6. States should encourage enterprises in the private sector to include disability issues in all aspects of their activity.

7. States should initiate and promote programmes aimed at raising the level of awareness of persons with disabilities concerning their rights and potential. Increased self-reliance and empowerment will assist persons with disabilities to take advantage of the opportunities available to them.

8. Awareness-raising should be an important part of the education of children with disabilities and in rehabilitation programmes. Persons with disabilities could also assist one another in awareness-raising through the activities of their own organizations.

9. Awareness-raising should be part of the education of all children and should be a component of teacher-training courses and training of all professionals.

Rule 2 Medical care

States should ensure the provision of effective medical care to persons with disabilities.

1. States should work towards the provision of programmes run by multidisciplinary teams of professionals for early detection, assessment

and treatment of impairment. This could prevent, reduce or eliminate disabling effects. Such programmes should ensure the full participation of persons with disabilities and their families at the individual level, and of organizations of persons with disabilities at the planning and evaluation level.

2. Local community workers should be trained to participate in areas such as early detection of impairments, the provision of primary assistance and referral to appropriate services.

3. States should ensure that persons with disabilities, particularly infants and children, are provided with the same level of medical care within the same system as other members of society.

4. States should ensure that all medical and paramedical personnel are adequately trained and equipped to give medical care to persons with disabilities and that they have access to relevant treatment methods and technology.

5. States should ensure that medical, paramedical and related personnel are adequately trained so that they do not give inappropriate advice to parents, thus restricting options for their children. This training should be an ongoing process and should be based on the latest information available.

6. States should ensure that persons with disabilities are provided with any regular treatment and medicines they may need to preserve or improve their level of functioning.

Rule 5 Accessibility

States should recognize the overall importance of accessibility in the process of the equalization of opportunities in all spheres of society. For persons with disabilities of any kind, States should (a) introduce programmes of action to make the physical environment accessible; and (b) undertake measures to provide access to information and communication.

(a) Access to the physical environment

1. States should initiate measures to remove the obstacles to participation in the physical environment. Such measures should be to develop standards and guidelines and to consider enacting legislation to ensure accessibility to various areas in society, such as housing, buildings, public transport services and other means of transportation, streets and other outdoor environments.

2. States should ensure that architects, construction engineers and others who are professionally involved in the design and construction of

the physical environment have access to adequate information on disability policy and measures to achieve accessibility.

3. Accessibility requirements should be included in the design and construction of the physical environment from the beginning of the designing process.

4. Organizations of persons with disabilities should be consulted when standards and norms for accessibility are being developed. They should also be involved locally from the initial planning stage when public construction projects are being designed, thus ensuring maximum accessibility.

(b) Access to information and communication

5. Persons with disabilities and, where appropriate, their families and advocates should have access to full information on diagnosis, rights and available services and programmes, at all stages. Such information should be presented in forms accessible to persons with disabilities.

6. States should develop strategies to make information services and documentation accessible for different groups of persons with disabilities. Braille, tape services, large print and other appropriate technologies should be used to provide access to written information and documentation for persons with visual impairments. Similarly, appropriate technologies should be used to provide access to spoken information for persons with auditory impairments or comprehension difficulties.

7. Consideration should be given to the use of sign language in the education of deaf children, in their families and communities. Sign language interpretation services should also be provided to facilitate the communication between deaf persons and others.

8. Consideration should also be given to the needs of people with other communication disabilities.

9. States should encourage the media, especially television, radio and newspapers, to make their services accessible.

10. States should ensure that new computerized information and service systems offered to the general public are either made initially accessible or are adapted to be made accessible to persons with disabilities.

11. Organizations of persons with disabilities should be consulted when measures to make information services accessible are being developed.

Rule 6 Education

States should recognize the principle of equal primary, secondary and tertiary educational opportunities for children, youth and adults with disabilities, in integrated settings. They should ensure that the education of persons with disabilities is an integral part of the educational system.

1. General educational authorities are responsible for the education of persons with disabilities in integrated settings. Education for persons with disabilities should form an integral part of national educational planning, curriculum development and school organization.

2. Education in mainstream schools presupposes the provision of interpreter and other appropriate support services. Adequate accessibility and support services, designed to meet the needs of persons with different disabilities, should be provided.

3. Parent groups and organizations of persons with disabilities should be involved in the education process at all levels.

4. In States where education is compulsory it should be provided to girls and boys with all kinds and all levels of disabilities, including the most severe.

5. Special attention should be given in the following areas:

   (a) Very young children with disabilities;

   (b) Pre-school children with disabilities;

   (c) Adults with disabilities, particularly women.

6. To accommodate educational provisions for persons with disabilities in the mainstream, States should:

   (a) Have a clearly stated policy, understood and accepted at the school level and by the wider community;

   (b) Allow for curriculum flexibility, addition and adaptation;

   (c) Provide for quality materials, ongoing teacher training and support teachers.

7. Integrated education and community-based programmes should be seen as complementary approaches in providing cost-effective education and training for persons with disabilities. National community-based programmes should encourage communities to use and develop their resources to provide local education to persons with disabilities.

8. In situations where the general school system does not yet adequately meet the needs of all persons with disabilities, special education may be considered. It should be aimed at preparing students for education in the general school system. The quality of such education should reflect the same standards and ambitions as general education and should be closely linked to it. At a minimum, students with disabilities should be afforded the same portion of educational resources as students

without disabilities. States should aim for the gradual integration of special education services into mainstream education. It is acknowledged that in some instances special education may currently be considered to be the most appropriate form of education for some students with disabilities.

9. Owing to the particular communication needs of deaf and deaf/blind persons, their education may be more suitably provided in schools for such persons or special classes and units in mainstream schools. At the initial stage, in particular, special attention needs to be focused on culturally sensitive instruction that will result in effective communication skills and maximum independence for people who are deaf or deaf/blind.

Rule 9 Family life and personal integrity

States should promote the full participation of persons with disabilities in family life. They should promote their right to personal integrity and ensure that laws do not discriminate against persons with disabilities with respect to sexual relationships, marriage and parenthood.

1. Persons with disabilities should be enabled to live with their families. States should encourage the inclusion in family counselling of appropriate modules regarding disability and its effects on family life. Respite-care and attendant-care services should be made available to families which include a person with disabilities. States should remove all unnecessary obstacles to persons who want to foster or adopt a child or adult with disabilities.

2. Persons with disabilities must not be denied the opportunity to experience their sexuality, have sexual relationships and experience parenthood. Taking into account that persons with disabilities may experience difficulties in getting married and setting up a family, States should encourage the availability of appropriate counselling. Persons with disabilities must have the same access as others to family-planning methods, as well as to information in accessible form on the sexual functioning of their bodies.

3. States should promote measures to change negative attitudes towards marriage, sexuality and parenthood of persons with disabilities, especially of girls and women with disabilities, which still prevail in society. The media should be encouraged to play an important role in removing such negative attitudes.

4. Persons with disabilities and their families need to be fully informed about taking precautions against sexual and other forms of abuse. Persons with disabilities are particularly vulnerable to abuse in the family, community or institutions and need to be educated on how to avoid the

occurrence of abuse, recognize when abuse has occurred and report on such acts.

4. Declaration of Commitment on HIV/AIDS, 2001

HIV/AIDS has become one of the most serious problems within the international legal and political community. The Declaration of Commitment on HIV/AIDS was consequently adopted in 2001 by General Assembly Resolution S-26/2 in order to assist all victims of HIV/AIDS. Although the Declaration has very high humanitarian aims for the protection of the rights of different persons including children, it appeared later that the prevention of the problem is not easy. Assistance to those who needed immediate humanitarian protection was rather difficult because of extortionate price of the relevant medical materials. This means that economically poor nations have not been able to procure the relevant medical care that they should have received on humanitarian grounds. Just the same, it should be noted that the Declaration is one of the most widely recognized human rights law instruments in the matter of AIDS response, although its intentions are not fully implemented. With regard to children, it states:

…

4. Noting with grave concern that all people, rich and poor, without distinction as to age, gender or race, are affected by the HIV/AIDS epidemic, further noting that people in developing countries are the most affected and that women, young adults and children, in particular girls, are the most vulnerable;

Prevention

Prevention must be the mainstay of our response

53. By 2005, ensure that at least 90 per cent, and by 2010 at least 95 per cent of young men and women aged 15 to 24 have access to the information, education, including peer education and youth-specific HIV education, and services necessary to develop the life skills required to reduce their vulnerability to HIV infection; in full partnership with youth, parents, families, educators and health-care providers;

54. By 2005, reduce the proportion of infants infected with HIV by 20 per cent, and by 50 per cent by 2010, by: ensuring that 80 per cent of pregnant women accessing antenatal care have information, counselling and other HIV prevention services available to them, increasing the availability of and by providing access for HIV-infected women and

babies to effective treatment to reduce mother-to-child transmission of HIV, as well as through effective interventions for HIV-infected women, including voluntary and confidential counselling and testing, access to treatment, especially anti-retroviral therapy and, where appropriate, breast milk substitutes and the provision of a continuum of care;

CARE, SUPPORT AND TREATMENT

Care, support and treatment are fundamental elements of an effective response

55. By 2003, ensure that national strategies, supported by regional and international strategies, are developed in close collaboration with the international community, including Governments and relevant intergovernmental organizations, as well as with civil society and the business sector, to strengthen health-care systems and address factors affecting the provision of HIV-related drugs, including anti-retroviral drugs, inter alia, affordability and pricing, including differential pricing, and technical and health-care system capacity. Also, in an urgent manner make every effort to provide progressively and in a sustainable manner, the highest attainable standard of treatment for HIV/AIDS, including the prevention and treatment of opportunistic infections, and effective use of quality-controlled anti-retroviral therapy in a careful and monitored manner to improve adherence and effectiveness and reduce the risk of developing resistance; and to cooperate constructively in strengthening pharmaceutical policies and practices, including those applicable to generic drugs and intellectual property regimes, in order further to promote innovation and the development of domestic industries consistent with international law;

56. By 2005, develop and make significant progress in implementing comprehensive care strategies to: strengthen family and community-based care, including that provided by the informal sector, and health-care systems to provide and monitor treatment to people living with HIV/AIDS, including infected children, and to support individuals, households, families and communities affected by HIV/AIDS; and improve the capacity and working conditions of health-care personnel, and the effectiveness of supply systems, financing plans and referral mechanisms required to provide access to affordable medicines, including anti-retroviral drugs, diagnostics and related technologies, as well as quality medical, palliative and psychosocial care;

57. By 2003, ensure that national strategies are developed in order to provide psychosocial care for individuals, families and communities affected by HIV/AIDS;

The vulnerable must be given priority in the response

Empowering women is essential for reducing vulnerability

62. By 2003, in order to complement prevention programmes that address activities which place individuals at risk of HIV infection, such as risky and unsafe sexual behaviour and injecting drug use, have in place in all countries strategies, policies and programmes that identify and begin to address those factors that make individuals particularly vulnerable to HIV infection, including underdevelopment, economic insecurity, poverty, lack of empowerment of women, lack of education, social exclusion, illiteracy, discrimination, lack of information and/or commodities for self-protection, and all types of sexual exploitation of women, girls and boys, including for commercial reasons. Such strategies, policies and programmes should address the gender dimension of the epidemic, specify the action that will be taken to address vulnerability and set targets for achievement;

63. By 2003, develop and/or strengthen strategies, policies and programmes which recognize the importance of the family in reducing vulnerability, inter alia, in educating and guiding children and take account of cultural, religious and ethical factors, to reduce the vulnerability of children and young people by ensuring access of both girls and boys to primary and secondary education, including HIV/AIDS in curricula for adolescents; ensuring safe and secure environments, especially for young girls; expanding good-quality, youth-friendly information and sexual health education and counselling services; strengthening reproductive and sexual health programmes; and involving families and young people in planning, implementing and evaluating HIV/AIDS prevention and care programmes, to the extent possible;

CHILDREN ORPHANED AND MADE VULNERABLE BY HIV/AIDS

Children orphaned and affected by HIV/AIDS need special assistance

65. By 2003, develop and by 2005 implement national policies and strategies to build and strengthen governmental, family and community capacities to provide a supportive environment for orphans and girls and boys infected and affected by HIV/AIDS, including by providing appropriate counselling and psychosocial support, ensuring their enrolment in school and access to shelter, good nutrition and health and social services on an equal basis with other children; and protect orphans and vulnerable children from all forms of abuse, violence, exploitation, discrimination, trafficking and loss of inheritance;

66. Ensure non-discrimination and full and equal enjoyment of all human rights through the promotion of an active and visible policy of de-stigmatization of children orphaned and made vulnerable by HIV/AIDS;

67. Urge the international community, particularly donor countries, civil society, as well as the private sector, to complement effectively national programmes to support programmes for children orphaned or made vulnerable by HIV/AIDS in affected regions and in countries at high risk and to direct special assistance to sub-Saharan Africa;

RESEARCH AND DEVELOPMENT

With no cure for HIV/AIDS yet found, further research and development is crucial

70. Increase investment and accelerate research on the development of HIV vaccines, while building national research capacity especially in developing countries, and especially for viral strains prevalent in highly affected regions; in addition, support and encourage increased national and international investment in HIV/AIDS-related research and development including biomedical, operations, social, cultural and behavioural research and in traditional medicine to: improve prevention and therapeutic approaches; accelerate access to prevention, care and treatment and care technologies for HIV/AIDS (and its associated opportunistic infections and malignancies and sexually transmitted diseases), including female controlled methods and microbicides, and in particular, appropriate, safe and affordable HIV vaccines and their delivery, and to diagnostics, tests, methods to prevent mother-to-child transmission; and improve our understanding of factors which influence the epidemic and actions which address it, inter alia, through increased funding and public/private partnerships; create a conducive environment for research and ensure that it is based on highest ethical standards;

HIV/AIDS IN CONFLICT AND DISASTER-AFFECTED REGIONS

Conflicts and disasters contribute to the spread of HIV/AIDS

75. By 2003, develop and begin to implement national strategies that incorporate HIV/AIDS awareness, prevention, care and treatment elements into programmes or actions that respond to emergency situations, recognizing that populations destabilized by armed conflict, humanitarian emergencies and natural disasters, including refugees, internally displaced persons, and in particular women and children, are at increased risk of exposure to HIV infection; and, where appropriate, factor HIV/AIDS components into international assistance programmes;

5. The Convention on the Rights of Persons with Disabilities, 2006

The Convention on the Rights of Persons with Disabilities is another international convention protecting the rights of persons who are not in a state of complete mental or physical health or social well-being. The provisions of the Convention have therefore created some optimism for 650 million disabled persons, including children. This Convention was adopted by the General Assembly in 2006, and entered into force in 2008. The key intention of the Convention is the protection of disabled persons under the fundamental principles of human rights, and it prohibits any kind of discrimination. For this reason, it calls on many international Conventions regarding the protection of the rights of minorities. For the confirmation of its statute, it also calls on the important value of different instruments, including the International Covenant on Economic, Social and Cultural Rights, the International Covenant on Civil and Political Rights, the International Convention on the Elimination of All Forms of Racial Discrimination, the Convention on the Elimination of All Forms of Discrimination against Women, the Convention against Torture and Other Cruel, Inhuman or Degrading Treatment or Punishment, the Convention on the Rights of the Child, and the International Convention on the Protection of the Rights of All Migrant Workers and Members of Their Families.

The Convention invites all governments to take effective legislative measures for the protection of the rights of disabled persons, and to promote social services including education, employment and sufficient health conditions. It requires that "children with disabilities should have full enjoyment of all human rights and fundamental freedoms on an equal basis with other children and recalling obligations to that end undertaken by States Parties to the Convention on the Rights of the Child". It also emphasises that the mobility of persons with a disability should not in any case be a reason to prevent such persons from attaining their rights. Thus, any discrimination which is based on the physical mobility of disabled persons is strongly condemned by the the Convention. The Convention also has an optional Protocol which creates a watch policy concerning the implementation of its provisions. The Protocol speaks about "the competence of the Committee on the Rights of Persons with Disabilities ("the Committee") to receive and consider communications from or on behalf of individuals or groups of individuals subject to its jurisdiction who claim to be the victims of a violation by that State Party of the provisions of the Convention". This means that states parties should be very cautious concerning the policy of the Convention and should not violate the principles of the human rights law regarding disabled persons. This includes, *inter alia*, any social, educational, work or any other matter relating to the members of the society of the state party. The Convention states:

Preamble

The States Parties to the present Convention,

(a) *Recalling* the principles proclaimed in the Charter of the United Nations which recognize the inherent dignity and worth and the equal and inalienable rights of all members of the human family as the foundation of freedom, justice and peace in the world,

(b) *Recognizing* that the United Nations, in the Universal Declaration of Human Rights and in the International Covenants on Human Rights, has proclaimed and agreed that everyone is entitled to all the rights and freedoms set forth therein, without distinction of any kind,

(c) *Reaffirming* the universality, indivisibility, interdependence and interrelatedness of all human rights and fundamental freedoms and the need for persons with disabilities to be guaranteed their full enjoyment without discrimination,

(d) *Recalling* the International Covenant on Economic, Social and Cultural Rights, the International Covenant on Civil and Political Rights, the International Convention on the Elimination of All Forms of Racial Discrimination, the Convention on the Elimination of All Forms of Discrimination against Women, the Convention against Torture and Other Cruel, Inhuman or Degrading Treatment or Punishment, the Convention on the Rights of the Child, and the International Convention on the Protection of the Rights of All Migrant Workers and Members of Their Families,

(e) *Recognizing* that disability is an evolving concept and that disability results from the interaction between persons with impairments and attitudinal and environmental barriers that hinders their full and effective participation in society on an equal basis with others,

(f) *Recognizing* the importance of the principles and policy guidelines contained in the World Programme of Action concerning Disabled Persons and in the Standard Rules on the Equalization of Opportunities for Persons with Disabilities in influencing the promotion, formulation and evaluation of the policies, plans, programmes and actions at the national, regional and international levels to further equalize opportunities for persons with disabilities,

(g) *Emphasizing* the importance of mainstreaming disability issues as an integral part of relevant strategies of sustainable development,

(h) *Recognizing also* that discrimination against any person on the basis of disability is a violation of the inherent dignity and worth of the human person,

(i) *Recognizing further* the diversity of persons with disabilities,

(j) *Recognizing* the need to promote and protect the human rights of all persons with disabilities, including those who require more intensive support,

(k) *Concerned* that, despite these various instruments and undertakings, persons with disabilities continue to face barriers in their participation as equal members of society and violations of their human rights in all parts of the world,

(l) *Recognizing* the importance of international cooperation for improving the living conditions of persons with disabilities in every country, particularly in developing countries,

(m) *Recognizing* the valued existing and potential contributions made by persons with disabilities to the overall well-being and diversity of their communities, and that the promotion of the full enjoyment by persons with disabilities of their human rights and fundamental freedoms and of full participation by persons with disabilities will result in their enhanced sense of belonging and in significant advances in the human, social and economic development of society and the eradication of poverty,

(n) *Recognizing* the importance for persons with disabilities of their individual autonomy and independence, including the freedom to make their own choices,

(o) *Considering* that persons with disabilities should have the opportunity to be actively involved in decision-making processes about policies and programmes, including those directly concerning them,

(p) *Concerned* about the difficult conditions faced by persons with disabilities who are subject to multiple or aggravated forms of discrimination on the basis of race, colour, sex, language, religion, political or other opinion, national, ethnic, indigenous or social origin, property, birth, age or other status,

(q) *Recognizing* that women and girls with disabilities are often at greater risk, both within and outside the home of violence, injury or abuse, neglect or negligent treatment, maltreatment or exploitation,

(r) *Recognizing* that children with disabilities should have full enjoyment of all human rights and fundamental freedoms on an equal basis with other children, and recalling obligations to that end undertaken by States Parties to the Convention on the Rights of the Child,

(s) *Emphasizing* the need to incorporate a gender perspective in all efforts to promote the full enjoyment of human rights and fundamental freedoms by persons with disabilities,

(t) *Highlighting* the fact that the majority of persons with disabilities live in conditions of poverty, and in this regard recognizing the critical need to address the negative impact of poverty on persons with disabilities,

(u) *Bearing in mind* that conditions of peace and security based on full respect for the purposes and principles contained in the Charter of the United Nations and observance of applicable human rights instruments are indispensable for the full protection of persons with disabilities, in particular during armed conflicts and foreign occupation,

(v) *Recognizing* the importance of accessibility to the physical, social, economic and cultural environment, to health and education and to information and communication, in enabling persons with disabilities to fully enjoy all human rights and fundamental freedoms,

(w) *Realizing* that the individual, having duties to other individuals and to the community to which he or she belongs, is under a responsibility to strive for the promotion and observance of the rights recognized in the International Bill of Human Rights,

(x) *Convinced* that the family is the natural and fundamental group unit of society and is entitled to protection by society and the State, and that persons with disabilities and their family members should receive the necessary protection and assistance to enable families to contribute towards the full and equal enjoyment of the rights of persons with disabilities,

(y) *Convinced* that a comprehensive and integral international convention to promote and protect the rights and dignity of persons with disabilities will make a significant contribution to redressing the profound social disadvantage of persons with disabilities and promote their participation in the civil, political, economic, social and cultural spheres with equal opportunities, in both developing and developed countries,

Have agreed as follows:

Article 1- Purpose

The purpose of the present Convention is to promote, protect and ensure the full and equal enjoyment of all human rights and fundamental freedoms by all persons with disabilities, and to promote respect for their inherent dignity.

Persons with disabilities include those who have long-term physical, mental, intellectual or sensory impairments which in interaction with various barriers may hinder their full and effective participation in society on an equal basis with others.

Article 2- Definitions

For the purposes of the present Convention:

"Communication" includes languages, display of text, Braille, tactile communication, large print, accessible multimedia as well as written, audio, plain-language, human-reader and augmentative and alternative modes, means and formats of communication, including accessible information and communication technology;

"Language" includes spoken and signed languages and other forms of non spoken languages;

"Discrimination on the basis of disability" means any distinction, exclusion or restriction on the basis of disability which has the purpose or effect of impairing or nullifying the recognition, enjoyment or exercise, on an equal basis with others, of all human rights and fundamental freedoms in the political, economic, social, cultural, civil or any other field. It includes all forms of discrimination, including denial of reasonable accommodation;

"Reasonable accommodation" means necessary and appropriate modification and adjustments not imposing a disproportionate or undue burden, where needed in a particular case, to ensure to persons with disabilities the enjoyment or exercise on an equal basis with others of all human rights and fundamental freedoms;

"Universal design" means the design of products, environments, programmes and services to be usable by all people, to the greatest extent possible, without the need for adaptation or specialized design. "Universal design" shall not exclude assistive devices for particular groups of persons with disabilities where this is needed.

Article 3 - General principles

The principles of the present Convention shall be:

(a) Respect for inherent dignity, individual autonomy including the freedom to make one's own choices, and independence of persons;

(b) Non-discrimination;

(c) Full and effective participation and inclusion in society;

(d) Respect for difference and acceptance of persons with disabilities as part of human diversity and humanity;

(e) Equality of opportunity;

(f) Accessibility;

(g) Equality between men and women;

(h) Respect for the evolving capacities of children with disabilities and respect for the right of children with disabilities to preserve their identities.

Article 4 - General obligations

1. States Parties undertake to ensure and promote the full realization of all human rights and fundamental freedoms for all persons with disabilities without discrimination of any kind on the basis of disability. To this end, States Parties undertake:

(a) To adopt all appropriate legislative, administrative and other measures for the implementation of the rights recognized in the present Convention;

(b) To take all appropriate measures, including legislation, to modify or abolish existing laws, regulations, customs and practices that constitute discrimination against persons with disabilities;

(c) To take into account the protection and promotion of the human rights of persons with disabilities in all policies and programmes;

(d) To refrain from engaging in any act or practice that is inconsistent with the present Convention and to ensure that public authorities and institutions act in conformity with the present Convention;

(e) To take all appropriate measures to eliminate discrimination on the basis of disability by any person, organization or private enterprise;

(f) To undertake or promote research and development of universally designed goods, services, equipment and facilities, as defined in article 2 of the present Convention, which should require the minimum possible adaptation and the least cost to meet the specific needs of a person with disabilities, to promote their availability and use, and to promote universal design in the development of standards and guidelines;

(g) To undertake or promote research and development of, and to promote the availability and use of new technologies, including information and communications technologies, mobility aids, devices and assistive technologies, suitable for persons with disabilities, giving priority to technologies at an affordable cost;

(h) To provide accessible information to persons with disabilities about mobility aids, devices and assistive technologies, including new technologies, as well as other forms of assistance, support services and facilities;

(i) To promote the training of professionals and staff working with persons with disabilities in the rights recognized in this Convention so as to better provide the assistance and services guaranteed by those rights.

2. With regard to economic, social and cultural rights, each State Party undertakes to take measures to the maximum of its available resources and, where needed, within the framework of international cooperation, with a view to achieving progressively the full realization of these rights, without prejudice to those obligations contained in the present Convention that are immediately applicable according to international law.

3. In the development and implementation of legislation and policies to implement the present Convention, and in other decision-making processes concerning issues relating to persons with disabilities, States Parties shall closely consult with and actively involve persons with disabilities, including children with disabilities, through their representative organizations.

4. Nothing in the present Convention shall affect any provisions which are more conducive to the realization of the rights of persons with disabilities and which may be contained in the law of a State Party or international law in force for that State. There shall be no restriction upon or derogation from any of the human rights and fundamental freedoms recognized or existing in any State Party to the present Convention pursuant to law, conventions, regulation or custom on the pretext that the present Convention docs not recognize such rights or freedoms or that it recognizes them to a lesser extent.

5. The provisions of the present Convention shall extend to all parts of federal states without any limitations or exceptions.

Article 5 - Equality and non-discrimination

1. States Parties recognize that all persons are equal before and under the law and are entitled without any discrimination to the equal protection and equal benefit of the law.

2. States Parties shall prohibit all discrimination on the basis of disability and guarantee to persons with disabilities equal and effective legal protection against discrimination on all grounds.

3. In order to promote equality and eliminate discrimination, States Parties shall take all appropriate steps to ensure that reasonable accommodation is provided.

4. Specific measures which are necessary to accelerate or achieve de facto equality of persons with disabilities shall not be considered discrimination under the terms of the present Convention.

Article 6- Women with disabilities

1. States Parties recognize that women and girls with disabilities are subject to multiple discrimination, and in this regard shall take measures to

ensure the full and equal enjoyment by them of all human rights and fundamental freedoms.

2. States Parties shall take all appropriate measures to ensure the full development, advancement and empowerment of women, for the purpose of guaranteeing them the exercise and enjoyment of the human rights and fundamental freedoms set out in the present Convention.

Article 7- Children with disabilities

1. States Parties shall take all necessary measures to ensure the full enjoyment by children with disabilities of all human rights and fundamental freedoms on an equal basis with other children.

2. In all actions concerning children with disabilities, the best interests of the child shall be a primary consideration.

3. States Parties shall ensure that children with disabilities have the right to express their views freely on all matters affecting them, their views being given due weight in accordance with their age and maturity, on an equal basis with other children, and to be provided with disability and age-appropriate assistance to realize that right.

Article 8- Awareness-raising

1. States Parties undertake to adopt immediate, effective and appropriate measures:

(a) To raise awareness throughout society, including at the family level, regarding persons with disabilities, and to foster respect for the rights and dignity of persons with disabilities;

(b) To combat stereotypes, prejudices and harmful practices relating to persons with disabilities, including those based on sex and age, in all areas of life;

(c) To promote awareness of the capabilities and contributions of persons with disabilities.

2. Measures to this end include:

(a) Initiating and maintaining effective public awareness campaigns designed:

(i) To nurture receptiveness to the rights of persons with disabilities;

(ii) To promote positive perceptions and greater social awareness towards persons with disabilities;

(iii) To promote recognition of the skills, merits and abilities of persons with disabilities, and of their contributions to the workplace and the labour market;

(b) Fostering at all levels of the education system, including in all children from an early age, an attitude of respect for the rights of persons with disabilities;
(c) Encouraging all organs of the media to portray persons with disabilities in a manner consistent with the purpose of the present Convention;
(d) Promoting awareness-training programmes regarding persons with disabilities and the rights of persons with disabilities.

Article 9- Accessibility

1. To enable persons with disabilities to live independently and participate fully in all aspects of life, States Parties shall take appropriate measures to ensure to persons with disabilities access, on an equal basis with others, to the physical environment, to transportation, to information and communications, including information and communications technologies and systems, and to other facilities and services open or provided to the public, both in urban and in rural areas. These measures, which shall include the identification and elimination of obstacles and barriers to accessibility, shall apply to, inter alia:

(a) Buildings, roads, transportation and other indoor and outdoor facilities, including schools, housing, medical facilities and workplaces;
(b) Information, communications and other services, including electronic services and emergency services.

2. States Parties shall also take appropriate measures to:

(a) Develop, promulgate and monitor the implementation of minimum standards and guidelines for the accessibility of facilities and services open or provided to the public;
(b) Ensure that private entities that offer facilities and services which are open or provided to the public take into account all aspects of accessibility for persons with disabilities;
(c) Provide training for stakeholders on accessibility issues facing persons with disabilities;
(d) Provide in buildings and other facilities open to the public signage in Braille and in easy to read and understand forms;
(e) Provide forms of live assistance and intermediaries, including guides, readers and professional sign language interpreters, to facilitate accessibility to buildings and other facilities open to the public;
(f) Promote other appropriate forms of assistance and support to persons with disabilities to ensure their access to information;
(g) Promote access for persons with disabilities to new information and communications technologies and systems, including the Internet;

(h) Promote the design, development, production and distribution of accessible information and communications technologies and systems at an early stage, so that these technologies and systems become accessible at minimum cost.

Article 10 - Right to life

States Parties reaffirm that every human being has the inherent right to life and shall take all necessary measures to ensure its effective enjoyment by persons with disabilities on an equal basis with others.

Article 11 - Situations of risk and humanitarian emergencies

States Parties shall take, in accordance with their obligations under international law, including international humanitarian law and international human rights law, all necessary measures to ensure the protection and safety of persons with disabilities in situations of risk, including situations of armed conflict, humanitarian emergencies and the occurrence of natural disasters.

Article 12 - Equal recognition before the law

1. States Parties reaffirm that persons with disabilities have the right to recognition everywhere as persons before the law.

2. States Parties shall recognize that persons with disabilities enjoy legal capacity on an equal basis with others in all aspects of life.

3. States Parties shall take appropriate measures to provide access by persons with disabilities to the support they may require in exercising their legal capacity.

4. States Parties shall ensure that all measures that relate to the exercise of legal capacity provide for appropriate and effective safeguards to prevent abuse in accordance with international human rights law. Such safeguards shall ensure that measures relating to the exercise of legal capacity respect the rights, will and preferences of the person, are free of conflict of interest and undue influence, are proportional and tailored to the person's circumstances, apply for the shortest time possible and are subject to regular review by a competent, independent and impartial authority or judicial body. The safeguards shall be proportional to the degree to which such measures affect the person's rights and interests.

5. Subject to the provisions of this article, States Parties shall take all appropriate and effective measures to ensure the equal right of persons with disabilities to own or inherit property, to control their own financial affairs and to have equal access to bank loans, mortgages and other forms

of financial credit, and shall ensure that persons with disabilities are not arbitrarily deprived of their property.

Article 13 - Access to justice

1. States Parties shall ensure effective access to justice for persons with disabilities on an equal basis with others, including through the provision of procedural and age-appropriate accommodations, in order to facilitate their effective role as direct and indirect participants, including as witnesses, in all legal proceedings, including at investigative and other preliminary stages.

2. In order to help to ensure effective access to justice for persons with disabilities, States Parties shall promote appropriate training for those working in the field of administration of justice, including police and prison staff.

Article 14 - Liberty and security of the person

1. States Parties shall ensure that persons with disabilities, on an equal basis with others:

(a) Enjoy the right to liberty and security of person;

(b) Are not deprived of their liberty unlawfully or arbitrarily, and that any deprivation of liberty is in conformity with the law, and that the existence of a disability shall in no case justify a deprivation of liberty.

2. States Parties shall ensure that if persons with disabilities are deprived of their liberty through any process, they are, on an equal basis with others, entitled to guarantees in accordance with international human rights law and shall be treated in compliance with the objectives and principles of this Convention, including by provision of reasonable accommodation.

Article 15 - Freedom from torture or cruel, inhuman or degrading treatment or punishment

1. No one shall be subjected to torture or to cruel, inhuman or degrading treatment or punishment. In particular, no one shall be subjected without his or her free consent to medical or scientific experimentation.

2. States Parties shall take all effective legislative, administrative, judicial or other measures to prevent persons with disabilities, on an equal basis with others, from being subjected to torture or cruel, inhuman or degrading treatment or punishment.

Article 16 - Freedom from exploitation, violence and abuse

1. States Parties shall take all appropriate legislative, administrative, social, educational and other measures to protect persons with disabilities, both within and outside the home, from all forms of exploitation, violence and abuse, including their gender-based aspects.

2. States Parties shall also take all appropriate measures to prevent all forms of exploitation, violence and abuse by ensuring, inter alia, appropriate forms of gender- and age-sensitive assistance and support for persons with disabilities and their families and caregivers, including through the provision of information and education on how to avoid, recognize and report instances of exploitation, violence and abuse. States Parties shall ensure that protection services are age-, gender- and disability-sensitive.

3. In order to prevent the occurrence of all forms of exploitation, violence and abuse, States Parties shall ensure that all facilities and programmes designed to serve persons with disabilities are effectively monitored by independent authorities.

4. States Parties shall take all appropriate measures to promote the physical, cognitive and psychological recovery, rehabilitation and social reintegration of persons with disabilities who become victims of any form of exploitation, violence or abuse, including through the provision of protection services. Such recovery and reintegration shall take place in an environment that fosters the health, welfare, self-respect, dignity and autonomy of the person and takes into account gender- and age-specific needs.

5. States Parties shall put in place effective legislation and policies, including women- and child-focused legislation and policies, to ensure that instances of exploitation, violence and abuse against persons with disabilities are identified, investigated and, where appropriate, prosecuted.

Article 17 - Protecting the integrity of the person

Every person with disabilities has a right to respect for his or her physical and mental integrity on an equal basis with others.

Article 18 - Liberty of movement and nationality

1. States Parties shall recognize the rights of persons with disabilities to liberty of movement, to freedom to choose their residence and to a nationality, on an equal basis with others, including by ensuring that persons with disabilities:

(a) Have the right to acquire and change a nationality and are not deprived of their nationality arbitrarily or on the basis of disability;

(b) Are not deprived, on the basis of disability, of their ability to obtain, possess and utilize documentation of their nationality or other documentation of identification, or to utilize relevant processes such as immigration proceedings, that may be needed to facilitate exercise of the right to liberty of movement;

(c) Are free to leave any country, including their own;

(d) Are not deprived, arbitrarily or on the basis of disability, of the right to enter their own country.

2. Children with disabilities shall be registered immediately after birth and shall have the right from birth to a name, the right to acquire a nationality and, as far as possible, the right to know and be cared for by their parents.

Article 19 -Living independently and being included in the community

States Parties to this Convention recognize the equal right of all persons with disabilities to live in the community, with choices equal to others, and shall take effective and appropriate measures to facilitate full enjoyment by persons with disabilities of this right and their full inclusion and participation in the community, including by ensuring that:

(a) Persons with disabilities have the opportunity to choose their place of residence and where and with whom they live on an equal basis with others and are not obliged to live in a particular living arrangement;

(b) Persons with disabilities have access to a range of in-home, residential and other community support services, including personal assistance necessary to support living and inclusion in the community, and to prevent isolation or segregation from the community;

(c) Community services and facilities for the general population are available on an equal basis to persons with disabilities and are responsive to their needs.

Article 20 - Personal mobility

States Parties shall take effective measures to ensure personal mobility with the greatest possible independence for persons with disabilities, including by:

(a) Facilitating the personal mobility of persons with disabilities in the manner and at the time of their choice, and at affordable cost;

(b) Facilitating access by persons with disabilities to quality mobility aids, devices, assistive technologies and forms of live assistance and intermediaries, including by making them available at affordable cost;

(c) Providing training in mobility skills to persons with disabilities and to specialist staff working with persons with disabilities;

(d) Encouraging entities that produce mobility aids, devices and assistive technologies to take into account all aspects of mobility for persons with disabilities.

Article 21 -Freedom of expression and opinion, and access to information

States Parties shall take all appropriate measures to ensure that persons with disabilities can exercise the right to freedom of expression and opinion, including the freedom to seek, receive and impart information and ideas on an equal basis with others and through all forms of communication of their choice, as defined in article 2 of the present Convention, including by:

(a) Providing information intended for the general public to persons with disabilities in accessible formats and technologies appropriate to different kinds of disabilities in a timely manner and without additional cost;

(b) Accepting and facilitating the use of sign languages, Braille, augmentative and alternative communication, and all other accessible means, modes and formats of communication of their choice by persons with disabilities in official interactions;

(c) Urging private entities that provide services to the general public, including through the Internet, to provide information and services in accessible and usable formats for persons with disabilities;

(d) Encouraging the mass media, including providers of information through the Internet, to make their services accessible to persons with disabilities;

(e) Recognizing and promoting the use of sign languages.

Article 22 - Respect for privacy

1. No person with disabilities, regardless of place of residence or living arrangements, shall be subjected to arbitrary or unlawful interference with his or her privacy, family, home or correspondence or other types of communication or to unlawful attacks on his or her honour and reputation. Persons with disabilities have the right to the protection of the law against such interference or attacks.

2. States Parties shall protect the privacy of personal, health and rehabilitation information of persons with disabilities on an equal basis with others.

Article 23 - Respect for home and the family

1. States Parties shall take effective and appropriate measures to eliminate discrimination against persons with disabilities in all matters relating to marriage, family, parenthood and relationships, on an equal basis with others, so as to ensure that:

(a) The right of all persons with disabilities who are of marriageable age to marry and to found a family on the basis of free and full consent of the intending spouses is recognized;

(b) The rights of persons with disabilities to decide freely and responsibly on the number and spacing of their children and to have access to age-appropriate information, reproductive and family planning education are recognized, and the means necessary to enable them to exercise these rights are provided;

(c) Persons with disabilities, including children, retain their fertility on an equal basis with others.

2. States Parties shall ensure the rights and responsibilities of persons with disabilities, with regard to guardianship, wardship, trusteeship, adoption of children or similar institutions, where these concepts exist in national legislation; in all cases the best interests of the child shall be paramount. States Parties shall render appropriate assistance to persons with disabilities in the performance of their child-rearing responsibilities.

3. States Parties shall ensure that children with disabilities have equal rights with respect to family life. With a view to realizing these rights, and to prevent concealment, abandonment, neglect and segregation of children with disabilities, States Parties shall undertake to provide early and comprehensive information, services and support to children with disabilities and their families.

4. States Parties shall ensure that a child shall not be separated from his or her parents against their will, except when competent authorities subject to judicial review determine, in accordance with applicable law and procedures, that such separation is necessary for the best interests of the child. In no case shall a child be separated from parents on the basis of a disability of either the child or one or both of the parents.

5. States Parties shall, where the immediate family is unable to care for a child with disabilities, undertake every effort to provide alternative care within the wider family, and failing that, within the community in a family setting.

Article 24 - Education

1. States Parties recognize the right of persons with disabilities to education. With a view to realizing this right without discrimination and

on the basis of equal opportunity, States Parties shall ensure an inclusive education system at all levels and life long learning directed to:

(a) The full development of human potential and sense of dignity and self-worth, and the strengthening of respect for human rights, fundamental freedoms and human diversity;

(b) The development by persons with disabilities of their personality, talents and creativity, as well as their mental and physical abilities, to their fullest potential;

(c) Enabling persons with disabilities to participate effectively in a free society.

2. In realizing this right, States Parties shall ensure that:

(a) Persons with disabilities are not excluded from the general education system on the basis of disability, and that children with disabilities are not excluded from free and compulsory primary education, or from secondary education, on the basis of disability;

(b) Persons with disabilities can access an inclusive, quality and free primary education and secondary education on an equal basis with others in the communities in which they live;

(c) Reasonable accommodation of the individual's requirements is provided;

(d) Persons with disabilities receive the support required, within the general education system, to facilitate their effective education;

(e) Effective individualized support measures are provided in environments that maximize academic and social development, consistent with the goal of full inclusion.

3. States Parties shall enable persons with disabilities to learn life and social development skills to facilitate their full and equal participation in education and as members of the community. To this end, States Parties shall take appropriate measures, including:

(a) Facilitating the learning of Braille, alternative script, augmentative and alternative modes, means and formats of communication and orientation and mobility skills, and facilitating peer support and mentoring;

(b) Facilitating the learning of sign language and the promotion of the linguistic identity of the deaf community;

(c) Ensuring that the education of persons, and in particular children, who are blind, deaf or deafblind, is delivered in the most appropriate languages and modes and means of communication for the individual, and in environments which maximize academic and social development.

4. In order to help ensure the realization of this right, States Parties shall take appropriate measures to employ teachers, including teachers

with disabilities, who are qualified in sign language and/or Braille, and to train professionals and staff who work at all levels of education. Such training shall incorporate disability awareness and the use of appropriate augmentative and alternative modes, means and formats of communication, educational techniques and materials to support persons with disabilities.

5. States Parties shall ensure that persons with disabilities are able to access general tertiary education, vocational training, adult education and lifelong learning without discrimination and on an equal basis with others. To this end, States Parties shall ensure that reasonable accommodation is provided to persons with disabilities.

Article 25 - Health

States Parties recognize that persons with disabilities have the right to the enjoyment of the highest attainable standard of health without discrimination on the basis of disability. States Parties shall take all appropriate measures to ensure access for persons with disabilities to health services that are gender-sensitive, including health-related rehabilitation. In particular, States Parties shall:

(a) Provide persons with disabilities with the same range, quality and standard of free or affordable health care and programmes as provided to other persons, including in the area of sexual and reproductive health and population-based public health programmes;

(b) Provide those health services needed by persons with disabilities specifically because of their disabilities, including early identification and intervention as appropriate, and services designed to minimize and prevent further disabilities, including among children and older persons;

(c) Provide these health services as close as possible to people's own communities, including in rural areas;

(d) Require health professionals to provide care of the same quality to persons with disabilities as to others, including on the basis of free and informed consent by, inter alia, raising awareness of the human rights, dignity, autonomy and needs of persons with disabilities through training and the promulgation of ethical standards for public and private health care;

(e) Prohibit discrimination against persons with disabilities in the provision of health insurance, and life insurance where such insurance is permitted by national law, which shall be provided in a fair and reasonable manner;

(f) Prevent discriminatory denial of health care or health services or food and fluids on the basis of disability.

Article 26 - Habilitation and rehabilitation

1. States Parties shall take effective and appropriate measures, including through peer support, to enable persons with disabilities to attain and maintain maximum independence, full physical, mental, social and vocational ability, and full inclusion and participation in all aspects of life. To that end, States Parties shall organize, strengthen and extend comprehensive habilitation and rehabilitation services and programmes, particularly in the areas of health, employment, education and social services, in such a way that these services and programmes:

(a) Begin at the earliest possible stage, and are based on the multidisciplinary assessment of individual needs and strengths;

(b) Support participation and inclusion in the community and all aspects of society, are voluntary, and are available to persons with disabilities as close as possible to their own communities, including in rural areas.

2. States Parties shall promote the development of initial and continuing training for professionals and staff working in habilitation and rehabilitation services.

3. States Parties shall promote the availability, knowledge and use of assistive devices and technologies, designed for persons with disabilities, as they relate to habilitation and rehabilitation.

Article 27 - Work and employment

1. States Parties recognize the right of persons with disabilities to work, on an equal basis with others; this includes the right to the opportunity to gain a living by work freely chosen or accepted in a labour market and work environment that is open, inclusive and accessible to persons with disabilities. States Parties shall safeguard and promote the realization of the right to work, including for those who acquire a disability during the course of employment, by taking appropriate steps, including through legislation, to, inter alia:

(a) Prohibit discrimination on the basis of disability with regard to all matters concerning all forms of employment, including conditions of recruitment, hiring and employment, continuance of employment, career advancement and safe and healthy working conditions;

(b) Protect the rights of persons with disabilities, on an equal basis with others, to just and favourable conditions of work, including equal opportunities and equal remuneration for work of equal value, safe and healthy working conditions, including protection from harassment, and the redress of grievances;

(c) Ensure that persons with disabilities are able to exercise their labour and trade union rights on an equal basis with others;
(d) Enable persons with disabilities to have effective access to general technical and vocational guidance programmes, placement services and vocational and continuing training;
(e) Promote employment opportunities and career advancement for persons with disabilities in the labour market, as well as assistance in finding, obtaining, maintaining and returning to employment;
(f) Promote opportunities for self-employment, entrepreneurship, the development of cooperatives and starting one's own business;
(g) Employ persons with disabilities in the public sector;
(h) Promote the employment of persons with disabilities in the private sector through appropriate policies and measures, which may include affirmative action programmes, incentives and other measures;
(i) Ensure that reasonable accommodation is provided to persons with disabilities in the workplace;
(j) Promote the acquisition by persons with disabilities of work experience in the open labour market;
(k) Promote vocational and professional rehabilitation, job retention and return-to-work programmes for persons with disabilities.

2. States Parties shall ensure that persons with disabilities are not held in slavery or in servitude, and are protected, on an equal basis with others, from forced or compulsory labour.

Article 28 - Adequate standard of living and social protection

1. States Parties recognize the right of persons with disabilities to an adequate standard of living for themselves and their families, including adequate food, clothing and housing, and to the continuous improvement of living conditions, and shall take appropriate steps to safeguard and promote the realization of this right without discrimination on the basis of disability.

2. States Parties recognize the right of persons with disabilities to social protection and to the enjoyment of that right without discrimination on the basis of disability, and shall take appropriate steps to safeguard and promote the realization of this right, including measures:

(a) To ensure equal access by persons with disabilities to clean water services, and to ensure access to appropriate and affordable services, devices and other assistance for disability-related needs;
(b) To ensure access by persons with disabilities, in particular women and girls with disabilities and older persons with disabilities, to social protection programmes and poverty reduction programmes;

(c) To ensure access by persons with disabilities and their families living in situations of poverty to assistance from the State with disability-related expenses, including adequate training, counselling, financial assistance and respite care;
(d) To ensure access by persons with disabilities to public housing programmes;
(e) To ensure equal access by persons with disabilities to retirement benefits and programmes.

Article 29 - Participation in political and public life

States Parties shall guarantee to persons with disabilities political rights and the opportunity to enjoy them on an equal basis with others, and shall undertake to:

a. Ensure that persons with disabilities can effectively and fully participate in political and public life on an equal basis with others, directly or through freely chosen representatives, including the right and opportunity for persons with disabilities to vote and be elected, inter alia, by:

(i) Ensuring that voting procedures, facilities and materials are appropriate, accessible and easy to understand and use;
(ii) Protecting the right of persons with disabilities to vote by secret ballot in elections and public referendums without intimidation, and to stand for elections, to effectively hold office and perform all public functions at all levels of government, facilitating the use of assistive and new technologies where appropriate;
(iii) Guaranteeing the free expression of the will of persons with disabilities as electors and to this end, where necessary, at their request, allowing assistance in voting by a person of their own choice;

(b) Promote actively an environment in which persons with disabilities can effectively and fully participate in the conduct of public affairs, without discrimination and on an equal basis with others, and encourage their participation in public affairs, including:

(i) Participation in non-governmental organizations and associations concerned with the public and political life of the country, and in the activities and administration of political parties;
(ii) Forming and joining organizations of persons with disabilities to represent persons with disabilities at international, national, regional and local levels.

Article 30 - Participation in cultural life, recreation, leisure and sport

1. States Parties recognize the right of persons with disabilities to take part on an equal basis with others in cultural life, and shall take all appropriate measures to ensure that persons with disabilities:

(a) Enjoy access to cultural materials in accessible formats;

(b) Enjoy access to television programmes, films, theatre and other cultural activities, in accessible formats;

(c) Enjoy access to places for cultural performances or services, such as theatres, museums, cinemas, libraries and tourism services, and, as far as possible, enjoy access to monuments and sites of national cultural importance.

2. States Parties shall take appropriate measures to enable persons with disabilities to have the opportunity to develop and utilize their creative, artistic and intellectual potential, not only for their own benefit, but also for the enrichment of society.

3. States Parties shall take all appropriate steps, in accordance with international law, to ensure that laws protecting intellectual property rights do not constitute an unreasonable or discriminatory barrier to access by persons with disabilities to cultural materials.

4. Persons with disabilities shall be entitled, on an equal basis with others, to recognition and support of their specific cultural and linguistic identity, including sign languages and deaf culture.

5. With a view to enabling persons with disabilities to participate on an equal basis with others in recreational, leisure and sporting activities, States Parties shall take appropriate measures:

(a) To encourage and promote the participation, to the fullest extent possible, of persons with disabilities in mainstream sporting activities at all levels;

(b) To ensure that persons with disabilities have an opportunity to organize, develop and participate in disability-specific sporting and recreational activities and, to this end, encourage the provision, on an equal basis with others, of appropriate instruction, training and resources;

(c) To ensure that persons with disabilities have access to sporting, recreational and tourism venues;

(d) To ensure that children with disabilities have equal access with other children to participation in play, recreation and leisure and sporting activities, including those activities in the school system;

(e) To ensure that persons with disabilities have access to services from those involved in the organization of recreational, tourism, leisure and sporting activities.

Article 31 - Statistics and data collection

1. States Parties undertake to collect appropriate information, including statistical and research data, to enable them to formulate and implement policies to give effect to the present Convention. The process of collecting and maintaining this information shall:

(a) Comply with legally established safeguards, including legislation on data protection, to ensure confidentiality and respect for the privacy of persons with disabilities;

(b) Comply with internationally accepted norms to protect human rights and fundamental freedoms and ethical principles in the collection and use of statistics.

2. The information collected in accordance with this article shall be disaggregated, as appropriate, and used to help assess the implementation of States Parties' obligations under the present Convention and to identify and address the barriers faced by persons with disabilities in exercising their rights.

3. States Parties shall assume responsibility for the dissemination of these statistics and ensure their accessibility to persons with disabilities and others.

Article 32- International cooperation

1. States Parties recognize the importance of international cooperation and its promotion, in support of national efforts for the realization of the purpose and objectives of the present Convention, and will undertake appropriate and effective measures in this regard, between and among States and, as appropriate, in partnership with relevant international and regional organizations and civil society, in particular organizations of persons with disabilities. Such measures could include, inter alia:

(a) Ensuring that international cooperation, including international development programmes, is inclusive of and accessible to persons with disabilities;

(b) Facilitating and supporting capacity-building, including through the exchange and sharing of information, experiences, training programmes and best practices;

(c) Facilitating cooperation in research and access to scientific and technical knowledge;

(d) Providing, as appropriate, technical and economic assistance, including by facilitating access to and sharing of accessible and assistive technologies, and through the transfer of technologies.

2. The provisions of this article are without prejudice to the obligations of each State Party to fulfil its obligations under the present Convention.

Article 33 - National implementation and monitoring

1. States Parties, in accordance with their system of organization, shall designate one or more focal points within government for matters relating to the implementation of the present Convention, and shall give due consideration to the establishment or designation of a coordination mechanism within government to facilitate related action in different sectors and at different levels.

2. States Parties shall, in accordance with their legal and administrative systems, maintain, strengthen, designate or establish within the State Party, a framework, including one or more independent mechanisms, as appropriate, to promote, protect and monitor implementation of the present Convention. When designating or establishing such a mechanism, States Parties shall take into account the principles relating to the status and functioning of national institutions for protection and promotion of human rights.

3. Civil society, in particular persons with disabilities and their representative organizations, shall be involved and participate fully in the monitoring process.

Article 34 - Committee on the Rights of Persons with Disabilities

1. There shall be established a Committee on the Rights of Persons with Disabilities (hereafter referred to as "the Committee"), which shall carry out the functions hereinafter provided.

2. The Committee shall consist, at the time of entry into force of the present Convention, of twelve experts. After an additional sixty ratifications or accessions to the Convention, the membership of the Committee shall increase by six members, attaining a maximum number of eighteen members.

3. The members of the Committee shall serve in their personal capacity and shall be of high moral standing and recognized competence and experience in the field covered by the present Convention. When nominating their candidates, States Parties are invited to give due consideration to the provision set out in article 4.3 of the present Convention.

4. The members of the Committee shall be elected by States Parties, consideration being given to equitable geographical distribution, representation of the different forms of civilization and of the principal legal systems, balanced gender representation and participation of experts with disabilities.

5. The members of the Committee shall be elected by secret ballot from a list of persons nominated by the States Parties from among their

nationals at meetings of the Conference of States Parties. At those meetings, for which two thirds of States Parties shall constitute a quorum, the persons elected to the Committee shall be those who obtain the largest number of votes and an absolute majority of the votes of the representatives of States Parties present and voting.

6. The initial election shall be held no later than six months after the date of entry into force of the present Convention. At least four months before the date of each election, the Secretary-General of the United Nations shall address a letter to the States Parties inviting them to submit the nominations within two months. The Secretary-General shall subsequently prepare a list in alphabetical order of all persons thus nominated, indicating the State Parties which have nominated them, and shall submit it to the States Parties to the present Convention.

7. The members of the Committee shall be elected for a term of four years. They shall be eligible for re-election once. However, the term of six of the members elected at the first election shall expire at the end of two years; immediately after the first election, the names of these six members shall be chosen by lot by the chairperson of the meeting referred to in paragraph 5 of this article.

8. The election of the six additional members of the Committee shall be held on the occasion of regular elections, in accordance with the relevant provisions of this article.

9. If a member of the Committee dies or resigns or declares that for any other cause she or he can no longer perform her or his duties, the State Party which nominated the member shall appoint another expert possessing the qualifications and meeting the requirements set out in the relevant provisions of this article, to serve for the remainder of the term.

10. The Committee shall establish its own rules of procedure.

11. The Secretary-General of the United Nations shall provide the necessary staff and facilities for the effective performance of the functions of the Committee under the present Convention, and shall convene its initial meeting.

12. With the approval of the General Assembly, the members of the Committee established under the present Convention shall receive emoluments from United Nations resources on such terms and conditions as the Assembly may decide, having regard to the importance of the Committee's responsibilities.

13. The members of the Committee shall be entitled to the facilities, privileges and immunities of experts on mission for the United Nations as laid down in the relevant sections of the Convention on the Privileges and Immunities of the United Nations.

Article 35 - Reports by States Parties

1. Each State Party shall submit to the Committee, through the Secretary-General of the United Nations, a comprehensive report on measures taken to give effect to its obligations under the present Convention and on the progress made in that regard, within two years after the entry into force of the present Convention for thc State Party concerned.

2. Thereafter, States Parties shall submit subsequent reports at least every four years and further whenever the Committee so requests.

3. The Committee shall decide any guidelines applicable to the content of the reports.

4. A State Party which has submitted a comprehensive initial report to the Committee need not, in its subsequent reports, repeat information previously provided. When preparing reports to the Committee, States Parties are invited to consider doing so in an open and transparent process and to give due consideration to the provision set out in article 4.3 of the present Convention.

5. Reports may indicate factors and difficulties affecting the degree of fulfilment of obligations under the present Convention.

Article 36 - Consideration of reports

1. Each report shall be considered by the Committee, which shall make such suggestions and general recommendations on the report as it may consider appropriate and shall forward these to the State Party concerned. The State Party may respond with any information it chooses to the Committee. The Committee may request further information from States Parties relevant to the implementation of the present Convention.

2. If a State Party is significantly overdue in the submission of a report, the Committee may notify the State Party concerned of the need to examine the implementation of the present Convention in that State Party, on the basis of reliable information available to the Committee, if the relevant report is not submitted within three months following the notification. The Committee shall invite the State Party concerned to participate in such examination. Should the State Party respond by submitting the relevant report, the provisions of paragraph 1 of this article will apply.

3. The Secretary-General of the United Nations shall make available the reports to all States Parties.

4. States Parties shall make their reports widely available to the public in their own countries and facilitate access to the suggestions and general recommendations relating to these reports.

5. The Committee shall transmit, as it may consider appropriate, to the specialized agencies, funds and programmes of the United Nations, and other competent bodies, reports from States Parties in order to address a request or indication of a need for technical advice or assistance contained therein, along with the Committee's observations and recommendations, if any, on these requests or indications.

Article 37 - Cooperation between States Parties and the Committee

1. Each State Party shall cooperate with the Committee and assist its members in the fulfilment of their mandate.

2. In its relationship with States Parties, the Committee shall give due consideration to ways and means of enhancing national capacities for the implementation of the present Convention, including through international cooperation.

Article 38 - Relationship of the Committee with other bodies

In order to foster the effective implementation of the present Convention and to encourage international cooperation in the field covered by the present Convention:

(a) The specialized agencies and other United Nations organs shall be entitled to be represented at the consideration of the implementation of such provisions of the present Convention as fall within the scope of their mandate. The Committee may invite the specialized agencies and other competent bodies as it may consider appropriate to provide expert advice on the implementation of the Convention in areas falling within the scope of their respective mandates. The Committee may invite specialized agencies and other United Nations organs to submit reports on the implementation of the Convention in areas falling within the scope of their activities;

(b) The Committee, as it discharges its mandate, shall consult, as appropriate, other relevant bodies instituted by international human rights treaties, with a view to ensuring the consistency of their respective reporting guidelines, suggestions and general recommendations, and avoiding duplication and overlap in the performance of their functions.

Article 39 - Report of the Committee

The Committee shall report every two years to the General Assembly and to the Economic and Social Council on its activities, and may make suggestions and general recommendations based on the examination of reports and information received from the States Parties. Such suggestions and general recommendations shall be included in the report of the Committee together with comments, if any, from States Parties.

Article 40 - Conference of States Parties

1. The States Parties shall meet regularly in a Conference of States Parties in order to consider any matter with regard to the implementation of the present Convention.

2. No later than six months after the entry into force of the present Convention, the Conference of the States Parties shall be convened by the Secretary-General of the United Nations. The subsequent meetings shall be convened by the Secretary-General of the United Nations biennially or upon the decision of the Conference of States Parties.

Article 41 - Depositary

The Secretary-General of the United Nations shall be the depositary of the present Convention.

Article 42 - Signature

The present Convention shall be open for signature by all States and by regional integration organizations at United Nations Headquarters in New York as of 30 March 2007.

Article 43 - Consent to be bound

The present Convention shall be subject to ratification by signatory States and to formal confirmation by signatory regional integration organizations. It shall be open for accession by any State or regional integration organization which has not signed the Convention.

Article 44 - Regional integration organizations

1. "Regional integration organization" shall mean an organization constituted by sovereign States of a given region, to which its member States have transferred competence in respect of matters governed by this Convention. Such organizations shall declare, in their instruments of formal confirmation or accession, the extent of their competence with respect to matters governed by this Convention. Subsequently, they shall inform the depositary of any substantial modification in the extent of their competence.

2. References to "States Parties" in the present Convention shall apply to such organizations within the limits of their competence.

3. For the purposes of article 45, paragraph 1, and article 47, paragraphs 2 and 3, any instrument deposited by a regional integration organization shall not be counted.

4. Regional integration organizations, in matters within their competence, may exercise their right to vote in the Conference of States Parties, with a number of votes equal to the number of their member States that are Parties to this Convention. Such an organization shall not exercise its right to vote if any of its member States exercises its right, and vice versa.

Article 45 - Entry into force

1. The present Convention shall enter into force on the thirtieth day after the deposit of the twentieth instrument of ratification or accession.

2. For each State or regional integration organization ratifying, formally confirming or acceding to the Convention after the deposit of the twentieth such instrument, the Convention shall enter into force on the thirtieth day after the deposit of its own such instrument.

Article 46 - Reservations

1. Reservations incompatible with the object and purpose of the present Convention shall not be permitted.

2. Reservations may be withdrawn at any time.

Article 47 - Amendments

1. Any State Party may propose an amendment to the present Convention and submit it to the Secretary-General of the United Nations. The Secretary-General shall communicate any proposed amendments to States Parties, with a request to be notified whether they favour a conference of States Parties for the purpose of considering and deciding upon the proposals. In the event that, within four months from the date of such communication, at least one third of the States Parties favour such a conference, the Secretary-General shall convene the conference under the auspices of the United Nations. Any amendment adopted by a majority of two thirds of the States Parties present and voting shall be submitted by the Secretary-General to the General Assembly for approval and thereafter to all States Parties for acceptance.

2. An amendment adopted and approved in accordance with paragraph 1 of this article shall enter into force on the thirtieth day after the number of instruments of acceptance deposited reaches two thirds of the number of States Parties at the date of adoption of the amendment. Thereafter, the

amendment shall enter into force for any State Party on the thirtieth day following the deposit of its own instrument of acceptance. An amendment shall be binding only on those States Parties which have accepted it.

3. If so decided by the Conference of States Parties by consensus, an amendment adopted and approved in accordance with paragraph 1 of this article which relates exclusively to articles 34, 38, 39 and 40 shall enter into force for all States Parties on the thirtieth day after the number of instruments of acceptance deposited reaches two thirds of the number of States Parties at the date of adoption of the amendment.

Article 48 - Denunciation

A State Party may denounce the present Convention by written notification to the Secretary-General of the United Nations. The denunciation shall become effective one year after the date of receipt of the notification by the Secretary-General.

Article 49 - Accessible format

The text of the present Convention shall be made available in accessible formats.

Article 50 - Authentic texts

The Arabic, Chinese, English, French, Russian and Spanish texts of the present Convention shall be equally authentic.

In witness thereof the undersigned plenipotentiaries, being duly authorized thereto by their respective Governments, have signed the present Convention.

6. Optional Protocol to the Convention on the Rights of Persons with Disabilities, 2006

The Optional Protocol to the Convention on the Rights of Persons with Disabilities was adopted by General Assembly Resolution 61/106 in 2006, and came into force in 2008. The Protocol has strengthened the policy of its original Convention. Its purposes are to limit the juridical and political power of states concerning violations of the principles of the human rights law. It encourages all states to recognize the competence of the Committee on the Rights of Persons with Disabilities. In this way, the Optional Protocol provides legal possibilities for those who have been discriminated against by the state on the grounds of their disability. This means that the policy of the Protocol, like its basic Convention, protects the rights of disabled children under the provisions of international human rights law. The Protocol states:

The States Parties to the present Protocol have agreed as follows:

Article 1

1. A State Party to the present Protocol ("State Party") recognizes the competence of the Committee on the Rights of Persons with Disabilities ("the Committee") to receive and consider communications from or on behalf of individuals or groups of individuals subject to its jurisdiction who claim to be victims of a violation by that State Party of the provisions of the Convention.

2. No communication shall be received by the Committee if it concerns a State Party to the Convention that is not a party to the present Protocol.

Article 2

The Committee shall consider a communication inadmissible when:

(a) The communication is anonymous;

(b) The communication constitutes an abuse of the right of submission of such communications or is incompatible with the provisions of the Convention;

(c) The same matter has already been examined by the Committee or has been or is being examined under another procedure of international investigation or settlement;

(d) All available domestic remedies have not been exhausted. This shall not be the rule where the application of the remedies is unreasonably prolonged or unlikely to bring effective relief;

(e) It is manifestly ill-founded or not sufficiently substantiated; or when

(f) The facts that are the subject of the communication occurred prior to the entry into force of the present Protocol for the State Party concerned unless those facts continued after that date.

Article 3

Subject to the provisions of article 2 of the present Protocol, the Committee shall bring any communications submitted to it confidentially to the attention of the State Party. Within six months, the receiving State shall submit to the Committee written explanations or statements clarifying the matter and the remedy, if any, that may have been taken by that State.

Article 4

1. At any time after the receipt of a communication and before a determination on the merits has been reached, the Committee may transmit to the State Party concerned for its urgent consideration a request that the State Party take such interim measures as may be necessary to avoid possible irreparable damage to the victim or victims of the alleged violation.

2. Where the Committee exercises its discretion under paragraph 1 of this article, this does not imply a determination on admissibility or on the merits of the communication.

Article 5

The Committee shall hold closed meetings when examining communications under the present Protocol. After examining a communication, the Committee shall forward its suggestions and recommendations, if any, to the State Party concerned and to the petitioner.

Article 6

1. If the Committee receives reliable information indicating grave or systematic violations by a State Party of rights set forth in the Convention, the Committee shall invite that State Party to cooperate in the examination of the information and to this end submit observations with regard to the information concerned.

2. Taking into account any observations that may have been submitted by the State Party concerned as well as any other reliable information available to it, the Committee may designate one or more of its members to conduct an inquiry and to report urgently to the Committee. Where warranted and with the consent of the State Party, the inquiry may include a visit to its territory.

3. After examining the findings of such an inquiry, the Committee shall transmit these findings to the State Party concerned together with any comments and recommendations.

4. The State Party concerned shall, within six months of receiving the findings, comments and recommendations transmitted by the Committee, submit its observations to the Committee.

5. Such an inquiry shall be conducted confidentially and the cooperation of the State Party shall be sought at all stages of the proceedings.

Article 7

1. The Committee may invite the State Party concerned to include in its report under article 35 of the Convention details of any measures taken in response to an inquiry conducted under article 6 of the present Protocol.

2. The Committee may, if necessary, after the end of the period of six months referred to in article 6, paragraph 4, invite the State Party concerned to inform it of the measures taken in response to such an inquiry.

Article 8

Each State Party may, at the time of signature or ratification of the present Protocol or accession thereto, declare that it does not recognize the competence of the Committee provided for in articles 6 and 7.

Article 9

The Secretary-General of the United Nations shall be the depositary of the present Protocol.

Article 10

The present Protocol shall be open for signature by signatory States and regional integration organizations of the Convention at United Nations Headquarters in New York as of 30 March 2007.

Article 11

The present Protocol shall be subject to ratification by signatory States of the present Protocol which have ratified or acceded to the Convention. It shall be subject to formal confirmation by signatory regional integration organizations of the present Protocol which have formally confirmed or acceded to the Convention. It shall be open for accession by any State or regional integration organization which has ratified, formally confirmed or acceded to the Convention and which has not signed the Protocol.

Article 12

1. Regional integration organization" shall mean an organization constituted by sovereign States of a given region, to which its member States have transferred competence in respect of matters governed by the Convention and the present Protocol. Such organizations shall declare, in their instruments of formal confirmation or accession, the extent of their competence with respect to matters governed by the Convention and the present Protocol. Subsequently, they shall inform the depositary of any substantial modification in the extent of their competence.

2. References to "States Parties" in the present Protocol shall apply to such organizations within the limits of their competence.

3. For the purposes of article 13, paragraph 1, and article 15, paragraph 2, of the present Protocol, any instrument deposited by a regional integration organization shall not be counted.

4. Regional integration organizations, in matters within their competence, may exercise their right to vote in the meeting of States Parties, with a number of votes equal to the number of their member States that are Parties to the present Protocol. Such an organization shall not exercise its right to vote if any of its member States exercises its right, and vice versa.

Article 13

1. Subject to the entry into force of the Convention, the present Protocol shall enter into force on the thirtieth day after the deposit of the tenth instrument of ratification or accession.

2. For each State or regional integration organization ratifying, formally confirming or acceding to the present Protocol after the deposit of the tenth such instrument, the Protocol shall enter into force on the thirtieth day after the deposit of its own such instrument.

Article 14

1. Reservations incompatible with the object and purpose of the present Protocol shall not be permitted.

2. Reservations may be withdrawn at any time.

Article 15

1. Any State Party may propose an amendment to the present Protocol and submit it to the Secretary-General of the United Nations. The Secretary-General shall communicate any proposed amendments to States Parties, with a request to be notified whether they favour a meeting of States Parties for the purpose of considering and deciding upon the proposals. In the event that, within four months from the date of such communication, at least one third of the States Parties favour such a meeting, the Secretary-General shall convene the meeting under the auspices of the United Nations. Any amendment adopted by a majority of two thirds of the States Parties present and voting shall be submitted by the Secretary-General to the General Assembly of the United Nations for approval and thereafter to all States Parties for acceptance.

2. An amendment adopted and approved in accordance with paragraph 1 of this article shall enter into force on the thirtieth day after the number

of instruments of acceptance deposited reaches two thirds of the number of States Parties at the date of adoption of the amendment. Thereafter, the amendment shall enter into force for any State Party on the thirtieth day following the deposit of its own instrument of acceptance. An amendment shall be binding only on those States Parties which have accepted it.

Article 16

A State Party may denounce the present Protocol by written notification to the Secretary-General of the United Nations. The denunciation shall become effective one year after the date of receipt of the notification by the Secretary-General.

Article 17

The text of the present Protocol shall be made available in accessible formats.

Article 18

The Arabic, Chinese, English, French, Russian and Spanish texts of the present Protocol shall be equally authentic.